Commencement-Level

PHYSICAL SETTING:

PHYSICS

STAREVIEW

PHYSICS

Author
Nancy Ann Moreau
Physics Teacher, NYS Physics Mentor
Roy C. Ketcham High School, Wappingers Falls, NY

Editors
Wayne Garnsey & Paul Stich
Fran Harrison, Associate Editor

Artwork & Graphics
Eugene B. Fairbanks & Wayne Garnsey

N&N Publishing Company, Inc.
18 Montgomery Street   Middletown, NY 10940-5116

For Ordering & Information
1-800-NN 4 TEXT
Website: www.nn4text.com   email: nn4text@warwick.net

DEDICATION

To my family –
Wayne,
Dave, Zory, and Maria
Deborah, Jeff, Logan, and Lauren
– all the joy of my life.

SPECIAL THANKS

The author thanks these dedicated educational professionals
for their hard work, subject and curricula contributions, and technical proofing
of our *Physical Setting: Physics STAReview*:

Kenneth Evans
LeRoy Leonard
Carl Preske

John Hanley
Dr. Wayne Moreau
Judith Shuback

CREDITS

Some material used in this book was adapted from
the material of these fine authors, researchers, teachers:

Laboratory Experiments in Physics for High School
by Thomas D. Miner and William C. Kelly

The Physics Classroom by Tom Henderson of Glenbrook South High School,
http://www.glenbrook.k12.il.us/gbssci/phys/Class/BBoard.html

Hands on Physics (HOP)

C³P Comprehensive Conceptual Curriculum in Physics

front cover and divider page photos: © PhotoDisc

© Copyright 2002, **2nd Revision 2004**

N&N Publishing Company, Inc.

phone: 1-800-NN 4 TEXT
internet: www.nn4text.com   email: nn4text@warwick.net
SAN - 216-4221   ISBN - 0935487 76 X

3 4 5 6 7 8 9 0 BookMart 2007 2006 2005 2004

TABLE OF CONTENTS

CONTEXT OF THE
PHYSICAL SETTING: PHYSICS

Note: Process Skills (most often assessed in Parts B and C of the Test) and Lab Skills (assessed in Part D on the Test) appear, not as separate areas, but in direct association with Key Ideas and Major Understandings throughout the chapters. For specific information see Appendix B.

RUBRIC FOR PHYSICS LABS

	QUALITY WORK	POINTS POSSIBLE	POINTS EARNED
Format	Name Lab Title		
Organization	Statement of the problem		
	Materials list		
	Summary of Procedures		
	Data table drawn with ruler		
	Graphs - axes drawn with ruler (if needed)		
	Data analysis *a* Sample calculation shown for each problem type *b* Calculations accurate *c* Units labeled in all steps and answer		
	Error analysis		
	Conclusion		
Mechanics	Correct spelling, capitalization and punctuation		
Neatness	Typed or written in pen (except graphs)		
	All sections in order		
Total Points			

TO THE STUDENT & TEACHER

PHYSICAL SETTING: PHYSICS STAREVIEW is written based on the new standards and assessments for physics. It is a comprehensive review of the Key Ideas, Major Understandings, Performance Indicators, Process Skills, and Real World Connections as set forth in the University of the State of New York Education Department: *Physical Setting: Physics Core Curriculum.*

"OPEN FIRST"

The student should upon receiving this *STAReview* begin by reading this section: "To the Student."

- Start by reviewing the Table of Contents (previous 6 pages). This will give an overview of the major topics reviewed in this book.

- Now, become familiar with Appendix C – Index & Glossary. This section is an extensive listing of the key physical terms that one needs to know in order to understand the material. A brief definition or explanation of the term is given together with cross-referenced pages to direct the student to additional material directly related to the term.

ORGANIZATION

The book is organized "conceptually" through Major Understandings, but the review is linked through the following organizational parts.

- **Standards** are the overall, general goals that apply to all scientific and indeed most general learning. For example, each Standard contains several goals, such as "Analysis, Scientific Inquiry, and Engineering Design in order to pose questions, seek answers, and develop solutions."

- Within each Standard, **Key Ideas** are used to further define the generalized objectives to be reached. For example, Standard 1 has several Key Ideas such as Key Idea 1 within the Scientific Inquiry part of Standard 1, that is, "to develop explanations of natural phenomena in a continuing, creative process."

- For each Key Idea there are several related **Process Skills** which specifically identify what processes the student must learn in order to demonstrate the particular Key Ideas of a general Standard. These Skills are identified and found in all chapters followed by explanations of the Skill and questions to test the student's abilities in preparation for the final, year-end test.

- Associated with both Standards and their Key Ideas are the **Performance Indicators**. These tell the student specifically what he/she is expected to know in order to answer correctly the questions on the final, year-end test. In other words, the Performance Indicators are the testing objectives. These are identified at the beginning of each chapter and again at the end of each unit with the Part A, B, and C questions.

- Finally, there are the **Major Understandings**. Each Performance Indicator has specific concepts and physical understandings to learn. This is the "meat and potatoes" of *Physical Setting: Physics STAReview*. These Major Understandings are first listed at the beginning of each chapter, are further developed in the text, examples, sample problems, and illustrations that follow, and are tested throughout the Unit in the Skills and at the end of each chapter in Parts *A*, *B*, and *C*.

MEANING OF SYMBOLS

Symbols are critical in all science. So, the author has developed a mini-help system. Stars are used to help navigate the student through the more complex Major Understandings in physics.

☆   Stars indicate two important things: Some starred material may not be *specifically* referred to in the *Core Curriculum*, but this text is needed for better understanding of major concepts. Also, stars may note special material that further explains Major Understandings, Skills, and Real World Connections. The dash-dot line (–·–·–) in the left margin identifies the extent of this specially identified material.

SKILL M 1.1 ☆ TRY IT

In addition, the ☆ identifies for the student "**Try It**" problems that should be solved in order to better understand the Performance and Lab Skills. The solid gray line (━━━━━━) in the left margin identifies the the extent of the Skill and/or Lab and any associated "Try It" problems being identified.

FINALLY, STUDY

Success comes through study. The author and editors of *Physical Setting: Physics STAReview* are teachers. This book has been written to provide the student with the best "outside help" possible. However, it can only help the student, if the student uses it consistently, with purpose and focused study.

We wish you good studying and success on your final, year-end test.
    – the author and editors, the teachers of N&N Publishing

CHAPTER 1
PHYSICS
FOR THE
NEXT
GENERATION

KEY IDEA 5
ENERGY AND MATTER INTERACT THROUGH
FORCES THAT RESULT IN CHANGES IN MOTION.

> PERFORMANCE INDICATOR 5.3 *STUDENTS CAN COMPARE ENERGY*
> *RELATIONSHIPS WITHIN AN ATOM'S NUCLEUS TO THOSE OUTSIDE THE NUCLEUS.*

CHAPTER 1 – MAJOR UNDERSTANDINGS

☆ 5.3b Charge is quantized on two levels. On the atomic level, charge is restricted to multiples of the elementary charge (charge on the electron or proton). On the subnuclear level, charge appears as fractional values of the elementary charge (quarks).

☆ 5.3f Among other things, mass-energy and charge are conserved at all levels (from sub-nuclear to cosmic).

☆ 5.3g The Standard Model of Particle Physics has evolved from previous attempts to explain the nature of the atom and states that:
• atomic particles are composed of subnuclear particles
• the nucleus is a conglomeration of quarks which manifest themselves as protons and neutrons
• each elementary particle has a corresponding antiparticle

☆ 5.3h Behaviors and characteristics of matter, from the microscopic to the cosmic levels, are manifestations of its atomic structure. The macroscopic characteristics of matter, such as electrical and optical properties, are the result of microscopic interactions.

☆ 5.3i The total of the fundamental interactions is responsible for the appearance and behavior of the objects in the universe.

☆ 5.3j The fundamental source of all energy in the universe is the conversion of mass into energy.*

Note: When an * (asterisk) appears with a *Major Understanding* (such as 5.3j), the student should recognize that these items are treated mathmatically.

CHAPTER 1
PHYSICS FOR THE
NEXT GENERATION

EINSTEIN'S E = mc²

In 1905, Albert Einstein concluded that: "The mass of a body is a measure of its energy content." We can write this in the more familiar form. This is probably the most famous formula in physics.

$$E = mc^2$$

Energy = mass x (speed of light)²

This equivalence has exciting significance. First, it means that the two great classical laws of conservation of mass and conservation of energy were simply an alternate statement of the same law. Second, the possibility arises that some of the rest mass might be transformed into another form of energy. A small amount of mass could produce a tremendous amount of power. This was the science behind nuclear energy and it signaled the beginning of a new era in physics. Scientists realized that the fundamental source of all energy in the universe is the conversion of mass into energy. Third, particle physics has demonstrated that mass can be created from energy.

SKILL M 1.1 (see Appendix B: Process Skills...)

a   How much energy is produced when 2.50 kilograms of matter are completely converted into energy?

Given: **m** = 2.50 kilograms

         c = 3.00×10^8 m/s (the speed of light from the *Reference Tables for Physical Setting / PHYSICS*)

Find: energy in joules

Solution: $E = mc^2$

            $E = (2.50 \text{ kg})(3.00 \times 10^8 \text{m/s})^2$

            $E = 2.25 \times 10^{17}$ Joules

Note: Joules is the MKS unit for energy.

b   One **universal** (atomic) **mass unit** (u) is equivalent to an energy of 931 MeV. [M represents a million or 10^6]. One **electron volt (eV)** is equivalent to an energy of 1.6×10^{-19} joules. Calculate the mass in kilograms of one universal mass unit (u).

Solution:

$$1 \text{ u} \times 931 \frac{\text{MeV}}{\text{u}} \times \frac{10^6 \text{eV}}{\text{MeV}} \times 1.60 \times 10^{-19} \frac{\text{J}}{\text{eV}} = 1.49 \times 10^{-10} \text{ J}$$

$$E = 1.49 \times 10^{-10} \text{ J}$$

$$E = mc^2$$

$$m = \frac{E}{c^2} = \frac{(1.49 \times 10^{-10}) \text{ J}}{(3.00 \times 10^8 \text{ m/s})^2}$$

$$m = 1.66 \times 10^{-27} \text{ kg}$$

Note: The mass of a *u* is equivalent to the mass of a proton.

c   How much energy in million electron volts (MeV) and joules (J) is produced when 2.10 universal mass units (u) of matter are completely converted into energy? (to three significant digits)

$$(2.10 \text{ u}) \, (9.31 \times 10^2 \text{ MeV/u}) = 1960 \text{ MeV} = 1.96 \times 10^3 \text{ MeV}$$

$$1.96 \times 10^3 \text{ MeV} \times \frac{10^6 \text{eV}}{\text{MeV}} \times 1.6 \times 10^{-19} \frac{\text{J}}{\text{eV}} = 3.14 \times 10^{-10} \text{ J}$$

☆ TRY IT

1   How much mass in kilograms is required to produce 1 joule, assuming all of the mass is converted into energy?

2   How much energy is produced in MeVs and joules when one atom of carbon-14 (14 u) is converted into energy?

3   The average high school student has a mass of 70 kilograms. What is the equivalent energy in joules?

4   In many nuclear reactions, less than one percent of the mass is converted into energy. Using that fact, how much mass must be used in the reaction in kilograms, would be necessary to produce 10^3 joules of energy?

5   Calculate the energy equivalent of the electron in MeV.

In the early 19th century, scientists began looking deeper into the atom to discover the fundamental forces and particles. The science of quantum mechanics, spurred on by the work of Albert Einstein, Max Planck, Paul Dirac, and others became the dominant theory of the twentieth century. In 1963, American physicist Murray Gell-Mann (1929-) proposed the existence of quarks as the fundamental particles for which he won the Nobel Prize in 1969. By the year 2000, six quarks had been identified and physicists had created The Standard Model to further enhance the understanding of matter and interactions.

THE STANDARD MODEL

The **Standard Model** encompasses all that we currently know about the most fundamental constituents of matter and the interactions among these constituents. The model states that all matter is composed of hadrons and leptons. The chart at the right summarizes the classification of all matter.

Classification of Matter

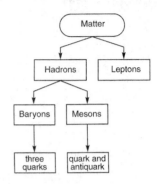

CLASSIFICATION OF MATTER

Quarks are the fundamental particles of the Standard Model. Despite extensive research, no isolated quark has ever been observed. **Mesons** are unstable and consist of one quark and one anti-quark. **Baryons** have masses equal to or greater than the proton. Baryons are formed by three quarks. The most common examples of baryons include protons and neutrons. Together, the baryons and mesons are called **hadrons**.

Leptons include the stable electron, and other charged (muon, tau) and neutral (neutrino) species. Lepton numbers and baryon numbers are conserved in all interactions. These numbers represent the charge of the particle.

Note: For each particle there is a corresponding antiparticle with a charge opposite that of its associated particle.

Note: Anti-up is represented by $\bar{u}$, down by $\bar{d}$ (bar over letter).

Particles of the Standard Model

Quarks

Name	up	charm	top
Symbol	u	c	t
Charge	$+\frac{2}{3}e$	$+\frac{2}{3}e$	$+\frac{2}{3}e$

down	strange	bottom
d	s	b
$-\frac{1}{3}e$	$-\frac{1}{3}e$	$-\frac{1}{3}e$

Leptons

electron	muon	tau
e	μ	τ
$-1e$	$-1e$	$-1e$

electron neutrino	muon neutrino	tau neutrino
ν_e	ν_μ	ν_τ
0	0	0

Anti-Matter

The predictions of antiparticles began in the 1920s with early quantum theories. The equations that resulted from the theory suggested the existence of particles with negative energy states, something like an electron with a positive charge. At the time, there was no experimental evidence of these antiparticles. Then in 1932, the American

COMBINING QUARKS TO GET NUCLEAR PARTICLES		
QUARKS	COMMON PARTICLE	CHARGE
up up down	Proton	+1
down down up	Neutron	0
Anti-up, anti-up, anti-down	Antiproton	-1

physicist Carl Anderson discovered such a particle called a positron. The antielectron has the same mass as an electron, but is positively charged. For each particle of the Standard Model, there is a corresponding antiparticle with a charge opposite that of its associated particle.

The Fundamental Forces

At a fundamental level, a force is not just something that happens to particles. It is an exchange which is passed between two particles.

The **strong nuclear force** which can hold a nucleus together against the enormous forces of repulsion of the protons is very powerful and very short ranged. However, it is not an inverse square force like the electromagnetic force. **Hideki Yukawa** modeled the strong force as an exchange force in which the exchange particles are pions and other heavier particles. The range of a particle exchange force is limited by the uncertainty principle. The strong force is the strongest of the four fundamental forces.

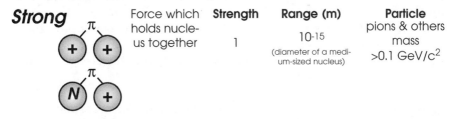

Strong	Force which holds nucleus together	Strength	Range (m)	Particle
		1	10^{-15} (diameter of a medium-sized nucleus)	pions & others mass >0.1 GeV/c^2

The **electromagnetic force** manifests itself through the forces between charges (**Coulomb's Law**) and the magnetic force. Fundamentally, both magnetic and electric forces are manifestations of an exchange force involving the exchange of **photons**. The electromagnetic force is a force of infinite range, which obeys the **inverse square law**. The force can be attractive or repulsive.

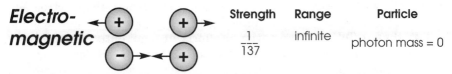

Electro-magnetic	Strength	Range	Particle
	$\frac{1}{137}$	infinite	photon mass = 0

The **weak interaction** involves the exchange of the **W** and the **Z** particles. Since the mass of these particles is on the order of 80 GeV/c^2, the uncertainty principle dictates a range which is about 0.1% of the diameter of a proton.

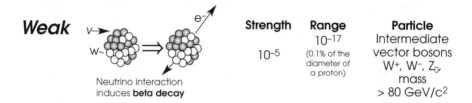

Weak		Strength	Range	Particle
			10^{-17}	Intermediate
		10^{-5}	(0.1% of the diameter of a proton)	vector bosons W^+, W^-, Z_0, mass > 80 GeV/c^2

Neutrino interaction induces **beta decay**

The role of the weak force in the interacton of quarks makes it involved in many decays of nuclear particles, which require a change of a quark from one flavor to another. The weak force is responsible for the fusion of the Sun and the conversion of the neutrons to protons in the nuclei. Were it not for the weak force, large elements would not be possible.

The discovery of the W and Z particles in 1983 was hailed as a confirmation of the theories which connect the weak force to the electromagnetic force by **electro-weak unification**.

Gravity is the weakest of the four fundamental forces, yet it is the dominant force in the universe for shaping the large-scale structure of galaxies, stars, etc. The force is always attractive and acts along the line joining the centers of mass of the two masses. The forces on the two masses are equal in size but opposite in direction, obeying **Newton's third law**. Viewed as an exchange force, the massless exchange particle is called the (not yet observed) **graviton**. Gravity and the electromagnetic force are both inverse square laws.

Gravity	Strength	Range (m)	Particle
	6×10^{-39}	infinite	graviton mass = 0

Our understanding of the fundamental forces involved in physics is still incomplete. The **Higgs boson** has been proposed as being a particle which might exist only at the high temperatures where the electromagnetic and weak forces begin to merge, has been proposed. Its mass should be less than 1 TeV/c^2. International efforts are currently underway to build a device capable of reaching 1 TeV to search for the Higgs boson.

There are many questions about the realm of the constituents of the standard model and the very large universe that still remain unanswered. With rapid advances and new discoveries in the field of particle physics, some of these questions may be answered by the time you finish this course. You could be involved in asking the questions, which will push forward the frontiers of physics. There is still much in science to be discovered and understood. A strong background in physics will prepare you to understand the developments of the next generation.

RADIOACTIVE DECAY

The three types of nuclear **radioactive decay** are alpha, beta, and gamma emissions.

$$^{263}_{106}Sg \rightarrow {}^{259}_{104}Rf + {}^{4}_{2}He$$

(alpha particle)
$^{4}_{2}He$

ALPHA DECAY

$^{263}_{106}Sg$ $^{259}_{104}Rf$

| before | after |

An **alpha particle** is a Helium 4 nucleus (two protons and two neutrons). It is produced by nuclear fission in which a massive nucleus breaks apart into two smaller nuclei (one of them the alpha particle).

A **beta particle** is an electron. It emerges from a weak decay process in which one of the neutrons inside an atom decays to produce a proton, a beta electron and an anti-electron-type **neutrino**. Some nuclei instead undergo beta decay. A beta decay can be of two types: a beta plus or a beta minus. In the beta plus, a proton decays to become a neutron plus a positron (anti-electron or beta-plus particle) and an electron-type neutrino.

$$^{14}_{6}C \rightarrow {}^{14}_{7}N + {}^{0}_{-1}e + \bar{v} \quad \text{(anti-neutrino)}$$

$$^{18}_{9}F \rightarrow {}^{18}_{8}O + {}^{0}_{+1}e + v \quad \text{(neutrino)}$$

$\bar{v}_e$

BETA MINUS DECAY

$^{14}_{6}C$ $^{14}_{7}N$

e^-
(beta particle)

v_e

BETA PLUS DECAY

$^{18}_{9}F$ $^{18}_{8}O$

e^+
(beta particle)

| before | after |

A **gamma particle** is a photon produced as a step in a radioactive decay chain. When a massive nucleus produced by fission relaxes from the excited state in which it first formed towards its lowest energy or ground-state configuration, a photon is emitted.

$$^{152}_{66}\text{Dy} \;\rightarrow\; ^{152}_{66}\text{Dy} \;+\; ^{0}_{0}\gamma$$

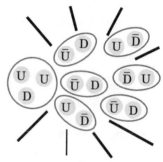

(gamma ray)
photon

GAMMA
DECAY

$^{152}_{66}\text{Dy}$

$^{152}_{66}\text{Dy}$

| before | after |

WHY DON'T WE SEE ISOLATED QUARKS?

While the nucleus of an atom can decay into a less massive nucleus by splitting apart, how does a fundamental particle change into other fundamental particles? Fundamental particles cannot split apart because they have no constituents, but rather they somehow turn into other particles.

For example, consider that the quarks are in an elastic bag which allows the quarks to move freely around as long as you do not try to pull them farther apart. If you try to pull a quark out, the bag stretches and resists.

The quarks of a proton are free to move within the proton volume.

If you try to pull one of the quarks out, the energy required is on the order of 1 GeV.

The energy required to produce a separation far exceeds the pair production energy of a quark-anti-quark pair, so instead of pulling out an isolated quark, you form mesons as the quark-anti-quark pairs combine.

This model helps in understanding why we have not seen isolated quarks. If one of the constituent quarks of a particle is given enough energy, it can create a meson as the energy imparted to the quark is used to produce quark-anti-quark pairs.

☆ TRY IT

6   Explain why we do not see isolated quarks.

THE VERY LARGE AND THE VERY SMALL

In order to communicate numbers which are very large or very small, prefixes are used for powers of ten. In physics, wavelengths are often expressed in nanometers and energy may be expressed in TeV.

SKILL 3.2 (see Appendix B: Process Skills...)

The distance between the Earth and the Sun is 1.50×10^{13} cm. Express this distance in m and in km.

Given: distance = 1.50×10^{13} cm

Find: distance = _____ m   distance = _____ km

Use the conversions found on your *Reference Tables for Physical Setting / PHYSICS*.

Prefix	Symbol	Notation	Alternate Useful Relationships
centi	c	10^{-2}	100 cm/m or m/100 cm
kilo	k	10^{3}	1000 m/km or km/1000m

$(1.50 \times 10^{13} \text{ cm}) \times (\frac{\text{m}}{100 \text{ cm}}) = 1.50 \times 10^{11}$ m

Take this answer and change it to km with another conversion factor.

$(1.50 \times 10^{11} \text{ m}) \times (\frac{\text{km}}{1000 \text{ m}}) = 1.50 \times 10^{8}$ km

☆ TRY IT

7   The wavelength of red light is 650 nm. What is the wavelength in meters and in centimeters?

8   The speed of light in a vacuum is 3.00×10^{8} m/s. What is the speed of light in cm/s and km/s?

9   A hydrogen atom has a diameter of approximately 0.1 nm.

   a   What is the diameter in meters?

   b   What is the diameter in millimeters?

   c   What is the diameter in micrometers?

SKILL 3.2 (see Appendix B: *Process Skills...*)

In scientific notation, the measurement is recorded to a power of 10 and all of the figures given are significant. To write a number in scientific notation, move the decimal point so that there is one digit to the left of the decimal point. That first digit is a number from one to nine and follow it by the correct power of 10. Each time you move the decimal point you change the power of 10. For example, 103.561 m can be written in a number of ways, but only one way is considered scientific notation.

---

a Moving the decimal point to the left one position is the same as multiplying the new number by 10^1 or 10.

103.561 m = 10.3561 x 10 m

b Moving the decimal point two positions to the left is the same as multiplying the new number by 10^2.

103.561m = 1.03561 x 10^2 m

c Moving the decimal point to the right one position is the same as multiplying the new number by 10^{-1}.

103.561 m = 1035.61 x 10^{-1} m

d Moving the decimal point two positions to the right is the same as multiplying the new number by 10^{-2}.

103.561 m = 10356.1 x 10^{-2} m

Example (*b*) is the only one written in scientific notation.

In science, the term **significant figures** refers to the precision with which a measurement is known. [The number of significant figures include all of those which were measured and one estimated digit.] Use the following rules to determine whether zeros are significant.

a All digits which are not zero *are counted*.

b Zeros at the beginning of a number *are not counted*.

c Zeros at the end of a number *are not counted* if the number has no decimal point.

d Final zeros *are counted* if the number has a decimal point.

e Zeros in the middle of a number *are counted*.

f When a number is written in scientific notation, all digits before the times sign (x) *are counted*.

☆ TRY IT

Practice using the *Reference Tables for Physical Setting/PHYSICS* and writing the following in scientific notation. For example, 345 nanometers = 345 x 10⁻⁹ m = 3.45 x 10⁻⁷ m. Now, write the numbers below in scientific notation with the correct number of significant figures.

10 6.5 decimeters   _____

11 230.0 gigawatts   _____

12 4.73 centimeters   _____

13 145 teravolts   _____

14 1550 picometers   _____

WHAT IS A FERMI QUESTION?

A Fermi question requires estimation of physical quantities to arrive at an answer. It challenges the student to ask more questions, not just provide "an answer." Fermi used a process of "zeroing in" on problems by saying that the value in question was certainly larger than one number and less than some other amount. He would proceed through a problem in that fashion and, in the end, have a quantified answer within identified limits.

A Fermi question seems to have too little information. It requires assumptions and estimations. For example, we might ask, "How many alphabetic letters are there in last Sunday's *New York Times*?" Fermi would say, "What else must I estimate?"

🌎 REAL WORLD CONNECTIONS

ENRICO FERMI (1901-1954)

Enrico Fermi was an Italian-born American physicist best known for his contributions to nuclear physics and the development of quantum theory. In addition to his contribution to theory, he is also noted as a mathematical **experimentalist**. In 1938, Fermi was awarded the *Nobel Prize* for his physics work on artificial radioactivity caused by neutron bombardment. In 1942, he produced the first controlled nuclear chain reaction, in a squash court at the University of Chicago.

Text Source: American Heritage Dictionary©2001
Photo: US postage stamp in celebration of centenary of his birth on 29 September 1001.

You must ask and answer more questions. For example, how many pages were in last Sunday's paper? How much text is on one page? How many letters are in the text? Do we want to estimate by columns and inches? How many columns to a page and how long is each column? How many pictures and illustrations are there? Should we deduct for that?

In a Fermi question, the goal is to get an answer to an order of magnitude (typically a power of ten) by making reasonable assumptions about the situation, not necessarily relying upon definite knowledge for an "exact" answer. A Fermi question emphasizes the process rather than "the" answer.

☆ TRY IT

15 How many jelly beans fill a one-liter jar?

16 What is the mass in kilograms of the student body in your school?

17 How many golf balls will fill-in a suitcase?

18 How many gallons of gasoline are used by cars each year in the United States?

19 How high would the stack reach if you piled up one trillion dollar bills in a single stack?

20 How many hairs are on your head?

21 What is the weight of solid garbage thrown away by American families every year?

22 How many water balloons will it take to fill the school gymnasium?

23 How many hot dogs will be eaten at major league baseball games during a one year season?

24 How many pizzas will be ordered in your state this year?

LAB 1 – INDIRECT MEASUREMENTS

BACKGROUND

Atoms and their nuclei are not visible with light because they are much smaller than the wavelength of light. Physicists measure the cross-sectional area of a nucleus of an atom by counting the number of particles from a beam that are scattered out of the beam when they hit a nucleus. The particles shot at the nucleus are often alpha particles. By knowing the target area and the number of particles shot from the experimental setup and recording the number of hits, the scientist can estimate the size of the nucleus.

PROBLEM

Determine the area of a coin using a method similar to one nuclear physicists use to determine the cross-sectional area of the nucleus. Do not measure the diameter of the coin until *after* you have completed the experiment.

EXPERIMENT

On a blank sheet of paper, use a ruler to draw a square approximately 10.0 cm on each side. Using any denomination of coin, place a number of the same coins in the square. Now put the paper on the floor near your feet. Without looking, drop a pencil from shoulder height towards the square on the paper. Drop the pencil so it makes a random mark in the box at least 50 times. Only drops which land in the box count as a hit or miss. Collect the data (pencil hits and locations) and set up a data table to record your results.

DATA ANALYSIS

The ratio of the area of the coins to the area of the square should be in the same proportion as the ratio of the hits on the coin to the number of hits on the square. First, set up this proportion and solve for the area of the coins. The total area of the coins divided by the number of coins should give you the area of each coin.

ERROR ANALYSIS

Measure the diameter of the coin. Calculate the actual area of the coins you used. Determine the Percentage Error based on your measured value.

$$\text{Percentage Error} = \left| \frac{\text{Your Answer - Correct Answer}}{\text{Correct Answer}} \right| \text{ x } 100\%$$

CONCLUSION

In completing your write-up be sure to cover each of the following:

- *Why* was the experiment done.
- *How* was it done.
- *What* were the results.
- *How* well did the results agree with the correct answer.

☆ TRY IT – GOING BEYOND

The experiments you do in science should be stepping stones to advanced thinking.

25 Where else might this technique be used?

26 How could you improve your results?

SKILLS M 2.1, S2.1 (see **Appendix B**: *Process Skills...*)
LAB 2 – PSYCHING OUT THE SYSTEM
BACKGROUND

When scientists study any system, they must ask two basic questions:

1   What are the basic objects or "building blocks" from which this system is made?

2   What are the interactions between these objects?

The answers to these questions depend on the scale at which you study the system. Particle physics plays this game on the smallest possible scales – seeking to discover the basic building blocks of all matter and the fundamental interactions between them.

The connecting rules of these interactions or basic forces explain why some composite objects are observed and others are not observed. The basic forces are as important as the building blocks in explaining data. *Note:* What does not happen is as important a clue as what does.

PROBLEM

To determine the size, shape, and connecting rules for a new set of fundamental particles.

PROCEDURE

This puzzle shows the challenge that particle physicists face. Imagine that the puzzle presents information that was obtained about particles from an accelerator. The black figures represent objects that were observed, while the objects shown in white have not been observed. In this puzzle, "objects" are all two-dimensional shapes, and "interactions" are ways in which they can combine.

The shapes that are not observed provide important clues to the answers. *Note:* You need to answer both questions to explain why the objects that are not observed are not possible.

Source: Puzzle adapted from Helen Quinn, "Of Quarks, Anti-quarks, and glue." *The Stanford Magazine*, Fall, 1983, p.29.

- Identify the shapes which are present.

- State the rules for connecting these shapes.

CHAPTER ONE ASSESSMENTS

PART A QUESTIONS

1   Compared to the gravitational force between two nucleons in an atom, the strong nuclear force between the nucleons is
    (1) weaker and has a shorter range
    (2) weaker and has a longer range
    (3) stronger and has a shorter range
    (4) stronger and has a longer range

2   A baryon may have a charge of
    (1) $-\frac{1}{3}$ e   (2) 0 e   (3) $+\frac{2}{3}$ e   (4) $+\frac{4}{3}$ e

3   Which force between the protons in an atom will have the greatest magnitude?
    (1) gravitational force   (3) strong nuclear force
    (2) electromagnetic force   (4) magnetic force

4   Which one of the following statements is true concerning the proton?
    (1) The proton is composed of two up quarks and a down quark.
    (2) The proton is composed of two down quarks and an up quark.
    (3) The proton is composed of a down quark and an up anti-quark.
    (4) The proton is composed of an up quark and a down anti-quark.

5   Which graph best represents the relationship between energy and mass in the mass-energy equation?

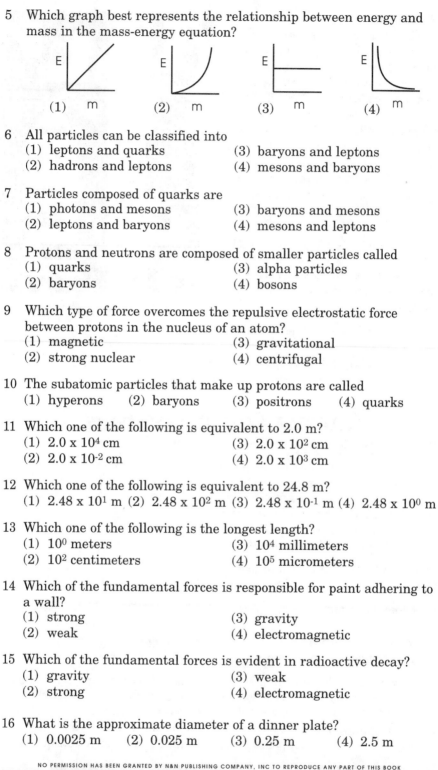

(1) m   (2) m   (3) m   (4) m

6   All particles can be classified into
(1) leptons and quarks   (3) baryons and leptons
(2) hadrons and leptons   (4) mesons and baryons

7   Particles composed of quarks are
(1) photons and mesons   (3) baryons and mesons
(2) leptons and baryons   (4) mesons and leptons

8   Protons and neutrons are composed of smaller particles called
(1) quarks   (3) alpha particles
(2) baryons   (4) bosons

9   Which type of force overcomes the repulsive electrostatic force between protons in the nucleus of an atom?
(1) magnetic   (3) gravitational
(2) strong nuclear   (4) centrifugal

10 The subatomic particles that make up protons are called
(1) hyperons   (2) baryons   (3) positrons   (4) quarks

11 Which one of the following is equivalent to 2.0 m?
(1) 2.0×10^4 cm   (3) 2.0×10^2 cm
(2) 2.0×10^{-2} cm   (4) 2.0×10^3 cm

12 Which one of the following is equivalent to 24.8 m?
(1) 2.48×10^1 m (2) 2.48×10^2 m (3) 2.48×10^{-1} m (4) 2.48×10^0 m

13 Which one of the following is the longest length?
(1) 10^0 meters   (3) 10^4 millimeters
(2) 10^2 centimeters   (4) 10^5 micrometers

14 Which of the fundamental forces is responsible for paint adhering to a wall?
(1) strong   (3) gravity
(2) weak   (4) electromagnetic

15 Which of the fundamental forces is evident in radioactive decay?
(1) gravity   (3) weak
(2) strong   (4) electromagnetic

16 What is the approximate diameter of a dinner plate?
(1) 0.0025 m   (2) 0.025 m   (3) 0.25 m   (4) 2.5 m

17 The length of a high school physics classroom is probably closest to
    (1) 10^{-2} m   (2) 10^{-1} m   (3) 10^1 m   (4) 10^4 m

18 A mass of one kilogram of nickels has a monetary value in United
    States dollars of approximately
    (1) $1.00   (2) $0.10   (3) $10.00   (4) $1000.00

Part B Questions

19 How much energy is released when 1.00×10^{-3} kilogram of matter is
    converted to energy?
    (1) 3.00×10^5 J   (3) 9.00×10^{13} J
    (2) 3.00×10^8 J   (4) 9.00×10^{16} J

20 Approximately how much energy is produced when 0.500 atomic
    mass unit of matter is completely converted into energy?
    (1) 9.31 MeV   (3) 4.65 MeV
    (2) 9.31×10^2 MeV   (4) 4.65×10^2 MeV

21 If the mass of one proton is totally converted into energy, it will yield
    a total energy of
    (1) 5.10×10^{-19} J   (3) 9.31×10^8 J
    (2) 1.50×10^{-10} J   (4) 9.00×10^{16} J

22 Approximately how much energy would be generated if the mass in a
    nucleus of a $^2_1$H atom were completely converted to energy? [The
    mass of $^2_1$H is 2.00 universal mass units.]
    (1) 3.21×10^{-19} J   (3) 9.31×10^2 MeV
    (2) 2.98×10^{-10} J   (4) 9.00×10^3 MeV

23 The length of a lake is 15.5 km. What is the length of the lake in m?
    (1) 1.55×10^4m   (3) 1.55×10^6m
    (2) 3.06×10^5m   (4) 1.55×10^7m

24 A bead has a mass of one *milli*gram. Which one of the following
    statements indicates the correct mass of the bead in grams?
    (1) The bead has a mass of 1×10^3 grams.
    (2) The bead has a mass of 1×10^{-1} grams.
    (3) The bead has a mass of 1×10^{-3} grams.
    (4) The bead has a mass of 1×10^{-6} grams.

25 A physics text has 1060 pages and is 33.5 millimeters thick between
    the inside front cover and the inside back cover. What is the thick-
    ness of a page? The answer should be expressed in scientific notation
    with the correct number of significant figures.
    (1) 3.55×10^{-4} m   (3) 3.6×10^{-6} m
    (2) 3.2×10^{-3} m   (4) 3.16×10^{-5} m

26 The graph at the right represents the relationship between mass and its energy equivalent. The slope of the graph represents: [1]

Energy Equivalent vs. Mass

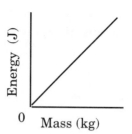

27 The composition of a meson is: [1]

28 Which quarks combine to form a neutron? [1]

29 A particle with the quark composition "down down charm" would have what electrical charge? [1]

30 How many particles combine to form a baryon? [1]

31 List the four fundamental forces in order of strength, beginning with the weakest force. [4]

32 What are two basic interactions that have a finite range?

33 What is the mass of a u in kilograms to three significant figures?

PART C QUESTIONS

34 How much more energy in joules would a proton yield than an electron if both were completely converted into energy? [Show all work including formula, and substitutions with units.] [2]

35 If the mass of one neutron is totally converted into energy, determine the energy in both joules and MeV. [Show all work including formula, and substitutions with units.] [2]

CHAPTER 2
VECTORS

KEY IDEA 5

ENERGY AND MATTER INTERACT THROUGH FORCES THAT RESULT IN CHANGES IN MOTION.

PERFORMANCE INDICATOR 5.1 *STUDENTS CAN EXPLAIN AND PREDICT DIFFERENT PATTERNS OF MOTION OF OBJECTS (E.G., LINEAR AND UNIFORM CIRCULAR MOTION, VELOCITY AND ACCELERATION, MOMENTUM AND INERTIA).*

CHAPTER 2 – MAJOR UNDERSTANDINGS

☆ 5.1a Measured quantities can be classified as either vector or scalar.

☆ 5.1b A vector may be resolved into perpendicular components.*

☆ 5.1c The resultant of two or more vectors, acting at any angle, is determined by vector addition.

☆ M1.1 Use algebraic and geometric representations to describe and compare data. Use scaled diagrams to represent and manipulate vector quantities. Represent physical quantities in graphical form. Construct graphs of real-world data (scatter plots, line or curve of best fit). Manipulate equations to solve for unknowns. Use dimensional analysis to confirm algebraic solutions

CHAPTER 2
VECTORS

ROLE OF UNITS IN PROBLEM SOLVING

Units are very important in the study of physics in that all physical quantities have units. These units are classified as either fundamental units of length (m), mass (kg) and time (s) or derived units such as the joule (kg m²/s²).

When used in algebraic expressions, the units which accompany the numbers can be used to check not only the accuracy of the calculation but also the validity of the equation. Units will always be displayed along with the number in this review book. Remember, if the units do not work out, the solution is not correct.

SKILL M 1.1

EXAMPLE 2.1 – WHEN MANIPULATING EQUATIONS TO SOLVE FOR UNKNOWNS, USE DIMENSIONAL ANALYSIS.

Convert 10 mi/h to m/s.

Conversion factors:

1 mi = 5280 ft	1 ft = 0.305 m
1 km = 1000 m	1 h = 3600 s

Each of the equalities above can be used to form a fraction or conversion factor that is equal to unity (or one). When we multiply by one we do not change the value of the physical quantities; we just express the same quantity in a different set of units. One side of the equality will appear in the numerator and the other side will appear in the denominator of a fraction. The specific way that the equality is written is decided so that the unwanted units cancel and the desired units appear in the final answer.

$$10.0\,\frac{mi}{h} = 10.0\,\frac{mi}{h}\left(\frac{5280\,ft}{1\,mi}\right)\left(\frac{0.305\,m}{1\,ft}\right)\left(\frac{1\,h}{3600\,s}\right) = 4.47\,\frac{m}{s}$$

The first conversion factor changes the miles to feet, the second factor changes the feet to meters, and the third conversion factor changes hours to seconds. Notice that in each conversion factor, the numerator is equal to the denominator, and the conversion factor is equal to one.

☆ Try It

1   Convert 10.0 m/s to miles per hour using the factor label method as shown above.

Note: The Physics Regents Exam will not ask you to convert between the English engineering system and the MKS system. This example was included to give you a real world example of speed.

SCALARS AND VECTORS

A **scalar** quantity is a physical quantity which has **magnitude** (size) only. It is completely described by a single number plus an appropriate unit. Scalar calculations involve only ordinary arithmetic operations.

A **vector** quantity is a physical quantity that has both magnitude and direction. Calculations involving vectors require vector mathematical methods.

VECTORS	SCALARS
Displacement	Distance
Velocity	Speed
Acceleration	Energy
Force	Time
Weight	Power
Momentum	Mass
Torque	Charge

PROPERTIES OF VECTORS

- A vector can be moved anywhere in the plane that contains it as long as the magnitude and the direction of the vector are not changed.
- Two vectors are identical (equal) if they have the same magnitude and direction.
- Vectors are concurrent if they act at the same point.
- A vector multiplied by a positive scalar quantity gives the vector with a different magnitude but the same direction.
- A vector multiplied by a negative scalar quantity gives the vector with a different magnitude and an exactly opposite direction.
- Two or more vectors can be added together to give a **resultant**. The resultant is a single vector that can replace the other vectors acting on the body and produce the same effect as the set of vectors.

- The maximum value two vectors can have occurs when the angle between the two vectors is zero degrees.
- The minimum value two vectors can have occurs when the angle between the two vectors is 180 degrees.
- The **equilibrant** is a vector exactly equal in magnitude to the resultant but in the opposite direction. When a system is in equilibrium, there are no unbalanced forces working on the system. The system may be at rest or in motion with constant velocity.

DISTANCE AND DISPLACEMENT

Distance is a scalar quantity that represents the length of a path from one point to another. **Displacement** is a vector quantity that represents the length and direction of a straight line path from one point to another. Total displacement is a vector sum. A jogger is concerned with distance and a pilot with displacement. The **SI unit** for distance or displacement is the meter.

To illustrate the difference between displacement and distance, consider that an object moves from **A** to **C** along the path **ABC**. The magnitude of the displacement is the length of the vector **AC**. The distance the object actually moves along path **ABC** is greater than the magnitude of the displacement.

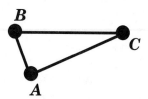

SOLVING VECTOR PROBLEMS GRAPHICALLY

You will need a centimeter ruler and a protractor to begin. To solve vector problems graphically, first select an appropriate scale. (For example, 1 cm = 10 m.) Draw one vector with the proper angle orientation and scaled length.

Vector addition is accomplished by moving the vectors so that the tail of each successive vector in the addition is connected to the head of the next vector in the addition. The resultant vector is then drawn from the starting point of the first vector to the ending point of the last vector.

The order in which the vectors are added does not matter. All combination will give a resultant with the same magnitude and direction.

IMPORTANT DEFINITIONS
Velocity is the time rate of change of displacement.
Speed is the time rate of change of distance.
Acceleration is the time rate of change of velocity.

SKILL 5.1IV
EXAMPLE - ADDING TWO CONCURRENT VECTORS

Consider two forces acting on a point. These forces are said to be **concurrent** vectors. One force acts due east and has a magnitude of 30 N. A second force has a magnitude of 40 N and acts due North. Calculate the resultant force. *Note:* before beginning any problem, it is helpful to sketch the situation. After the sketch is completed, the problem may be solved either by graphical or mathematical methods.

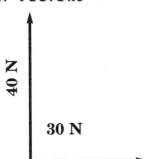

GRAPHICAL METHOD

Construct a scaled vector diagram. In this diagram, 1.0 cm represents 10.0 N. Add the vectors "head to tail." The resultant (**R**) starts where the first vector begins and ends where the last vector ends.

Measure the resultant with a ruler and determine the amount of force it represents. Determine the angle with a protractor.

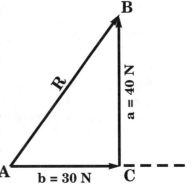

☆ TRY IT

2   Using the graphical method, add the following vectors and determine the resultant.

  a   3.0 meters north, 4.0 meters west

  b   8.0 meters south, 6.0 meters east

  c   16.0 meters east, 8.0 meters north

  d   250. meters south, 300. meters north

  e   660. meters east, 1000. meters south

  f   380 cm west, 790 cm south

Skills 5.1, M 1.1

Mathematical Technique — Applying the right triangle rule of the preceding figure:

$$c^2 = a^2 + b^2$$

Substituting:
$$c^2 = (40. \text{ N})^2 + (30. \text{ N})^2$$
$$= 1600 \text{ N}^2 + 900 \text{ N}^2$$
$$= 2500 \text{ N}^2$$

$$c^2 = 50. \text{ N}$$

$$\sin A = \frac{\text{opposite}}{\text{hypotenuse}} = \frac{40.\text{N}}{50.\text{N}} = .80$$

$$A = 53°$$

The final answer is a 50 N force at an angle of 53°.

☆ Try It

3   Check your work for the previous graphing skill by solving (2 *a – f*) above algebraically (mathematical technique).

Skill 5.1iv

Example 2.3 – Adding Three Vectors Graphically

A bus heads 3.5 km north, then 6.0 km east, then 1.5 km southwest.

Draw a vector diagram to represent the bus trip. Determine the bus' displacement and distance traveled. Southwest is exactly forty five degrees south of west. This technique requires a ruler and a protractor.

Step One: Select an appropriate scale. For this example, 1 cm = 1 km was selected. The scale should allow the diagram to fit into the space provided.

Step Two: Draw each vector the correct length and the correct direction. Label each vector in the original units.

Step Three: Draw the resultant displacement vector from the original starting position to the end of the last vector arrow. Be careful to measure the length. Record this length and use the scale to convert it back to km. Measure the angle of the resultant with a protractor. Angles must be properly described to avoid confusion.

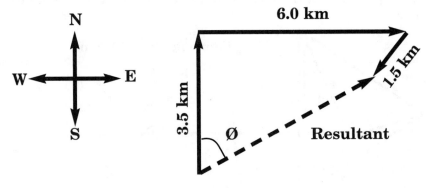

$$\emptyset = 63° \text{ East of North}$$

$$\text{Resultant} = 5.5 \text{ cm} = 5.5 \text{ km}$$

$$\text{Displacement} = 5.5 \text{ km at } 63° \text{ E of N}$$

Note: Do not say 63° NE because the angle is not exactly 45 degrees.

$$\text{Distance} = 3.5 \text{ km} + 6.0 \text{ km} + 1.5 \text{ km} = 11.0 \text{ km}$$

☆ TRY IT

4   Add the following vectors and determine the resultant.

  a   6 meters south, 3 meters north, 4 meters west

  b   14 meters west, 8 meters south, 6 meters east

  c   16 meters east, 8 meters north, 10 meters west

  d   250 meters south, 150 meters west, 300 meters north

  e   660 meters east, 100 meters south, 450 meters west

SKILL 5.1 VI
EXAMPLE – COMPONENTS OF A VECTOR

Every vector can be resolved into any number of components. Most often, two perpendicular components are selected. The components represent the projection of the vector onto the **x-** and **y-axis** of a coordinate system.

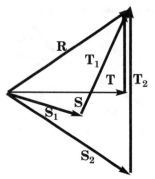

Components of a Vector:

$$R = S + T$$

$$R = S_1 + T_1$$

$$R = S_2 + T_2$$

Consider a vector, **F**, resolved into two perpendicular vectors of magnitude F_y and F_x.

Resolving a vector into two perpendicular components from trigonometry:

$$F_x = F \cos \phi \qquad F_y = F \sin \phi$$

REAL WORLD CONNECTIONS – SKILLS M1.1 AND M3.1
THE PLANE TRUTH ABOUT VELOCITY

A plane is traveling at a velocity of 300 m/s in a direction 30° North of East. At what velocity is the plane traveling to the north? To the east?

This problem can be solved by the graphical method or the mathematical method. Graphically, a vector whose length is 3 cm will represent the velocity of 300 m/s. The top of the page is normally considered North. First draw the vector to scale at the proper angle. Next resolve the vector into components by constructing a perpendicular to each axis. Measure the lengths of the projection along the east and north axis. This length represents the magnitude of the velocity in each direction.

The Concord ©PhotoDisc

The Concord ©PhotoDisc

| Graphical Method: | Mathematical Solution: |

Graphical Method:

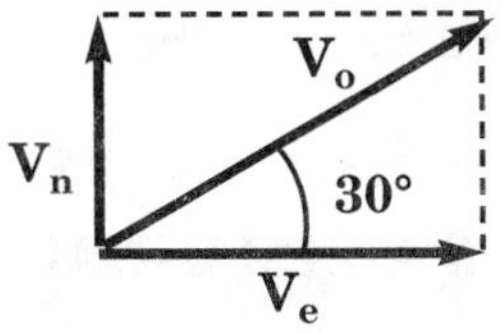

scale: 1 cm = 100 m/s

V_{north} = 1.5 cm
= 150 m/s

V_{east} = 2.6 cm

= 2.60 c̶m̶ x $\dfrac{100 \text{ m/s}}{\text{c̶m̶}}$

= 260 m/s

Mathematical Solution:

$$\sin 30° = \dfrac{V_{north}}{V_0}$$

$$V_n = V_0 \sin 30°$$

$$V_n = (300 \text{ m/s})(0.5) = 150 \text{ m/s}$$

$$\cos 30° = \dfrac{V_{east}}{V_0}$$

$$V_e = V_0 \cos 30°$$

$$V_e = (300 \text{ m/s})(0.866)$$

$$= 260 \text{ m/s}$$

🌎 REAL WORLD CONNECTIONS – ☆ TRY IT

A rocket can be launched at various angles. Assume the horizontal is at zero degrees and a vertical launch is straight up. Complete the table below by determining the components of the velocity in an x and y direction for each launch angle. You may solve this either graphically or mathematically.

5 Complete the following table:

Velocity (m/s)	Angle (degrees)	x-component (m/s)	y-component (m/s)
100	10	_____	_____
100	30	_____	_____
100	45	_____	_____
100	60	_____	_____
100	90	_____	_____

VECTOR ADDITION BY COMPONENTS

The resultant vector can also be determined by summing of the vector components. This technique will be used in the next example to illustrate how to determine the resultant of multiple vectors mathematically.

SKILLS 5.1VI, M 3.1 – EXAMPLE 2.5 – FINDING THE RESULTANT OF TWO OR MORE VECTORS MATHEMATICALLY

Note: This technique will require a scientific calculator.

A bus heads 3.50 km north, then 6.00 km east, then 1.50 km southwest. First, decide on the zero degree orientation. Determine all angles relative to that position. The zero position is typically taken as due east, but it can be any direction you choose. The reference of southwest refers to exactly 45 degrees between south and west.

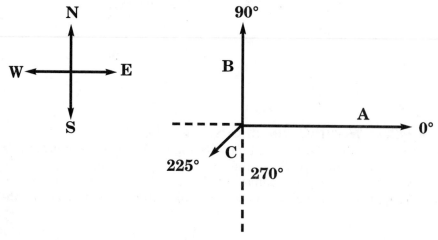

Next, determine the x and y components of each vector. Set up a table like the one below and complete the entries. For this problem, the zero position was selected as due east.

Vector	Magnitude (km)	Direction (degrees)	$F_x = F\cos(\emptyset)$ x-Component (km)	$F_y = F\sin(\emptyset)$ y-Component (km)
Vector A	6.00	0.00	6.00	0
Vector B	3.50	90.0	0	3.50
Vector C	1.50	225.	-1.06	-1.06
		Totals	$\Sigma F_x = 4.94$	$\Sigma F_y = 2.44$

The symbol Σ (sigma) represents "the sum of."

Resultant Magnitude:

$$R = \sqrt{(\Sigma F_x)^2 + (\Sigma F_y)^2}$$

$$R = \sqrt{(4.94\text{ km})^2 + (2.44\text{ km})^2}$$

$$R = 5.5\text{ km}$$

Direction is given by:

$$\tan \emptyset = \frac{\Sigma F_y}{\Sigma F_x} = \frac{4.94\text{ km}}{2.44\text{ km}}$$

$$\emptyset = 26.3° \text{ as measured from the due East position.}$$

This mathematical technique can be used for any number of vectors.

END SKILL

 TRY IT

6   A soccer player runs 53 m due south, 14 m due west, 35 m southeast and 22 m northeast. Determine the soccer player's displacement both graphically and mathematically.

7   Determine the resultant mathematically (or graphically).
   a   150 m at 10 degrees, 75 m at 45 degrees, 200 m at 80 degrees

   b   500 m at 40 degrees, 280 m at 110 degrees, 375 m at 210 degrees

8   Why do you need to receive the signal from three satellites in order to determine your location?

REAL WORLD CONNECTIONS
GLOBAL POSITIONING SYSTEM

The Global Positioning System (GPS) is a worldwide radio-navigation system formed from a constellation of 24 satellites and their ground stations. GPS uses these "man-made stars" as reference points to calculate positions.

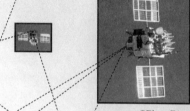

©PhotoDisc

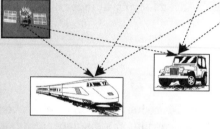

HERE'S HOW GPS WORKS:

a The basis of GPS is "triangulation" from satellites. The signals from three satellites identify your position on Earth. A fourth satellite signal gives altitude. The intersection of these vectors can locate your position to within 1 cm.

b To "triangulate," a GPS receiver measures distance using the travel time of radio signals.

c To measure travel time, GPS needs accurate timing from atomic clocks that are precise to within a billionth of a second.

d Along with distance, you need to know exactly where the satellites are in space.

e Finally you must correct for any delays the signal experiences as it travels through the atmosphere.

Although originally developed for the military, GPS is used for most all guidance systems and navigation, from hikers to commercial airlines and fishermen. It tracks emergency vehicles, construction equipment, and computers. It might even be in your next car.

SKILLS 5.1B,C, 5.1VI, M 1.1
LAB 3 – DISPLACEMENT VECTORS

Vectors are quantities that have both magnitude and direction. The displacement from one location to another is a vector. Vectors can be added graphically by drawing a diagram in which each vector is represented by an arrow pointing in the correct direction and of a length proportional to the magnitude of the vector. These arrows are drawn to scale and placed consecutively end-to-tip. The sum, or resultant, is represented by the vector arrow that joins the end of the first arrow to the tip of the last.

THE PROBLEM

In this lab, we shall determine the displacements between various points on a map. By treating these displacements as vectors and drawing a scale vector diagram, we can add the displacements. Then go back to the map to check the precision of your work. Carefully drawn vector diagrams can be made with good accuracy. A 1% error is a reasonable expectation. Use a sharp pencil and make measurements with care.

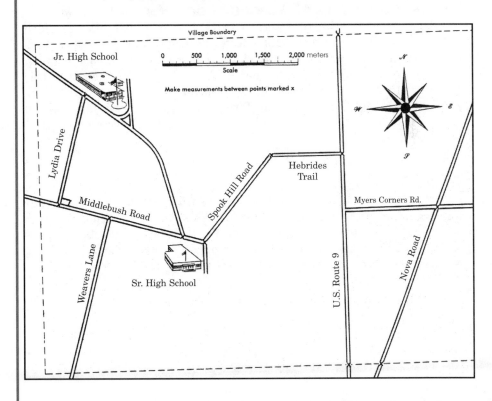

ADD TWO VECTORS

Imagine that you are going from the Senior High School to the Junior High School by Middlebush Road and Lydia Drive. Find the magnitude in meters of each of the necessary displacements. Using a scale of 1.0 cm = 200 m, draw on your report sheet a vector diagram representing this trip. On your diagram, measure the resultant displacement and express it in meters. Knowing that your figure is a right triangle, calculate the result algebraically. How many significant figures should your answer have? Now return to the map and measure the actual displacement, using the map scale. Compare your results and evaluate your accuracy.

ADD THREE VECTORS

Using a scale of 1.0 cm = 200 m, draw a vector diagram representing a trip: starting at the intersection of Weaver's Lane and Middlebush Road, travel along Middlebush Road to Spook Hill Road, up Spook Hill Road to Hebrides Trail and along Hebrides Trail to the intersection with U.S. Route 9. Compare the resultant displacement from your diagram with that obtained by making a measurement on the map.

FIND THE RECTANGULAR COMPONENTS OF A VECTOR

It is often useful to represent a single vector by two others, which when combined produce the same effect. These are called the components of the original vector. Assume Myers Corners Road runs east to west. Draw a vector diagram in your notebook to obtain the answer to this question: In a trip along Nova Road from Myers Corners Road to the south boundary of the village, how far south and how far west would you travel? This process is called resolving a vector into its rectangular components.

GOING BEYOND

See if you can devise a method of measuring the distance from your physics laboratory to some outside feature such as a flagpole, church steeple, or water tower without leaving the building. If the object is less than a half-mile distant, the job can be done to within about 10% using only a protractor and meter stick and drawing a vector diagram to scale.

CHAPTER TWO ASSESSMENTS

PART A QUESTIONS

1 Which terms both represent scalar quantities?
(1) displacement and velocity
(2) distance and speed
(3) displacement and speed
(4) distance and velocity

2 A softball player leaves the batter's box, overruns first base by 3.0 meters, and then returns to first base. Compared to the total distance traveled by the player, the magnitude of the player's total displacement from the batter's box is
(1) smaller   (2) larger   (3) the same

3 The vector at the right represents the resultant of two forces acting concurrently on an object at point P. Which pair of vectors best represents two concurrent forces that combine to produce this resultant force vector?

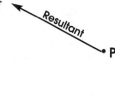

(1)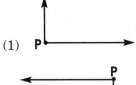

(3)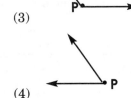

(2)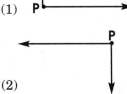

(4)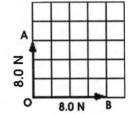

4 Two forces (OA and OB) act simultaneously at point O as shown on the diagram to the right. The magnitude of the resultant force is closest to
(1) 8.0 N   (3) 15 N
(2) 11 N   (4) 16 N

5 A force of 3 newtons and a force of 5 newtons act concurrently to produce a resultant of 8 newtons. The angle between the forces must be
(1) 0°   (2) 60°   (3) 90°   (4) 180°

6 Two concurrent forces have a maximum resultant of 45 newtons and a minimum resultant of 5.0 newtons. What is the magnitude of each of these forces?
(1) 0.0 N and 45 N
(2) 5.0 N and 9.0 N
(3) 20. N and 25 N
(4) 0.0 N and 50. N

7 As the angle between a force and level ground decreases from 60° to 30°, the vertical component of the force
(1) decreases   (2) increases   (3) remains the same

8   Which two terms represent a vector quantity and the scalar quantity
    of the vector's magnitude, respectively?
    (1) acceleration and velocity   (3) speed and time
    (2) weight and force   (4) displacement and distance

9   Which pair of terms are vector quantities?
    (1) force and mass   (3) momentum and acceleration
    (2) distance and displacement   (4) speed and velocity

10 Distance is to displacement as
    (1) force is to weight   (3) velocity is to acceleration
    (2) speed is to velocity   (4) impulse is to momentum

11 A ship changes direction several times and finishes 20 miles north of
    its starting point. This displacement is a vector quantity because it has
    (1) both magnitude and direction
    (2) magnitude but no direction
    (3) direction but no magnitude
    (4) neither magnitude nor direction

12 Which diagram represents the vector with the largest downward
    component? (Assume each vector has the same magnitude.)

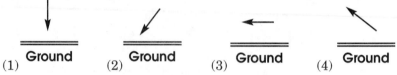

13 The maximum number of components that a single force may be
    resolved into is
    (1) one   (2) two   (3) three   (4) unlimited

14 A lawn mower is pushed with a constant force of F,
    as shown in the diagram at the right. As angle Ø
    between the lawn mower handle and the horizontal
    increases, the horizontal component of F
    (1) decreases   (2) increases   (3) remains the same

PART B QUESTIONS

15 Two students push on a sled. One pushes
    with a force of 30. newtons east and the
    other exerts a force of 40. newtons south,
    as shown in the top view diagram at the
    right. Which vector best represents the
    resultant of these two forces?

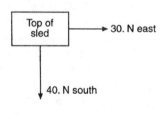

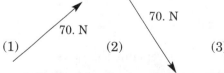

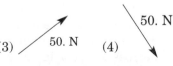

16 An object is displaced 3 meters to the west and then 4 meters to the south. Which vector shown below best represents the resultant displacement of the block?

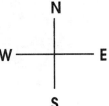

(1) 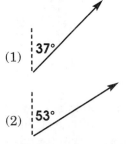 37°

(3) 37°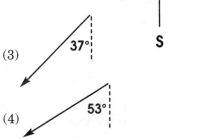

(2) 53°

(4) 53°

17 A 3.0-newton force and a 4.0-newton force act concurrently on a point. In which diagram below would the orientation of these forces produce the greatest net force on the point?

(1) 3.0 N 4.0 N

(3) 3.0 N 4.0 N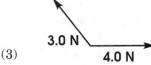

(2) 3.0 N 4.0 N

(4) 4.0 N 3.0 N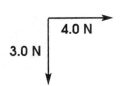

18 The diagram at the right represents a force acting at point P. Which pair of concurrent forces would produce equilibrium when added to the force acting at point P?

P • Force

(1) P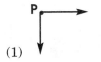

(2) P

(3) P

(4) P

19 If the force vector shown in the diagram at the right is resolved into two components, these two components could best be represented by which diagram at the right?

(1)

(3)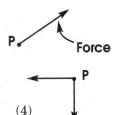

(2)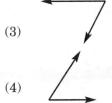

(4)

20 The horizontal component of F in the diagram at the right is

(1) $F \sin 55°$
(2) $F \cos 55°$
(3) $F/\sin 55°$
(4) $F/\cos 55°$

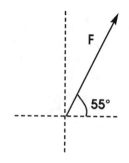

21 A car travels 12.0 kilometers due north and then 8.00 kilometers due west going from town A to town B. What is the magnitude of the displacement of a helicopter that flies in a straight line from town A to town B? [1]

22 A 100.–newton force acts on point P, as shown in the diagram at the right.

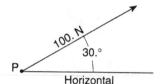

a The magnitude of the vertical component of this force is _____ N [1]

b The magnitude of the horizontal component of this force is _____ N [1]

23 As shown in the diagram at the right, a painter climbs 7.3 meters up a vertical scaffold from A to B and then walks 11.0 meters from B to C along a level platform. The magnitude of the painter's total displacement while moving from A to C is _____ m [1]

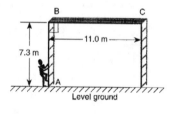

24 The map at the right shows the route traveled by a school bus. What is the magnitude of the total displacement of the school bus from the start to the end of its trip?
_____ m [1]

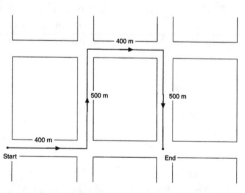

25 The diagram at the right shows a child pulling a 50.-kilogram friend on a sled by applying a 300.-newton force on the sled rope at an angle of 40.° with the horizontal.

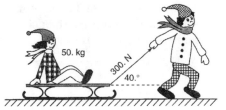

a   The vertical component of the 300.-newton force is approximately _____ N [1]

b   The horizontal component of the 300 newton force is approximately _____ N [1]

26 A student follows the path ABC, as illustrated in the diagram at the right. There is a difference between the distance traveled and the displacement. What is the difference between these two quantities? [1]

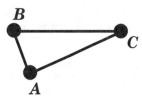

_____

27 A student walks 3 blocks south, 4 blocks west, and 3 blocks north. What is the displacement of the student? [1] _____

28 If a woman runs 100 meters north and then 70 meters south, her total displacement will be [1] _____

29 A student walks 1.0 kilometer due east and 1.0 kilometer due south. Then she runs 2.0 kilometers due west. The magnitude of the student's distance is [1] _____

30 What is the total displacement of a student who walks 3 blocks east, 2 blocks north, 1 block west, and then 2 blocks south? [1] _____

31 A force of 100. newtons is applied to an object at an angle of 30° from the horizontal as shown in the diagram at the right. What is the magnitude of the vertical component of this force? [1]

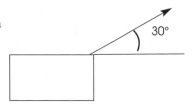

32 A plane flies 400. kilometers south and then 300. kilometers east. The magnitude of the displacement is [1] _____

33 A resultant force of 10. newtons is made up of two component forces acting at right angles to each other. If the magnitude of one of the components is 6.0 newtons, the magnitude of the other component must be [1] _____

PART C QUESTIONS

34 A 300.-newton force acts on point P, as shown in the diagram at the right. The magnitude of the vertical and horizontal components of this force are [2] _____
   [show all work]

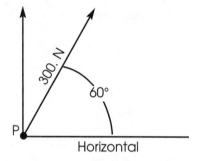

35 A student sailed 10. km north, 5.0 km northeast, then 6.0 km east. Select an appropriate scale and draw a graphical solution of the student's trip.

   a   What was the total displacement of the student? [1]

   b   What was the total distance the student sailed? [1]

CHAPTER 3
KINEMATICS

KEY IDEA 5
ENERGY AND MATTER INTERACT THROUGH FORCES THAT RESULT IN CHANGES IN MOTION.

PERFORMANCE INDICATOR 5.1 *STUDENTS CAN EXPLAIN AND PREDICT DIFFERENT PATTERNS OF MOTION OF OBJECTS (E.G., LINEAR AND UNIFORM CIRCULAR MOTION, VELOCITY AND ACCELERATION, MOMENTUM AND INERTIA).*

CHAPTER 3 – MAJOR UNDERSTANDINGS

☆ 5.1d An object in linear motion may travel with a constant velocity* or with acceleration*. (Note: Testing of acceleration will be limited to cases in which acceleration is constant.)

☆ M1.1 Use algebraic and geometric representations to describe and compare data. Use scaled diagrams to represent and manipulate vector quantities. Represent physical quantities in graphical form. Construct graphs of real-world data (scatter plots, line or curve of best fit). Manipulate equations to solve for unknowns. Use dimensional analysis to confirm algebraic solutions

☆ M2.1 Use deductive reasoning to construct and evaluate conjectures and arguments, recognizing that patterns and relationships in mathematics assist them in arriving at these conjectures and arguments. Interpret graphs of real world data to determine the mathematical relationship between the variables.

☆ M3.1 Apply algebraic and geometric concepts and skills to the solution of problems. Explain the physical relevance of properties of a graphical representation of real-world data, e.g., slope, intercepts, area under the curve.

CHAPTER 3
KINEMATICS

MOTION OF OBJECTS

Kinematics is the science of describing the motion of objects using words, diagrams, graphs, and equations without regard to the forces which produced it. These motions are described in terms of their position as a function of time. The goal of any study of kinematics is to develop mental models to describe and explain the motion of real-world objects.

VOCABULARY OF MOTION

Remember, all vector quantities have a direction associated with them. The words that follow, describe motion. *Note:* Scalar quantities have no direction associated with them.

- **Distance** is a scalar quantity, which refers to how much ground an object has covered during its motion.

- **Displacement** is a vector quantity, which refers to the object's change in position.

- **Speed** is a scalar quantity, which refers to how fast an object is moving. **Instantaneous Speed** is speed at any given instant in time. The instantaneous speed is the reading on a car's speedometer or the slope of a distance-time curve. **Average Speed** – computed from the distance/time ratio.

$$\text{Average Speed} = \frac{\text{Distance Traveled}}{\text{Time of Travel}}$$

- **Velocity** is a vector quantity, which refers to the rate at which an object changes its position and is computed from the displacement/time ratio.

$$\text{Average Velocity} = \frac{\text{Change in Position}}{\text{Change in Time}}$$

- **Acceleration** is a vector quantity, which is defined as the time rate of change of velocity. An object is accelerating if it is changing its velocity, by either changing the magnitude or the direction.

$$a = \frac{\text{Change in Velocity}}{\text{Change in Time}}$$

Since acceleration is a vector quantity, it will always have a direction associated with it. The direction of the acceleration vector depends on two things:

- whether the object is speeding up or slowing down

- whether the object is moving in the + or – direction

General Rule: If an object is slowing down, then its acceleration is in the opposite direction of its motion.

Note: An object moving along a circular path may have a constant speed. Since its direction is changing, it cannot have a constant velocity. The object is being accelerated because its velocity direction is changing. Any change in either the magnitude or the direction of the velocity vector over a period of time indicates acceleration.

DESCRIBING MOTION WITH DIAGRAMS

Diagrams are another way to describe motion. The two most common types of diagrams used to describe the motion of objects include the ticker tape diagrams and the vector diagrams.

TICKER TAPE DATA

One way of analyzing the motion of objects in physics labs is to perform a ticker tape analysis. A long tape is attached to a moving object and threaded through a device that places a tick upon the tape at regular time intervals. As the object moves, it drags the tape through the timing device, and leaves a trail of dots, which provides a history of the object's motion.

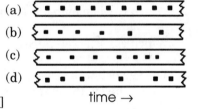

At the right is a sampling of ticker tapes. Select the one which represents each of the following: [Defend your choice.]

- The slowest moving object at t = 5 dots.

- An object which is moving at constant speed.

- An object which is accelerating.

- An object which has negative acceleration (slowing down).

☆ TRY IT

1   What would a ticker tape look like for a car which is stopped? Draw it at the right:

VECTOR DIAGRAMS

Vector diagrams show the direction and magnitude of a vector quantity by a vector arrow. Vector diagrams can be used to describe the velocity of a moving object during its motion. In a vector diagram, the magnitude of a vector is represented by the length of the vector arrow. The direction of the arrow is the same as the direction of the vector. If the length of the arrow in each consecutive frame of the vector diagram is the same, then the magnitude of that vector is constant. The diagrams below depict the velocity of a car during its motion.

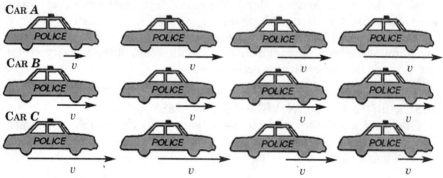

☆ TRY IT

Directions: Based on the vector diagrams for Car A, Car B, and Car C, answer the next two questions.

2   Which car is moving at constant speed?

3   Which car is accelerating?

4   The car below is slowing down at a constant rate. Draw a series of vectors below the car(s) to represent the acceleration.

Note: Vector diagrams can be used to represent any vector quantity.

DESCRIBING MOTION WITH
POSITION (DISPLACEMENT) VS. TIME GRAPHS

Position v. time graphs are another way to describe motion. The specific features of the motion of objects are demonstrated by the shape and the slope of the lines on a position vs. time (**p-t**) graph.

There are two basic shapes of the position vs. time graphs.

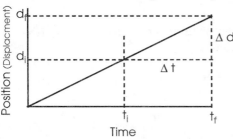

Uniform Motion

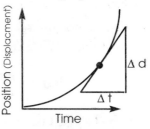

Accelerated Motion

These two *p-t* graphs represent two different kinds of motion – constant velocity motion and accelerated motion. The slope of the line on a position-time graph reveals information about the velocity of the object. It is common to say, "As the slope goes, so goes the velocity." A small slope means a small velocity; a negative slope means a negative velocity; a constant slope (straight line) means a constant velocity; and a changing slope (curved line) means a changing velocity. The shape of the line on the graph is descriptive of the object's motion. *Note:* Directions of positive and negative velocity can be determined by the student.

SKILLS M 2.1, M 3.1
DETERMINING THE
SLOPE ON A *P-T* GRAPH

The line is sloping upwards to the right. Mathematically, by how much does it slope upwards per second along the horizontal (time) axis? To answer this question, we must use the slope equation or graphically determine it.

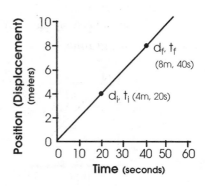

$$\textbf{Slope} = \frac{\textbf{rise}}{\textbf{run}} = \frac{\textbf{d}_f - \textbf{d}_i}{\textbf{t}_f - \textbf{t}_i} = \frac{\mathbf{\Delta d}}{\mathbf{\Delta t}}$$ The units are m/s.

The slope equation says that the slope of a line is found by determining the amount of *rise* of the line between any two points divided by the amount of *run* of the line between the same two points. In other words,

- Pick two points *on the line* and determine their coordinates on the x and y axes.

- Determine the difference in y-coordinates of these two points (*rise*).

- Determine the difference in x-coordinates for these two points (*run*).

- Divide the difference in y-coordinates by the difference in x-coordinates (rise/run or slope).

$$\text{Slope} = \frac{\text{rise}}{\text{run}} = \frac{4 \text{ m}}{20 \text{ s}} = \frac{1 \text{ m}}{5\text{s}} = 0.2 \text{ m/s}$$

SKILLS 5.1I, 5.1II

Students can also determine the slope graphically, by drawing a triangle. The diagram at the right shows this method being applied to determine the slope of the line. The slope is 0.20 m/s.

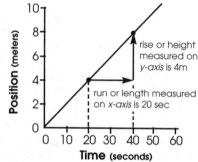

- Pick two points on the line.
- Construct a right triangle by constructing a perpendicular to the horizontal and vertical axes.
- Measure the height of the triangle on the y axis (rise).
- Measure the length of your triangle on the x axis (run).
- If the graph is a curve, a tangent line must be drawn at a point. The slope will then represent the instantaneous speed at that point.
- Divide the rise by the run.

Examples: *p-t* graphs:

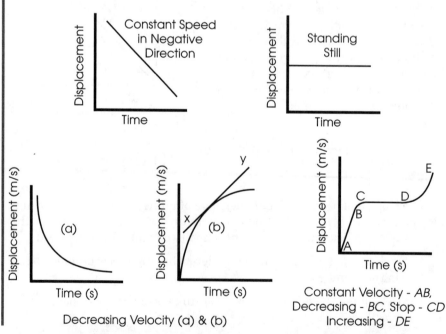

Decreasing Velocity (a) & (b)

Constant Velocity - *AB*,
Decreasing - *BC*, Stop - *CD*
Increasing - *DE*

☆ TRY IT

Directions: Check your understanding of *p-t* graphs by graphically determining the slope of each of the following graphs. Show all work.

(5) Graph 1

(6) Graph 2

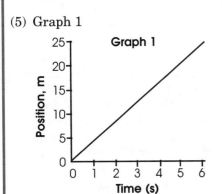

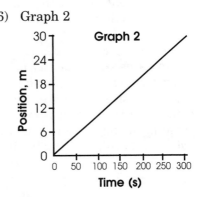

DESCRIBING MOTION WITH VELOCITY VS. TIME GRAPHS

SKILLS M 3.1, 5.1I, 5.1II
THE MEANING OF THE SLOPE OF A *V-T* GRAPH

Uniform Motion   **Accelerated Motion**

$$\text{slope} = \frac{\Delta v}{\Delta t} = \frac{m/s}{s} = m/s^2$$

These two velocity vs. time (*v-t*) graphs represent two different kinds of
motion – constant velocity motion and accelerated motion. The slope of the
line on a velocity-time graph reveals information about the acceleration of
the object. A small slope means a small acceleration, a negative slope
means a negative acceleration; a constant slope (straight line) means a

constant acceleration and a changing slope (curved line) means a changing acceleration. The shape of the line on the graph is descriptive of the object's motion.

How can one tell whether the object is moving in the positive direction (i.e., positive velocity) or in the negative direction (i.e., negative velocity)?

A positive velocity means the object is moving in the positive direction; and a negative velocity means the object is moving in the negative direction. An object is moving in the positive direction if the line is located in the positive region of the graph (regardless if it is sloping up or sloping down). An object is moving in the negative direction if the line is located in the negative region of the graph (regardless if it is sloping up or sloping down). And finally, if a line crosses over the x-axis from the positive region to the negative region of the graph, then the object has changed directions.

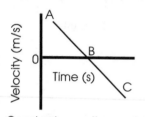

Constant negative acceleration. Describe the velocity from A to B to C. *Note,* this could be a v-t graph of a baseball thrown straight up into the air. the slope would represent the acceleration of gravity.

How can one tell if the object is speeding up or slowing down? The magnitude of the velocity (the number itself, not the sign or direction) is increasing; the speed is getting bigger. To the left is a graph which illustrates an object speeding up and slowing down. When an object is slowing down (*AB*), the line approaches the x-axis; when an object is speeding up (*BC*) the line moves away from the x-axis. What happens at position *B*?

☆ TRY IT

Directions: Draw a velocity-time graph to show each of the following cases.

7   moving with a constant velocity

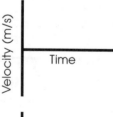

8   moving with a constant negative velocity

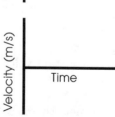

9   slowing down at a constant rate

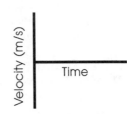

10 changing directions

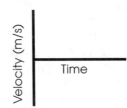

11 speeding up

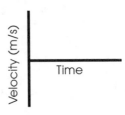

12 moving with a positive acceleration

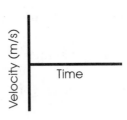

13 moving with a negative acceleration

Skills M 3.1, 5.1ı, 5.1ıı
Getting Information from a v-t Graph
Slope Gives Acceleration

The slope of a velocity vs. time graph reveals pertinent information about an object's acceleration. For example, if the acceleration is zero, then the velocity-time graph is a horizontal line (i.e., the slope is zero). If the acceleration is positive, then the line is an upward sloping line (i.e., the slope is positive). If the acceleration is negative, then the velocity-time graph is a downward sloping line (i.e., the slope is negative). Thus the shape of the line on the graph is descriptive of the object's motion.

Area Gives Distance Traveled

A plot of velocity vs. time can also be used to determine the distance traveled by an object. For velocity vs. time graphs, the area bound by the line and the axes represents the distance. The diagram below shows a velocity-time graph; the shaded regions between the line and the time-axis represents the distance traveled during the stated time interval.

☆ Try It – Example

A toy train heads north on a long straight track as plotted on the graph below:

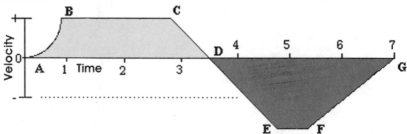

From the data on the graph (above), answer the following questions:

14 At what time(s) was the train stopped?

15 During what interval(s) was acceleration constant and not zero?

16 Identify the interval(s) of non-uniform acceleration.

17 Identify the interval where the uniform acceleration was the greatest magnitude.

18 Did the train arrive back at the starting point?

☆ TRY IT – 🌎 REAL WORLD CONNECTIONS

The graph below represents an acceleration curve for a Porsche 968. As the transmission moves to a different gear, there is a different acceleration for each portion of the curve. (*Note:* Use 1 mph = .448 m/s.)

19 At 30 seconds, what was the speed of the car?

    a   in m/s?

    b   in km/hr?

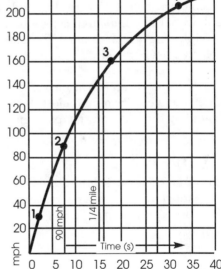

20 According to the graph, what time did the vehicle take to go from 0-60 mph?

21 Calculate the slope of the graph at position
    a 1 _____

    b 2 _____

    c 3 _____

    d 4 _____

22 Describe the changes in acceleration as time increases.

DESCRIBING MOTION WITH ACCELERATION VS. TIME GRAPHS
SKILLS 5.1ı, 5.1ıı
INFORMATION FROM AN A-T GRAPH

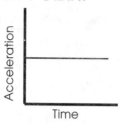

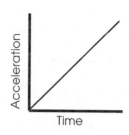

Uniform Motion
(no acceleration)

Uniformly Acc. Motion
(constant acceleration)

Changing Acceleration
(at a constant rate)

These three acceleration vs. time (*a-t*) graphs represent three different kinds of motion – constant velocity motion, uniformly accelerated motion and non-uniform accelerated motion. The slope of the line on an acceleration-time graph reveals information about the change of acceleration of the object. A zero slope indicates no change in acceleration, while a diagonal line indicated constant slope (straight line) indicates uniformly changing acceleration. The slope of an acceleration-time graph is referred to as the jerk.

A graph of acceleration vs. time can also be used to determine the change in velocity of an object. For acceleration vs. time graphs, the area bound by the line and the axes represents the change in velocity.

☆ TRY IT

23 From the slopes determined in the last exercise, sketch an acceleration vs. time graph for the Porsche's velocity.

24 What are the units for acceleration on this graph?

25 What does the shape of this curve indicate?

FREELY FALLING OBJECTS
THE ACCELERATION OF GRAVITY (*g*)

A free-falling object is an object which is falling under the sole influence of gravity. Such an object has an acceleration of 9.81 m/s², downward (on Earth). This numerical value for the acceleration of a free-falling object is such an important value that it is given a special name: the **acceleration of gravity** with the symbol ***g***. The numerical value for the acceleration of gravity is 9.81 m/s².

REPRESENTING FREE-FALL BY GRAPHS

There are a variety of means of describing the motion of objects. One such means of describing the motion of objects is through the use of graphs – position vs. time and velocity vs. time graphs. In this set of graphs, the origin was picked where the object was released. Upward is the positive direction. Downward is the negative direction.

A position vs. time graph for a free-falling object is shown at the right. Observe that the line on the graph curves. A curved line on a position vs. time graph signifies an accelerated motion. Since a free-falling object is undergoing an acceleration, it would be expected that its position-time graph would be curved. Since the slope of any position vs. time graph is the velocity of the object, the small initial slope indicates a small initial velocity and the large final slope indicates a large final velocity. Finally, the negative slope of the line indicates a negative (i.e., downward) velocity.

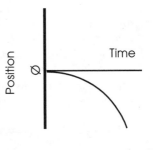

A velocity vs. time graph for a free-falling object is shown at the right. The line on the graph is a straight, diagonal line. A diagonal line on a velocity vs. time graph signifies an accelerated motion. Since a free-falling object is undergoing constant acceleration (*g* = 9.81 m/s²), it would be expected that its velocity-time graph would be diagonal. The velocity-time graph shows that the object starts with a zero velocity (as read from the graph) and finishes with a large, negative velocity; that is, the object is moving in the negative direction and speeding up. The constant, negative slope indicates a constant, negative acceleration.

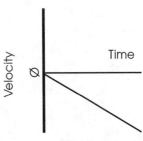

ANOTHER GRAPH OF THE SAME MOTION

In physics, you have the freedom to label your axes in a number of ways. It is just as "right" to identify down as the positive direction, again starting with the origin at zero. With that in mind, the following set of graphs would represent free fall also.

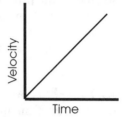

 REAL WORLD CONNECTIONS – WEIGHTLESSNESS

While orbiting Earth, an astronaut isn't really weightless. Earth's gravity is still pulling her toward the center of Earth and her weight is almost as large as it would be on Earth's surface. What makes her feel weightless is the fact that she is in free fall all the time! She is falling just as she would be if she had jumped off a diving board or a cliff. If it were not for the astronaut's enormous sideways velocity, she would plunge toward Earth faster and faster and soon crash into Earth's surface. But her sideways velocity carries her past the horizon so fast that she keeps missing Earth as she falls. Instead of crashing into Earth, she orbits it.

During her orbit, the astronaut feels weightless because all of her "pieces" are falling together. Those pieces do not need to push on one

---

 REAL WORLD CONNECTIONS

THE "VOMIT COMET"

To prepare for this weightless feeling, the astronaut needs to fall. Jumping off a diving board or riding a roller coaster will help, but the classic training technique is a ride on the "Vomit Comet" – an airplane that follows a parabolic arc through the air that allows everything inside it to fall freely. The airplane's arc is just that of a freely falling object and everything inside it floats around in free fall, too – including the astronaut trainee. The plane starts the arc heading upward. It slows its rise until it reaches a peak height and then continues arcing downward faster and faster. The whole trip lasts at most 20 seconds, during which everyone inside the plane feels weightless.

another to keep their relative positions as they fall, so she feels none of the internal forces that she interprets as weight when she stands on the ground. A falling astronaut cannot feel her weight.

TRY IT

26 Describe a situation where you would feel weightless.

WHICH FALLS FASTER – A MORE MASSIVE OBJECT OR A LESS MASSIVE OBJECT?

The acceleration of a free-falling object (on Earth) is 9.81 m/s². This value is the same for all free-falling objects regardless of how long they have been falling, or whether they were initially dropped from rest or thrown up into the air. The question is often asked "doesn't a more massive object fall faster?" This question is a reasonable inquiry that is probably based in part upon personal observations made of falling objects in the physical world. Nearly everyone has observed the difference in the rate of fall of a single piece of paper and a textbook. The two objects clearly travel to the ground at different rates - with the more massive book falling faster.

But, the answer to the question is, "absolutely not," if we are considering free-fall. Free-fall is the motion of objects, which move under the sole influence of gravity. Free-falling objects do not encounter air resistance. More massive objects will only fall faster if there is an appreciable amount of air resistance present.

The actual explanation of why all objects accelerate at the same rate involves the concepts of force and mass. The force to mass ratio of all objects is the same. The value of that ratio is the acceleration of gravity *g*.

THE KINEMATIC EQUATIONS

The kinematic equations are a set of four equations which can be utilized to determine unknown information about an object's motion if other information is known. The equations can be utilized for any motion that can be described as being either a constant velocity motion or a constant acceleration motion. Each of the kinematic equations include four variables. If the values of three of the four variables are known, then the value of the fourth variable can be calculated. In this manner, the kinematic equations provide a useful means of predicting information about an object's motion if other information is known. One equation is written a little bit differently on the *Reference Tables for Physical Setting/PHYSICS* and includes average velocity ($\bar{v}$) instead of $\frac{1}{2}(v_i + v_f)$. The two equations are equivalent. The four kinematic equations which describe an object's motion are described below.

SOLVING KINEMATIC PROBLEMS (WORKSHEET)

Number	Equation	d	v_i	v_f	a	t
1	$v_f = v_i + at$					
2	$d = \frac{1}{2}(v_i + v_f)t$					
3	$d = v_i t + \frac{1}{2}(at^2)$					
4	$v_f^2 = v_i^2 + 2ad$					

SKILLS 5.1, M 1.1
APPLYING THE KINEMATIC EQUATIONS

a   Make a drawing to represent the situation described in the problem.

b   Decide which direction will be called (+) positive and (–) negative. Do not change your decision during the course of a calculation.

c   In an organized way, write down what values are given for the kinematic variables. Use a table or write down the givens for the problem. *Note:* Be alert for unstated or implied data, such as "starting from rest" which indicates $v_i = 0$. Free-falling indicates an acceleration of gravity at 9.81 m/s^2.

d	v_i	v_f	a	t

d   Before attempting to solve a problem, identify at least three of the variables. Once you know what variables you have and what is the unknown variable, select the appropriate equation. The fact that the motions are interrelated is an important piece of data. They may have a common variable.

e   Keep in mind that there may be two possible answers to a kinematic problem. Try to visualize the different physical situations to which the answers correspond.

f   Remember, when a problem asks you for the velocity with which an object hits the ground, the answer is not zero. The problem requires the final velocity at impact.

g   An object projected upward takes as long to go up as to go down because the acceleration of gravity is a constant.

h   In relative motion, simplify the problem.

j   Make sure you have included units in your answer.

k   Finally, does your answer make sense?

EXAMPLE

An object increases its speed from 10. m/s to 24. m/s in 2.0 s.

Find: *a*   the average speed of the object,
            b   the acceleration of the object, and
            c   the distance the object traveled during 2.0 seconds.

Solution: Given:

$$v_i = 10. \text{ m/s} \qquad v_f = 24. \text{ m/s} \qquad t = 2.0 \text{ s}$$

Find: v, a, and **distance**

a   for average speed use:

$$v = \tfrac{1}{2}(v_i + v_f) = \tfrac{1}{2}(10. \text{ m/s} + 24. \text{m/s}) = 17. \text{ m/s}$$

b for acceleration use the definition for acceleration:

$$a = \frac{\text{change in velocity}}{\text{change in time}} = \frac{(24. \text{ m/s} - 10. \text{ m/s})}{2 \text{ s}} = 7.0 \text{ m/s}^2$$

c for distance use:

$$d = v_i t + \tfrac{1}{2}a(t)^2$$

$$d = (10. \text{ m/s})(2.0s) + 1/2(7.0 \text{ m/s}^2)(2.0 \text{ s})^2 = 34. \text{ m}$$

☆ TRY IT

FREE-FALL – HOW FAST AND HOW FAR?

27 Using the kinematic formulae, complete the following table:

TABLE - FREE FALL OF AN OBJECT STARTING FROM REST

Time of fall(s)	0.00s	1.00s	2.00s	3.00s	4.00s	5.00s	6.00s
Speed (m/s)	0.00	9.81					
Distance traveled (m)	0.00						

SKILLS M3.1, 5.1D

WALK A GRAPH

In this activity, the student will be given an index card with a position-time or velocity-time graph on it. The student determines the origin point in the front of the classroom and indicates the positive direction to the class. No other words may be spoken. The student's task will be to walk the graph properly so another can draw the correct graph. This can be a team or a full class activity. Below are a series of graphs to get you started. The **p-t** and **v-t** graphs do not describe the same motion. Students should be encouraged to draw their own graphs for this activity.

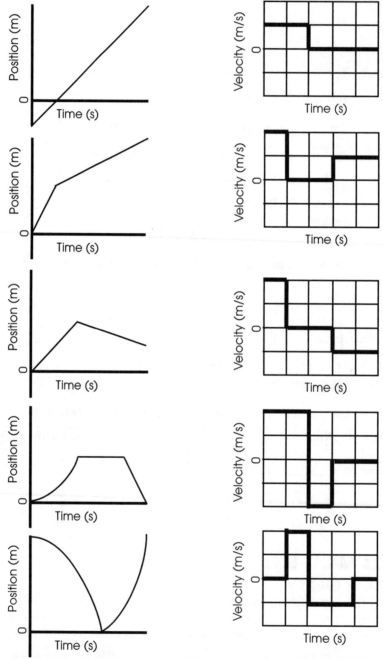

Skills M3.1, 5.1D
Story Graphs

Draw a position-time graph and a velocity-time graph for the following story:

Lauren left her house and walked east at a constant speed to the bus stop (*AB*). At the bus stop she waited for a short time before the bus arrived (*BC*). When she got on the bus, she was accelerated eastward for a few minutes until the bus reached cruising speed (*CD*). She traveled for several miles at a constant speed (*DE*) still in the eastward direction until the bus decelerated to a stop at school.

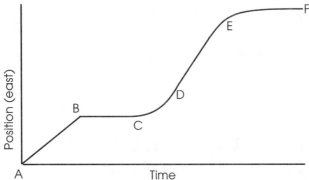

That is just half of the story. After school, Lauren returned home on the bus heading west.

☆ Try It

28 Write the words and draw the graphs to describe her motion back home.

29 Create some story-graphs of your own to share in class.

Nursery Rhymes and Children's Songs

These familiar items can also be graphed. For example, a position-time graph of "Itsy, Bitsy Spider" might look like this.

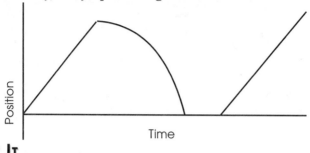

☆ Try It

29 Try to graph some of your favorite rhymes or songs to share with the class.

Skills M 1.1, M 2.1, M 3.1, 5.1ı, 5.1ıı
Lab 4 – Creating Motion Graphs

The Problem

As an object moves down a hill its speed increases. It is accelerating. If the slope of the incline is constant, the object gains speed at a constant rate – its acceleration is constant. Because of the object's increasing speed, the distances that it travels in successive time intervals also increase. We shall study this process and learn the relationships between distance, speed, and acceleration as demonstrated by an object moving down an incline of constant slope.

The Experiment

Prepare the incline first. You can use Hot Wheels® Tracks, molding or even two meter sticks taped to create a V for the incline. You can use a ball or a Hot Wheels® car, or any other object which will move down your track and accelerate at a constant speed. Prop up one end so that the object obviously accelerates, but does not move so fast at the bottom that you cannot easily time it. Sight along the incline to make sure that the slope is constant. If not, support the incline near the center. Using masking tape, mark the object's starting point and at least six points distributed at random along the incline. After marking these points, measure the distance of each from the object's starting point.

Measure the time required for the object to roll from the starting point to each of the marks. These are very critical measurements. You should practice the procedure and repeat each measurement several times until you are certain that your results are as accurate as you can make them.

ANALYZING THE DATA

To start the analysis of data, plot distance (vertical axis) against time (horizontal axis). Is the origin a part of your data? Draw the best smooth curve you can. It is probable that the best curve will not pass through some of the plotted points. How would you describe the slope of this curve? What is the significance of its slope? Select one of the points that lies on the curve near the middle of the graph and draw a tangent to the curve at this point. Calculate the slope of the tangent, which is the same as the slope of the curve at the selected point. Do not forget the units!

Using the original data for the same point, calculate the speed of the object at this point. Since you know the distance and the time, you can calculate the average speed over that distance. The ball started from rest, and the inclination of its path was constant. Are you justified in doubling the average speed to find the ball's instantaneous speed as it passed the point in question? Compare the result of this calculation with the slope of the tangent.

Using either method (determining the slope of the tangent or doubling the average speed) find the speed of the ball at several different instants. Obtain all your data from the curve. Plot a graph of speed versus time. What is the significance of the shape of the graph? Measure the slope of this line. What is the significance of the slope? Check by calculating the acceleration of the ball from the speed and time at one of the "good" data points.

What is the significance of the area under the speed-time graph? Devise a way to check this area against your original data.

Extension I: This is an excellent setup for using computer interfacing equipment. Motion detectors will plot the position-time, the velocity-time and the acceleration time graphs for this activity. Compare the computer generated graphs with your own.

Extension II: An interesting extension of this lab is to determine the kinematics of a student. Using stopwatches, student timers, student runners and a tape measure, design a procedure to take data of a student moving at constant speed and a student accelerating over a distance of 30-40 meters. After deciding on a procedure for the entire class to use, go outside or down a long hallway and determine the velocity and acceleration of several students in class. Compare graphs to determine who was able to produce constant acceleration.

CHAPTER THREE ASSESSMENTS

PART A QUESTIONS

1 Which two graphs best represent the motion of an object falling freely from rest near Earth's surface?

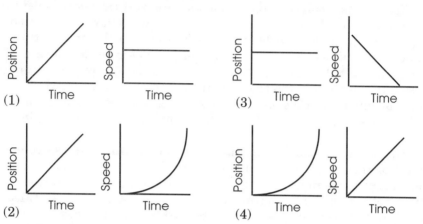

2 Which pair of graphs represent the same motion?

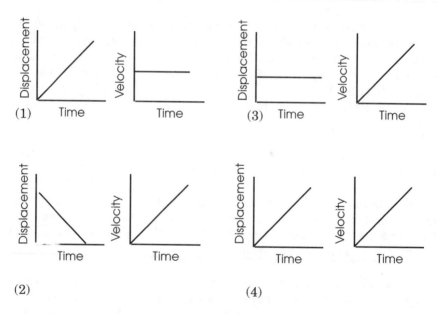

3 A car having an initial velocity of 12 meters per second east slows uniformly to 2 meters per second east in 4.0 seconds. The acceleration of the car during this 4.0-second interval is
(1) 2.5 m/s² west
(3) 6.0 m/s² west
(2) 2.5 m/s² east
(4) 6.0 m/s² east

4 What is the average velocity of a car that travels 30. kilometers due west in 0.50 hour?
   (1) 15 km/hr   (3) 15 km/hr west
   (2) 60. km/hr   (4) 60. km/hr west

5 An object initially traveling in a straight line with a speed of 5.0 m/s is accelerated at 2.0 m/s^2 for 4.0 seconds. The total distance traveled by the object in the 4.0 seconds is
   (1) 36 m   (2) 40 m   (3) 16 m   (4) 4.0 m

6 Which graph best represents the motion of an object whose speed is increasing?

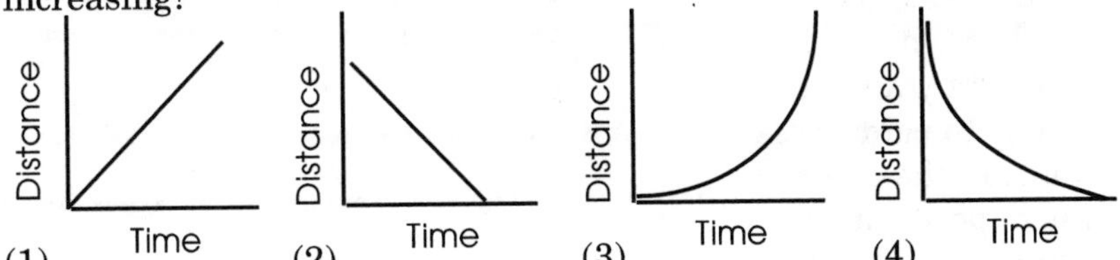

   (1)   Time   (2)   Time   (3)   Time   (4)   Time

7 The displacement-time graph below represents the motion of a cart along a straight line. During which interval was the cart accelerating?

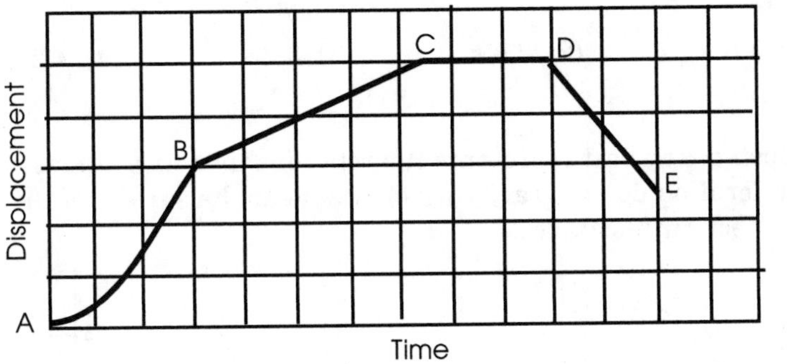

   (1) *AB*   (2) *BC*   (3) *CD*   (4) *DE*

8 A blinking light of constant period is situated on a lab cart. Which diagram best represents a photograph of the light as the cart moves with constant velocity?

   (1) . . .   .   .   .

   (2) .   .   .   . . .

   (3) .   .   .   .

   (4) . .   .   .

9 A moving body must undergo a change of
   (1) velocity   (3) position
   (2) acceleration   (4) direction

10 The graph at the right represents the motion of a
   body that is moving with
   (1) increasing acceleration
   (2) decreasing acceleration
   (3) increasing speed
   (4) constant speed

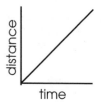

11 A jogger accelerates at a
   constant rate as she
   travels 5.0 meters along
   a straight track from
   point A to point B, as
   shown in the diagram.
   If her speed was 2.0
   meters per second at
   point A and will be 3.0
   meters per second at
   point B, how long will it take her to go from A to B.

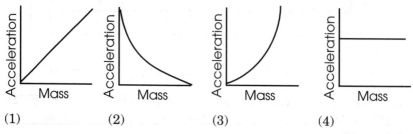

   (1) 1.0 s   (2) 2.0 s   (3) 3.3 s   (4) 4.2 s

12 Which graph best represents the relationship between mass and
   acceleration due to gravity for objects near the surface of the Earth?
   (Neglect air resistance.)

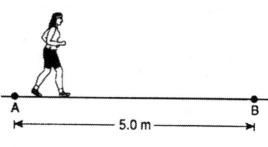

   (1)   (2)   (3)   (4)

13 Acceleration is a vector quantity that represents the time-rate of
   change in
   (1) momentum   (2) velocity   (3) distance   (4) energy

14 A 4.0-kilogram rock and a 1.0-kilogram stone fall freely from rest
   from a height of 100. meters. After they fall for 2.0 seconds, the ratio
   of the rock's speed to the stone's speed is
   (1) 1:1   (2) 2:1   (3) 1:2   (4) 4:1

15 Which graph best represents the relationship between velocity and time for an object which accelerates uniformly for 2 seconds, then moves at a constant velocity for 1 second, and finally decelerates for 3 seconds?

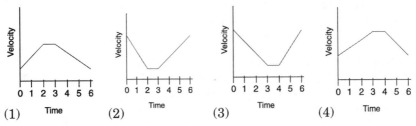

(1)   (2)   (3)   (4)

16 Which graph represents an object moving at a constant speed for the entire time interval?

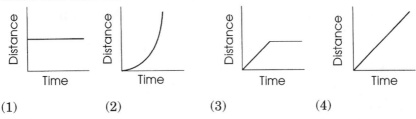

(1)   (2)   (3)   (4)

17 As shown in the diagram at the right, an astronaut on the Moon is holding a baseball and a balloon. The astronaut releases both objects at the same time. What does the astronaut observe? (*Note:* The Moon has no atmosphere.)

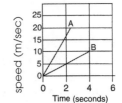

(1) The baseball falls slower than the balloon.
(2) The baseball falls faster than the balloon.
(3) The baseball and balloon fall at the same rate.
(4) The baseball and balloon remain suspended and do not fall.

18 The graph at the right shows the relationship between speed and time for two objects, *A* and *B*. Compared with the acceleration of object *B*, the acceleration of object *A* is approximately

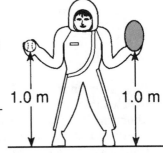

(1) one-third as great
(2) twice as great
(3) three times as great
(4) the same

19 A locomotive starts from rest and accelerates at 0.12 meter per second^2 to a speed of 2.4 meters per second in 20. seconds. This motion could best be described as
(1) constant acceleration and constant velocity
(2) increasing acceleration and constant velocity
(3) constant acceleration and increasing velocity
(4) increasing acceleration and increasing velocity

20 The speed-time graph shown on the right represents the motion of an object. Which graph best represents the relationship between acceleration and time for this object?

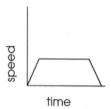

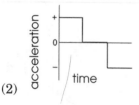

(1)

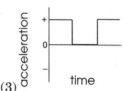

(3)

(2)

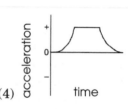

(4)

21 Base your answer on the diagram below which shows a 1-kilogram mass and a 2-kilogram mass being dropped from a building 100 meters high. [neglect friction] Halfway down, the acceleration is
(1) greater for the 1-kilogram mass
(2) greater for the 2-kilogram mass
(3) the same for both masses

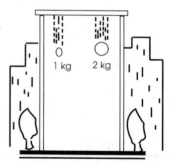

PART B QUESTIONS

22 A car having an initial speed of 16 meters per second is uniformly brought to rest in 4.0 seconds. How far does the car travel during this 4.0-second interval? [1] _____ m

23 A baseball pitcher throws a fastball at 42 meters per second. If the batter is 18 meters from the pitcher, approximately how much time does it take for the ball to reach the batter? [1] _____ s

24 A stone is dropped from a bridge 45 meters above the surface of a river. Approximately how many seconds does the stone take to reach the water's surface? [1] _____ s

Base your answers to questions 25 and 26 on the graph at the right, which represents the relationship between the displacement of an object and its time of travel along a straight line.

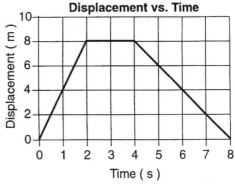

25 What is the magnitude of the object's total displacement after 8.0 seconds? [1] _____ m

26 What is the average speed of the object during the first 4.0 seconds? [1] _____ m/s

27 A runner starts from rest and accelerates uniformly to a speed of 8.0 meters per second in 4.0 seconds. The magnitude of the acceleration of the runner is [1] _____ m/s^2

28 A ball is thrown straight up with a speed of 12 meters per second near the surface of Earth. What is the maximum height reached by the ball? [Neglect air friction.] [1] _____ m

29 An airplane originally at rest on a runway accelerates uniformly at 6.0 m/s^2 for 12 seconds. During this 12-second interval, the airplane travels a distance of approximately [1] _____ m

30 A truck with an initial speed of 12 meters per second accelerates uniformly at 2.0 m/s^2 for 3.0 seconds. What is the total distance traveled by the truck during this 3.0- second interval? [1] _____ m

31 Two cars, A and B, are 400. meters apart. Car A travels due east at 30. meters per second on a collision course with car B, which travels due west at 20. meters per second. How much time elapses before the two cars collide? [1] _____ s

Base your answers to questions 32 through 36 on the information and diagram below.

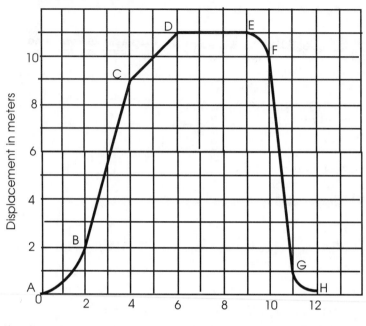

Time in seconds

The graph represents the trip of a cart along a straight line. The total trip takes 12 seconds and starts at $t = 0$.

32 What was the total distance covered by the cart during the trip (*AH*)? [1] _____ m

33 The part of the trip during which the cart was at rest is represented by line [1] _____

34 What is the average speed of the cart during the part of the trip labeled *CD*? [1] _____ m/s

35 The part of the trip during which the cart was moving with a constant speed is represented by line [1] _____

36 The part of the trip during which acceleration was not 0 is represented by line [1] _____

Base your answers to questions 37 and 38 on the graphs below which represent various phenomena in physics. (*Note:* A graph may be used more than once.)

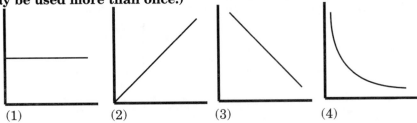

(1)   (2)   (3)   (4)

37 Which graph best represents the relationship between speed and time for an object in free fall near Earth's surface? [1] _____

38 Which graph best represents the relationship between velocity and time for an object thrown vertically upward near the surface of Earth? [1] _____

39 A bicyclist accelerates from rest to a speed of 5.0 meters per second in 10. seconds. During the same 10. seconds, a car accelerates from a speed of 22 meters per second to a speed of 27 meters per second. Compared to the acceleration of the bicycle, the acceleration of the car is [1] _____

40 A rock dropped off a bridge takes 5 seconds to hit the water. What was the rock's velocity just before impact? [1] _____ m/s

41 An object, initially at rest, falls freely near Earth's surface. How long does it take the object to attain a speed of 98 meters per second? [1] _____ s

42 An object is allowed to fall freely near the surface of a planet. The object has an acceleration due to gravity of 24 m/s². How far will the object fall during the first second? [1] _____ m

43 In an experiment that measures how fast a student reacts, a meter stick dropped from rest falls 0.20 meter before the student catches it. The reaction time of the student is approximately [1] _____ s

44 A clam dropped by a sea gull takes 3.0 seconds to hit the ground. What is the sea gull's approximate height above the ground at the time the clam was dropped? [1] _____ m

Base your answers to questions 45 through 47 on the graph at the right which represents the displacement of an object as a function of time.

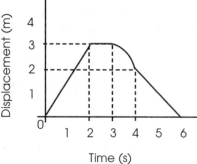

45 During which interval is the object accelerating? [1] _____ s to _____ s

46 What is the average velocity of the object from $t = 0$ to $t = 3$ seconds? [1] _____

47 During which time interval is the object at rest? _____ s to _____ s

Base your answers to questions 48 on the information and diagram at the right.
   An inclined plane is 10 meters long and is elevated 5 meters on one end as shown. Starting from rest at the top of the incline, a box weighing 100 newtons accelerates down the incline at a rate of 2.5 meters per second^2.

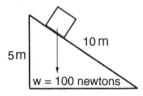

48 How many seconds will it take the box to reach the bottom of the incline? [1] _____ s

Base your answers to questions 49 through 55 on the diagram below right.

49 What is the velocity at $t = 3$ s? [1] _____

50 What is the acceleration at $t = 3$ s? [1] _____

51 How far has the object traveled at the end of 7 s? [1] _____

52 When is the object traveling with greatest velocity? [1] _____

53 When does the object have the greatest acceleration? [1] _____

54 What is the object's velocity at $t = 9$ s? [1] _____

55 What is the object's acceleration at $t = 9$ s? [1] _____

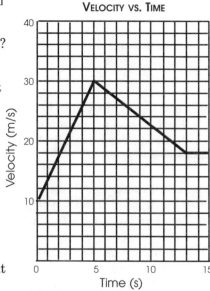

VELOCITY VS. TIME

PART C QUESTIONS

Base your answers to questions 56 through 58 on the information and data table at the right.

Time (s)	Velocity (m/s)
0.0	24.0
1.0	19.0
2.0	14.0
3.0	10.0
4.0	4.0

A car is traveling due north at 24.0 meters per second when the driver sees an obstruction on the highway. The data table above shows the velocity of the car at 1.0-second intervals as it is brought to rest on the straight, level highway.

Using the information in the data table, construct a graph on the gird provided following the directions below.

56 Plot the data points for velocity versus time. [1]

57 Draw the best-fit line. [1]

58 Using your graph, determine the acceleration of the car. (Show all calculations including the equation and substitution with units.) [2]

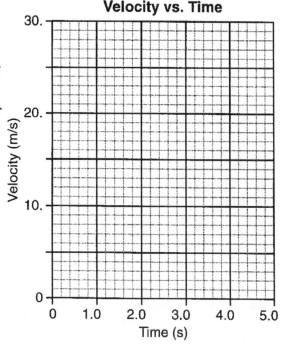

Base your answers to questions 59 and 60 on the speed-time graph at the right which represents the linear motion of a cart. For each question be sure to show all calculations, including the equation and substitution with units.

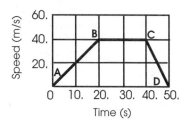

59 Calculate the distance traveled by cart during interval *BC*. [2]

60 Determine the magnitude of the acceleration of the cart during interval *AB*. [1]

Base your answers to questions 61 through 64 on the information and diagram below, which is drawn to a scale of 1.0 centimeter = 30. meters.

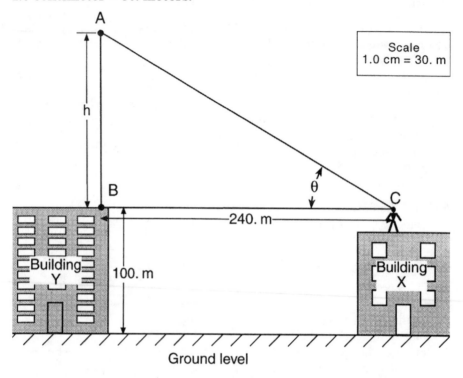

A student on building X is located 240. meters from the launch site B of a rocket on building Y. The rocket reaches its maximum altitude at point A. The student's eyes are level with the launch site on building Y.

61 Using the scale diagram and a protractor, measure the angle of elevation, θ, of the rocket and record it to the *nearest degree.* [1]

62 Determine the height, h, of the rocket above the student's eye level. [1]

63 What is the total distance the rocket must fall from its maximum altitude to reach the ground? [1]

64 Determine how much time is required for the rocket to fall freely from point A back to ground level. [Show all calculations, including the equation and substitution with units. [1]

FORCES AND FRICTION

KEY IDEA 5

ENERGY AND MATTER
INTERACT THROUGH
FORCES THAT RESULT IN
CHANGES IN MOTION.

PERFORMANCE INDICATOR 5.1 *STUDENTS CAN EXPLAIN AND PREDICT DIFFERENT PATTERNS OF MOTION OF OBJECTS (E.G., LINEAR AND UNIFORM CIRCULAR MOTION, VELOCITY AND ACCELERATION, MOMENTUM AND INERTIA).*

CHAPTER 4 – MAJOR UNDERSTANDINGS

☆ 5.1e An object in free fall accelerates due to the force of gravity.* Friction and other forces cause the actual motion of a falling object to deviate from its theoretical motion. *(Note: Initial velocities of objects in free fall may be in any direction.)*

☆ 5.1i According to Newton's First Law, the inertia of an object is directly proportional to its mass. An object remains at rest or moves with constant velocity, unless acted upon by an unbalanced force.

☆ 5.1j When the net force on a system is zero, the system is in equilibrium.

☆ 5.1k According to Newton's

Second Law, an unbalanced force causes a mass to accelerate*.

☆ 5.1l Weight is the gravitational force with which a planet attracts a mass*. The mass of an object is independent of the gravitational field in which it is located.

☆ 5.1o Kinetic friction* is a force that opposes motion.

☆ 5.1q According to Newton's Third Law, forces occur in action/ reaction pairs. When one object exerts a force on a second, the second exerts a force on the first that is equal in magnitude and opposite in direction.

continued on page 82

CHAPTER 4
FORCES AND FRICTION

FORCES

A **force** is a vector quantity that may be defined as a push or a pull. The MKS unit of force is the **newton (N)**. Forces may act upon an object at a distance without physical contact. The **newton** is the force which imparts to a mass of one kilogram an acceleration of one meter per second squared. It is a derived unit. A medium size apple weighs approximately 1 N. The English unit for force is the **pound**. The English unit for mass is the **slug**. The acceleration is 32 ft/s² in the English system. An average student has a mass of 60 kg and a weight of approximately 600 N.

EQUILIBRIUM

If the vector sum of the concurrent forces acting on an object is zero, the object is in equilibrium. In physics, the word *normal* means perpendicular.

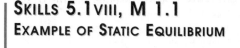

SKILLS 5.1VIII, M 1.1
EXAMPLE OF STATIC EQUILIBRIUM

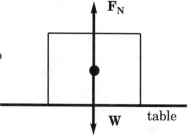

F_N = normal force of table pushing up
  (*Note:* The table *can* push.)

W = force of block pushing down

(Free Body Diagram)

An object in static equilibrium experiences no relative motion. An object in dynamic equilibrium moves at a constant velocity.

CHAPTER 4 – MAJOR UNDERSTANDINGS (CONTINUED FROM PAGE 81)	
☆ 5.1s Field strength* and direction are determined using a suitable test particle. (Notes: 1) Calculations are limited to electrostatic and gravitational fields. 2) The gravitational field near the surface of Earth and the electrical field between two oppositely charged parallel plates are treated as uniform.)	☆ 5.1t Gravitational forces are only attractive, whereas electrical and magnetic forces can be attractive or repulsive. ☆ 5.1u The inverse square law applies to electrical* and gravitational* fields produced by point sources.

EXAMPLE OF DYNAMIC EQUILIBRIUM

An object is moving with a 10. N vector force pulling forward to overcome a 10. N friction force. Vector sum is zero force, so the net force is zero. The object keeps moving at constant speed in a straight line.

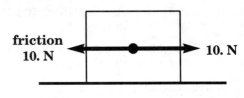

If you are told that a system is in equilibrium, the sum of all vectors acting on that system must equal zero. If any vector force is removed, the resultant of all the remaining vectors is equal to the magnitude of that vector at a direction 180° from the direction of the vector which was removed.

SKILL M 2.1
EXAMPLE OF VECTORS IN EQUILIBRIUM

Can the three vectors 6.0 N, 8.0 N, and 12.N be in equilibrium?

SOLUTION

To determine if a system of vectors is in equilibrium, add any two vectors. Note the sum. Next, subtract the two vectors and note the difference. If the third vector is between the sum and difference of the first two, the system can be in equilibrium.

$$8.0 \text{ N} + 6.0 \text{ N} = 14. \text{ N (sum)}$$
$$8.0 \text{ N} - 6.0 \text{ N} = 2.0 \text{ N (difference)}$$

Any vector value between 2.0 N and 14. N could provide equilibrium if placed at the proper angle.

☆ TRY IT

1   In this diagram, the vector forces are balanced. **B** has a force of 10 Newtons balancing **A** and **C**.

   a   What is the resultant of **A** + **C**?

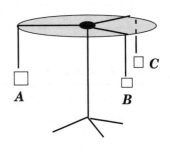

   b   If **B** were removed, what would happen to the system?

2   Which of the following vectors (*a-c*) could be in equilibrum? Show why.

   (a) 10. N   10. N   10. N

   (b) 15. N   8.0 N   4.0 N

   (c) 570. N   1200. N   7500 N

REAL WORLD CONNECTIONS
SEAT BELTS

Thousands of people, apparently believing themselves immune to the laws of physics, die each year as a result of motor vehicle accidents because they were not wearing seat belts. According to the laws of physics, if a vehicle is traveling at 30 miles per hour, its contents and passengers are also moving at 30 mph. Proper use of seat belts – should a vehicle suddenly stop at 30 mph – can mean the difference between life or death. *Wear your seat belt...it's the law.*

Source: *National Transportation Safety Board*

NEWTON'S THREE LAWS OF MOTION

First Law — an object remains at rest or in uniform motion unless acted upon by an unbalanced force. An object in uniform motion will continue to move in a straight line unless acted upon by an unbalanced force. This law is sometimes referred to as the **Law of Inertia**. The first law is a special case of the second law, when $\mathbf{F = 0}$. The inertia of an object is proportional to the object's mass.

Second Law — an unbalanced force acting on an object causes an acceleration which is directly proportional to the force and in the direction of the force. The law is represented by the equation $\mathbf{F = ma}$, where $\mathbf{F}$ is the net force in newtons, $\mathbf{m}$ is the mass in kilograms, and $\mathbf{a}$ is the acceleration in m/s². Graphic and timing tape examples of Newton's Second Law are illustrated below:

Start   **Timing Tape**   Stop

The timing tape above indicates accelerated motion. When the distance between the marks on the tape increases, the object is being accelerated. *Figure A* is a displacement-time graph of an object acted upon by a constant force. The graph indicates constant acceleration.

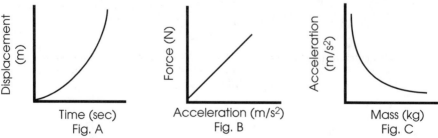

Time (sec)
Fig. A

Acceleration (m/s²)
Fig. B

Mass (kg)
Fig. C

Force can be plotted against acceleration according to the formula **F = ma.** The slope of this graph (*Figure B*) represents the inertial mass. *Inertial mass is a scalar quantity.* Acceleration can be plotted against mass. The graph (*Figure C*) indicates that the acceleration varies inversely with the mass, with the force held constant.

Weight, the measurement of Earth's gravitational attraction for any object, is an example of Newton's Second Law (**W = mg**). The slope of a weight-mass graph (*Figure D*) is the acceleration of gravity.

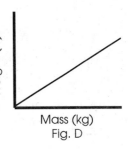

Mass (kg)
Fig. D

SKILL M 1.1
EXAMPLE: NORMAL
Calculate **F** if the acceleration of the block is 2 m/s² to the right. There is a 5.0 N frictional force opposing the motion.

SOLUTION:
The normal force is balanced by the weight. There is no net force in the vertical direction. In the horizontal direction, the net force (F – friction) causes the 5.0 kg block to accelerate at 2.0 m/s² to the right.

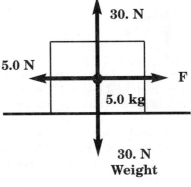

$$F_{net} = ma$$
$$F - 5N = (5.0 \text{ kg})(2.0 \text{ m/s}^2)$$
$$F - 5.0 \text{ N} = 10N$$
$$F = 15. \text{ N}$$

☆ TRY IT

3   A 4.0 N force is pulling horizontally on a 2.0 kg block. Calculate the acceleration of the block.

4   Four forces are applied to the block: A 5.0 N force is pulling north, a 5.0 N force is pulling south, a 5.0 N force is pulling west, and a 5.0 N force is pulling east. Can the block be in motion? Explain.

5   Lauren pulls a 50 kg mass eastward with a force of 30 Newtons. Logan pulls westward with a force of 40 N. What is the acceleration of the box? (*Note:* magnitude and direction.)

REAL WORLD CONNECTIONS – THE ELEVATOR

The elevator is an interesting application of Newton's Second Law. The force exerted by the cable of an elevator at rest, is equal to the weight of the elevator (**Tension = mg**). When the elevator begins to rise, it is accelerated upward. The cable must now provide an additional force to lift and accelerate the elevator (**Tension = mg + ma**). Soon the elevator reaches a constant speed. There is no acceleration and the force on the cable is calculated by the formula **F = mg + m(0)**. As the elevator begins to decelerate, the cable now provides a force calculated by **F = mg + m(-a)**. The process is repeated on the way down as indicated in the diagram:

$F = mg + m(-a)$ Decelerate	TOP	$F = mg + m(-a)$ Accelerate
Constant Velocity $F = mg$		Constant Velocity $F = mg$
Accelerate $F = mg + ma$	BOTTOM	Decelerate $F = mg + ma$

If a 70.0 kg person is accelerating upward at a rate of 2.00 m/s^2 and standing on a scale, the scale would read:

$$F = mg + ma$$
$$= (70.0 \text{ kg})(9.81 \text{ m/s}^2) + (70.0 \text{ kg})(2.00 \text{ m/s}^2)$$
$$= 687 \text{ N} + 140 \text{ N} = 827 \text{ N}$$

☆ TRY IT

6 What would the scale read if the elevator were accelerating downward at 2.0 m/s^2 ?

Newton's Third Law — forces always occur in pairs. For any applied force there is an equal and opposing force.

When a book is placed on a table, the book pushes down with a force equal to the book's weight. The table pushes up on the book with an equal and opposite reaction force. The force pairs do not cancel each other. Each force acts on a different object. The Law of Conservation of Momentum is the basis for Newton's Third Law.

"Going Down"

REAL WORLD CONNECTIONS
BASEBALL HITTER HITTING BALL

When a player hits the baseball, the force of the ball on the bat is exactly the same as the force of the bat on the ball according to Newton's Third Law. Since the baseball has a smaller mass it flies off with a larger velocity than the bat which has a large mass and a small velocity. The Law of Conservation of Momentum is the basis for Newton's Third Law.

UNIVERSAL GRAVITATION

Newton's Law of Universal Gravitation states that the force of attraction between any two point masses is directly proportional to the product of their masses, and inversely proportional to the square of the distance between them. It can be illustrated by the following formula:

$$F_g = Gm_1m_2/r^2$$

Where:

F_g is the force between the two masses, measured in Newtons

G   is the Universal Gravitation Constant, $6.67 \times 10^{-11} \dfrac{N \bullet m^2}{kg^2}$

  m_1 and m_2 are masses, measured in kilograms

r   is the distance between the two masses, measured center to center in meters

The law indicates that there is a force of Earth pulling on the Moon and an equal and opposite force of the Moon pulling on Earth. Every object experiences this force of attraction, but when the masses are relatively small, the forces are also small. This law is limited to point or spherical masses with uniform mass distribution.

EXAMPLE

Calculate the force of attraction between a 50. kg mass and a 3000. kg mass two meters apart.

Given: **G**   =   constant = 6.67×10^{-11} N m²/kg²
     $\mathbf{m_1}$ =   50. kg
     $\mathbf{m_2}$ =   3000. kg
     r   =   2.0 m

Find: Force

Solution:

  F_g = Gm_1m_2/r^2
     = $(6.67 \times 10^{-11}$ N m²/kg²$)(50.$ kg$)(3000.$ kg$)/(2.0$ m$)^2$
     = 2.5×10^{-6} N

REAL WORLD CONNECTIONS

TIDES

©PhotoDisc

At the surface of Earth, Earth's force of gravitational attraction acts in a direction inward toward its center of mass, and thus holds the ocean water confined to this surface. However, the gravitational forces of the Moon and Sun also act externally upon Earth's ocean waters. These external forces are exerted as tide-producing forces. Their effects are superimposed upon Earth's gravitational force and act to draw the ocean waters to positions on Earth's surface directly beneath the Sun and the Moon. High tides are produced in the ocean waters by the "heaping" action resulting from the horizontal flow of water toward two regions of Earth representing positions of maximum attraction of combined lunar and solar gravitational forces. Low tides are created by a compensating maximum withdrawal of water from regions around Earth midway between these two humps. The alternation of high and low tides is caused by the daily rotation of Earth with respect to these two tidal humps and two tidal depressions.

GRAVITATIONAL FIELDS

The concept of field was introduced by **Michael Faraday** to deal with the problems of forces acting at a distance. Every mass may be considered to be surrounded by a gravitational field. The interaction of the fields results in attraction. An object can push or pull you without touching you.

Mass measured by gravitational attraction is called **gravitational mass**. The most sensitive experiments possible to date conclude that gravitational mass is equivalent to inertial mass, and both are expressed in the same units.

The magnitude of the strength of a gravitational field at any point is the force per unit mass at that point in the gravitational field. The relationship:

$$g = F_g/m$$

Where: g is the acceleration of gravity (in m/s^2)
F_g is the force (in Newtons)
m is the mass (in kilograms)

TRY IT

The gravitational field at any planet can be calculated from the formula:

$$g = \frac{Gm}{r^2}$$

Where: **G** = universal gravitational constant
            m = mass of planet
            r = radius of planet

7   Using the constants from the *Reference Tables for Physical Setting/PHYSICS*, calculate **g** on Earth from this equation.

Note: The direction of the gravitational field is the direction of the force on a test mass. The force to mass ratio is the same for all objects.

 REAL WORLD CONNECTIONS

MASSING THE EARTH?

It is a smaller world after all – that is, if new measurements by University of Washington physicists turn out to be correct. Their new calculations for the Earth's mass came from work that could establish the most precise measurement ever achieved of Isaac Newton's gravitational constant. The measurement of the planet's weight is derived from the gravitational attraction that Earth has for objects near it.

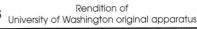
Rendition of
University of Washington original apparatus

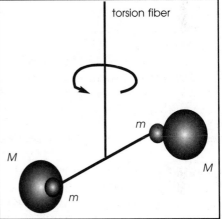

Newton's gravitational constant allows us to calculate the gravitational force there is between two masses in newtons.

To make their measurements, the researchers are using a device called a torsion balance that records nearly imperceptible accelerations from the gravitational effects of four 8.14-kilogram stainless steel balls on a 3- by 1.5-inch gold-coated Pyrex plate just 1.5 millimeters thick. The device, operating inside an old cyclotron hall in the UW nuclear physics laboratory, is similar in nature to one used 200 years ago to make the first Big G measurement. However, it is computer controlled and contains numerous mechanical refinements that make the more precise measurement possible. These new findings will probably not affect the average person, but advance the frontiers of science.

So, what is the mass of planet Earth? The quick answer to that is: approximately 5,980,000,000,000,000,000,000,000 (5.98 x 10^{24}) kilograms.

WEIGHT

The weight of an object is equal to the net gravitational force acting on it. The weight of an object is equal to the product of its mass and the gravitational force.

$$F_g = mg$$

Where: F_g is weight in newtons
             m is mass in kilograms
             g is acceleration of gravity in m/s²

Weight is a vector quantity that varies in magnitude with the location of the object with reference to the Earth. Spring scales may be used in weight measurements, but comparison of masses ("weighing") on a balance should be referred to as measurement of mass. To one significant figure, 100 grams has a weight of one newton. The average apple has a weight of one newton. Kilograms and grams are commonly misused as if they were weight units, especially on grocery package labeling.

 REAL WORLD CONNECTIONS

WORLD TRADE CENTER – 11 SEPTEMBER 2001

(Publisher's Note: On 11 September 2001, four U.S. planes hijacked by terrorists crashed in New York, Washington, and Pennsylvania killing more than 3,000 people. It is important that all of us remember the tragic human loss, because in so doing, we honor the memory of the victims and heroes of that dark day in U.S. history. It is also necessary that we study the physics of the destruction, as hopefully with research and understanding, engineering to prevent this kind of tragedy will be discovered and implemented.)

The World Trade Center "twin towers" were completed in 1970 as state of the art buildings designed with one of the earliest applications of computer stress analysis. The foundations extended more than 70 feet into the ground, resting on solid bedrock. 200,000 tons of steel and 425,000 cubic yards of concrete were used to build the towers. They were some of the best examples of "tube buildings," with closely spaced columns and beams in the outer walls, designed to withstand hurricane winds, fire, and the impact of an airplane. Even the sky lobby elevators could hold 10,000 pounds each. So, what caused the collapse of the Twin Towers?

Photo: Garnsey

The first jetliner banked into the north tower at a 45-degree angle, damaging floors 92 to 95. About 40 minutes later, the second jet crashed into the south tower, hitting floors 78 to 84. It is believed that the hijackers intentionally flew the aircraft into the lowest part of the buildings to which they had access.

Photo: USCG

The impact of the jetliners shattered and fractured two-thirds of the support columns on one face of each tower, causing the partial collapse of several floors. Debris penetrated each building's core and may have damaged the core columns located in the center of the 110-story structures.

The damaged columns held up the weight of the building, so it was logical to think that the building would fall, but that didn't happen. Because of its great structural redundancy, the load was distributed to other parts of the building. There is reason to believe that, without the fire, the buildings could have stood indefinitely and been repaired.

The fuel in both jetliners burned off rapidly, despite media reports that the aircraft continued burning long after the crash. The fuel ignited several floors in the building, which had a devastating effect on the steel support beams. When steel is reheated, it expands and loses its rigidity. Above 1,000 degrees Fahrenheit, it loses a significant amount of its strength.

The extreme heat from the fires might have caused the steel floors to expand and bow, which may have caused the support columns to bend inward and buckle. Heat also may have caused the steel flooring to separate from the columns, or the columns themselves may have heated up and buckled outward. The exact scenario is yet to be determined by a

team of structural engineers, but there is little doubt that the collapse of the upper floors of the WTC towers brought down both structures. The impact of 25-stories falling downward was more than any force safety factor which could have been built into the building. Both towers completely collapsed.

Photo: USCG

Static And Kinetic Friction

Friction is a force that opposes motion. It is the result of contact of irregular surfaces. The amount of force depends on the roughness of the surface and how much force pushes them together. It is calculated by multiplying the coefficient of friction (signified by the Greek letter mu, μ) by the force perpendicular to the surface or the normal force. The coefficient of friction is defined as the frictional force divided by the normal force. When the object is on a level surface, the force perpendicular is equal to the weight of the object.

There are two types of friction encountered in elementary physics problems: **static** and **kinetic** friction. Static friction is the force that must be overcome in order to start an object moving. Kinetic friction is frictional force that must be overcome to keep the object moving. The static friction is always greater than the kinetic friction. Both frictions are calculated using the same formula with the proper coefficient for static or kinetic friction.

Skill 5.1x

As illustrated below right, if a force of 10.0 newtons is applied to a 200.0 newton block and the block does not move, the force of friction is exactly 10.0 newtons. The force of friction will never oppose more than the force applied. If the force is increased to exactly 20.0 newtons, and the block just starts moving, there are no unbalanced forces acting on the block. Therefore, the force of static friction was 20.0 newtons.

The coefficient of static friction can be calculated from the equation:

$\mathbf{F}_f$ = force of friction = $(\mu_s)\mathbf{F}_N$
μ_s = $\mathbf{F}_f/\mathbf{F}_N$
μ_s = 20.0 newtons/200. newtons
= 0.1 (*no units*)

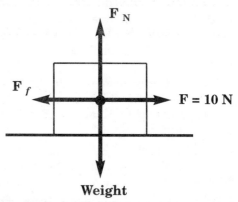

Weight

Starting friction is the maximum static friction force. Once started a force of 10. newtons keeps the block moving at constant velocity. Therefore, the coefficient of kinetic friction or moving friction is

$\mu_k = \dfrac{\mathbf{F}_f}{\mathbf{F}_N} = \dfrac{10.\text{ N}}{200.\text{ N}} = .05$

$\mathbf{F}_f$ = force of friction = $(\mu_k)\mathbf{F}_N$
μ_k = 0.05 (no units)

The amount of friction depends on the coefficient of friction and the normal force only.

Kinetic friction is independent of the surface area and the relative velocity of the object.

Rolling friction is the friction that occurs when objects are rolled over a surface. Rolling friction is generally less than sliding friction. Examples include roller skates, ball bearings, and bicycles.

Approximate Coefficients of Friction		
	Kinetic	Static
Rubber on concrete (dry)	0.68	0.90
Rubber on concrete (wet)	0.58	
Rubber on asphalt (dry)	0.67	0.85
Rubber on asphalt (wet)	0.53	
Rubber on ice	0.15	
Waxed ski on snow	0.05	0.14
Wood on wood	0.30	0.42
Steel on steel	0.57	0.74
Copper on steel	0.36	0.53
Teflon on Teflon	0.04	

Fluid friction is the friction that results from an object moving through a fluid such as water or air. Examples include parachutes and the streamlining of cars.

 REAL WORLD CONNECTIONS

FRICTION SAVES LIVES

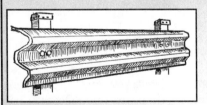

Automobiles, trains, planes, and trucks rely upon hydraulic brakes which use pads made of composite materials of high coefficient of friction to slow and stop vehicles. For highway traffic, guardrails are made of horizontal metal or wooden planks which slow down errant vehicles by collision with the metal side panels of a car. The average coefficient friction of metal to metal is 0.5 and the coefficient of friction of rubber against textured concrete is 1.0. Improved road safety is achieved through the design of concrete barriers (Jersey Barriers) with a wide base. When an errant car hits these newer concrete barriers, it is slowed down when the rubber tires strike the base of the concrete barrier.

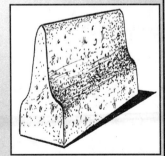

ANALYSIS OF AN OBJECT ON AN INCLINE

When the object is on an incline, the force perpendicular ($F_\perp$) to the surface of the ramp is calculated by:

$$F_N$$
$$F_N = F_\perp$$

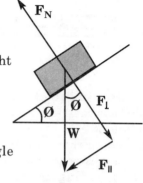

$F_\perp$ is the perpendicular component of the weight
$F_\parallel$ is the parallel component of the weight

$$\cos \emptyset = F_\perp / \text{ weight or } F_\perp = W \cos \emptyset$$
$$\sin \emptyset = F_\parallel / \text{ weight or } F_\parallel = W \sin \emptyset$$

The force of friction decreases as the angle increases since:

$$F_f = \text{ Force of friction } = (\mu)F_\perp = (\mu)W \cos \emptyset$$

As the angle increases, the component of the force pushing the block down the ramp increases. $F_\parallel$ increases; $F_\perp$ decreases. When one tries to push the block up the ramp, friction acts in a downhill direction.

If you adjust the angle so with a slight tap the block will just slide down by itself, then

$$F_\parallel = F_f$$

$$W \sin \emptyset = \mu_k \, W \cos \emptyset$$

$$\frac{W \sin \emptyset}{W \cos \emptyset} = \mu_k$$

$$\tan \emptyset = \mu_k = \text{coefficient of sliding friction}$$

To pull the block up the ramp at constant speed, you must apply a force equal to $F_\parallel + F_f$. If the applied force is greater than the kinetic force of friction and the component of gravity, the block will accelerate according to Newton's Second Law.

☆ TRY IT –

8   A cross country skier using waxed skis is starting to move on a level surface.

　　a   What is the initial force of static friction the 70 kg skier must overcome?

REAL WORLD CONNECTIONS

EXTREME SPORTS

The first person to break the 200 km/hr speed barrier in downhill skiing had a record-setting run of 200.222 km/hr or 124.34 mph. In comparison, the speed of a sky diver at terminal velocity is quoted at 120 mph. How is it possible for a downhill skier to move faster than a sky diver?

©PhotoDisc

The sky diver assumes a "spread-eagle" position as he falls and presents to the air a relatively large area. As a result, he doesn't have to move very fast to make the air resistance force equal to his weight. When that occurs, he will achieve terminal velocity. After that, he will continue to fall at this maximum velocity without further change.

The speed skier crouches in a "tuck" position in order to present the smallest area possible to the air, typically only half of his area when upright. The skier would have to move very fast to make the air resistance force equal to the downhill component of his weight.

Discussion: What is the current downhill record? What is currently done to help the skier increase his/her speed? Is there a maximum speed for each skier based on the slope angle and the skier's mass?

Source: *The Physics Teacher*, February 1984

©PhotoDisc

Try It 8 continued:

 b   As the skier continues to push forward with the force necessary to overcome the static friction, describe the motion of the skier as she continues along on a level surface.

9   A force of 40. N is applied to a 5.0 kg rubber box. The box accelerates at a rate of 2.4 m/s².

   a   What is the force of friction between the block and the concrete floor?

   b   What is the coefficient of friction between the rubber and the concrete?

   c   Is the concrete wet or dry? Defend your answer.

10 Identify and describe two (2) things which can be done to reduce friction between two surfaces?

   a   Reduce friction by...

   b   Reduce friction by...

SKILL 5.1IX
LAB 5 – FORCES THAT ACCELERATE

BACKGROUND

Newton's second law is a famous and far-reaching generalization of mechanics. It describes the motion of an object when the object is *not* in equilibrium; that is, when an unbalanced force acts on the object. This is an extremely important idea, covering the behavior of objects from electrons and alpha particles, to rockets and satellites, and even Earth itself. In addition, it clarifies the very fundamental idea of mass.

THE PROBLEM

There are two specific goals in this experiment: (1) to show how the acceleration of an object depends on the resultant force if the mass is unchanged, and (2) to show how the acceleration depends on the mass for a constant applied force. The principal piece of apparatus is a cart that travels across a level tabletop. The cart is acted upon by force supplied by an object of known weight hanging from a string passed over a pulley.

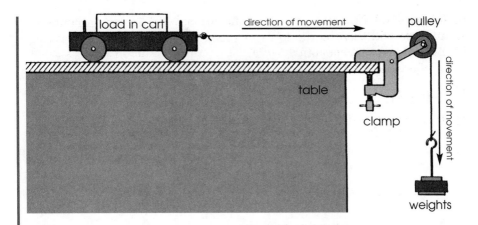

You will measure the time required for the cart to move a measured distance from rest. From your observations, make conclusions about the cart's motion.

Relating Acceleration to the Unbalanced Force

Set up the apparatus as shown. Hang an object on a string, heavy enough to start the cart (from rest) moving on the string to the end of the table. Describe the cart's motion. Does it appear to be in equilibrium? How would you describe its motion?

In making the measurements that follow, you must plan the procedure so that, as you vary the force, the mass remains constant. What, in addition to the cart and its load, is being accelerated? To keep the mass of the entire accelerating system from changing as you change the weight of the hanging object, the object to be added to the string must have been riding on the cart on the previous trial. When you start the series of measurements, the cart must carry, in addition to any other load being used, all the objects subsequently used to supply the force.

Measure the acceleration of the cart for a number of different unbalanced forces, keeping the total mass constant. Also, by trial and error, find what force must be applied to the cart and the hanging weight so that, once started, they move with constant velocity (zero acceleration). What is the significance of this measurement? Plot a graph of the acceleration as a function of the resultant force. What do you conclude from the shape of the graph about the way acceleration depends on unbalanced force?

Effect of Mass on Acceleration

Make a series of trials in which you vary the total mass being accelerated and measure the acceleration produced by a constant unbalanced force. Changing the mass of the cart will cause the friction in its wheels to change also. Thus, for each trial you must first measure the friction by finding the force that will cause uniform motion. The constant unbalanced force will then be the force in excess of friction. The accelerating force should remain constant.

☆ TRY IT

11 Draw a graph showing how the acceleration varies with the mass.

12 What type of relationship does your graph suggest?

13 How can you test your results mathematically to confirm this relationship? Do this test.

14 Draw a conclusion based on your measurements about the way acceleration depends on mass if the resultant force is constant.

SKILL 5.1x
LAB 6 – COEFFICIENT OF FRICTION

BACKGROUND

Whenever a force is applied to on object resting on a surface, a resisting force of friction may be observed. There are two types of friction present. Static friction is the amount of friction, which must be overcome to begin moving an object. Kinetic friction is the amount of friction, which must be overcome to keep an object in motion at a constant speed. In this lab, we will be calculating the coefficient of kinetic friction.

THE PROBLEM

Determine the coefficient of kinetic friction between several materials.

HOW FRICTION DEPENDS ON MASS

Set up the inclined plane at an angle of zero steepness so its in the horizontal position. After you determine the mass of the block, place it on the incline. Attach the string to the block, over the pulley and to a mass attached to the end. Add masses to the hanger until the wooden block moves at a constant velocity after giving it a tap. The purpose of the slight tap is to break the bond of static friction. Draw the vector forces on the block at this point. Make sure all of the forces are recorded in the proper units. Add additional mass to the top of the block and repeat. Determine the coefficient of friction for each case.

HOW FRICTION DEPENDS ON SURFACE AREA

Turn the block on its side and repeat the experiment. Make sure that the string is parallel to the plane at all time. What is the effect of the surface area on the coefficient of friction?

HOW FRICTION DEPENDS ON ANGLE

A block of wood resting on an incline at some angle Ø is being pulled up by a string at constant velocity. The acceleration of the system is zero since there is no unbalanced force.

The tension (**T**) on the block must provide enough force to overcome the friction and lift the parallel component of the weight (**W$_\parallel$**). Friction is determined by the formula:

Where: μ is the coefficient of friction.

$$F_f = \mu F_\perp$$

$$T = F_\parallel + F_f$$

$$T = mg\sin\emptyset + \mu\, mg \cos \emptyset$$

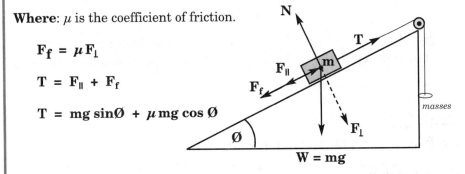

Incline the plane at several angles between five degrees and twenty degrees. Note that now you are pulling the block up the incline. Note the vectors acting on the block when it is moving up at a constant velocity. Draw them to scale in your report. The dashed lines are only the compliments of the weight vector. Calculate the coefficient for several angles.

DETERMINING THE COEFFICIENT FROM THE ANGLE

There is one angle where the block will just begin to slide down the incline by itself after tapping it. Remove the string from the block. Place the block on the incline and find that angle where the block just slides down by itself after tapping it. The tangent of this angle will be the coefficient of friction for this block-incline surface. Using the forces acting on the block, show how tan (Ø) could equal mu (μ).

COMPARING MU

Compare all of the mu's (μ) you determined. How do these values compare to tan (Ø)? Can you account for any discrepancies?

THE MU OF THE SHOE

Now that you know how to determine the coefficient of kinetic friction for a wood block, look at your shoes. Some sneakers are especially "tacky" while some shoes are very slippery. Calculate the mu (μ) of several shoes in your lab group. Include these calculations in the lab report.

CHAPTER FOUR ASSESSMENTS

PART A QUESTIONS

1   In the diagram at the right, surface B of the wooden block has the same texture as surface A, but twice the area of surface A. If force F is required to slide the block at constant speed across the table on surface A, approximately what force is required to slide the block at constant speed across the table on surface B?

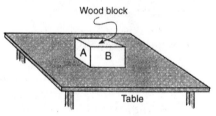

(1) F (2) $2F$ (3) $\frac{1}{2}F$ (4) $4F$

2   A different force is applied to each of four 1-kilogram blocks to slide them across a uniform steel surface at constant speed as shown below. In which diagram is the coefficient of friction between the block and steel smallest?

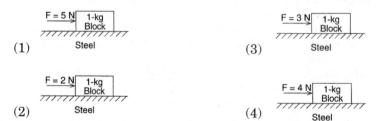

3   Sand is often placed on an icy road because the sand
    (1) decreases the coefficient of friction between the tires of a car and
        road
    (2) increases the coefficient of friction between the tires of a car and
        road
    (3) decreases the gravitational force on a car
    (4) increases the normal force of a car on the road

4   Which combination of three concurrent forces acting on a body could
    not produce equilibrium?
    (1) 1 N, 3 N, 5 N   (3) 3 N, 4 N, 5 N
    (2) 2 N, 2 N, 2 N   (4) 4 N, 4 N, 5 N

5   Equilibrium exists in a system where three forces are acting concur-
    rently on an object. If the system includes a 5.0-newton force due
    north and a 2.0-newton force due south, the third force must be
    (1) 7.0 N south   (3) 3.0 N south
    (2) 7.0 N north   (4) 3.0 N north

6   Forces F_1 and F_2 act concurrently on
    point P, as shown in the diagram at the
    right. The equilibrant of F_1 and F_2 is
    (1) 14 N southwest
    (2) 14 N southeast
    (3) 20. N southwest
    (4) 20. N southeast

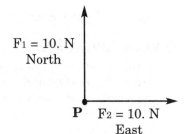

7   In the diagram at the right, a force, F, is applied to the handle of a
    lawn mower inclined at angle θ, to the ground. The
    magnitude of the horizontal component of force F
    depends on
    (1) the magnitude of force F, only
    (2) the measure of angle θ, only
    (3) both the magnitude of force F and the measure of angle θ
    (4) neither the magnitude of force F nor the measure of angle θ

8   Net force F causes mass m_1 to accelerate at rate a. A net force of $3F$
    causes mass m_2 to accelerate at rate $2a$. What is the ratio of mass m_1
    to mass m_2?
    (1) 1:3   (2) 2:3   (3) 1:2   (4) 1:6

9   Which combination of fundamental units can be used to express the
    weight of an object?
    (1) kilogram/second   (3) kilogram•meter/second
    (2) kilogram•meter   (4) kilogram•meter/second²

10 Compared to 8 kilograms of feathers, 6 kilograms of lead has
   (1) less mass and less inertia
   (2) less mass and more inertia
   (3) more mass and less inertia
   (4) more mass and more inertia

11 Two students are pulling on a rope, each with a force of 50. N. What is the tension in the rope?
   (1) 0 N
   (2) 50 N
   (3) 100 N
   (4) 200 N

12 Two forces are applied to a 2.0-kilogram block on a frictionless horizontal surface, as shown in the diagram at the right. The acceleration of the block is
   (1) 1.5 m/s² to the right
   (2) 2.5 m/s² to the left
   (3) 2.5 m/s² to the right
   (4) 4.0 m/s² to the left

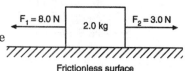

Frictionless surface

13 A series of unbalanced forces was applied to each of two blocks, *A* and *B*. The graphs at the right show the relationship between unbalanced force and acceleration for each block.

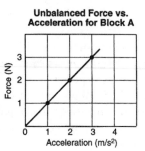

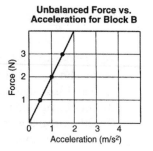

Compared to the mass of block *A*, the mass of block *B* is
   (1) the same
   (2) twice as great
   (3) half as great
   (4) four times as great

14 A 6-newton force and an 8-newton force act concurrently on a box located on a frictionless horizontal surface. Which top-view diagram shows the forces producing the *smallest* magnitude of acceleration of the box?

(1)

(2)

(3)

(4)

15 A man weighs 900 newtons standing on a scale in a stationary elevator. If some time later the reading on the scale is 1200 newtons, the elevator must be moving with
   (1) constant acceleration downward
   (2) constant speed downward
   (3) constant acceleration upward
   (4) constant speed upward

16 A 150.–newton force, F_1, and a 200.–newton force, F_2, are applied simultaneously to the same point on a large crate resting on a frictionless, horizontal surface. Which diagram shows the forces positioned to give the crate the greatest acceleration?

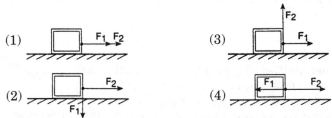

17 Which graph best represents the relationship between the mass (m) of a satellite launched from Earth and the satellite's distance (r) away from Earth?

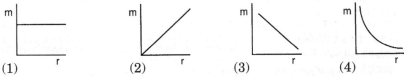

18 The gravitational force of attraction between two objects would be increased by
   (1) doubling the mass of both objects, only
   (2) doubling the distance between the objects, only
   (3) doubling the mass of both objects and doubling the distance between the objects
   (4) doubling the mass of one object and doubling the distance between the objects

19 The radius of Mars is approximately one-half the radius of Earth, and the mass of Mars is approximately one-tenth the mass of Earth. Compared to the acceleration due to gravity on the surface of Earth, the acceleration due to gravity on the surface of Mars is
   (1) smaller   (2) larger   (3) the same

20 A 1.0-kilogram block is placed on each of four frictionless planes inclined at different angles. On which inclined plane will the acceleration of the block be greatest?

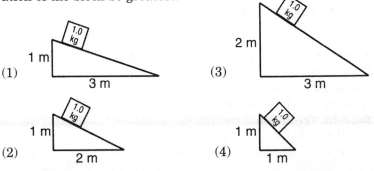

21 A cart moving across a level surface accelerates uniformly at 1.0 m/s^2 for 2.0 seconds. What additional information is required to determine the distance traveled by the cart during this 2.0-second interval?
(1) coefficient of friction between the cart and the surface
(2) mass of the cart
(3) net force acting on the cart
(4) initial velocity of the cart

22 A book weighing 20. newtons slides at constant velocity down a ramp inclined 30.° to the horizontal as shown in the diagram at the right. What is the force of friction between the book and the ramp?

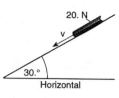

(1) 10. N up the ramp   (3) 10. N down the ramp
(2) 17 N up the ramp   (4) 17 N down the ramp

23 In the diagram at the right, a block rests on a ramp, making angle θ with the horizontal. If angle θ is increased, what will occur?
(1) The block's mass will decrease.
(2) The block's weight will increase.
(3) The block's component of weight parallel to the ramp will decrease.
(4) The block's component of weight parallel to the ramp will increase.

PART B QUESTIONS

24 A person kicks a 4.0-kilogram door with a 48-newton force causing the door to accelerate at 12 meters per second^2. What is the magnitude of the force exerted by the door on the person?[1] _____ N

25 What is the magnitude of the net force acting on a 2.0 x 10^3 kg car as it accelerates from rest to a speed of 15 meters per second in 5.0 seconds? [1] _____ N

26 When a person walks forward, the foot pushes backward against the ground. What causes the person to move forward? [1]

27 A mosquito flying over a highway strikes the windshield of a moving truck. Compared to the magnitude of the force of the truck on the mosquito during the collision, the magnitude of the force of the mosquito on the truck is [1]
(1) smaller   (2) larger   (3) the same

28 The diagram below shows a student applying a 10.-newton force to slide a piece of wood at constant speed across a horizontal surface. After the wood is cut in half, one piece is placed on top of the other, as shown.

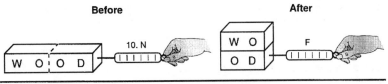

Uniform horizontal surface

What is the magnitude of the force, *F*, required to slide the stacked wood at constant speed across the surface? [1] _____ N

29 The diagram at the right represents a block sliding down an incline. Draw a vector which best represents the frictional force acting on the block. [1]

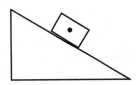

30 A 50.-newton horizontal force is needed to keep an object weighing 500. newtons moving at a constant velocity of 2.0 meters per second across a horizontal surface. The magnitude of the frictional force acting on the object is [1] _____ N

31 If a 30-newton force is required to accelerate a 2-kilogram object at 10 m/s², over a level floor, then the magnitude of the frictional force acting on the object is [1] _____ N

32 The graph at the right shows the relationship between weight and mass for a series of objects on the Moon. The acceleration due to gravity on the Moon is approximately [1] _____ m/s²

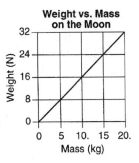

33 An astronaut weighs 500 newtons on Earth and 25 newtons on Asteroid X. The acceleration due to gravity on Asteroid X is approximately [1] _____ m/s²

34 The graph at the right shows the weight of three objects on Planet X as a function of their mass. The acceleration due to gravity on Planet X is approximately [1] _____ m/s²

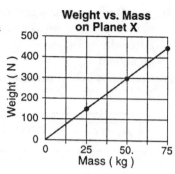

Weight vs. Mass on Planet X

35 A 15-kilogram mass weights 60. newtons on Planet X. The mass is allowed to fall freely from rest near the surface of the planet. After falling for 6.0 seconds, the acceleration of the mass is [1] _____ m/s²

36 The magnitude of the gravitational force of attraction between Earth and the Moon is [1] _____ N

37 What is the magnitude of the gravitational force between an electron and a proton separated by a distance of 1.0×10^{-10} meter?
v_____ N

38 On the surface of Planet X, the acceleration due to gravity is 16 meters per second². What is the weight of a 6.0-kilogram mass located on the surface of Planet X? [1] _____ N

PART C QUESTIONS

Base your answers to questions 39 and 40 on the information below.

A 5.0-kilogram block weighing 49 newtons sits on a frictionless, horizontal surface. A horizontal force of 20. newtons towards the right is applied to the block. [Neglect air resistance.]

39 On the diagram, draw a vector to represent each of the three forces acting on the block. Use a ruler and a scale of 1.0 centimeter = 10. newtons. Begin each vector at point C and label its magnitude in newtons. [3]

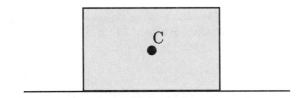

40 Calculate the magnitude of the acceleration of the block. [Show all calculations, including the equation and substitution with units.] [2]

Base your answers to questions 41 through 45 on the information and vector diagram at the right.

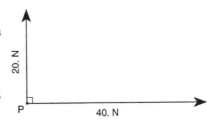

A 20.–newton force due north and a 40.–newton force due east act concurrently on a 10.–kilogram object, located at point P.

41 Using a ruler, determine the scale used in the vector diagram by finding the number of newtons represented by each centimeter. [1]

42 On the vector diagram below, use a ruler and protractor to construct the vector that represents the resultant force. [1]

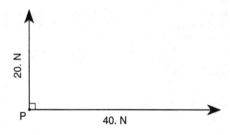

43 What is the magnitude of the resultant force? [1]

44 What is the measure of the angle (in degrees) between east and the resultant force? [1]

45 Calculate the magnitude of the acceleration of the object. [Show all calculations, including the equation and substitution with units.] [2]

CHAPTER 5
MOTION IN A PLANE

KEY IDEA 5
ENERGY AND MATTER INTERACT THROUGH FORCES THAT RESULT IN CHANGES IN MOTION.

> **PERFORMANCE INDICATOR 5.1** *STUDENTS CAN EXPLAIN AND PREDICT DIFFERENT PATTERNS OF MOTION OF OBJECTS (E.G., LINEAR AND UNIFORM CIRCULAR MOTION, VELOCITY AND ACCELERATION, MOMENTUM AND INERTIA).*

CHAPTER 5 – MAJOR UNDERSTANDINGS

☆ 5.1e An object in free fall accelerates due to the force of gravity.* Friction and other forces cause the actual motion of a falling object to deviate from its theoretical motion. (Note: Initial velocities of objects in free fall may be in any direction.)

☆ 5.1f The path of a projectile is the result of the simultaneous effect of the horizontal and vertical components of its motion; these components act independently.

☆ 5.1g A projectile's time of flight is dependent upon the vertical component of its motion.

☆ 5.1h The horizontal displacement of a projectile is dependent upon the horizontal component of its motion and its time of flight.

☆ 5.1n Centripetal force* is the net force which produces centripetal acceleration.* In uniform circular motion, the centripetal force is perpendicular to the tangential velocity.

CHAPTER 5
MOTION IN A PLANE

The motion of an object traveling in a plane (two dimensions) may be described by separating the motion of the object into horizontal (**x**) and vertical (**y**) components of the vector quantities displacement, velocity, and acceleration. (Once the object is free, it is subject to only one force, the force of gravity. Air friction will be ignored in the following discussion.)

SECTION I
TWO DIMENSIONAL MOTION AND TRAJECTORIES
HORIZONTAL PROJECTILE

When the initial velocity (speed and direction) of a projectile in the gravitational field of the Earth is given, the subsequent motion of the projectile may be described.

EXAMPLE OF A FIRED BULLET

A projectile fired horizontally has an initial vertical velocity of zero.

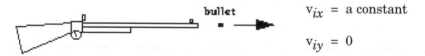

$$v_{ix} = \text{a constant}$$

$$v_{iy} = 0$$

Assuming no friction from the air, there is nothing in the horizontal direction to accelerate the bullet. As soon as the bullet leaves the gun, gravity accelerates the bullet in the vertical direction. The same principle is used in supply drops from an airplane.

 REAL WORLD CONNECTIONS
DROPPING A FREE FALLING OBJECT (EXAMPLE: BOMB)

Suppose that a bomb is dropped from an airplane which is moving parallel to the Earth. Its horizontal velocity is **v**, the same as the airplane. Once it is dropped, no horizontal force acts on the package; therefore, the horizontal velocity will remain unchanged. Its **x** component (horizontal) remains **v** until the bomb hits the ground, as indicated in the illustration at the top of the next page.

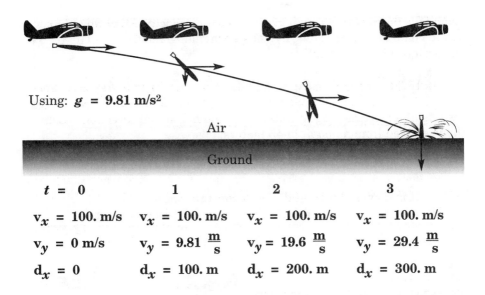

Using: $g = 9.81$ m/s²

Air

Ground

$t = 0$	1	2	3
$v_x = 100.$ m/s	$v_x = 100.$ m/s	$v_x = 100.$ m/s	$v_x = 100.$ m/s
$v_y = 0$ m/s	$v_y = 9.81 \frac{m}{s}$	$v_y = 19.6 \frac{m}{s}$	$v_y = 29.4 \frac{m}{s}$
$d_x = 0$	$d_x = 100.$ m	$d_x = 200.$ m	$d_x = 300.$ m

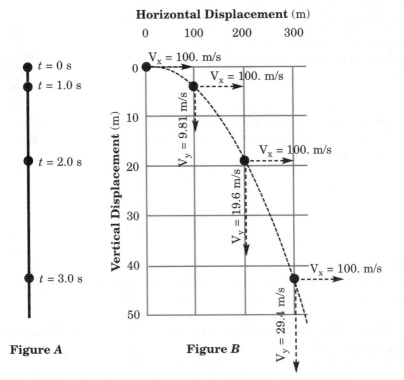

Figure A   Figure B

In the *falling bomb* example, a plane traveling at 100 meters per second releases a bomb. When the bomb is first released, it has no vertical velocity. The vertical pull of gravity will accelerate it downward at a rate of 9.81 m/s². The vertical (**y** component) velocity will increase by 9.81 m/s (or approximately 10 m/s) each second. As shown in the example, the bomb falls downward with an ever-increasing velocity. All of this happens as the bomb moves horizontally with unchanging velocity $\mathbf{v}_x$. The resultant path is a half of a parabola.

In the drop object example (middle of previous page), *figure A* represents an object at rest dropped from a height of 45 meters. *Figure B* represents an object moving at 100 m/s in the horizontal direction which is then released from a height of 45 meters.

Note: A projectile in flight does two things at the same time:

a   It is moving horizontally with constant speed.
b   It is moving up or down with downward acceleration **g**.

☆ TRY IT

Consider changing the object (free falling bomb) in the previous example with dropping from an airplane a humanitarian package, such as a crate of food and medicine descending attached to a parachute.

1   Using your knowledge of physics, suggest how the two flight paths would be different and give at least two examples of what forces would be involved in changing the path of descent.

SKILL 5.1 VII

For a horizontal projectile, the time of flight is determined by the height above the ground where the object is released.

Once you recognize this, the solution of projectile problems is easy. Simply split each problem into two problem parts. One part involves a horizontal motion at constant velocity. For that motion:

$$\mathbf{v}_{ix} = \mathbf{v}_{fx} = \mathbf{v}_x$$

The vertical part of the motion is exactly the same as the free-fall motion discussed earlier.

The following mechanics formula is applied to trajectory motion:

$$d_y = v_{iy}t + \tfrac{1}{2} a_y t^2 \quad \text{and} \quad d_x = v_{ix}t + \tfrac{1}{2} a_x t^2$$

Where:
$$
\begin{aligned}
d_y &= \text{vertical displacement} \\
a_y &= \text{gravity} = 9.81 \text{ m/s}^2 \\
t &= \text{time in the air} \\
v_{iy} &= 0 \text{ (zero), when fired horizontally} \\
d_x &= \text{horizontal displacement} \\
a_x &= \text{zero in horizontal direction} \\
v_{ix} &= \text{velocity initial in the horizontal direction}
\end{aligned}
$$

EXAMPLE

An airplane traveling at 100. m/s drops a package from a height of 3000. meters. Calculate the time it takes to reach the ground. How far in front of the target must the package be dropped?

Given:
$$
\begin{aligned}
v_{iy} &= 0.0 \text{ m/s} \\
v_{ix} &= 100. \text{ m/s} \\
d_y &= 3,000. \text{ m} \\
a_y &= g = 9.81 \text{ m/s}^2
\end{aligned}
$$

Take the downward direction as positive to eliminate negative signs.

Find: (1) time to reach ground
(2) distance from drop point to target

Solution: Divide the problem into two portions, vertical and horizontal:

a **Vertical:** At the beginning, the plane was moving horizontally; therefore: $v_{iy} = 0$

$$d_y = v_{iy}t + \tfrac{1}{2} a_y t^2$$

$$
\begin{aligned}
3,000. \text{ m} &= (0)(t) + \tfrac{1}{2}(9.8 \text{ m/s}^2)(t^2) \\
25 \text{ sec} &= t
\end{aligned}
$$

b **Horizontal:** The plane and the package were traveling at a speed of 100 m/s horizontally. Since we can ignore friction, $v_{ix} = \textbf{100 m/s}$, there is no force acting on it in the x direction; therefore: $a_x = \textbf{0 m/s}^2$

$$
\begin{aligned}
d_x &= v_{ix}t + \tfrac{1}{2} a_x t^2 \\
d_x &= (100 \text{ m/s})(25 \text{ s}) + 0 \\
d_x &= 2,500 \text{ m}
\end{aligned}
$$

The package should be released 2,500 m before the target.

2   An airplane traveling at 90 m/s drops an object from 1000 m. Calculate the time it takes to reach the ground? Determine how far in front of the target the package must be dropped. Repeat the calculation for a drop height of 2000 m.

PROJECTILE FIRED AT AN ANGLE

For a projectile fired at an angle with the surface of the Earth, the initial vertical and horizontal components of the velocity may be determined and the motion treated as two separate linear motion problems.

PROJECTILE MOTION

When an object is fired into the air at an angle, the vertical component of the velocity is accelerated and the horizontal component remains in uniform motion.

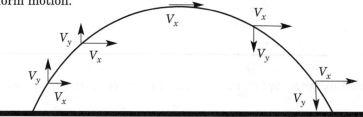

At the top of the parabola, the projectile has a velocity in the **x** direction but the velocity in the **y** direction is zero. The acceleration at every point is 9.81 m/s^2 and directed downward.

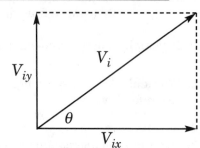

SKILLS M1.1, 5.1 VII

SKETCH THE THEORETICAL PATH OF A PROJECTILE

The motion of all objects is affected by gravity as soon as the object is released. An object fired horizontally will follow a path of half of a parabola while an object fired at an angle will follow a full parabola as long as it is launched and it lands at the same elevation. Below is the general path of a projectile fired horizontally. On the diagram, draw the path of another projectile fired at a greater initial horizontal velocity. Next draw another path representing another projectile fired horizontally with a lower velocity than the first projectile. Label both paths.

The diagram at the right is the general path of a projectile fired at an angle. On the diagram, draw the path of another projectile fired at a greater initial velocity but at the same angle. Next draw another path representing a projectile traveling at an initial velocity slower than the first. Label each diagram.

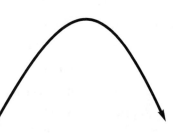

To solve a projectile problem, first resolve the vector into components. The vertical component, v_{iy}, is calculated using the sine function.

$$\sin \varnothing = v_{iy}/v_i \quad \text{or} \quad v_{iy} = v_i \sin \varnothing$$

The horizontal component, v_{ix}, is calculated using the cosine function.

$$\cos \varnothing = v_{ix}/v_i \quad \text{or} \quad v_{ix} = v_i \cos \varnothing$$

Next, determine the time to reach the maximum height at which time velocity final, v_f, equals zero. Since gravity is acting to slow down the projectile use 9.81 m/s² for g.

$$v_{fy} = v_{iy} + a_y t \quad \text{where:} \quad g = 9.81 \text{ m/s}^2$$

The maximum height can be calculated from the formula:

$$d_y = v_{iy} t + \tfrac{1}{2} a_y (t)^2$$

Since the time to fall is the same as the time to reach the highest point, the total time in the air is **2t**. During the total time in the air, the horizontal velocity remains constant. The distance traveled horizontally can be calculated from the equation:

$$d_x = v_{ix} 2t$$

EXAMPLE

A projectile is shot into the air at a 30° angle with a velocity of 100 meters per second. Calculate the maximum height, the time in the air and the horizontal range of the projectile.

Given:
$$v_i = 100 \text{ m/s} \qquad \varnothing = 30°$$

Find: time in air, maximum height, horizontal range

Solution:

a
$$v_{iy} = v_i \sin \emptyset = 100 \text{ m/s}(.5)$$
$$= 50 \text{ m/s}$$
$$v_f = v_{iy} + at$$
$$0 = 50 \text{ m/s} + (-9.81 \text{ m/s}^2)(t)$$
$$t_{up} = 5.1 \text{ sec time to reach maximum height}$$
$$\text{total time} = 2t_{up}$$
$$= 10.2 \text{ sec}$$

b
$$d_y = v_{iy}t + \tfrac{1}{2} a(t)^2$$
$$= 50 \text{ m/s } (5.1s) + (\tfrac{1}{2}) (-9.81 \text{m/s}^2) (5.1s)^2$$
$$= 130 \text{ m}$$

c   horizontal d_x
$$= v_{ix} \text{ (total time)}$$
$$= v_i \cos \emptyset (2t_{up})$$
$$= (86.6 \text{m/s})10.2 \text{ s}$$
$$= 883 \text{ m}$$

Axis **x** and axis **y** must be perpendicular to each other so that the **x** and **y** motions are independent. The horizontal motion has no force acting on it horizontally so there is uniform motion. The vertical motion has a constant gravitational force and undergoes uniformly accelerated motion. The connection between these independent motions is that they take place simultaneously on the same time scale.

A projectile's maximum distance is obtained at a 45° projection angle (if friction is ignored).

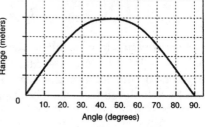
Range vs. Angle of Inclination

Range (meters)

0 10. 20. 30. 40. 50. 60. 70. 80. 90.
Angle (degrees)

☆ Try It

3   Determine the horizontal and vertical components of the velocity, the time in the air, and the horizontal range for each set of data below.

a   .66 m/s at 46 degrees

b   145 m/s at 33 degrees

c   256 km/hr at 55 degrees

REAL WORLD CONNECTIONS
GAME OF GOLF
When an announcer at a golf tournament talks about the player's club selection, you will generally hear whether the player has chosen a wood or an iron, and then a number. The number is related to the angle at which the face slopes back from vertical when the club is held in its normal position facing the ball. A higher number for the club represents a greater degree of **slope** away from vertical, generally resulting in a higher, shorter shot. Although there are some slight variations between manufacturers, the club numbers and their related slopes generally look like the chart below.

©PhotoDisc

The slope is important for two reasons. First, the face will launch the ball on a path perpendicular to the plane of the face at impact, so a more "laid back" face will start the ball on a higher trajectory. This is crucial when a golfer tries to send the ball over some obstacle. The second important aspect of the slope is **spin** – the greater the slope, the greater the spin. This is important when the golfer wants the ball to come back down at a steep angle, which tends to result in a shorter roll after landing.

Adapted from: *How Stuff Works* ©2000

 TRY IT

4   Use the picture of the head of a golf club to answer this question.

   a   Determine the slope of this iron.

   b   What is the closest club value for the determined slope?

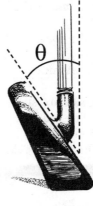

Club Slope* Guide	
Putter	0°
Sand Wedge	56°
Pitching Wedge	47°
9 iron	43°
8 iron	39°
7 iron	35°
6 iron	31°
5 iron	27°
4 iron	24°
3 iron	21°
5 wood	20°
3 wood	15°
Driver	10°
*in degrees from vertical	

CHAPTER FIVE (SECTION 1) ASSESSMENTS

PART A QUESTIONS

1   In the diagram at the right, a stationary observer on the ground watches as a sea gull flying horizontally to the right drops a clamshell. Which diagram best represents the path of the falling clamshell as seen by the observer? [Neglect air resistance.]

Clamshell

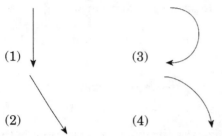

(1)   (3)

(2)   (4)

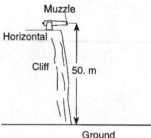

2   The diagram at the right shows the muzzle of a cannon located 50. meters above the ground. When the cannon is fired, a ball leaves the muzzle with an initial horizontal speed of 250. meters per second. [Neglect air resistance.] Which action would most likely increase the time of flight of a ball fired by the cannon?

Muzzle

Horizontal

Cliff   50. m

Ground

(1) pointing the muzzle of the cannon toward the ground
(2) moving the cannon closer to the edge of the cliff
(3) positioning the cannon higher above the ground
(4) giving the ball a greater initial horizontal velocity

3   A student throws a stone upward at an angle of 45°. Which statement best describes the stone at the highest point that it reaches?
(1) Its acceleration is zero.
(2) Its acceleration is at a maximum.
(3) Its velocity is zero.
(4) Its velocity is at a maximum.

4   A red ball and a green ball are simultaneously thrown horizontally from the same height. The red ball has an initial speed of 40. meters per second and the green ball has an initial speed of 20. meters per second. Compared to the time it takes the red ball to reach the ground, the time it takes the green ball to reach the ground will be
(1) the same   (3) half as much
(2) twice as much   (4) four times as much

5   A baseball player throws a ball horizontally. Which statement best describes the ball's motion after it is thrown? [Neglect the effect of friction.]
    (1) Its vertical speed remains the same, and its horizontal speed increases.
    (2) Its vertical speed remains the same, and its horizontal speed remains the same.
    (3) Its vertical speed increases, and its horizontal speed increases.
    (4) Its vertical speed increases, and its horizontal speed remains the same.

6   The diagram at the right shows a projectile moving with speed v at the top of its trajectory. Which vector best represents the acceleration of the projectile in the position shown?

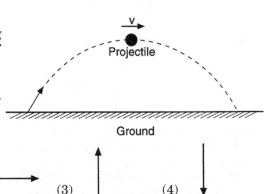

(1) ⟵   (2) ⟶   (3) ↑   (4) ↓

7   Four different balls are thrown horizontally off the top of four cliffs. In which diagram does the ball have the shortest time of flight?

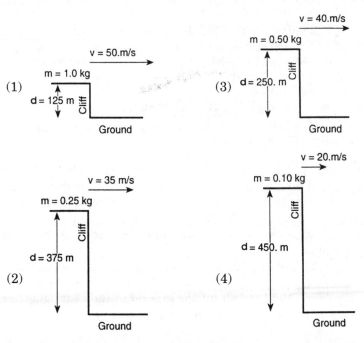

8 A soccer ball travels the path shown in the diagram at the right. Which vector best represents the direction of the force of air friction on the ball at point *P*?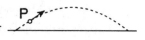

(1)   (2)   (3) | (4) ↓

9 A ball rolls through a hollow semicircular tube lying flat on a horizontal tabletop. Which diagram best shows the path of the ball after emerging from the tube, as viewed from above?

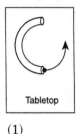   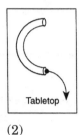   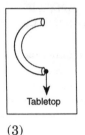   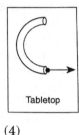

(1)   (2)   (3)   (4)

10 Projectiles are fired from different angles with the same initial speed of 14 meters per second. The graph at the right shows the range of the projectiles as a function of the original angle of inclination to the ground, neglecting air resistance. The graph shows that the range of the projectiles is

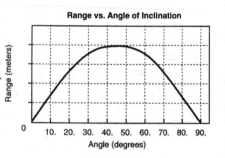

(1) the same for all angles
(2) the same for angles of 20.° and 80.°
(3) greatest for an angle of 45°
(4) greatest for an angle of 90.°

11 A 2-kilogram block is dropped from the roof of a tall building at the same time a 6-kilogram ball is thrown horizontally from the same height. Which statement best describes the motion of the block and the motion of the ball? [Neglect air resistance.]
(1) The 2-kg block hits the ground first because it has no horizontal velocity.
(2) The 6-kg ball hits the ground first because it has more mass.
(3) The 6-kg ball hits the ground first because it is round.
(4) The block and the ball hit the ground at the same time because they have the same vertical acceleration.

PART B QUESTIONS

Base your answers to questions 12 and 13 on the information and diagram at the right.

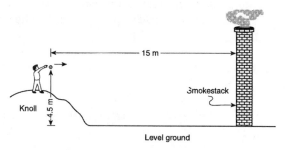

A student standing on a knoll throws a snow-ball horizontally 4.5 meters above the level ground toward a smokestack 15 meters away. The snowball hits the smokestack 0.65 second after being released. [Neglect air resistance.]

12 Approximately how far above the level ground does the snowball hit the smokestack? [1] _____ m

13 At the instant the snowball is released, the horizontal component of its velocity is approximately [1] _____ m/s

14 An artillery shell is fired at an angle to the horizontal. Its initial velocity has a vertical component of 150 meters per second and a horizontal component of 260 meters per second. What is the magnitude of the initial velocity of the shell? [1] _____ m/s

Base your answers to questions 15 through 18 on the diagram and information below.

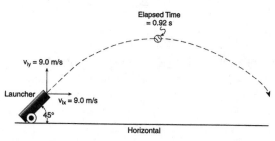

A machine launches a tennis ball at an angle of 45° with the horizontal, as shown. The ball has an initial vertical velocity of 9.0 meters per second and an initial horizontal velocity of 9.0 meters per second. The ball reaches its maximum height 0.92 second after its launch. [Neglect air resistance and assume the ball lands at the same height above the ground from which it was launched.]

15 The speed of the tennis ball as it leaves the launcher is approximately [1] _____ m/s

16 The total horizontal distance traveled by the tennis ball during the entire time it is in the air is approximately [1] _____ m

17 The speed at which the launcher fires tennis balls is constant, but the angle between the launcher and the horizontal can be varied. As the angle is decreased from 45 to 30, the range of the tennis balls [1] _____

18 Explain why the range changes for your answer to question 17. [1]

Base your answers to questions 19 and 20 on the information below and diagram at the right.

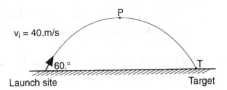

A projectile is launched at an angle of 60.° above the horizontal at an initial speed of 40. meters per second, as shown in the diagram above right. The projectile reaches its highest altitude at point P and strikes a target at point T. [Neglect air resistance.] [1]

19 What is the magnitude of the vertical component of the projectile's initial speed? [1] _____ m/s

20 Complete the graph at the right which represents the horizontal speed of the projectile as a function of time. [1] [Neglect air resistance.]

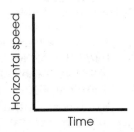

PART C QUESTIONS

21 Using the data from the graph at the right, select two angles which produce the same range for a projectile. [2]

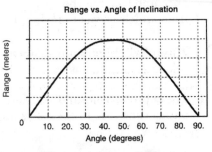

Range vs. Angle of Inclination

22 Determine the relationship between two angles which produce the same range. State the relationship. [2]

23 Projectile *A* is fired at a velocity of 100 m/s at an angle of 25 degrees. Projectile *B* is fired at the same initial velocity at an angle of 35 degrees. Compared to the quantities for projectile A, explain what will happen to the quantities of projectile B. [5]

Quantity	Increase, Decrease, or Remain the Same	Explanation
Initial horizontal velocity (V_x)		
Initial horizontal vertical velocity (V_y)		
Maximum vertical height		
Maximum vertical distance		
Time in air		

SECTION II
UNIFORM CIRCULAR MOTION

Uniform circular motion is the motion of an object at constant speed along a circular path.

CENTRIPETAL ACCELERATION

Centripetal acceleration is a vector quantity directed toward the center of curvature. Its magnitude is calculated by the formula:

$$a_c = v^2 / r$$

Where: a_c represents centripetal acceleration measured in m/s^2
v represents velocity in m/s
r is radius measured in meters

When an object moves in a circle, its velocity is constantly changing. This change in direction indicates that the object is being accelerated. Since velocity is a vector quantity, any change in magnitude (speed) or direction indicates acceleration.

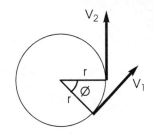

Centripetal acceleration occurs when magnitude and/or direction changes.

CENTRIPETAL FORCE

Centripetal force is a vector quantity directed towards the center of the circle. Its magnitude is calculated by using Newton's Second Law of Motion.

$$\mathbf{F_c} = \mathbf{ma_c}$$

$$= \frac{\mathbf{mv^2}}{\mathbf{r}}$$

Where: $\mathbf{F_c}$ represents the force measured in newtons
$\mathbf{m}$ is the mass in kilograms
$\mathbf{a_c}$ is centripetal acceleration

Centripetal force is the net force acting on a body. A body maintains its constant speed since there are no tangential forces. It is *not* in equilibrium. Centripetal force can be supplied by a variety of means such as tension in a rope, by the force of gravity, by friction on a road, or by the wall of an amusement park ride.

When the source of the centripetal force is removed, the object will move in a straight line tangent to the circle. Below is a diagram of an athlete in a hammer-throw event. The athlete pulls inward to keep the hammer moving in a horizontal circle of fixed radius at a constant speed. When the hammer is released at the position shown, it will travel along a tangent to the circle

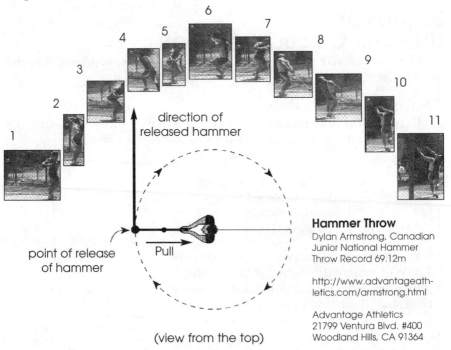

direction of released hammer

point of release of hammer

Pull

(view from the top)

Hammer Throw
Dylan Armstrong, Canadian Junior National Hammer Throw Record 69.12m

http://www.advantageath-letics.com/armstrong.html

Advantage Athletics
21799 Ventura Blvd. #400
Woodland Hills, CA 91364

REAL WORLD CONNECTIONS

RACE CALLED OFF AFTER SAFETY FEARS

Fears of drivers passing out at over 376 km/h have led to the Champ Car race in Texas being called off on April 30, 2001. Extremely high G-forces at the oval track were causing drivers dizziness, nausea, and vision problems on the Fort Worth track, which is new to the Championship Auto Racing Teams (CART)  series. The unprecedented move came after drivers expressed safety fears to race officials following speeds above 376 k/hr in the Saturday qualifying session at the 1.5-mile Texas Motor Speedway banked oval.

"The G-forces were beyond what I could have ever imagined," said Michael Andretti, the most successful driver in CART history. "You feel very compressed when you get down in the corners. Everything is just compressing your body. It's a feeling I've never felt before."

This time, series officials were caught off guard by the impact of the 24-degree banking at Texas as the carts were traveling at over 376 km/h. No other track in the CART series is steeper than 18 degrees.

The medical director said all but four of the 25 drivers on the starting grid experienced some sort of inner ear or vision problems after running more than 10 laps at a time.

Teams said the G-forces were above five, when a range in the threes is generally considered as high as drivers can endure for extended periods on oval tracks. The event was scheduled for 250 laps on the 1.5-mile (2.4-kilometer) four-turn oval.

 "At this point, I've got to really applaud CART for standing up for the drivers and safety and trying to find a solution and not going ahead with the event at this time," Andretti said. "This isn't something we could predict."

Source: CART – Champion Auto Racing Teams ©2001

EXAMPLE

An object weighing 49. newtons moves in a circular path of radius 0.50 meters at a speed of 10. meters per second. Calculate the (a) mass, (b) centripetal acceleration, and (c) the centripetal force.

Given: $F_g = 49.\ N$ $r = .50\ m$ $v = 10.\ m/s$

Find: mass, acceleration, and force

Solution:

a $m = \dfrac{F_g}{g}$

   $= $ 49. N/9.81 m/s^2

   $= $ 5.0 kg

b $a_c = \dfrac{v^2}{r}$

   $= $ (10. m/s)^2/(.50 m)

   $= $ 2.0 x 10^2 m/s^2

c $F_c = \dfrac{mv^2}{r}$

   $= $ (5.0 kg)(10. m/s)^2/(.50 m)

   $= $ 1.0 x 10^3 N

REAL WORLD CONNECTIONS

RIDING THE LOOPS AT THE AMUSEMENT PARK

TOP OF A HILL

The only forces acting on the rider are the upward normal force F_N exerted by the car and the downward force of gravity **mg**, the rider's weight. These add together, as vectors, to provide the net force F_{net} which is the centripetal force F_c, directed toward the center of the circle. The normal force may also be called the rider's "apparent weight" for this is the force of the seat on the rider and also describes what the rider "feels" (in addition to terror!).

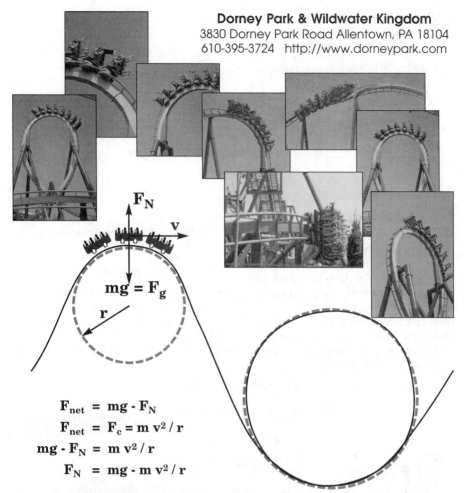

$$F_{net} = mg - F_N$$
$$F_{net} = F_c = m\,v^2\,/\,r$$
$$mg - F_N = m\,v^2\,/\,r$$
$$F_N = mg - m\,v^2\,/\,r$$

What does all this mean? The normal force or the rider's apparent weight is less than the rider's real weight. The seat cannot exert a negative force on the rider. If we approach a situation where the apparent weight might become negative, there should be a good safety restraint system – seat belts, lap bars, or shoulder restraints to keep the person inside the ride.

We might ask how fast the coaster can go until the rider just (barely) loses contact with the seat. That means the normal force between the seat and rider is zero. That occurs when the velocity at the top is equal to the product of radius and gravitational acceleration (**rg**).

$$F_N = mg - m\,v^2\,/\,r = 0$$
$$m\,v^2\,/\,r = mg$$
$$v^2\,/\,r = g$$
$$v^2 = rg$$

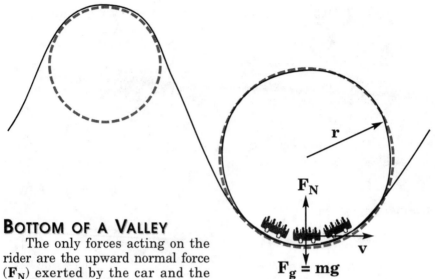

BOTTOM OF A VALLEY

The only forces acting on the rider are the upward normal force ($\mathbf{F_N}$) exerted by the car and the downward force of gravity (**mg**), the rider's weight. These add together, as vectors, to provide the net force ($\mathbf{F_{net}}$) which is the centripetal force ($\mathbf{F_c}$), directed toward the center of the circle. Notice, of course, that the center of the circle is now up from the rider. As always, the normal force may also be called the rider's "apparent weight" for this is the force of the seat on the rider and also describes what the rider "feels."

$$\mathbf{F_{net}} = \mathbf{F_N} - \mathbf{F_g} = \mathbf{F_N} - \mathbf{mg}$$

$$\mathbf{F_{net}} = \mathbf{F_c} = m\, v^2 / r$$

$$\mathbf{F_N} - mg = m\, v^2 / r$$

$$\mathbf{F_N} = mg + m\, v^2 / r$$

What does all this mean? The normal force or the rider's apparent weight is now more than the rider's real weight. The rider feels pressed down into the seat. The rider's hands and arms are hard to move. The rider's blood is even hard to move. Airplane pilots are in this situation as they pull out of a dive. The ratio of this "apparent weight" to real weight may be described as the apparent effect of gravity or may be described as "g-forces." "G-forces" of six or seven – meaning an apparent weight of six or seven times one's real weight – can mean that enough blood will not be circulated to the brain and a pilot – or other passenger – may pass out. Many pilots use pressurized suits to keep the blood from flowing out of the head.

UPSIDE-DOWN
AT THE TOP OF A LOOP

In this stage, both the normal force $\mathbf{F_N}$ and the weight $\mathbf{F_g}$ point in the same direction, so the net force is the sum of these two forces.

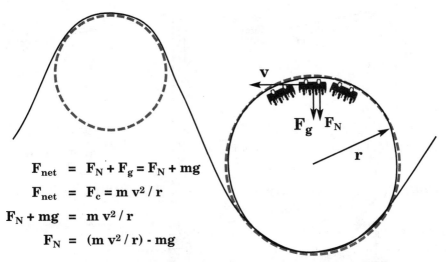

$$F_{net} = F_N + F_g = F_N + mg$$
$$F_{net} = F_c = m\,v^2/r$$
$$F_N + mg = m\,v^2/r$$
$$F_N = (m\,v^2/r) - mg$$

What does all this mean? If the speed is too low, this equation indicates the normal force will be negative. What does a negative normal force mean? Since the seat cannot reach out and pull the rider back, the rider will fall out of the car. And, since the track cannot reach out and pull back on the roller coaster car, the car would fall off the track! To prevent this, roller coasters have wheels on both sides of the track and the riders have safety restraints

☆ TRY IT

5 Design a ride so the normal force just vanishes and the riders do, indeed, feel weightless at the top. Or design a ride so the normal force is equal to the real weight at the top. Draw an illustration and describe in words.

LAB 7 – CENTRIPETAL FORCE
BACKGROUND

When an object moves along a curved path, its velocity is not constant because the direction is changing. The object is accelerating. An acceleration always involves the action of an unbalanced force. The force causing an acceleration toward the center of a circle is called the centripetal force. When an automobile rounds a curve, the centripetal force is supplied by the road surface pushing against the tires. Centripetal acceleration depends on the object's speed and the radius of curvature of its path.

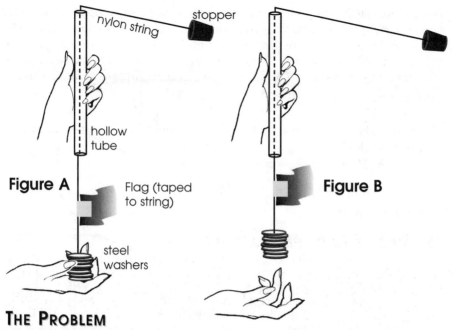

Figure A

Figure B

nylon string

stopper

hollow tube

Flag (taped to string)

steel washers

THE PROBLEM

In the following experiment we shall cause an object to move in a circular path and measure the centripetal force. The apparatus setup is shown above.

In this experiment, we will keep the mass at the end of the string constant. We will analyze the relationship between the force, the velocity, and the radius by separately varying each variable.

CHANGING THE FORCE

Fasten one end of the nylon cord securely to the rubber stopper. Pass the other end through the plastic tube and fasten 15 uniform washers to it, by slipping the washers through the attached paper clip. Adjust the cord so that there is about 0.75 m of cord between the top of the tube and the stopper. Attach a piece of tape as a flag to the cord just below the bottom of the tube. Support the washers with one hand and hold the plastic tube in the other (Figure A). Whirl the stopper by moving the tube in a circular motion.

Slowly release the washers and adjust the speed of the stopper so that the flag stays just below the bottom of the tube (Figure B). Make several trial runs before recording any data.

When you have learned how to keep the velocity of the stopper and the position of the paper clip relatively constant, have a classmate measure the time required for 20 revolutions. Record this time. How will you calculate the period (**T**)? (The period is the time it takes to complete one revolution.) How will you calculate the velocity of the stopper? Vary the force by adding or subtracting five washers at a time. Setup a data table to record results for force (in number of washers), radius, period, and velocity. In this trial what is kept constant? You will find that a graph of centripetal force versus velocity is helpful in revealing the relationship.

☆ TRY IT

6 How could you use this data to plot a straight line? State and justify your conclusions.

THE RADIUS AND THE VELOCITY

Using a fixed number of washers, repeat the experiment by varying the radius. Setup a data table to record results for force (in number of washers), radius, period, and velocity. In this trial, what is kept constant? You will find that a graph of radius versus velocity is helpful in revealing the relationship.

☆ TRY IT

7 How could you use this data to plot a straight line? State and justify your conclusions.

DATA ANALYSIS

You can compare your data with the actual formula for centripetal force if you measure the force of the washers (in newtons) and the mass of the stopper (in kilograms). If the centripetal force formula is valid, then the product FT^2 (force times period squared) should be constant for all values of F, and equal to $4\pi^2Rm$ (where R is the radius and m is the mass of the stopper). You can calculate the values of FT^2 from your data. Calculate the value for a number of tries and determine the average. Remember to change the washer number to a force value (newtons) and see how close the average is to the theoretical value of the proportionality constant ($4\pi^2Rm$).

☆ TRY IT

8 Within what percent of the theoretical value is the proportionality constant you have found?

CHAPTER FIVE (SECTION 2) ASSESSMENTS

PART A QUESTIONS

1   As a cart travels around a horizontal circular track, the cart must undergo a change in
    (1) velocity   (2) inertia   (3) speed   (4) weight

Base your answers to questions 2 through 4 on the information and diagram at the right.

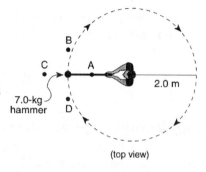

(top view)

An athlete in a hammer-throw event swings a 7.0-kilogram hammer in a horizontal circle at a constant speed of 12 meters per second. The radius of the hammer's path is 2.0 meters.

2   At the position shown, the centripetal force acting on the hammer is directed toward point
    (1) *A*   (2) *B*   (3) *C*   (4) *D*

3   What is the magnitude of the centripetal acceleration of the hammer?
    (1) 6.0 m/s²   (2) 24 m/s²   (3) 72 m/s²   (4) 500 m/s²

4   If the hammer is released at the position shown, it will travel toward point
    (1) *A*   (2) *B*   (3) *C*   (4) *D*

Base your answers to questions 5 through 7 on the diagram at the right which shows a 2.0-kilogram cart traveling at a constant speed in a horizontal circle of radius 3.0 meters. The magnitude of the centripetal force on the cart is 24 newtons.

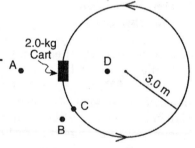

5   In the position shown, the acceleration of the cart is
    (1) 8.0 m/s² directed toward point *A*
    (2) 8.0 m/s² directed toward point *D*
    (3) 12 m/s² directed toward point *A*
    (4) 12 m/s² directed toward point *D*

6   What is the speed of the cart?
    (1) 6.0 m/s   (2) 16 m/s   (3) 36 m/s   (4) 4.0 m/s

7   Which statement correctly describes the direction of the cart's velocity and centripetal force in the position shown?
   (1) Velocity is directed toward point B, and the centripetal force is directed toward point A.
   (2) Velocity is directed toward point B, and the centripetal force is directed toward point D.
   (3) Velocity is directed toward point C, and the centripetal force is directed toward point A.
   (4) Velocity is directed toward point C, and the centripetal force is directed toward point D.

8   The diagram at the right shows a satellite of mass m orbiting Earth in a circular path of radius R. If centripetal force F_c is acting on the satellite, its speed is equal to

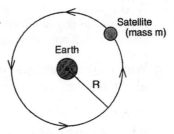

   (1) $\sqrt{\dfrac{F_c R}{m}}$ (3) $\sqrt{\dfrac{F_c m}{R}}$

   (2) $\dfrac{F_c R}{m}$ (4) $F_c\, mR$

9   An amusement park ride moves a rider at a constant speed of 14 meters per second in a horizontal circular path of radius 10. meters. What is the rider's centripetal acceleration in terms of g, the acceleration due to gravity?
   (1) $1g$ (2) $2g$ (3) $3g$ (4) $0g$

10 If the speed of the airplane is doubled and the radius of the path remains unchanged, the magnitude of the centripetal force acting on the airplane will be
   (1) half as much   (3) one-fourth as much
   (2) twice as much   (4) four times as much

PART B QUESTIONS

Base your answers to questions 11 and 12 on the information below and diagram at the right.

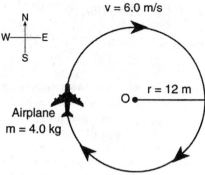

A 4.0-kilogram model airplane travels in a horizontal circular path of radius 12 meters at a constant speed of 6.0 meters per second.

11 At the position shown, what is the direction of the net force acting on the airplane? [1] _____

12 What is the magnitude of the centripetal acceleration of the airplane? [1] _____ m/s²

13 A ball attached to a string is whirled at a constant speed of 2.0 meters per second in a horizontal circle of radius 0.50 meter. What is the magnitude of the ball's centripetal acceleration? [1] _____ m/s²

Base your answers to questions 14 and 15 on the information below and diagram at the right.

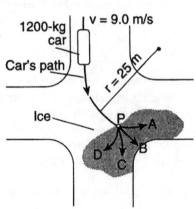

A 1200-kilogram car traveling at a constant speed of 9.0 meters per second turns at an intersection. The car follows a horizontal circular path with a radius of 25 meters to point P.

14 The magnitude of the centripetal force acting on the car as it travels around the circular path is approximately [1] _____ N

15 At point P, the car hits an area of ice and loses all frictional force on its tires. Which path does the car follow on the ice? [1] _____

PART C QUESTIONS

Base your answers to questions 16 through 18 on the information below and diagram to the right.

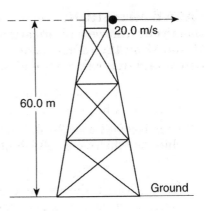

A ball is thrown horizontally with an initial velocity of 20.0 meters per second from the top of a tower 60.0 meters high.

16 What is the approximate total time required for the ball to reach the ground? [Show all calculations.] [2]

17 What is the vertical velocity of the ball just before it reaches the ground? [Neglect air resistance. Show all calculations.] [2]

18 In the above problem, the initial horizontal velocity changes to 30.0 meters per second.

   a   What is the approximate total time required for the ball to reach the ground? [Show all calculations.] [2]

   b   What is the vertical velocity of the ball just before it reaches the ground? [Neglect air resistance. Show all calculations.] [2]

Base your answers to questions 19 and 20 on the information below and diagram at the right.

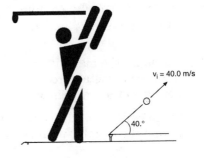

A golf ball leaves a golf club with an initial velocity of 40.0 meters per second at an angle of 40.° with the horizontal.

19 Calculate the vertical component of the golf ball's initial velocity. [Show all calculations.] [2]

20 What is the total horizontal distance traveled by the golf ball during the first 2.5 seconds of its flight? [1]

21 Describe any changes in initial velocity and/or angle that could increase the range of the ball. [2]

Base your answers to questions 22 and 23 on the information below and diagram at the right.

A 60.-kilogram car travels clockwise in a horizontal circle of radius 10. meters at 5.0 meters per second.

22 Draw a vector which represents the direction of the centripetal acceleration of the car at the position shown. [2]

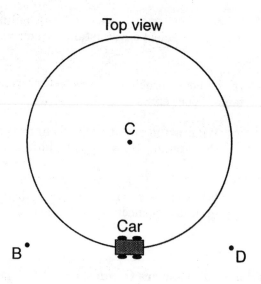

Top view

23 Calculate the magnitude of the centripetal force acting on the car. [Show all work.] [2]

CHAPTER 6
MOMENTUM

KEY IDEA 5 ENERGY AND MATTER INTERACT THROUGH FORCES THAT RESULT IN CHANGES IN MOTION.

PERFORMANCE INDICATOR 5.1 *STUDENTS CAN EXPLAIN AND PREDICT DIFFERENT PATTERNS OF MOTION OF OBJECTS (E.G., LINEAR AND UNIFORM CIRCULAR MOTION, VELOCITY AND ACCELERATION, MOMENTUM AND INERTIA).*

CHAPTER 6 – MAJOR UNDERSTANDINGS

☆ 5.1p The impulse* imparted to an object causes a change in its momentum*.

☆ 5.1q According to Newton's Third Law, forces occur in action/reaction pairs. When one object exerts a force on a second, the second exerts a force on the first that is equal in magnitude and opposite in direction.

☆ 5.1r Momentum is conserved in a closed system.* (Note: Testing will be limited to momentum in one dimension.)

CHAPTER 6
MOMENTUM

MOMENTUM – A VECTOR QUANTITY

Momentum is a vector quantity. It is the product of mass and velocity. The direction of the momentum is the same as the direction of the velocity. The unit for momentum is kg-m/s or newton-second.

When a body accelerates, its velocity changes; therefore, acceleration always produces a change in momentum. The momentum of an object will increase or decrease when a net external force acts on it.

In a system of objects, the individual components of a system will gain or lose momentum as they interact with one another. These interaction forces are internal forces and thus the momentum of the system does not change. As some components of the system gain momentum, other components of the system lose an equal amount of momentum. The momentum of the system is conserved.

©PhotoDisc

In special cases, called **elastic collisions**, there is also conservation of kinetic energy. That is, the sum of the kinetic energy before the collision equals the sum of the kinetic energy after the collisions. Unless otherwise specified, collisions are **inelastic**, meaning that kinetic energy is not conserved, but momentum is conserved.

Important Equations for Momentum:

$$\textbf{p} \; = \; \textbf{momentum} \; = \; \textbf{mass} \cdot \textbf{velocity}$$

$$\textbf{and}$$

$$\textbf{momentum before} \; = \; \textbf{momentum after}$$

EXAMPLES OF MOMENTUM PROBLEMS

The following examples illustrate applications of the Law of Conservation of Momentum:

Example 1: Cart A approaches cart B (initially at rest) with an initial velocity of 30 m/s. After the collision, cart A stops and cart B continues with what velocity?

Before Collision	After Collision

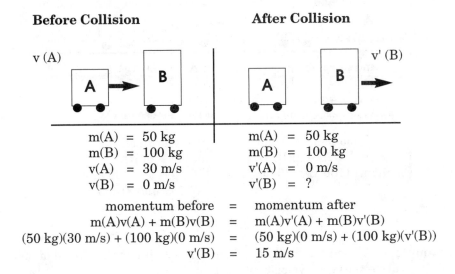

m(A) = 50 kg	m(A) = 50 kg
m(B) = 100 kg	m(B) = 100 kg
v(A) = 30 m/s	v'(A) = 0 m/s
v(B) = 0 m/s	v'(B) = ?

$$
\begin{aligned}
\text{momentum before} &= \text{momentum after} \\
m(A)v(A) + m(B)v(B) &= m(A)v'(A) + m(B)v'(B) \\
(50 \text{ kg})(30 \text{ m/s}) + (100 \text{ kg})(0 \text{ m/s}) &= (50 \text{ kg})(0 \text{ m/s}) + (100 \text{ kg})(v'(B)) \\
v'(B) &= 15 \text{ m/s}
\end{aligned}
$$

Example 2: Cart A approaches cart B (initially at rest) with an initial velocity of 30 m/s. After the collision, cart A locks together with cart B. Both travel with what velocity?

Before Collision	After Collision

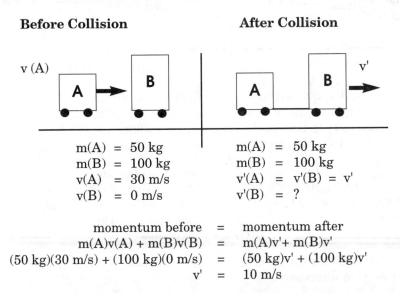

m(A) = 50 kg	m(A) = 50 kg
m(B) = 100 kg	m(B) = 100 kg
v(A) = 30 m/s	v'(A) = v'(B) = v'
v(B) = 0 m/s	v'(B) = ?

$$
\begin{aligned}
\text{momentum before} &= \text{momentum after} \\
m(A)v(A) + m(B)v(B) &= m(A)v' + m(B)v' \\
(50 \text{ kg})(30 \text{ m/s}) + (100 \text{ kg})(0 \text{ m/s}) &= (50 \text{ kg})v' + (100 \text{ kg})v' \\
v' &= 10 \text{ m/s}
\end{aligned}
$$

Example 3: Cart A moving with an initial velocity of 30 m/sec approaches cart B moving at an initial velocity of 20 m/s towards cart A. The two carts lock together and move as one. Calculate the magnitude and the direction of the final velocity. (*Note:* Velocity to the left is denoted by a (−) negative sign)

Before Collision	After Collision

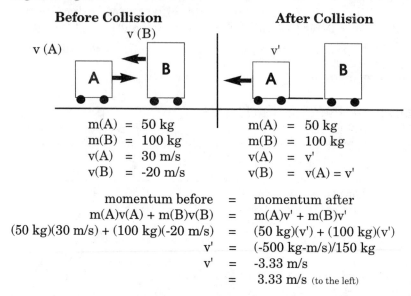

m(A) = 50 kg	m(A) = 50 kg
m(B) = 100 kg	m(B) = 100 kg
v(A) = 30 m/s	v(A) = v'
v(B) = -20 m/s	v(B) = v(A) = v'

$$
\begin{aligned}
\text{momentum before} &= \text{momentum after} \\
m(A)v(A) + m(B)v(B) &= m(A)v' + m(B)v' \\
(50 \text{ kg})(30 \text{ m/s}) + (100 \text{ kg})(-20 \text{ m/s}) &= (50 \text{ kg})(v') + (100 \text{ kg})(v') \\
v' &= (-500 \text{ kg-m/s})/150 \text{ kg} \\
v' &= -3.33 \text{ m/s} \\
&= 3.33 \text{ m/s} \text{ (to the left)}
\end{aligned}
$$

Example 4: A 1 gm bullet is fired from a 10 kg rifle with a speed of 300 m/s. Calculate the recoil velocity of the gun.

Before Explosion	After Explosion

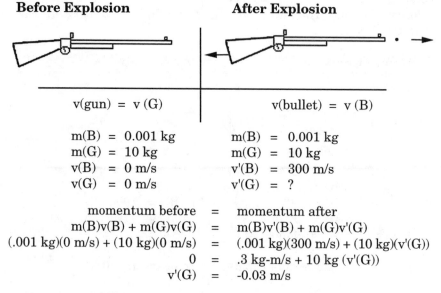

v(gun) = v (G)	v(bullet) = v (B)
m(B) = 0.001 kg	m(B) = 0.001 kg
m(G) = 10 kg	m(G) = 10 kg
v(B) = 0 m/s	v'(B) = 300 m/s
v(G) = 0 m/s	v'(G) = ?

$$
\begin{aligned}
\text{momentum before} &= \text{momentum after} \\
m(B)v(B) + m(G)v(G) &= m(B)v'(B) + m(G)v'(G) \\
(.001 \text{ kg})(0 \text{ m/s}) + (10 \text{ kg})(0 \text{ m/s}) &= (.001 \text{ kg})(300 \text{ m/s}) + (10 \text{ kg})(v'(G)) \\
0 &= .3 \text{ kg-m/s} + 10 \text{ kg } (v'(G)) \\
v'(G) &= -0.03 \text{ m/s}
\end{aligned}
$$

After an explosion, momentum in one direction is equal to momentum in the other direction.

IMPULSE

When an unbalanced force acts on an object for a period of time, a change in momentum is produced. **Impulse** is defined as the product of force and time. It is the cause of a change in momentum, and it is equal to the change in momentum.

$$\text{Impulse} = F\Delta t = m\Delta v = \Delta p$$

The units for impulse are the same as the units for momentum, newton-second or kg-m/s.

EXAMPLES OF IMPULSE PROBLEMS

Example 1: An impulse of 50 newton-seconds is applied to a 10 kg mass in the direction of motion. If the mass had a speed of 20 m/s before the impulse, its speed after the impulse could be

Given:

Impulse	=	50 N-s
v_i	=	20 m/s
m	=	10 kg
$m\Delta v$	=	impulse

Find:

new speed (v) $= v_i + \Delta v$

$\Delta v = \text{impulse}/m = 50 \text{ N-s}/10 \text{ kg} = 5 \text{ m/s}$

Therefore: v = $v_i + \Delta v$
So: v = **25 m/s**

Example 2: A 30 kg mass moving at a speed of 3 m/s is stopped by a constant force of 15 newtons. How many seconds must the force act on the mass to stop it?

Given:

m	=	30 kg
v_i	=	3 m/s
F	=	-15 N
v_f	=	0 m/s

Find: time

Solution:

Impulse	=	$F\Delta t = m\Delta v$
$F\Delta t$	=	$m\Delta v$
N-s	=	kg • m/s
Δt	=	$m\ \Delta v/F$
Δt	=	30 kg (0 m/s − 3 m/s) / -15 N
Δt	=	6 s

REAL WORLD CONNECTIONS

THE VEHICLE RESEARCH CENTER

For years, the Insurance Institute for Highway Safety has been a leader in finding out what works and doesn't work to prevent motor vehicle crashes in the first place and reduce injuries in the crashes that still occur. This work expanded with the 1992 opening of the Vehicle Research Center (VRC), which is the focus of all of the Institute's vehicle-related research. VRC activities include vehicle and component testing, including fully instrumented crash tests, plus in-depth study of serious, on-the-road crashes. Scrutinizing the outcomes of both controlled tests and real collisions gives researchers – and ultimately the public – a better idea of how and why occupants get injured in crashes. This research, in turn, leads to vehicle designs that reduce injuries.

HYBRID III FAMILY OF DUMMIES

The VRC has a fully equipped dummy calibration laboratory with a range of dummy sizes and configurations. Born in America in General Motors' labs, the 50th percentile Hybrid III family of dummies are the standard dummy used in frontal crash tests all over the world. They are called hybrids because their ancestors were created by combining parts of two different types of dummies.

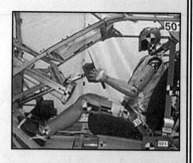

The 50th percentile male Hybrid III is the most widely used frontal crash test dummy, but the Hybrid III family also includes dummies representing different sizes, ages, and sexes. There is the 95th percentile or large male who is bigger than 95 percent of the adult male population. He is 6 feet 2 inches tall, 223 pounds. The 5th percentile or small female Hybrid III is smaller than 95 percent of the adult female population. She is 5 feet tall, 110 pounds. There are two child-size Hybrid III dummies. They are the 47-pound, 6 year-old and the 33-pound, 3 year-old.

Dummies are tough, but if they ever break, damaged parts can be repaired or replaced. This way, they are able to work a long, long time – a very good thing since new dummies are expensive. A fully instrumented one costs about $150,000.

Source: *Insurance Institute for Highway Safety* ©2002
http://www.highwaysafety.org/vehicle_ratings/vrc.htm

TRY IT

1   Two cars, weighing 11,120 N (2250 lb) and 13,344 N (3000 lb) are
    moving at 13.4 m/s (30 mph) and 22.3 m/s (50.0 mph) respectively.
    The latter car hits the rear end of the former car and their bumpers
    lock.

    a   What is the velocity of the two car combination after the colli-
        sion?

    b   What is the impulse given to the 712 N (160 lb) person riding in
        the 22.3 m/s (50.0 mph) car and wearing a seatbelt if the colli-
        sion time is 0.1 s? What is the average force acting on this per-
        son?

2   While waiting at a traffic light, a driver
    begins to daydream and unknowingly
    releases the foot brake on his car. His car
    moves a distance of 2.0 m down a grade
    which makes an angle of 6° with the hori-
    zontal and hits a stopped 2nd car.
    (Remember that the acceleration is g sin θ, not g)

    a   With what speed does his car hit the the 2nd car?

    b   What is the impulse given to an 801 N (180 lb) driver of the car
        when it is stopped by the second car?

    c   What is the average force exerted on the 1st car if the stopping
        time is 0.1 s? (The car has a weight of 11,120 N [2500 lb])

    d   What is the average force on the driver in (b) if he wears a seat-
        belt and stops with the car?

SKILL 5.1XII
LAB 8 – CONSERVATION OF MOMENTUM IN AN EXPLOSION

BACKGROUND

When a net force acts on an object, the object is accelerated. The acceleration of the object is directly proportional to the force and inversely proportional to the mass of the object. Algebraically this is expressed as $\mathbf{F} = \boldsymbol{ma}$. Since we know that acceleration is the rate of change of velocity, or $a = \Delta v/\Delta t$, we can write

$$\mathbf{F} = \boldsymbol{ma} = \boldsymbol{m}\,\frac{\Delta\mathbf{v}}{\Delta\mathbf{t}}$$

or

$$\mathbf{F}\Delta \boldsymbol{t} = \boldsymbol{m}\Delta\boldsymbol{v}$$

If the mass remains constant, $m\Delta v = \Delta(mv)$, and we have

$$\mathbf{F}\Delta \boldsymbol{t} = \Delta(\boldsymbol{mv}).$$

The product of an object's mass and its velocity (mv) is known as the momentum, a vector quantity. The product of the resultant force and the time interval during which it acts ($F\Delta t$) is known as the *impulse*. The formula above thus states that the change in an object's momentum is equal to the applied impulse.

THE PROBLEM

In this experiment we shall allow an "explosion" caused by a compressed spring to push two loaded carts apart. We can measure their masses and the comparative resulting velocities. This enables us to compare their momenta. Knowing their comparative momenta allows us to compare the impulses acting on the two objects and the forces the objects exerted on each other during explosion.

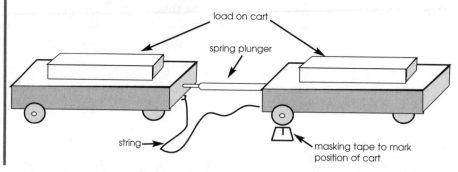

load on cart

spring plunger

string

masking tape to mark position of cart

COMPARING THE VELOCITIES OF THE CARTS

The apparatus consists of two carts, one of which has a spring-actuated plunger. The spring is compressed and the carts are placed together. The plunger can be released by a trigger, and the explosion causes the carts to fly apart. We shall use a trick to determine their comparative velocities. The carts are attached by a length of string that is slack before the separation explosion. The carts fly apart and move until the string is pulled tight; they are then abruptly stopped. Since the two carts (represented in the following by subscripts 1 and 2) move for the same length of time, the distances they travel (s_1 and s_2) away from their starting points must be in the same ratio as their speeds (v_1 and v_2), or

$$\frac{v_1}{v_2} = \frac{s_1}{s_2}$$

Knowing the masses of the carts, we can calculate the ratio of their momenta after the explosion has occurred.

MAKING THE MEASUREMENTS

Mark the starting position of one cart with a piece of masking tape on the table top. With another piece of masking tape, mark the position the cart reaches after the explosion. Repeat this several times to make sure that you have marked the correct distance. Place the two carts together in the starting position and mark the original position of the second cart. By placing the first in its final position and pulling the string tight, you can locate the final position of the second cart. You can now measure the distance each cart travels. Repeat this experiment for a variety of combinations of masses of the carts.

OBTAINING RESULTS FROM THE DATA

Compute the ratio of the momenta of the carts. What do the momentum ratios suggest about the comparative magnitudes of the momenta of the carts after the explosion? Recalling the momentum is a vector quantity, make a general statement about the total momentum of the two carts before the explosion and after the explosion.

Compare the times during which the spring pushed on the carts. Compare the forces on the two carts during the explosion.

CHAPTER SIX ASSESSMENTS

PART A QUESTIONS

1 What is the momentum of a 1,200-kilogram car traveling at 15 meters per second due east?
   (1) 80. kg•m/s due east
   (2) 80. kg•m/s due west
   (3) 1.8 x 10⁴ kg•m/s due east
   (4) 1.8 x 10⁴ kg•m/s due west

2 What is the momentum of a 1.5 x 10³-kilogram car as it travels at 30. meters per second due east for 60. seconds?
   (1) 4.5 x 10⁴ kg•m/s, east
   (2) 4.5 x 10⁴ kg•m/s, west
   (3) 2.7 x 10⁶ kg•m, east
   (4) 2.7 x 10⁶ kg•m, west

3 The velocity-time graph at the right represents the motion of a 3-kilogram cart along a straight line. The cart starts at $t = 0$ and initially moves north. What is the magnitude of the change in momentum of the cart between $t = 0$ and $t = 3$ seconds?
   (1) 20 kg•m/s   (3) 60 kg•m/s
   (2) 30 kg•m/s   (4) 80 kg•m/s

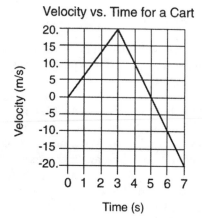
Velocity vs. Time for a Cart

4 As shown in the diagrams at the right, a lump of clay travels horizontally to the right toward a block at rest on a frictionless surface. Upon collision, the clay and the block stick together and move to the right. Compared to the total momentum of the clay and the block before the collision, the momentum of the clay-block system after the collision is
   (1) less   (2) greater   (3) the same

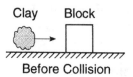
Before Collision

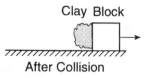
After Collision

5 A student drops two eggs of equal mass simultaneously from the same height. Egg A lands on the tile floor and breaks. Egg B lands intact, without bouncing, on a foam pad lying on the floor. Compared to the magnitude of the impulse on egg A as it lands, the magnitude of the impulse on egg B as it lands is
   (1) less   (2) greater   (3) the same

6   Which terms represent a vector quantity and its respective unit?
    (1) weight – kilogram   (3) force – newton
    (2) mass – kilogram   (4) momentum – newton

7   A 2,400-kilogram car is traveling at a speed of 20. meters per second.
    Compared to the magnitude of the force required to stop the car in
    12 seconds, the magnitude of the force required to stop the car in 6.0
    seconds is
    (1) half as great   (3) the same
    (2) twice as great   (4) four times as great

PART B QUESTIONS

8   A 0.60-kilogram softball initially at rest is hit with a bat. The ball is
    in contact with the bat for 0.20 second and leaves the bat with a
    speed of 25 meters per second. What is the magnitude of the average
    force exerted by the ball on the bat? [1] _____ N

9   A 1.2 x 10³-kilogram car is accelerated uniformly from 10. meters per
    second to 20. meters per second in 5.0 seconds. What is the magni-
    tude of the net force acting on the car during this 5.0-second inter-
    val? [1] _____ N

10 A 2.0 x 10³-kilogram car collides with a tree and is brought to rest in
    0.50 second by an average force of 6.0 x 10⁴ newtons. What is the
    magnitude of the impulse on the car during this 0.50-second inter-
    val? [1] _____N•s

11 Satellite A has a mass of 1.5 x 10³ kilograms and is traveling east at
    8.0 x 10³ meters per second. Satellite B is traveling west at 6.0 x 10³
    meters per second. The satellites collide head-on and come to rest.
    What is the mass of satellite B? [1] _____ kg

12 A 2.0-kilogram cart moving due east at 6.0 meters per second col-
    lides with a 3.0-kilogram cart moving due west. The carts stick
    together and come to rest after the collision. What was the initial
    speed of the 3.0-kilogram cart? [1] _____ m/s

13 The magnitude of the momentum of an object is
    64.0 kilogram•meter per second. If the velocity of the object is dou-
    bled, the magnitude of the momentum of the object will be [1]
    _____ kg•m/s

14 In an automobile collision, a 44-kilogram passenger moving at 15 meters per second is brought to rest by an air bag during a 0.10-second time interval. What is the magnitude of the average force exerted on the passenger during this time? [1] _____ N

15 In the diagram at the right, a 100.-kilogram clown is fired from a 500.-kilogram cannon. If the clown's speed is 15 meters per second after the firing, then the recoil speed (v) of the cannon is [1] _____ m/s

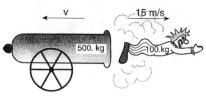

16 The diagram at the right shows two carts on a horizontal, frictionless surface being pushed apart when a compressed spring attached to one of the carts is released. Cart A has a mass of 3.0 kilograms and cart B has a mass of 5.0 kilograms. The speed of cart A is 0.33 meter per second after the spring is released. If the carts are initially at rest, what is the approximate speed of cart B after the spring is released? [1] _____ m/s

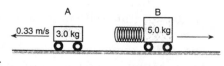

PART C QUESTIONS

Base your answers to questions 17 and 18 on the information below. Show all calculations including equations and substitution with units.

A 1,000–kilogram car traveling with a velocity of +20. meters per second decelerates uniformly at –5.0 meters per second^2 until it comes to rest.

17 What is the total distance the car travels as it decelerates to rest? [2]

18 What is the magnitude of the impulse applied to the car to bring it to rest? [2]

CHAPTER 7
SWINGS AND SPRINGS

KEY IDEA 4
ENERGY EXISTS IN MANY FORMS, AND WHEN THESE FORMS CHANGE ENERGY IS CONSERVED.

KEY IDEA 5
ENERGY AND MATTER INTERACT THROUGH FORCES THAT RESULT IN CHANGES IN MOTION.

CHAPTER 7 – MAJOR UNDERSTANDINGS

☆ 4.1c Potential energy is the energy an object possesses by virtue of its position or condition. Types of potential energy include gravitational* and elastic*.

☆ 4.1d Kinetic energy* is the energy an object possesses by virtue of its motion.

☆ 4.1e In an ideal mechanical system, the sum of the macroscopic kinetic and potential energies (mechanical energy) is constant.*

☆ 4.1f In a non-ideal mechanical system, as mechanical energy decreases there is a corresponding increase in other energies such as internal energy.*

☆ 4.1g When work* is done on or by a system, there is a change in the total energy* of the system.

☆ 5.1p The impulse* imparted to an object causes a change in its momentum*.

☆ 5.1m The elongation or compression of a spring depends upon the nature of the spring (its spring constant) and the magnitude of the applied force.*

CHAPTER 7
SWINGS AND SPRINGS

THINGS THAT SWING

The pendulum, the spring, and even the Pirate Ship and Sky Coaster at the amusement park are examples of **simple harmonic motion**. The motion always has a restoring force directed toward the center and the force is directly proportional to the displacement from the equilibrium position (center).

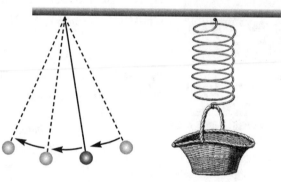

The pirate ship ride is basically a large pendulum. At the top of each swing, the participant feels a moment of zero-g. Gravity is still working, but for that short period of time, the force between the person and his or her seat drops to zero. Without that support force, we accelerate as gravity dictates, and we feel weightless. On this ride, the vertical accelerometer will indicate zero-g at the top of the swing.

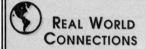
REAL WORLD CONNECTIONS

SWINGING PIRATES

The Pirate is a very common amusement park ride. One of the most famous pirate rides is installed at Six Flags Darien Lake. Appearing during the later years of the park, the Pirate was located next to the Giant Coaster.

Source: *Six Flags Darien Lake* - Buffalo, NY ©2002

Skills 2.2, 2.3, 2.4, 4.1iv
Lab 9 – Pendulum

Background

Some of the earliest timepieces were based on the workings of a simple pendulum. This predictable time for one swing of the pendulum is called the period. The **period** of a pendulum is the time it takes the pendulum to go through one complete swing. You might guess that the period of the pendulum depends on several factors. In this lab, we will try to determine how each of these factors influence the pendulum's period.

The Problem

Your task is to come up with an equation which will work for the pendulums set up in the lab. Decide in your lab group which factors might affect the period of the pendulum and devise a strategy to test each factor.

The Experiment

Do the experiment as you have planned it. Record all your data and the calculated results. Analyze your data looking for relationships between each variable and the pendulum's period. For every variable you investigated, graph Pendulum Period vs. Variable.

The Equation

Working with your group, write an equation for the period of a pendulum in terms of the variables which affect it. Test the validity of your formula using a pendulum.

☆ Try It

1   How would you adjust a pendulum clock that runs too *fast*?

2   How would you adjust a pendulum clock which runs too *slow*?

3   What is the formula you derived for the period of the pendulum?

4   What factors affect the period of a pendulum?

5   The spaceship is an amusement park ride with a giant pendulum
     and a counter weight. Additional energy is provided every time the
     pendulum passes the lowest point until it makes a full turn with rid-
     ers hanging upside down. The distance from the center is about
     12 m. What would be the period of a pendulum of this length?

HOOKE'S LAW

When a force is applied to a spring, the spring extends (or compresses) a specific amount. The amount of deformation was studied by Robert Hooke and the relationship which relates the amount of extension (or compression) and the force which caused it is now called **Hooke's Law**.

$$F_{spring} = k \bullet x$$

Where: **F** represents the force acting on the spring
k is the spring constant (for any spring) in N/m
x is the amount of deformation, either extension or compression

Note: Each spring may have a different spring constant (k), depending on the material of which it is made and how it is coiled.

When work is done on a spring in compressing or stretching it, potential energy is stored in the spring. The data was collected in a Hooke's Law demonstration. Then, it was plotted on a force vs. elongation graph below. When the data is graphed, the slope of the line represents the spring constant (**k**).

Data Table	
Force (N)	Elongation (m)
1	2
2	4
3	6
4	8
5	10

$$\textbf{Slope} = \frac{\Delta \textbf{y}}{\Delta \textbf{x}} = \frac{\textbf{2N}}{\textbf{4m}} = \frac{\textbf{1}}{\textbf{2}} \frac{\textbf{N}}{\textbf{m}}$$

$$\text{Slope} = k = \frac{1N}{2m}$$

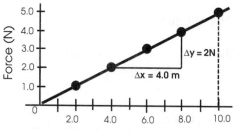

The area under the curve represents the work done on the spring and the potential energy stored in the spring system when a five newton force is applied to the system. Since the shape is a triangle, area can be calculated by multiplying one half the base times the height.

$$
\begin{aligned}
\textbf{Area} &= \frac{1}{2}\textbf{(base)(height)} \\
&= \frac{1}{2}(10.\,\text{m})\,5.0\,\text{N} \\
&= 25.\,\text{N} \bullet \text{m} = 25.\,\text{J}
\end{aligned}
$$

Another way to look at the graph is to substitute "elongation" (x) in the above formula for the (base) and "force" (kx) for the height. The equation now gives the formula for the potential energy stored in a spring.

$$
\begin{aligned}
\textbf{Area} &= \frac{1}{2}\textbf{(base)(height)} \\
&= \frac{1}{2}(x)(kx) \\
&= \frac{1}{2}kx^2
\end{aligned}
$$

Scale
1.0 m
2.0 m
4.0 m
6.0 m
8.0 m
10.0 m

3 N

SKILLS 2.3, 2.4
LAB 10 – THE PERIOD OF A VIBRATING SPRING SYSTEM
BACKGROUND

Like a pendulum, a spring can be displaced from its equilibrium position and caused to vibrate. The up and down motion of a vibrating spring has a definite period. The period is defined as the time for one complete vibration. This activity should be modeled after the pendulum lab, but of course different factors will influence the period.

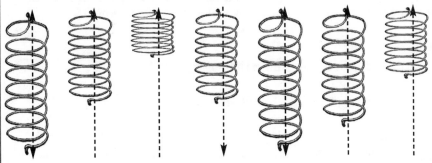

PROBLEM

Your task is going to be to determine the factors which affect a vibrating spring system. Your task is to come up with an equation which will work for the springs set up in the lab.

THE EXPERIMENT

Do the experiment as you have planned it. Record all your data and the calculated results. Analyze your data looking for relationships between each variable and the spring's period. For every variable you investigate, graph Spring Period vs. Variable.

THE EQUATION

Working with your group, write an equation for the period of a spring in terms of the variables which affect it. Test the validity of your formula using a spring.

☆ TRY IT

6   What is the formula you derived for the period of the vibrating spring?

7   What factors affect the period of a vibrating spring?

8   How does this formula compare to the formula for the period of a pendulum?

SKILL 5.1XIII
LAB 11 – HOOKE'S LAW
BACKGROUND
Springs are used all around us, in scales, in timepieces, in uphol-stered furniture and mattresses. Some springs are extended and some are compressed. As each spring is deformed from its equilibrium position it stores energy and is able to do work. Springs have an elastic limit. If you exceed the elastic limit of a spring, the spring will not return to its original equilibrium position, and it will lose its effectiveness.

PROBLEM
In this lab, first determine the spring constant for a given spring. Using a system of springs, predict and then determine the effective spring constant of a spring system.

THE EXPERIMENT
Collect data to determine the spring constant of each of your springs. How many data points are reasonable to take?

ANALYSIS OF DATA
Graph your data for each spring and calculate the slope of the graph. Show all work for your calculations. If your slope units were in N/m, what would be another name for the slope? If your slope units were in m/N, what is the sig-nificance of the slope?

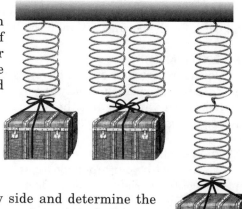

SYSTEM OF SPRINGS
Attach two springs side by side and determine the effective spring constant of the system. Attach the two springs to each other in a single line and determine the effective spring constant of the system.

SUMMING UP
Write a general rule to determine the spring constant of the combina-tion spring system.

GOING BEYOND
Other materials have the property of elasticity, but do they obey Hooke's Law? Try using a rubber band, a balloon, or a bungee cord to find out.

SKILL 5.1III – LAB 12 – DETERMINING THE ACCELERATION OF GRAVITY FROM A SIMPLE PENDULUM

The pendulum can be used to determine the acceleration of gravity anywhere on Earth with very simple equipment.

☆ TRY IT

9 Starting with the accepted formula for the period of the pendulum, design and carry out an experiment to determine the acceleration of gravity at your school. It may not turn out to be 9.81 m/s^2.

CHAPTER SEVEN ASSESSMENTS

PART A QUESTIONS

1 Graphs A and B at the right represent the results of applying an increasing force to stretch a spring which did not exceed its elastic limit. The spring constant can be represented by the
   (1) slope of graph A
   (2) slope of graph B
   (3) reciprocal of the slope of graph A
   (4) reciprocal of the slope of graph B

A   Spring Displacement

B   Work Done on Spring

2 A spring has a spring constant of 25 newtons per meter. The minimum force required to stretch the spring 0.25 meter from its equilibrium position is approximately
   (1) 1.0 x 10^{-4} N   (3) 6.3 N
   (2) 0.78 N   (4) 1.0 x 10^2 N

3 Which graph best represents the relationship between the elongation of a spring whose elastic limit has not been reached and the force applied to it?

(1) Elongation   (2) Elongation   (3) Elongation   (4) Elongation

4 Spring A has a spring constant of 140 newtons per meter, and spring B has a spring constant of 280 newtons per meter. Both springs are stretched the same distance. Compared to the potential energy stored in spring A, the potential energy stored in spring B is
   (1) the same   (3) half as great
   (2) twice as great   (4) four times as great

PART B QUESTIONS

5 The graph at the right represents the relationship between the force applied to a spring and the elongation of the spring. What is the spring constant? [1] _____ N/m

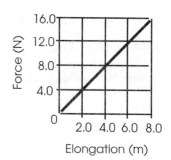

6 A 20.-newton weight is attached to a spring, causing it to stretch, as shown in the diagram at the right. What is the spring constant of this spring? [1] _____ N/m

Unstretched Spring

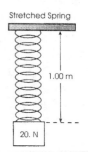

Stretched Spring

7 At the right is a graph representing the elongation of a spring as different forces are added to it. What is the value of the spring constant? [1] _____ N/m

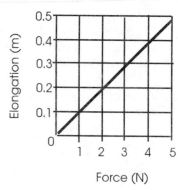

8 The graph at the right shows the relationship between the elongation of a spring and the force applied to the spring causing it to stretch. What is the spring constant for this spring? [1] _____ N/m

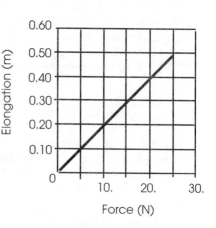

9   What is the spring constant of a spring of negligible mass which gained 8 joules of potential energy as a result of being compressed 0.4 meter? _____ N/m

10 The graph at the right represents the relationship between the force applied to a spring and the compression (displacement) of the spring. What is the spring constant for this spring? [1] _____ N/m

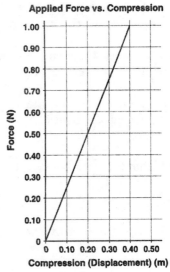

Applied Force vs. Compression

Force (N) vs. Compression (Displacement) (m)

Base your answers to questions 11 and 12 on the information below and the table at the right.

A student conducted a series of experiments to investigate the effect of mass, length, and amplitude (angle of release) on a simple pendulum. The table at the right shows the initial conditions for a series of trials.

Trial	Mass (kg)	Length (m)	Angle of release (°)
R	2	3	10.
S	3	2	15.
T	3	2	10.
U	1	3	10.
V	3	2	5.0
W	2	2	15.
X	2	1	15.
Y	3	3	10.
Z	2	3	15.

11 Which three trials should the student use to test the effect of mass on the period of the pendulum? [1]

12 Which three trials should the student use to test the effect of length on the period of the pendulum? [1]

PART C QUESTIONS

Base your answers to questions **13** through **16** on the information in the data table below right. The data were obtained by varying the force applied to a spring and measuring the corresponding elongation of the spring.

Directions: Construct a graph on the grid following the directions below.

13 Mark an appropriate scale on the axis labeled "Elongation (m)." [1]

14 Plot the data points for force versus elongation. [1]

15 Draw the best-fit line. [1]

16 Using the best-fit line, determine the spring constant of the spring. [Show all calculations, including the equation and substitution with units.] [2]

Applied Force (N)	Elongation of Spring (m)
0.0	0.00
4.0	0.16
8.0	0.27
12.0	0.42
16.0	0.54
20.0	0.71

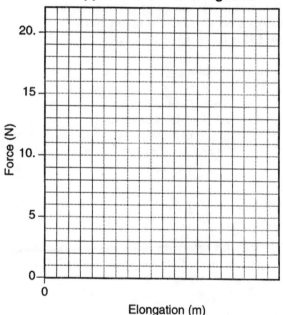

Applied Force vs. Elongation

Force (N)

Elongation (m)

CHAPTER 8
WORK, POWER, AND ENERGY

KEY IDEA **4** ENERGY EXISTS IN MANY FORMS, AND WHEN THESE FORMS CHANGE ENERGY IS CONSERVED.

PERFORMANCE INDICATOR 4.1
STUDENTS CAN OBSERVE AND DESCRIBE TRANSMISSION OF VARIOUS FORMS OF ENERGY.

CHAPTER 8 – MAJOR UNDERSTANDINGS

☆ 4.1c Potential energy is the energy an object possesses by virtue of its position or condition. Types of potential energy include gravitational* and elastic*.

☆ 4.1d Kinetic energy* is the energy an object possesses by virtue of its motion.

☆ 4.1g When work* is done on or by a system, there is a change in the total energy* of the system.

☆ 4.1h Work done against friction results in an increase in the internal energy of the system.

☆ 4.1j Energy may be stored in electric* or magnetic fields. This energy may be transferred through conductors or space and may be converted to other forms of energy.

CHAPTER 8
WORK, POWER, AND ENERGY

WORK - DEFINITION AND MATHEMATICS

In physics, **work** is defined as a force acting upon an object to cause a displacement. There are three key words in this definition - force, displacement, and cause. In order for a force to qualify as having done *work* on an object, there must be a displacement and the force must *cause* the displacement. There are many examples of work which can be observed in everyday life: a student pushing a lawn mower to cut the grass, a parent pushing a baby stroller in the park, a freshman lifting a backpack full of books upon his shoulder, a weightlifter lifting a barbell above her head, etc. In each case described, there is a force exerted upon an object to cause that object to be displaced.

Pushing a wall produces
no movement and no work

Pulling a box produces
movement and work

☆ TRY IT

1   Read the following statements and identify whether or not each is an example of work:

a   _____ A student applies a force to a wall and becomes exhausted.

b   _____ A calculator falls off a table and free falls to the ground.

c   _____ A waiter carries a tray full of beverages above his head by one arm across the room. (Careful! This is a trick question.)

d   _____ A rocket accelerates through space.

WORK – HOW TO MEASURE

Mathematically, work can be expressed by the following equation.

$$W = F \bullet d \bullet \cos \emptyset$$

Where **F** = force, **d** = displacement, and the **Ø** = angle (theta) is defined as the angle between the force and the displacement vector.

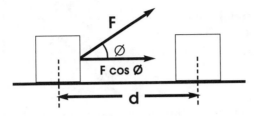

Example 1: A force acts towards the right upon an object as it is displaced to the right. In such an instance, the force vector and the displacement vector are in the same direction. Thus, the angle between **F** and **d** is 0 degrees.

Ø = 0°
work = positive

Example 2: A force acts towards the right upon an object, which is displaced towards the left. In such an instance, the force vector and the displacement vector are in the opposite direction. Thus, the angle between **F** and **d** is 180 degrees.

Ø = 180°
work = negative

Example 3: A force acts upward upon an object as it is displaced towards the right. In such an instance, the force vector and the displacement vector are at right angles to each other. Thus, the angle between **F** and **d** is 90 degrees.

Ø = 90°
work = 0

The equation for work lists three variables – each variable is associated with the one of the three key words mentioned in the definition of work (force, displacement, and cause). The angle Ø in the equation is associated with the component of the force, which causes a displacement.

When determining the measure of the angle in the work equation, it is important to recognize that the angle has a precise definition. It is the angle between the force and the displacement vectors. A force is applied to a cart to pull it up an incline at constant speed. The displacement of the cart is also parallel to the incline. Since **F** and **d** are in the same direction, the angle is 0 degrees.

Whenever **F** and **d** are in the same direction, Ø = 0°

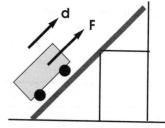

The joule is the metric unit used to measure work and also energy. One joule is equivalent to one newton of force causing a displacement of one meter.

1 joule = 1 newton • 1 meter
1 J = 1 N • m

Example 1: How much work is done in lifting a 5.0 kg box from the floor to a height of 1.2 m above the floor?

Given: m =   5.0 kg
           d = h = 1.2 m

Find: Work against gravity

$$W = Fd$$

Solution: F =   mg   = $(5.0 \text{ kg})(9.8 \text{ m/s}^2)$ = 49 N
            W =   Fd   =   (49 N)(1.2 m) = 58.8 J = 59 J
            W =   59 J

Example 2: A 600 N force pulls a 50 kg block a distance of 2.0 m along the floor. The force acts at a 37° angle to the horizontal. Calculate the work done. The force in the direction of the displacement is F_x.

Given: F_x =   F cos ø   =   600 N (cos 37°) = 480 N
            d =   2.0 m

Find: Work

Solution: W =   Fd   =   (480 N)(2.0 m) = 960 J

Work is a scalar quantity; it does not have a direction. Unlike displacement, velocity, acceleration, force, and momentum, the work done is completely described by magnitude alone.

FORCE VS. DISPLACEMENT GRAPH

The area under a force versus displacement graph is the work done by the force. Consider a block that is pulled along a table with a constant force of 10. N over a distance of 1.0 meter. The force is constant in this example.

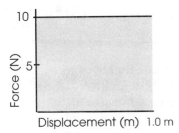

Area = base x height
= 1.0 m x 10 N
= 10. N • m
= 10. J

In this case, the 10. joules of work was done against friction and was changed to thermal energy (heat).

☆ TRY IT

2 A force of 50 N acts on the block at the angle shown in the diagram. The block moves a horizontal distance of 3.0 m over a frictionless surface. Calculate the work done by the force.

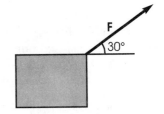

3 How much work is done by an applied force to lift a 35-newton block 3.0 meters vertically at a constant speed?

4 A student with a mass of 60.0 kg runs up three flights of stairs in 12.0 sec. The student has gone a vertical distance of 8.0 m. Determine the amount of work done by the student to elevate her body to this height. Assume that her speed is constant.

5   A tired kitten (mass of 1 kg) does push-ups by applying a force to elevate its center-of-mass by 6 cm. Determine the number of push-ups which a kitten must do in order to do 3.0 joules of work.

6   Calculate the work done by a 2.0-N force (directed at a 20° angle to the vertical) to move a 600 gram box a horizontal distance of 400 cm across a rough floor at a constant speed of 0.5 m/s. *Hint:* Be careful with the units.

7   Logan Thomas carries a 100-N suitcase up three flights of stairs (a height of 10.0 m) and then pushes it with a horizontal force of 40.0 N at a constant speed of 0.5 m/s for a horizontal distance of 35.0 meters. How much work does Logan do on his suitcase during this entire motion?

8   Before beginning its initial descent, a roller coaster car is always pulled up the first hill to a high initial height. Work is done on the car (usually by a chain) to achieve this initial height. A coaster designer is considering three different incline angles at which to drag the 2000-kg car train to the top of the 60-meter high hill. In each case, the force applied to the car will be applied parallel to the hill. The critical question is: Which angle would require the least work? Analyze the data, determine the work done in each case, and answer this critical question.

Trial	Angle	Force	Displacement	Work (Joules)	Potential Energy (Joules)
1	32°	1.10×10^4 N	106 m		
2	35°	1.44×10^4 N	84.4 m		
3	39°	1.64×10^4 N	75.3 m		

In summary, work is a force acting upon an object to cause a displacement. When a force acts to cause an object to be displaced, three quantities must be known in order to calculate the amount of work. Those three quantities are force, displacement, and the angle between the force and the displacement.

POWER

Work is energy. The quantity work has to do with a force causing a displacement. Work has nothing to do with the amount of time that this force acts to cause the displacement. Sometimes, the work is done very quickly and other times the work is done rather slowly. Power is the rate at which work is done. It is the work/time ratio. Mathematically, it is computed using the following equation.

$$\text{Power} = \frac{\text{Work done}}{\text{time required}} = \frac{W}{t}$$

Note: The units for power are $\dfrac{\text{joules}}{\text{sec}}$ = watts

The standard metric unit of power is the watt. A unit of power is equivalent to a unit of work divided by a unit of time. A watt is equivalent to a joule/second and was named for James Watt.

🌍 REAL WORLD CONNECTIONS
JAMES WATT'S ATMOSPHERIC STEAM ENGINE

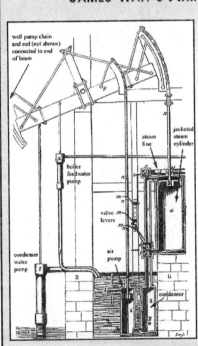

well pump chain
and rod (not shown)
connected to end
of beam

steam line

jacketed steam cylinder

boiler feedwater pump

valve levers

condenser water pump

air pump

condenser

Early steam engines were extremely inefficient, requiring much energy. The steam cylinder was heated and cooled repeatedly, which wasted energy to reheat the steel. James Watt (1736-1819) made a breakthrough development in the steam engine by using a separate condenser. Watt discovered the separate condenser in 1765. It took 11 years before he saw the device in practice!

The Watt engine operated on the principle of a vacuum pulling the steam piston down. However, Watt's steam cylinder remained hot at all times. Valves permitted the steam to be sucked into a separate condenser and then pumped along with any gases using the air pump. (Illustration of the Watt atmospheric engine for pumping water. The main pump is not shown.)

Adapted from: Michigan State University College of Engineering ©2001
http://www.egr.msu.edu/~lira/supp/steam/index.htm
Brief History of the Steam Engine, Summary by Carl Lira

MOTOR HORSEPOWER RATING

When James Watt greatly improved the steam engine, people naturally wanted to know how these new engines compared with the horses previously used to do the same sort of work. How many horses would one of his engines replace? Watt therefore decided to express the power of his engines in terms of the rate at which a horse could do work. To do this he got a horse and measured the rate at which it could pull a known weight up a mine shaft.

CHECK FOR UNDERSTANDING

Calculate the power-to-weight ratio for each vehicle in the table below. Fill in the table. Make a general statement about what the power to weight ratio should be for a fast car.

☆ TRY IT	Horse power	Weight (lbs)	Power Weight	0-60 mph (sec)	Price
Dodge Viper	450	3,320		4.1	$66,000
Ferrari 355 F1	375	2,975		4.6	$134,000
Shelby Series 1	320	2,650		4.4	$108,000
Lotus Esprit V8	350	3,045		4.4	$83,000
Chevrolet Corvette	345	3,245		4.8	$42,000
Porsche Carrera	300	2,900		5.0	$70,000
Mitsubishi 3000GT bi-turbo	320	3,740		5.8	$45,000
Ford Escort	110	2,470		10.9	$12,000

Most machines are designed and built to do work on objects. All machines are typically described by a power rating. The power rating indicates the rate at which that machine can do work upon other objects. The power equation suggests that a more powerful engine can do the same amount of work in less time.

A person is also a machine which has a power rating. Some people are more powerful than others; that is, they are capable of doing the same amount of work in less time or more work in the same amount of time. In the "Are You a Horse?" Lab (page 168), students will determine their own personal power by doing work on their bodies to elevate it up a flight of stairs. By measuring the force, displacement and time, we are able to measure our personal power rating.

Suppose that Jeff elevated his 80-kg body up the 2.0 meter staircase in 1.8 seconds. If this were the case, then we could calculate Jeff's power rating. It can be assumed that Jeff must apply a 785 N ($F_g = mg$) downward force upon the stairs to elevate his body. By so doing, the stairs would push upward on Jeff's body with just enough force to lift his body up the stairs. It can also be assumed that the angle between the force of the stairs on Jeff and Jeff's displacement is 0 degrees. With these two approximations, Jeff's power rating could be determined as shown below.

$$\textbf{Power} = \frac{\textbf{Work}}{\textbf{time}} = \frac{\textbf{785 N} \cdot \textbf{2.0 m}}{\textbf{1.8 seconds}}$$

$$\textbf{Power} = \textbf{872 Watts}$$

$$\frac{\textbf{872 Watts}}{\textbf{(746 watts / HP)}} = \textbf{1.17 HP}$$

The expression for power is work/time. Now since the expression for work is force•displacement, the expression for power can be rewritten as (force•displacement)/time. Yet since the expression for velocity is displacement/time, the expression for power can be rewritten once more as force•velocity. This is shown below.

Example 1: If the horse could walk at 1.49 m/s when raising a load of 500 N, how much work could it do every second? The power developed could be calculated from the formula:

$$P = \frac{W}{t} = \frac{Fd}{t} = F\left[\frac{d}{t}\right] = F\,\overline{v}$$

The expression, **Fd/t**, also represents average power generated when the speed of the object to which the force is applied varies with time.

Given: F = 500 N

$\overline{v}$ = 1.49 m/s

Find: Power

Solution: P = F x $\overline{v}$ = (500 N) (1.49 m/s) = 745 N-m / s

P = 745 J/s = 745 watts

Example 2: Suppose a $1/4$ horsepower motor (shown right) lifts its load at a speed of 0.20 m/s. What is the maximum load it could lift at this speed? (1 hp = 746 watts)

Given: v = 0.20 m/s

Ideally, $1/4$ hp can do work at the rate of:

$$1/4 \, (746)J/s \; = \; 187 \text{ watts}$$

Find: **F**

Solution:
$$P = \overline{F}v$$
$$F = \frac{P}{v} = \frac{187 \text{ J/s}}{.20 \text{ m/s}} = 935 \, \frac{J}{m}$$
$$F = 935 \text{ N}$$

Note: Because of friction and other energy losses, the actual maximum load would be less than this.

SKILL 4.1VII – COMPARE THE POWER DEVELOPED WHEN THE SAME WORK IS DONE AT DIFFERENT RATES

LAB 13 – ARE YOU A HORSE?

 BACKGROUND

There is a power rating for every machine including humans. By calculating the work done in positioning your body from one level to another level, and measuring the time, you should be able to calculate your horsepower. *Note:* On the exam, power will be expressed as watts or kilowatts but not in horsepower (hp). The watt and/or kilowatt will be tested.

PROBLEM

Calculate your horsepower as you walk or jog up a flight of stairs.

PROCEDURE

Refer to the formula, data, and calculations on page 167 to determine what measurements you need.

☆ TRY IT

9   Identify at least one (1) other way to calculate your horsepower.

10 What are some of the assumptions you had to make in this lab?

POTENTIAL ENERGY

An object can store energy as the result of its position. For example, the lamp on the edge of a table is storing energy when it is in this position related to the floor. This stored energy of position is referred to as **potential energy**. Likewise, a drawn bow is able to store energy as the result of its position. When the string on the bow is pulled back from its usual equilibrium position, the bow is able to store energy by virtue of its position. This stored energy of position is also referred to as potential energy. Potential energy is the stored energy due to the position possessed by an object.

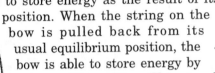

The examples above illustrate the two forms of potential energy to be discussed in this chapter: gravitational potential energy and elastic potential energy. **Gravitational potential energy** is the energy stored in an object as the result of its vertical position (i.e., height). The energy is stored as the result of the gravitational attraction of the Earth for the object. The gravitational potential energy of the box is dependent on two variables - the mass of the box and the height to which it is raised. These relationships are expressed by the following equation:

$$PE_{grav} = mass \cdot g \cdot height$$

$$PE_{grav} = m \cdot g \cdot h$$

In the above equation, **m** represents the mass of the object, **h** represents the height of the object and **g** represents the acceleration of gravity (9.81 m/s^2 on Earth).

To determine the gravitational potential energy of an object, a zero height position must first be assigned. Typically, the ground is considered to be a position of zero height. But, it doesn't have to be. The zero position could be a lab table, the bottom of a mountain or the lowest position on a roller coaster.

Since the gravitational potential energy of an object is directly proportional to its height above the zero position, a doubling of the height will result in a doubling of the gravitational potential energy. Potential energy is a scalar quantity; it does not have a direction. Like work, the potential energy of an object is completely described by magnitude alone.

☆ Try It

11 Use the formula, a ruler, and principle on the previous page to determine the blanks in the following diagram. Knowing that the potential energy at the top of the tall pole is 60 J, what is the potential energy at the other positions shown on the hill and the stairs

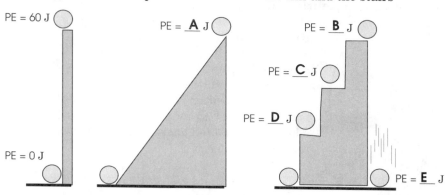

ELASTIC POTENTIAL ENERGY

The second form of potential energy which we will discuss in this STAReview is **elastic potential energy**. Elastic potential energy is the energy stored in elastic materials as the result of their stretching or compressing. Elastic potential energy can be stored in rubber bands, bungee cords, trampolines, springs, an arrow drawn into a bow, etc. The amount of elastic potential energy stored in such a device is related to the amount of stretch of the device - the more stretch, the more stored energy.

Springs are a special instance of a device which can store elastic potential energy due to either compression or stretching. A force is required to compress a spring; the more compression there is, the more force which is required to compress it further. For certain springs, the amount of force is directly proportional to the amount of stretch or compression (x); the constant of proportionality is known as the spring constant (k).

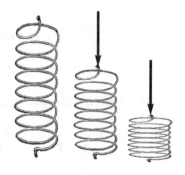

$$F_{spring} = k \cdot x$$

Such springs are said to follow Hooke's Law. If a spring is not stretched or compressed, then there is no elastic potential energy stored in it. The spring is said to be at its equilibrium position. The equilibrium position is the position that the spring naturally assumes when there is no force applied to it. In terms of potential energy, the equilibrium position could be called the zero-potential energy position. There is a special equation for springs which relates the amount of elastic potential energy to the amount of stretch (or compression) and the spring constant. The equation is

$$PE_{spring} \ = \ ^1/_2 \bullet k \bullet x^2$$

Where: k = spring constant
x = amount of compression or extension
(relative to equilibrium position)

To summarize, potential energy is the energy which an object has stored due to its position relative to some zero position. An object possesses gravitational potential energy if it is positioned at a height above (or below) the zero height position. The spring possesses elastic potential energy if it is at a position on an elastic medium other than the equilibrium position.

KINETIC ENERGY

Kinetic energy is the energy of motion. An object which has motion - whether it be vertical or horizontal motion - has kinetic energy. There are many forms of kinetic energy – vibrational, rotational, and translational (the energy due to motion from one location to another). For our purposes, the phrase kinetic energy refers to **translational kinetic energy**. It depends upon two variables: the mass (m) of the object and the velocity (v) of the object. The following equation is used to calculate the kinetic energy (KE) of an object.

$$KE \ = \ ^1/_2 \bullet m \bullet v^2$$

Where: m = mass of object
$|v|$ = speed of object   (absolute value of velocity is speed)

This equation reveals that the kinetic energy of an object is directly proportional to the square of its speed. That means that for a twofold increase in speed, the kinetic energy will increase by a factor of four. The kinetic energy is dependent upon the square of the speed.

Like work and potential energy, the standard metric unit of measurement for kinetic energy is the joule. As might be implied by the above equation, 1 joule is equivalent to 1 kg$\bullet$(m/s)^2.

SKILLS 4.1i, 4.1v
LAB 14 – FORCE, WORK, AND ENERGY
BACKGROUND

When work is done in lifting an object, the object is given additional gravitational potential energy. If the object is then released and falls, it gains velocity. Its kinetic energy increases as its potential energy decreases. When the object has fallen to the height from which it was originally lifted, the kinetic energy is equal to the original work minus whatever energy was lost to the air during the fall. The moving object can then do work that is nearly equal to the work done in lifting it.

cardboard
cylinder

THE PROBLEM

We can study these changes in energy by investigating the way a falling vegetable can drives a nail into dense Styrofoam or balsa wood. We will look at the amount of force exerted by the can on the nail when it drives the nail into the wood. The can is allowed to fall from a known height onto a nail. Knowing the mass of the can and the distance it falls, we can calculate the gravitational potential energy. This is equal to the work done on the nail. If we measure the distance the nail is driven by the blow, we can solve for the average force that the can exerts on the nail during the blow.

MEASURING THE DRIVING FORCE

Roll a file folder into a loose cylinder and attached it to a stand. This makes a guide for the falling can. Start a nail in a block of soft wood or dense styrofoam, being careful that the nail is vertical. Measure the height of the nail head from the block's surface, using a vernier caliper. Place the block under the cardboard cylinder so that the nail is centered. Now move the cylinder up or down so that its bottom opening is just above the head of the nail. This will keep the can from falling out of the guide after the blow. The mass of the can and the height from which it will be released must be measured.

Make several successive trials on the same nail until you have driven it through the block. Calculate the driving force for each trial. Does there appear to be any relationship between the height dropped and the total depth the nail has penetrated into the block?

☆ TRY IT

12 Using data from the previous lab, how did the force you calculated compare to the weight of the can on the nail?

13 How is it possible for the falling can to exert a force so much greater than its weight? Explain by referring to the deceleration of the can during the impact of the nail.

14 Use the same experimental procedure to determine the answer to this question: What is the relationship between the force produced and the depth to which the nail goes into the material?

15 Carpenters sometimes cut the point off a nail to prevent it from splitting the wood. Does a pointless nail require a different driving force in soft material?

CHAPTER EIGHT ASSESSMENTS

PART A QUESTIONS

1 Which combination of units can be used to express work?

(1) $\dfrac{\text{newton} \bullet \text{second}}{\text{meter}}$

(3) newton/meter

(2) $\dfrac{\text{newton} \bullet \text{meter}}{\text{second}}$

(4) newton•meter

2 Which action would require no work to be done on an object?
(1) lifting the object from the floor to the ceiling
(2) pushing the object along a horizontal floor along a frictionless surface
(3) decreasing the speed of the object until it comes to rest
(4) holding the object stationary above the ground

3 If the time required for a student to swim 500 meters is doubled, the power developed by the student will be
(1) halved   (2) doubled   (3) quartered   (4) quadrupled

4 Which variable expression is paired with a corresponding unit?

(1) $\dfrac{\text{mass} \bullet \text{distance}}{\text{time}}$ and watt

(3) $\dfrac{\text{mass} \bullet \text{distance}^2}{\text{time}^2}$ and joule

(2) $\dfrac{\text{mass} \bullet \text{distance}^2}{\text{time}}$ and watt

(4) $\dfrac{\text{mass} \bullet \text{distance}}{\text{time}^3}$ and joule

5   A 0.10-meter spring is stretched from equi-
    librium to position A and then to position B
    as shown in the diagram below. Compared
    to the spring's potential energy at A, what is
    its potential energy at B?
    (1) the same
    (2) twice as great
    (3) half as great
    (4) four times as great

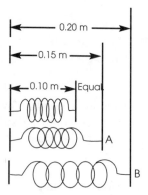

6   Which graph below best represents the relationship between the
    potential energy (PE) stored in a spring and the change in the length
    of the spring from its equilibrium position X?

(1)   (2)   (3)   (4)

7   The unstretched spring in the diagram
    at the right has a length of 0.40 meter
    and spring constant k. A weight is
    hung from the spring, causing it to
    stretch to a length of 0.60 meter. How
    many joules of elastic potential energy
    are stored in this stretched spring?
    (1) 0.020 x k (3) 0.18 x k
    (2) 0.080 x k (4) 2.0 x k

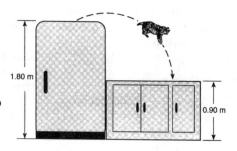

8   The diagram at the right
    shows a 1.5-kilogram kitten
    jumping from the top of a 1.80-
    meter-high refrigerator to a
    0.90 meter-high counter.
    Compared to the kitten's gravi-
    tational potential energy on top
    of the refrigerator, the kitten's
    gravitational potential energy
    on top of the counter is

    (1) half as great
    (2) twice as great
    (3) one-fourth as great
    (4) four times as great

9 Which graph best represents the relationship between gravitational potential energy (*PE*) and height (*h*) above the ground for an object near the surface of Earth?

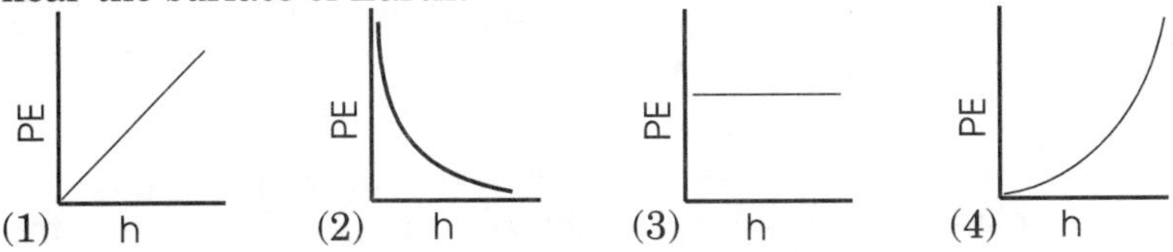

(1) h   (2) h   (3) h   (4) h

10 The diagram at the right shows block *A*, having mass 2m and speed *v*, and block *B* having mass m and speed 2v. Compared to the kinetic energy of block *A*, the kinetic energy of block *B* is

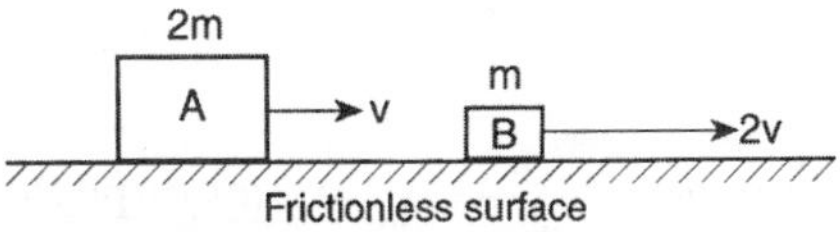

Frictionless surface

(1) the same   (3) one-half as great
(2) twice as great   (4) four times as

PART B QUESTIONS

11 How much work is done on a downhill skier by an average braking force of 9.8 x 10^2 newtons to stop her in a distance of 10. meters? [1]
_____ J

12 Zory does 300. joules of work pushing a cart 3.0 meters due east and then does 400. joules of work pushing the cart 4.0 meters due north. The total amount of work done by Zory is [1] _____ J

13 Jeff pulls a box across a horizontal floor at a constant speed of 4.0 meters per second by exerting a constant horizontal force of 45 newtons. Approximately how much work does Jeff do against friction in moving the box 5.5 meters across the floor? [1] _____ J

14 Deborah applies a 20.-newton force to move a crate at a constant speed of 4.0 meters per second across a rough floor. How much work is done by Deborah on the crate in 6.0 seconds? [1] _____ J

15 A 2000-watt motor working at full capacity can vertically lift a 400-newton weight at a constant speed of [1] _____ m/s

16 A 45-kilogram bicyclist climbs a hill at a constant speed of 2.5 meters per second by applying an average force of 85 newtons. How much power does the bicyclist develop? [1] _____ W

17 A 5.0 x 10^2-newton girl takes 10. seconds to run up two flights of stairs to a landing, a total of 5.0 meters vertically above her starting point. What power does the girl develop during her run? [1] _____ W

18 A motor having a maximum power rating of 8.1 x 10^4 watts is used to operate an elevator with a weight of 1.8 x 10^4 newtons. What is the maximum weight this motor can lift at an average speed of 3.0 meters per second? [1] _____ N

19 In the diagram at the right, Wayne compress-es the spring in a pop-up toy 0.020 meter. If the spring has a spring constant of 340 new-tons per meter, how much energy is being stored in the spring?

Uncompressed spring   Compressed spring

(1) 0.068 J   (3) 3.4 J
(2) 0.14 J   (4) 6.8 J

20 When a spring is stretched 0.200 meter from its equilibrium posi-tion, it possesses a potential energy of 10.0 joules. What is the spring constant for this spring? [1] _____ N/m

21 A 3.0-kilogram mass is attached to a spring having a spring constant of 30. newtons per meter. The mass is pulled 0.20 meter from the spring's equilibrium position and released. What is the maximum kinetic energy achieved by the mass-spring system? [1] _____ J

22 A force of 0.2 newton is needed to compress a spring a distance of 0.02 meter. The potential energy stored in this compressed spring is [1] _____ J

23 A spring has a spring constant of 120 newtons per meter. How much potential energy is stored in the spring as it is stretched 0.20 meter? [1] _____ J

24 In the diagram at the right, an average force of 20. newtons is used to pull back the string of a bow 0.60 meter. As the arrow leaves the bow, its kinetic energy is [1] _____ J

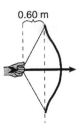

0.60 m

25 The kinetic energy of a 980-kilogram race car traveling at 90. meters per second is [1] _____ J

PART C QUESTIONS

Base your answers to questions 26 through 28 on the information below.

A 680-newton student runs up a flight of stairs 3.5 meters high in 11.4 seconds. On a second run, the same student completes the same stair run in 8.5 seconds.

26 Determine the work done by the 680-newton student in climbing the stairs. [Show all calculations, including the equation and substitution with units.] [2]

27 Determine the power developed by the student during the 11.4-second climb. [Show all calculations, including the equation and substitution with units.] [2]

28 Using one or more complete sentences, compare the power developed by the student climbing the stairs in 11.4 seconds to the power developed during a 8.5-second climb. [1]

Base your answers to questions 29 through 31 on the diagram, information, and data table below.

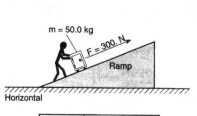

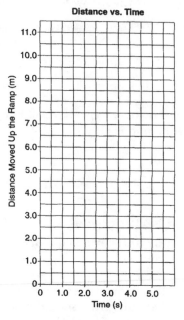

Time (s)	Distance Moved up the Ramp (m)
0.0	0.0
1.0	2.2
2.0	4.6
3.0	6.6
4.0	8.6
5.0	11.0

The diagram shows a worker moving a 50.0 kilogram safe up a ramp by applying a constant force of 300. newtons parallel to the ramp. The data table shows the distance the safe has moved as a function of time.

29 Using one or more complete sentences, explain the physical significance of the slope of the graph. [2]

30 Calculate the work done by the worker in the first 3.0 seconds. [Show all calculations, including the equation and substitution with units.] [2]

31 Using the information in the data table, plot the data points and draw the best-fit line. [2]

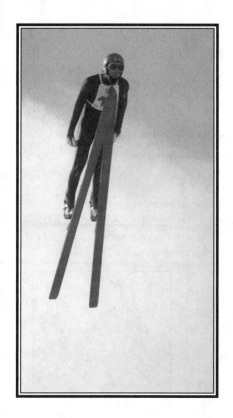

CHAPTER 9
CONSERVATION
OF ENERGY

KEY IDEA 4

ENERGY EXISTS IN MANY
FORMS, AND WHEN THESE
FORMS CHANGE ENERGY
IS CONSERVED.

PERFORMANCE INDICATOR 4.1 *STUDENTS CAN OBSERVE
AND DESCRIBE TRANSMISSION OF VARIOUS FORMS OF ENERGY.*

CHAPTER 9 – MAJOR UNDERSTANDINGS

☆ 4.1a All energy transfers are
governed by the law of
conservation of energy.*
☆ 4.1b Energy may be converted
among mechanical,
electromagnetic, nuclear, and
thermal forms.
☆ 4.1e In an ideal mechanical
system, the sum of the
macroscopic kinetic and
potential energies (mechanical
energy) is constant.*
☆ 4.1f In a non-ideal mechanical
system, as mechanical energy
decreases there is a
corresponding increase in other
energies such as internal
energy.*

CHAPTER 9
CONSERVATION OF ENERGY

CONSERVATION OF ENERGY

Conservation of energy mass is one of the universal laws of physics. It states that energy mass cannot be created or destroyed but can be changed from one form to another. It is also a valuable tool for solving physics problems. Let us begin with the pendulum.

THE PENDULUM

As a 2.00 kg pendulum bob swings to and fro, its height above the table top (and in turn its speed) is constantly changing. The total mechanical energy is 19.6 J when the height is 1.00 meters above the lowest point. As the height decreases, potential energy is lost. And, simultaneously the kinetic energy is gained. Yet at all times, the sum of the potential and kinetic energies of the bob remains constant. There is no loss or gain of mechanical energy, only a transformation from kinetic energy to potential energy (and vice versa). In other words, total mechanical energy is conserved as the potential energy is converted into kinetic energy. This is depicted in the diagram below.

The pendulum principle can be not only seen, but experienced as well in many amusement parks across the world on thrill rides, such as the Pirate.

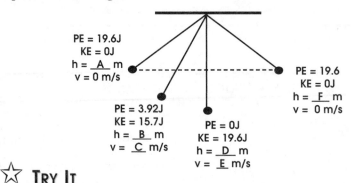

PE = 19.6J
KE = 0J
h = _A_ m
v = 0 m/s

PE = 3.92J
KE = 15.7J
h = _B_ m
v = _C_ m/s

PE = 0J
KE = 19.6J
h = _D_ m
v = _E_ m/s

PE = 19.6
KE = 0J
h = _F_ m
v = 0 m/s

☆ TRY IT

1   From the diagram of the pendulum and information above, complete the follow table:

   (a) **A** = _____m   (c) **C** = _____m/s   (e) **E** = _____m/s
   (b) **B** = _____m   (d) **D** = _____m   (f) **F** = _____m

ROLLER COASTER

A roller coaster operates on the principle of energy transformation. Work is initially done on a roller coaster car to lift the car to the first and highest hill. The roller coaster car has a large quantity of potential energy and virtually no kinetic energy as it begins the trip down the first hill. As the car descends hills and loops, its potential energy is transformed into kinetic energy (as the car speeds up); as the car ascends hills and loops, its kinetic energy is transformed into potential energy (as the car slows down). In the absence of external forces such as friction and air resistance doing work, the total mechanical energy of the car is conserved.

Conservation of energy on a roller coaster ride means that the total amount of mechanical energy is the same at every location along the track. The amount of kinetic energy is constantly changing, as is the amount of potential energy; yet, the sum of the kinetic and potential energies is the same everywhere.

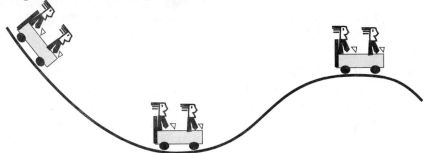

As a coaster car loses height, it gains speed; PE is transformed into KE. As a coaster car gains height, it loses speed; KE is transformed into PE. The sum of the KE and PE is a constant.

THE SKIER

Transformation of energy from the potential to the kinetic also occurs for a ski jumper. As a ski jumper glides down the hill towards the jump ramp and off the jump ramp towards the ground, potential energy is transformed into kinetic energy. If it can be assumed that no external forces are doing work upon the ski jumper as he travels from the top of the hill to the completion of the jump, then the total mechanical energy of the ski jumper is conserved. Our skier starts at rest on top of a 100-meter hill, skis down the 45-degree incline and makes a world-record setting jump. Assuming that friction and air resistance have a negligible effect upon the skier's motion and assuming that he never uses his poles for propulsion, his total mechanical energy would never change.

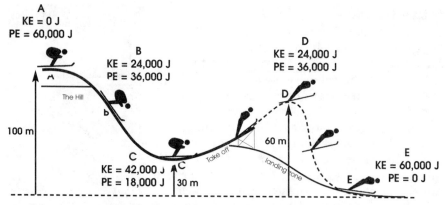

Of course, it should be noted that the original assumption that was made for the ski jumper and the roller coaster is that there were no external forces doing work. In actuality, there are external forces doing work. Both the roller coaster and the ski jumper experience the force of friction and the force of air resistance during the course of the motion. The presence of friction and air resistance would do negative work and cause the total mechanical energy to decrease during the course of the motion. The decrease in mechanical energy usually appears as an increase in thermal energy of the object or the system. While the assumption that mechanical energy is conserved is an invalid assumption, it is a useful approximation, which assists in the analysis of an otherwise complex motion.

INTERNAL VS. EXTERNAL FORCES

Forces can be categorized as internal forces or external forces. External forces include applied forces, normal forces, tensional forces, friction forces, and air resistance forces. If we specify "the system," internal forces include gravitational forces, magnetic forces, electrical forces, and spring forces.

When work is done on an object by an external force, the total mechanical energy (**KE + PE**) of that object is changed. When the work is positive work, then the object will gain energy. When the work is negative work, then the object will lose energy. The gain or loss in energy can be in the form of potential energy, kinetic energy, or both. The work done will be equal to the change in mechanical energy of the object.

When work is done on an object by an internal force (for example, gravitational and spring forces), the total mechanical energy (**KE + PE**) of that system remains constant. The system's energy simply changes form. As an object is pulled from a high elevation to a lower elevation by gravity, some of the potential energy of that object is transformed into kinetic energy. The sum of the kinetic and potential energies remain constant. This is called the conservation of energy.

Mechanical energy is often defined as the ability to do work. Any object which possesses mechanical energy – whether it be in the form of potential energy or kinetic energy – is able to do work.

WORK ENERGY THEOREM

Whenever work is done upon an object by an external force, there will be a change in the total mechanical energy of the object. The quantitative relationship between work and the two forms of mechanical energy is expressed by the following equation:

$$KE_i + PE_i + W_{ext} = KE_f + PE_f$$

Where: KE_i is the initial kinetic energy

PE_i is the initial potential energy

W_{ext} is the work done by the external force

KE_f is the final kinetic energy

PE_f is the final potential energy

A physics lab cart is pulled up an inclined plane at constant speed by a student. The applied force (20 N) on the cart is directed parallel to the incline to cause the cart to be displaced parallel to the incline for a given displacement (0.80 m). According to the work-energy theorem, the initial energy plus the work done by the external force equals the final energy. If our reference level is the top of the lab table, the cart will begin with 0 joules of energy. When the student does 16. joules of work ($F \cdot d = 20$ N $\cdot 0.80$ m $= 16.$ J), the cart will finish with 16. joules of mechanical energy. The final energy (16. J) is equal to the initial energy (0 J) plus the work done by external forces (16. J).

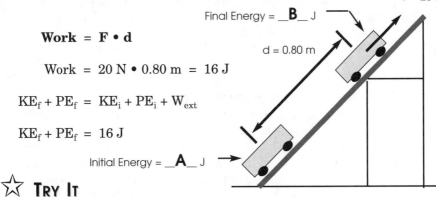

F = 20 N

Final Energy = __B__ J

Work = F • d

d = 0.80 m

Work = 20 N • 0.80 m = 16 J

$KE_f + PE_f = KE_i + PE_i + W_{ext}$

$KE_f + PE_f = 16$ J

Initial Energy = __A__ J

☆ TRY IT

2 From the diagram of the cart and table and formulas above, complete the follow table:

(a) A _____ J

(b) B _____ J

REAL WORLD CONNECTIONS

BUNGEE JUMPING

Bungee jumping is a dramatic demonstration of the conversion of energy. Depending on the reference level, all or part of the gravitational potential energy at the top of the jump is converted to elastic potential energy at the bottom. The basic equations involved have been used for years to describe events in which loads are suddenly applied to springs. The bungee cord is simply a very weak spring yielding large spring deflections and rather small force magnitudes.

Jumping in Zambia
Bungee Zone Photo Gallery ©1998

When taking a jump, the operator must select the right height and cord for each jumper. It seems plausible to match a heavy person (1112 N) with the stiff cord, a medium person (800 N) with the medium cord, and the soft cord with a jumper of about 490 N. The extension of the bungee cord on the jump is twice the static load. So if the cord will stretch 9.0 meter when a 490 N person hangs from it, it will stretch 18 m when the person jumps from the platform.

A typical facility will drop the jumpers from a jump height of 36 m, producing a maximum acceleration of under 29.4 m/s^2 (or 3 g). Some daredevilish embellishments may tempt the adventurous participants. "Sling-shotting" (from the ground up), "sandbagging" (jumping with extra weight), and "body-dipping" (over water) are examples. Extreme care and proper application of the physics involved are vitally important in these challenges.

LONG TERM PROJECT: THE ESCAPE BUNGEE

There is a need for a safe way to escape quickly from a tall building. During a fire, using an elevator could be dangerous and internal stairs might be blocked. A personal, quick, and direct means of escape would seem to be best. Inventors are trying various escape systems, such as the Escapechute (a personal parachute), the ZEC (vertical escape chute), the toboggan rigid and pneumatic escape chutes, and the "Trolley Wheel" cable escape system. Is it possible that a bungee cord escape system could work?

Your task will be to design and evaluate a bungee jump escape system. If the right length cord were used, the jumper could stop just at the ground, get off, and walk safely away from the building. A bungee cord is relatively small, easy to store, inexpensive, and a quick way to get out!

A large insurance company is interested in the project. The company was thrilled by the possibility of saving lives (and money) and wanted to find out the answer to the questions below. Your job in this project is to see whether you could save lives with a bungee cord escape system. To start out, you might study a small-scale model of the bungee jump. If you can understand this model, then you could later scale it up to a full-sized test.

QUESTIONS TO THINK ABOUT

a   Will there be too much force on a jumper?

b   Would it be possible to "get off" safely at the bottom of the drop?

c   Would a jumper crash into the side of the building?

d   What might be some of the problems that would limit the use of this escape system?

e   Can you understand the behavior of the small bungee drop mathematically?

f   How can you scale up the small model to figure out how much cord would be needed for a person of given weight to use to escape from an eight story building?

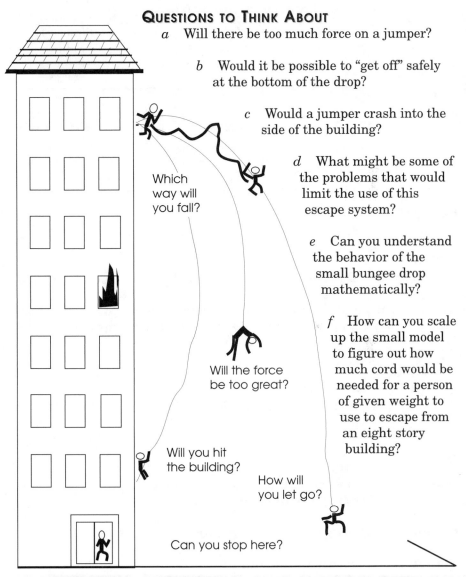

Which way will you fall?

Will the force be too great?

Will you hit the building?

How will you let go?

Can you stop here?

Do your work carefully because lives might depend on getting the right answers. Would you stake your life on your results by jumping out of a building attached to a bungee cord?

Skill 4.1 vi
Lab 15 – A Potpourri Of Energy

Background
Energy comes in many types. At each lab station is an object which can have energy. Think about other examples which should be included.

Examples of Energy Types

	Kinetic	Potential	Heat	Light	Chemical	Electrical
Kinetic	*****	Pendulum	Rocket Nozzle	Solar Sail	Muscles	Electric Motor
Potential	Pendulum	*****	Steam Boiler	X	X	Elevator Winch
Heat	Friction	X	*****	Solar Heater	Fire	Electric Stove
Light	X	X	Lightbulb, Sun	*****	Firefly light	Light Emitting Diode
Chemical	X	Chemical reactions	Quicklime Kiln	Green Plants	*****	Car Battery
Electrical	Windmill Power	Hydroelectric Power	Thermo-couple	Solar	X	*****

Problem
How do you classify energy?

Activity
You are to visit the various stations around the room and classify the energy that you feel is represented. You are to include the units that you would give the energy. Organize your information in a data table that includes a description of the station–energy type and energy unit.

The Stations

Station 1: **Wind up toy**
 a Wind up the toy and identify the energy available to the toy.
 b Let the toy go. What type of energy do you think the toy has now?

Station 2: **An assortment of batteries such as a car battery, a dry cell, a fruit or potato cell**

Station 3: **A spring and/or a pogo stick**

Station 4: **A picture of the Sun**

Station 5: **A hand cranked generator**

Station 6: **A Hot Wheels™ track including a loop the loop**
  a Car at the top of the track "hill"
  b Car at the bottom of the hill just entering the loop
  c Car at the top of the loop

Station 7: **Hand warmer and ice packs for athletic injuries**

Station 8: **Candles**
  a An unlit candle
  b A burning candle

Station 9: **Electric Circuits**
  a An open electric circuit
  b A closed electric circuit

Station 10: **A portable stereo with a small Styrofoam™ ball on a string hanging in front of the speaker**

Station 11: **Microwave oven**

Station 12: **Glow in the dark materials, phosphorescent and fluorescent materials**

Station 13: **A Geiger Counter and old Coleman™ lantern mantles or smoke detector**

Station 14: **Spring-loaded hand strengtheners**

Station 15: **A container representing gasoline**

Station 16: **Assorted food items**

Station 17: **A hot plate**

Station 18: **A container of hot water**

Station 19: **A Penguin Race toy**

Discussion
Be ready to discuss
- the basic types of energy you used in your classification
- how many of the energies involved motion
- how energies were stored
- which stations involved more than one type of energy
- in which station energy was being added or removed

Adapted with permission from C³P material.

SKILL 4.1 ॥
SPRING CONSTANT AND MOMENTUM CART

In order to store energy in a momentum cart whose mass is 490. g, the student pushed the plunger in a distance of 2.0 cm. The spring constant of the spring in the momentum cart has been determined to be 40 N/m. Calculate the initial velocity of the cart when it is released on the floor against a wall.

Given:

$$m = 490 \text{ g} = .49 \text{ kg}$$
$$x = 2.0 \text{ cm} = .020 \text{ m}$$

Find: v

load on cart   spring plunger

$$PE_{spring} = KE_{cart}$$

$$(^1/_2)kx^2 = {^1/_2} mv^2$$

$$.5 \,(40 \text{ N/m}) \,(.020 \text{ m})^2 = .5 \,(.49 \text{ kg}) \,v^2$$
$$v^2 = .0326 \text{ m}^2/_{s^2}$$
$$v = .18 \text{ m}/_s$$

The cart will move until it is stopped by friction. The work done by friction will be the same as the initial stored spring energy which was transferred to kinetic energy at launch.

☆ TRY IT

3   Using the same spring, the student pushes the plunger in 3.0 cm. Calculate the velocity with which it leaves the wall.

4   If the force of friction is .15 N, how far will the car move before stopping?

5   Calculate the coefficient of friction between the cart and the floor. [*Hint*: Refer back to page 92.]

Skills 4.1i, 4.1vi
Lab 16 – Is Mechanical Energy Conserved?
Background
A popular toy consists of part of a hollow rubber sphere that pops up when inverted and dropped. A homemade version of this toy can be made by cutting off the bottom 1/3 of a racquetball. We call it the "popper."

Problem
What work is needed to energize a "hopper-popper"? Using your knowledge of physics determine whether or not mechanical energy is conserved as it "pops" up.

Determining the Work
It is suggested that you use a 10 kg scale to measure the force needed to energize the popper. Over what distance does that force need to be applied? Try energizing the popper several times with your hands to determine this distance, as the maximum force is not needed over the whole distance.

Calculating Energy
Determine a way to calculate the energy of the system. Take careful measurement. Repeat at least five times.

Was Mechanical Energy Conserved? Or, Not.
In your discussion, identify the forces on the system and the part each played in the activity.

Chapter Nine Assessments
Part A Questions
1   Maria rides an escalator that moves her upward at constant speed. As the Maria rises, how do her gravitational potential energy and kinetic energy change?
    (1) Gravitational potential energy decreases and kinetic energy decreases.
    (2) Gravitational potential energy decreases and kinetic energy remains the same.
    (3) Gravitational potential energy increases and kinetic energy decreases.
    (4) Gravitational potential energy increases and kinetic energy remains the same.

2   A cart of mass M on a frictionless 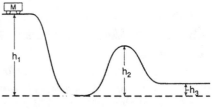 track starts from rest at the top of a hill having height h_1, as shown in the diagram at the right. What is the kinetic energy of the cart when it reaches the top of the next hill, having height h_2?

(1) Mgh_1 (2) $Mg(h_1-h_2)$ (3) $Mg(h_2-h_3)$ (4) 0

3   The diagram at the right shows a cart at four positions. Where is the sum of the potential energy and kinetic energy of the cart the same?
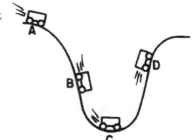
(1) A and B, only
(2) B and C, only
(3) C and D, only
(4) all position, A through D

4   A 20.-kilogram object strikes the ground with 1,960 joules of kinetic energy after falling freely from rest. How far above the ground was the object when it was released?

(1) 10. m   (2) 14 m   (3) 98 m   (4) 200 m

5   A 1.0-kilogram mass gains kinetic energy as it falls freely from rest a vertical distance, d. How far would a 2.0-kilogram mass have to fall freely from rest to gain the same amount of kinetic energy?

(1) d (2) $2d$ (3) $d/2$ (4) $d/4$

6   A 500.-newton girl lifts a 10.-newton box vertically over a distance of 0.50 meter. The work done on the box is

(1) 5.0 J   (2) 50. J   (3) 250 J   (4) 2,500 J

7   The work done in accelerating an object along a frictionless horizontal surface is equal to the object's change in

(1) momentum   (3) potential energy
(2) velocity   (4) kinetic energy

8   A ball is thrown vertically upward. As the ball rises, its total energy (neglecting friction)

(1) decreases   (2) increases   (3) remains the same

9   The wrecking crane is moving toward a brick wall which is to be torn down. At what point in the swing of the wrecking ball should the ball make contact with the wall to make a collision with the greatest kinetic energy?
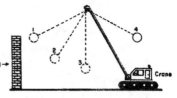
(1) 1   (2) 2   (3) 3   (4) 4

PART B QUESTIONS

10 A 0.10-kilogram ball dropped vertically from a height of 1.0 meter above the floor bounces back to a height of 0.80 meter. The mechanical energy lost by the ball as it bounces is [1] _____ J

11 The diagram at the right shows a 5.0-kilogram mass sliding 9.0 meters down an incline from a height of 2.0 meters in 3.0 seconds. The object gains 90. joules of kinetic energy while sliding. How much work is done against friction as the mass slides the 9.0 meters?

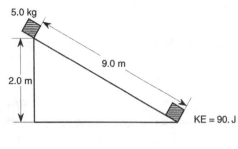

(1) 0 J   (2) 8 J   (3) 45 J   (4) 90. J

12 Which graph best represents the kinetic energy (KE) of an object as a function of its speed v?

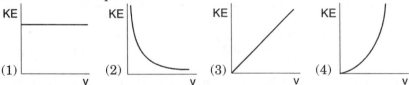

(1)   (2)   (3)   (4)

13 The diagram at the right shows three positions, A, B, and C, in the swing of a pendulum, released from rest at point A. [Neglect friction.] Which statement is true about this swinging pendulum?

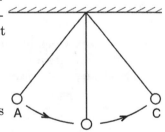

(1) The potential energy at A equals the kinetic energy at C.
(2) The speed of the pendulum at A equals the speed of the pendulum at B.
(3) The potential energy at B equals the potential energy at C.
(4) The potential energy at A equals the kinetic energy at B.

14 Base your answer on the diagram at the right which represents an object M suspended by a string from point P. When object M is swung to a height of h and released, it passes through the rest position at a speed of 10 meters per second. The height h from which the object was released is [1]

_____ m

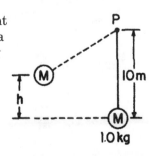

Base your answers to questions 15 and 16 on the diagram at the right which shows a 1.0-kilogram stone being dropped from a bridge 100 meters above a gorge.

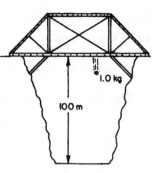

15 What will be the kinetic energy of the stone after it has fallen 50 meters? [1] ____ J

16 As the stone falls, the gravitational potential energy of the stone [1] _____ .

Base your answers to questions 17 and 18 on the diagram below that shows an object at *A* that moves over a frictionless surface from *A* to *E*. The object has a mass of m.

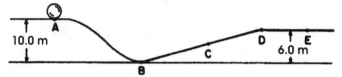

17 The object's kinetic energy at point *D* is equal to
    (1) mgd   (2) mg(d–h)   (3) mgh   (4) mg(h–d)

18 As the object moves from point *A* to point *D*, the sum of its gravitational potential and kinetic energies [1] _____.

Base your answers to questions 19 and 20 on the diagram below which represents a frictionless track. A 10-kilogram block starts from rest at point *A* and slides along the track.

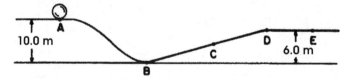

19 As the block moves from point *A* to point *B*, the total amount of gravitational potential energy changed to kinetic energy is [1] _____ J

20 What is the speed of the block at point *B*? [1] _____ m/s

PART C QUESTIONS

Base your answers to questions 21 and 22 on the information and diagram below.

A block of mass m starts from rest at height h on a frictionless incline. The block slides down the incline across a frictionless level surface and comes to rest by compressing a spring through distance x, as shown in the diagram below.

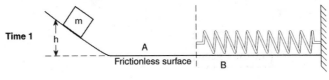

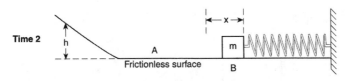

21 Name the forms of mechanical energy possessed by the system when the block is in position A and in position B. [2]

22 Determine the spring constant, k, in terms of g, h, m, and x. [Show all work including formulas and an algebraic solution for k.] [2]

23 A 0.65-meter-long pendulum consists of a 1.0-kilogram mass at the end of a string. The pendulum is released from rest at position A, 0.25 meter above its lowest point. The pendulum is timed at five positions, A through E.

Data Table

Position	Elapsed Time
A	0.00 s
B	0.20 s
C	0.40 s
D	0.60 s
E	0.80 s

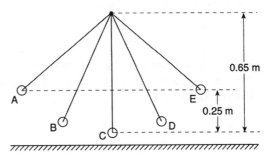

Based on the information in the diagram and the data table, determine the period of the pendulum. [1]

Base your answers to questions 24 through 26 on the information and diagram below, which is drawn to a scale of 1.0 centimeter = 3.0 meters.

A 650-kilogram roller coaster car starts from rest at the top of the first hill of its track and glides freely. [Neglect friction.]

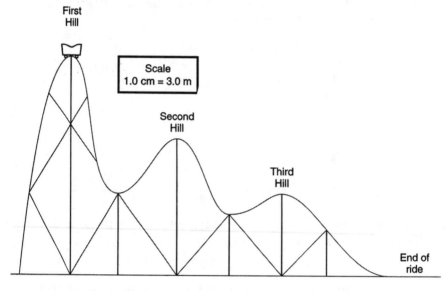

24 Using a metric ruler and the scale of 1.0 cm = 3.0 m, determine the height of the first hill. [1]

25 Determine the *gravitational potential energy* of the car at the top of the first hill. [Show all calculations, including the equation and substitution with units.] [2]

26 Using one or more complete sentences, compare the kinetic energy of the car at the top of the second hill to its kinetic energy at the top of the third hill. [1]

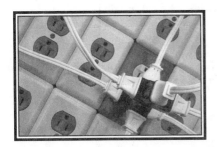

CHAPTER 10
ELECTRIC
FIELDS
AND FORCES

KEY IDEA **4** ENERGY EXISTS IN MANY FORMS, AND WHEN THESE FORMS CHANGE ENERGY IS CONSERVED.

KEY IDEA **5**

ENERGY AND MATTER INTERACT THROUGH FORCES THAT RESULT IN CHANGES IN MOTION.

PERFORMANCE INDICATOR 4.1

STUDENTS CAN OBSERVE AND DESCRIBE TRANSMISSION OF VARIOUS FORMS OF ENERGY.

CHAPTER 10 – MAJOR UNDERSTANDINGS

☆ 5.1t Gravitational forces are only attractive, whereas electrical and magnetic forces can be attractive or repulsive.

☆ 5.1u The inverse square law applies to electrical* and gravitational* fields produced by point sources.

☆ 4.1j Energy may be stored in electric* or magnetic fields. This energy may be transferred through conductors or space and may be converted to other forms of energy.

CHAPTER 10
ELECTRIC FIELDS AND FORCES

STATIC ELECTRICITY

Static electricity deals with electrical charges at rest. The term "at rest" indicates that there is no net transfer of charge in any given direction. The charges can vibrate, but there is no flow of charge, which would be called current. Static charges are most evident in dry environments such as the clothes dryer or indoors during winter months.

MICROSTRUCTURE OF MATTER

Atoms consist of three main particles. The **proton** has a positive charge and is found in the nucleus. The **neutron** has no charge and is also located in the nucleus. The **electron** has a negative charge and orbits the nucleus. The magnitude of the positive and negative charges is the same. The unit of charge in the SI system is the coulomb. One coulomb (C) represents the charge of 6.25×10^{18} electrons. Each electron has a charge of 1.6×10^{-19} coulomb. The electron and the proton are among a class of particles called **charge carriers**.

The electron has the smallest negative charge, and the proton has the smallest positive charge. These charges are equal in magnitude and opposite in sign. One **negative elementary charge** is defined as the charge on an electron. One **positive elementary charge** is the charge on one proton. The symbol for an elementary charge is **e**.

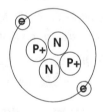

Neutral atoms have an equal number of positive and negative charges. The protons are difficult to remove because they are held together by very strong nuclear forces. Electrons are much easier to remove, because they are more loosely bound by the electrical force. Objects are said to be charged when they have an excess or a deficiency of electrons

When electrons are lost or gained by a neutral atom, the resulting particle is electrically charged and is called an **ion**. The charge on an ion depends on the excess charge. For example, an atom with 10 protons and

10 electrons is neutral. If two electrons (two elementary units of negative charge) are removed from this atom, the resulting ion is said to have a charge of +2 elementary units.

CHARGE DETECTION

Example A: A positively charged object sets up an **electric field** around it. This field attracts a neutral pith ball because the electrons migrate to one side of the pith ball, causing one side of the pith ball to be more negative than the other side. The positively charged object attracts the negative side of the pith ball. The pith ball moves towards the charged object.

Example B: A negatively charged object will also attract a pith ball. The electrons are repelled by the electric field of the charged object leaving one side of the pith ball more positive than the other side. Positive and negative charges attract each other. The pith ball moves towards the object.

Example C: When a neutral object is in the region of a neutral pith ball, there is no attraction.

Note: The only proof that an object is charged is repulsion. If two objects are repelled, they have the same charge.

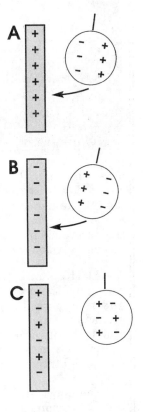

TYPES OF CHARGE

Certain neutral objects can become charged by rubbing them with wool or fur. During the rubbing, electrons are removed from one object and placed on the other object. When rubber is rubbed with wool, electrons are removed from the wool and left on the rubber. The rubber has an excess of electrons. This gives the rubber a negative charge. The wool has a deficiency of electrons so it has a positive charge.

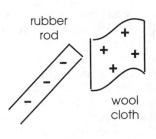

The concept of negative and positive charges was studied by Benjamin Franklin. Franklin made the choice on which charge would be called positive. The charge gained by one object exactly equals the charge lost by the other object. This principle is known as the **conservation of charge**. It states that the net charge in a closed system is constant.

REAL WORLD CONNECTIONS

LIGHTNING

Thunderstorms are a common event. At any one time, about 2,000 thunderstorms exist worldwide, producing about 100 lightning flashes per second. Without lightning, there could be no thunder, and there are specific conditions that must occur for such storms to form. When the clouds begin to form, their molecules have no electrical charge, positive and negative ions being paired. As the thunderhead develops, a negative electrical charge forms at the bottom of the cloud. Exactly how this happens is not fully understood, but it is probably related to quickly rising air currents. Most often, the top of the cloud has a positive charge, and when the difference in charge overcomes the resistance of the air, lightning strikes between the top and bottom of the cloud.

At the same time, things are happening near the ground. Normally, the ground has both positive and negative charges paired and is neutral. When a thunderhead passes over the ground, it attracts positive charges from the ground below, and in the air just above the ground. When the difference in negative and positive charges between ground and cloud gets large enough, the stage is set for the lightning show.

The show begins quite subtly, a faintly visible lightning "leader" leaves the cloud and streaks for the ground in a zig-zag manner. When the leader is about sixty to one hundred feet above the ground, a return stroke of lightning explodes from the ground. This return stroke is what we actually see as "lightning" and is several inches in diameter, surrounded by about a four inch thick sleeve of superheated air. The return stroke carries a charge of 20,000 to 200,000 amperes.

It is with the return stroke that thunder occurs. Temperatures, such as 50,000 degrees Fahrenheit, superheat the surrounding air, causing it to expand violently, which we hear as thunder. As soon as the return stroke reaches the cloud, another leader forms, and several dozen cycles may occur. These strokes travel at 90,000 miles per second, and we see all these cycles as one bolt of lightning.

There are some people who fear thunder and lightning, and others who enjoy watching the show. But whether we love it or hate it, we must all agree lightning can be deadly. Between 100 and 300 people are killed by lightning strikes each year in the United States.

COULOMB'S LAW

Charges exert forces on each other. These forces have been shown experimentally to be directly proportional to the magnitude of the charge and inversely proportional to the square of the distance between the charges. Coulomb's Law is limited to point charges that are small in size.

$$F = \frac{kq_1 q_2}{r^2}$$

Where:

k = constant of proportionality = 8.99×10^9 N•m²/C²

q_1, q_2 = charges measured in coulombs

r = distance between charged particles in meters

EXAMPLE

What is the force between two point charges, that each have a charge of –0.003 coulombs at a separation of 10 meters?

Given: $q_1 = q_2 = -0.0030$ C

$r = 10.0$ m

Find: F

Solution: $F = \dfrac{kq_1q_2}{r^2}$

$$= \frac{(8.99 \times 10^9 \text{ N•m}^2 / \text{C}^2)\,(-0.0030\text{C})\,(-0.0030\text{C})}{(10. \text{ m})^2}$$

$$= 8.09 \times 10^2 \text{ N} = 810 \text{ N}$$

A positive value for force indicates repulsion.

SKILLS M 2.1, M 3.1, S 2.1
LAB 17 – STATIC CHARGES

BACKGROUND

The observation that some substances when rubbed with others will attract small pieces of lint or dust was first made more than two thousand years ago. This is the simplest experiment in **electrostatics**, the study of electric charges at rest.

THE PROBLEM

In the experiment that follows, you will produce and study electric charges. Question each observation and see that you can explain it. Write a log of your observations as you work, explaining each point.

THE APPARATUS

The apparatus consists of rods of assorted plastic and glass, Scotch Brand Magic Tape, wool and nylon cloth, cotton balls, and a short piece of wire. The detector of charges is a triangle of aluminum foil about a half inch on each edge. Attach one corner of the triangle around a piece of silk thread and hang it from a support rod. *Note:* Any unnecessary handling of the detector can spoil your results because a moist surface will allow the charges to leak off.

CHARGED OBJECTS

Determine which pair of substances produces the greatest effect when rubbed together. Charge the adhesive cellophane tape by placing a strip on the desk, rubbing the surface and then removing the strip of tape quickly from the desk. How does the strength of the charge produced on the tape compare to the charge produced in other ways? Now stick two pieces of adhesive cellophane tape together, and then pull them apart. What can you say about the charges on the pair of tapes? Can you find any other ways to charge the tape?

ELECTROSTATIC FORCE AND DISTANCE

Devise a simple experiment to show whether the distance between two charges affects the force they exert on each other. For this section of the laboratory, you might want to use balloons to develop your experiment. Briefly describe the experiment and its result. Be sure to include vector diagrams in your report, when appropriate.

TWO KINDS OF CHARGE

Show experimentally that there are two different kinds of charge. *Note:* The attraction between two objects shows only that one of the two is charged. The other may or may not be. Repulsion, on the other hand, shows that both are charged. State your evidence for the existence of two kinds of charge.

CONSERVATION OF CHARGE

In any closed system, the total charge remains constant.

*   Consider one of your charging pairs as a closed system. What evidence of conservation of charge can you observe?

*   What happens to the charge on the foil when you touch the foil with your finger? How do you explain this with reference to conservation of charge?

*   Charge the foil, then quickly pass a lighted match under it. Is the effect the same for either type of charge? Explain.

CONDUCTORS AND INSULATORS

Some materials are insulators and others are conductors. Touch a charged piece of foil with a cotton ball. Repeat using a short piece of wire. Compare the results and explain what happened.

TRY IT

Describe and explain each of the following by referring to the two substances which produced the greatest electrostatic effect.

1 The behavior of the uncharged foil when a charged object is brought near it.

2 The behavior of the foil after it has been touched by a charged object when the same charged object is brought near again.

3 The action of the charged foil when the other member of the charging pair is brought near.

4 The behavior of the charged foil when your finger is slowly brought near—and also after the finger has touched it.

5 The behavior of the foil when charged weakly, as a strongly and similarly charged object is brought near.

THE ELECTRIC FIELD

An electric field is said to exist in any region of space in which an electric force acts on a charge. The field exists around every charged object. A similarity exists between the electric field around a uniformly charged spherical body and the gravitational field around a sphere. The electric field intensity is a vector quantity. The SI unit for electric field strength is the newton/coulomb. In comparison, the gravitational field strength can be expressed in newtons/kilogram ($g = F/m$). The magnitude of the field at any point is equal to:

$$E = F/q$$

Where:

        q is the charge in coulombs on the test charge
        F is the force in newtons on the test charge q
        E is the electric field intensity in newtons/coulomb

The direction of the electric field is defined as the direction of force on a positive test charge placed in the field.

An **electric field line** is the line along which a charged particle would move as a result of its interaction with the electric field. The direction of a field line is the direction of the force exerted on a positively charged particle placed at that location on the field line.

Electric field lines leave the surface of the charge at right angles and extend away from a positive charge. The lines around a negative charge point toward the charge. Charges interact through their fields. Below are several examples of interacting fields:

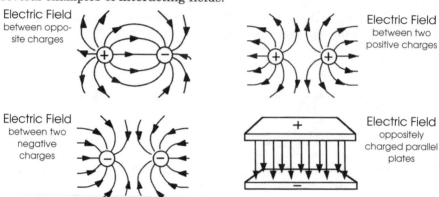

Electric Field between opposite charges

Electric Field between two positive charges

Electric Field between two negative charges

Electric Field oppositely charged parallel plates

Note: The field lines do not cross each other.

As charges distribute on the surface of a conductor, the field lines are normal to the surface. The field around the charged sphere acts as though all of the charges were concentrated at the center. The field within the charged conducting sphere is zero. The intensity of the electric field around a point charge varies inversely with the square of the distance from the point charge. If you double the distance from the charge, the field intensity is quartered.

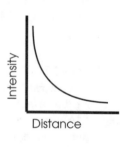

Example: Calculate the force exerted on an electron in an electric field, whose intensity is 2.0×10^2 N/C

Given: $E = 2.0 \times 10^2$ N/C $q = 1.6 \times 10^{-19}$ C

Find: F

Solution: $F = Eq$
$F = (2.0 \times 10^2 \text{ N/C})(1.6 \times 10^{-19} \text{ C})$
$F = 3.2 \times 10^{-17}$ N

The electric field around a point charge is calculated from:

$$E_{point} = \frac{kq}{r^2}$$

The electric field between parallel charged plates is essentially uniform if the distance between the plates is small compared to the dimensions of the plates. This uniform field produces a constant force on a charge placed anywhere in the field.

ELECTRIC POTENTIAL

The **electric potential** at any point in an electric field is the work required to bring a unit positive charge from infinity to that point. When a charge is moved against the force of an electric field, work is done on the charge and the potential energy of the system is increased. When the charge moves in response to the field, work is done by the field and the potential energy of the charge is decreased.

In order to move a proton from point B to point A, work must be done on the charge. The work increases the potential energy.

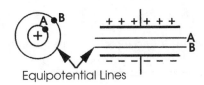

Equipotential Lines

Equipotential lines cross electric field lines at right angles. They connect positions of equal potential energy. As a charge moves on an equipotential line, there is no change in potential energy. As the charge crosses equipotential lines, the potential energy changes.

POTENTIAL DIFFERENCE OR POTENTIAL DROP

The potential difference between two points in an electric field is the change in energy per unit charge, as the charge is moved from one point to another. The SI unit of electric potential is the **volt**.

$$V = W/q$$

When: V is potential difference (measured in volts)
W is work (measured in joules)
q is charge (measured in coulombs)

1 volt = 1 joule/1 coulomb

One volt is the potential difference that exists between two points, when one joule of work is required to transfer one coulomb of charge from one point to the other against the electric force.

REAL WORLD CONNECTIONS

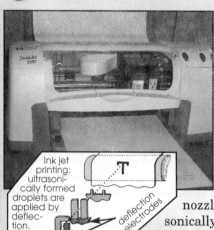

Ink jet printing: ultrasonically formed droplets are applied by deflection.

CHARGE IT – INK JETS

For tiny particles (1000 nm-1,000,000 nm), electrostatic forces can control the motion of the particle and has led to a wide range of real world applications. Low cost, high-resolution printers produce better quality and at a lower per copy cost.

A jet of ink is produced by forcing the liquid though a fine nozzle. The droplets are formed ultrasonically into a stream of uniform equally spaced droplets, which are then charged by a voltage applied to the nozzle. These droplets are first accelerated and then deflected by two pairs of plates. A potential difference is applied to the plates to give a deflection in two perpendicular directions. Computer control of the deflection plate allows for extremely rapid printing.

As an electron moves along an equipotential line, there is no change in potential energy. As the electron is moved from the negative plate to the positive plate, it crosses equipotential lines. The electron gains kinetic energy as it crosses the gap between the plates. The energy can be calculated in the unit of electron volts. An **electron volt** (eV) is the energy required to move one elementary charge (that is, 1.6×10^{-19} coulombs) through a potential of one volt.

$$W = Vq$$

$$1.6 \times 10^{-19} \text{ J} = (1.0 \text{ Volt})(1.6 \times 10^{-19} \text{ coulombs})$$

Therefore,   **1.0 eV = 1.0 V x 1 elementary charge = 1.6×10^{-19} J**

At location A, the electron has 100 eV of electric potential energy. At location B, the electron has 100 eV of kinetic energy.

100 v

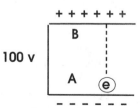

Volts (V) are related to the electric field intensity (E).

Where: E = electric field intensity
V = volts
d = distance between parallel plates

$$E = \frac{V}{d} \quad \text{(measured in volts/meter or newtons/coulomb for parallel plates)}$$

$$\frac{\text{volt}}{\text{meter}} = \frac{\text{joules/coulomb}}{\text{meter}} = \frac{\text{joules}}{\text{coulomb} \cdot \text{meter}} = \frac{\text{newton} \cdot \text{meter}}{\text{coulomb} \cdot \text{meter}} = \frac{\text{newton}}{\text{coulomb}}$$

In 1911, American physicist **Robert Andrews Millikan** (1868-1953) won the *Nobel Prize* in 1923 for determining the fundamental unit of charge. He measured the forces on a charged oil drop in a uniform electric field. The field between two parallel plates can be adjusted so the oil drop remains suspended in the space between the plates. At that time the forces acting on the oil drop are balanced.

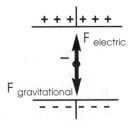

F (electric) = F (gravitational)

$$Eq = mg$$

Once balanced, the amount of charge on the oil drop can be calculated. Millikan found that the charge was always an integral multiple of a small constant. He determined the elementary charge to be equal to 1.6×10^{-19} coulomb. It is the charge of an electron or proton. It is the smallest charge possible.

Example: Two large parallel metal plates are separated by a distance of 2.0×10^{-3} meters. The plates are attached to a 4.0×10^3 volt source.

- Calculate the field intensity between the plate.

- Determine the force on an electron in the field.

- Calculate the work necessary to move an electron from the positive plate to the negative plate in electron volts and in joules.

Given: d = 2.0×10^{-3} m
V = 4.0×10^3 V
q = e = 1.6×10^{-19} C = 1 eV

Find: a Field intensity
b Force
c Work

Solution:

a $E = V/d$
   $= (4.0 \times 10^3 \text{ V}) / (2.0 \times 10^{-3} \text{ m})$
   $= 2.0 \times 10^6 \text{ V/m}$

b $F = qE$
   $= (1.6 \times 10^{-19} \text{ C})(2.0 \times 10^6 \text{ N/C})$
   $= 3.2 \times 10^{-13} \text{ N}$

c $W = qV = 1 \text{ electron} \times (4.0 \times 10^3 \text{ V})$
   $= 4.0 \times 10^3 \text{ eV}$

Since: $1 \text{ eV} = 1.6 \times 10^{-19} \text{ J}$
    $W = (1.6 \times 10^{-19} \text{ J/eV})(4.0 \times 10^3 \text{ eV})$
     $= 6.4 \times 10^{-16} \text{ J}$

CHAPTER TEN ASSESSMENTS

PART A QUESTIONS

1   A sphere has a net excess charge of -4.8×10^{-19} coulomb. The sphere must have an excess of
  (1) 1 electron   (2) 1 proton   (3) 3 electrons   (4) 3 protons

2   The diagram at the right shows the initial charge and position of three metal spheres, X, Y, and Z, on insulating stands. Sphere X is brought into contact with sphere Y and then removed. Then sphere

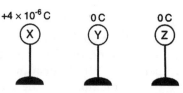

Y is brought into contact with sphere Z and removed. What is the charge on sphere Z after this procedure is completed?
  (1) $+1 \times 10^{-6}$ C   (2) $+2 \times 10^{-6}$ C   (3) $+3 \times 10^{-6}$ C   (4) $+4 \times 10^{-6}$ C

3   The diagram at the right shows two metal spheres suspended by strings and separated by a distance of 3.0 meters. The charge on sphere A is $+5.0 \times 10^{-4}$ coulomb and the charge on sphere B is $+3.0 \times 10^{-5}$ coulomb. Which statement best describes the electrical force between the spheres?

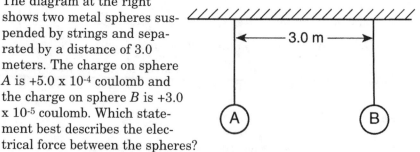

  (1) It has a magnitude of 15 N and is repulsive.
  (2) It has a magnitude of 45 N and is repulsive.
  (3) It has a magnitude of 15 N and is attractive.
  (4) It has a magnitude of 45 N and is attractive.

4   Two similar metal spheres possessing +1.0 coulomb of charge and
    −1.0 coulomb of charge, respectively, are brought toward each other.
    Which graph best represents the relationship between the magni-
    tude of the electric force between the spheres and the distance
    between them?

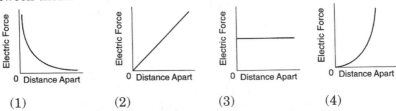

    (1)   (2)   (3)   (4)

5   Compared to the charge on a proton, the charge on an electron has
    the
    (1) opposite sign and a smaller magnitude
    (2) opposite sign and a same magnitude
    (3) same sign and a smaller magnitude
    (4) same sign and a same magnitude

6   Three identical metal spheres are mounted on insulating stands.
    Initially, sphere A has a net charge of q and spheres B and C are
    uncharged. Sphere A is touched to sphere B and removed. Then
    sphere A is touched to sphere C and removed. What is the final
    charge of sphere A?

    (1) q (2) $\frac{q}{2}$ (3) $\frac{q}{3}$ (4) $\frac{q}{4}$

7   Two plastic rods, A and B, each possess a net nega-
    tive charge of 1.0 x 10^{-3} coulomb. The rods and a
    positively charged sphere are positioned as shown.
    Which vector best represents the resultant electro-
    static force on the sphere?

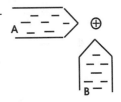

    (1)   (2)   (3)   (4)

8   Which diagram best represents the electric field around a negatively
    charged conducting sphere?

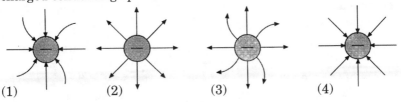

    (1)   (2)   (3)   (4)

9   Which diagram best represents the electric field near a positively
    charged conducting sphere?

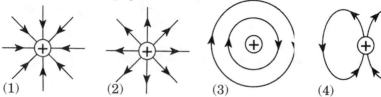

(1)   (2)   (3)   (4)

10 The diagram at the right shows a point,
    P, located midway between two opposite-
    ly charged parallel plates. If an electron
    is introduced at Point *P*, the electron will

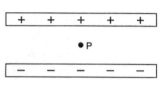

    (1) travel at constant speed toward the positively charged plate
    (2) travel at constant speed toward the negatively charged plate
    (3) accelerate toward the positively charged plate
    (4) accelerate toward the negatively charged plate

11 Gravitational field strength is to newtons per kilogram as electric
    field strength is to
    (1) coulombs per joule   (3) joules per coulomb
    (2) coulombs per newton   (4) newtons per coulomb

12 Two oppositely charged parallel plates are a fixed distance apart.
    Which graph best represents the relationship between the electric
    field intensity (*E*) between the plates and the potential difference (*V*)
    across the plates?

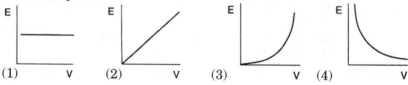

(1)   V   (2)   V   (3)   V (4)   V

13 An electron is located between two oppositely
    charged parallel plates as shown in the diagram
    at the right. As the electron moves toward the
    positive plate, the magnitude of the electric force
    acting on the electron

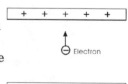

    (1) decreases
    (2) increases
    (3) remains the same

14 An electron is located between a pair of oppositely charge parallel
    plates. As the electron approaches the positive plate, the kinetic
    energy of the electron
    (1) decreases   (2) increases   (3) remains the same

15 The diagram below, which illustrates the Millikan oil drop experiment, shows a 3.2×10^{-14}-kilogram oil drop with a charge of -1.6×10^{-18} coulomb. The oil drop was in equilibrium when the upward electric force on the drop was equal in magnitude to the gravitational force on the drop. What was the magnitude of the electric field intensity when this oil drop was in equilibrium?

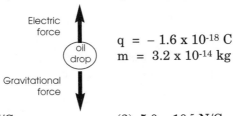

$q = -1.6 \times 10^{-18}$ C
$m = 3.2 \times 10^{-14}$ kg

(1) 2.0×10^{-5} N/C
(2) 2.0×10^{5} N/C
(3) 5.0×10^{-5} N/C
(4) 5.0×10^{5} N/C

16 The graph at the right shows the relationship between the work done on a charged body in an electric field and the net charge on the body. What does the slope of this graph represent?
(1) power
(2) potential difference
(3) force
(4) electricity field intensity

Base your answers to questions 17 and 18 on the information and diagram at the right.

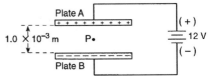

Two parallel plates separated by a distance of 1.0×10^{-3} meter are charged to a potential difference of 12 volts. An alpha particle with a charge of +2 elementary charges is located at Point P in the region between the plates.

17 What is the magnitude and direction of the electric field intensity between the plates?
(1) 1.2×10^3 V/m toward Plate A   (3) 1.2×10^4 V/m toward Plate A
(2) 1.2×10^3 V/m toward Plate B   (4) 1.2×10^4 V/m toward Plate B

18 The electric field between the plates will cause the alpha particle, starting from rest at Point P, to
(1) accelerate toward the positive plate
(2) accelerate toward the negative plate
(3) move at constant speed toward the positive plate
(4) move at constant speed toward the negative plate

PART B QUESTIONS

19 Moving 2.0 coulombs of charge a distance of 6.0 meters from Point A to Point B within an electric field requires a 56.0-newton force. What is the electric potential difference between points A and B? [1]
_____ V

20 If 15 joules of work is required to move 3.0 coulombs of charge between two points, the potential difference between these two points is [1] _____ V

21 An alpha particle consists of two protons and two neutrons. The alpha particle's charge of +2 elementary charges is equivalent to [1] _____ C

22 A metal sphere having an excess of +5 elementary charges has a net electric charge of [1] _____ C

23 What is the net static electric charge on a metal sphere having an excess of +3 elementary charges? [1] _____ C

24 The diagram at the right shows two metal spheres charged to $+1.0 \times 10^{-6}$ coulomb and $+3.0 \times 10^{-6}$ coulomb, respectively, on insulating stands separated by a distance of 0.10 meter. The spheres are touched together and then returned to their original positions. As a result, the magnitude of the electrostatic force between the spheres changes from 2.7 N to [1] _____ N

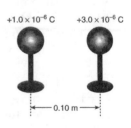

25 Two aluminum spheres of identical mass and identical charge q hang from strings of equal length. If the spheres are in equilibrium, which diagram best represents the direction of each force acting on the spheres?

Key
F_s = Force (tension) in string
F_e = Electrostatic force
F_g = Gravitational force

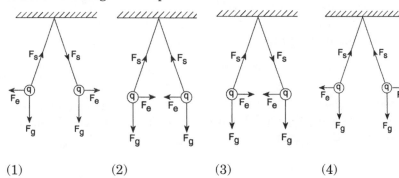

(1)   (2)   (3)   (4)

26 An electrostatic force of 20. newtons is exerted on a charge of 8.0×10^{-2} coulomb at Point P in an electric field. The magnitude of the electric field intensity at P is [1] _____ N/C

27 The diagram at the right shows proton P located at Point A near a positively charge sphere. If a 6.4×10^{-19} joule of work is required to move the proton from point A to Point B, the potential difference between A and B is [1] _____ V

Sphere

28 A distance of 1.0×10^3 meters separates the charge at the bottom of a cloud and the ground. The electric field intensity between the bottom of the cloud and the ground is 2.0×10^4 newtons per coulomb. What is the potential difference between the bottom of the cloud and the ground? [1] _____ V

29 A point charge of $+3.0 \times 10^{-7}$ coulomb is placed 2.0×10^{-2} meter from a second point charge of $+4.0 \times 10^{-7}$ coulomb. The magnitude of the electrostatic force between the charges is [1] _____ N

Base your answers to questions 30 through 34 on the following information and diagram. Two parallel plates are charged to a potential difference of 20.0 volts. Points A, B, and C are located in the region between the plates.

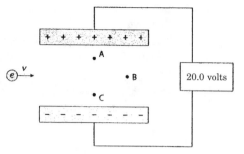

30 Sketch at least two electric field lines in the region between the oppositely charged parallel plates. Draw lines with arrowheads in the proper direction. [2]

31 If an electron were projected into the electric field with a velocity v, as shown, it would
(1) deflect into the page
(2) deflect out of the page
(3) deflect toward the top of the page
(4) deflect toward the bottom of the page

32 Compared to the magnitude of the electric field strength at Point B, the magnitude of the electric field strength at Point A is
(1) less
(2) greater
(3) the same

33 Compared to the work done in moving an electron from Point A to Point B to Point C, the work done in moving an electron directly from Point A to Point C is
(1) less
(2) greater
(3) the same

34 As a proton moves from A to B to C, the magnitude of the electric force on the proton
(1) less
(2) greater
(3) the same

PART C QUESTIONS

Base your answers to questions 35 through 37 on the information and diagram below.

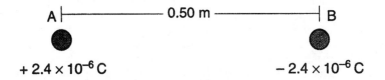

Two small charged spheres, A and B, are separated by a distance of 0.50 meter. The charge on sphere A is +2.4 x 10^{-6} coulomb and the charge on sphere B is -2.4 x 10^{-6} coulomb.

35 On the diagram, sketch *three* electric field lines to represent the electric field in the region between Sphere A and Sphere B. [Draw an arrowhead on each field line to show the proper direction.] [2]

36 Calculate the magnitude of the electrostatic force that sphere A exerts on Sphere B. [Show all calculations, including the equation and substitution with units.] [2]

37 Using the axes provided, sketch the general shape of the graph that shows the relationship between the magnitude of the electrostatic force between the two charged spheres and the distance separating them. The Charge on each sphere remains constant as the distance separating them is varied. [1]

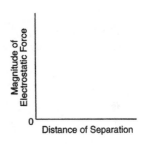

38 Four small metal Spheres R, S, T, and U on insulating stands act on each other by means of electrostatic forces. It was known that sphere S is negatively charged. The following observations were made:

- Sphere S attracts all the other spheres.
- Spheres T and U repel each other.
- Sphere R attracts all the other spheres.

Determine the charge on each sphere and complete the table provided noting for each sphere if it is positive (+), negative (−), or neutral (0). [3]

Sphere	Charge
R	
T	
U	

Base your answers to questions 39 through 41 on the passage below and on your knowledge of physics.

Forces of Nature

Our understanding of the fundamental forces has evolved along with our growing knowledge of the particles of matter. Many everyday phenomena seemed to be governed by a long list of unique forces. Observations identified the gravitational, electrical, and magnetic forces as distinct. A large step toward simplification came in the mid-19th century with James C. Maxwell's unification of the electrical and magnetic forces into a single electromagnetic force. Fifty years later came the recognition that the electromagnetic force also governed atoms. By the late 1800s, all commonly observed phenomena could be understood with only the electromagnetic and gravitational forces.

Particle Physics–Perspectives and Opportunities (adapted)

A hydrogen atom, consisting of an electron in orbit about a proton, has an approximate radius of 10^{-10} meter.

39 Determine the order of magnitude of the electrostatic force between the electron and the proton. [1]

40 Determine the order of magnitude of the gravitational force between the electron and the proton. [1]

41 In the above passage, there is an apparent contradiction. The author stated that "the electromagnetic force also governed atoms." He concluded with "all commonly observed phenomena could be understood with only the electromagnetic and gravitational forces."

Use your responses to questions 39 and 40 to explain why the gravitational interaction is negligible for the hydrogen atom. [2]

42 Two parallel plates separated by a distance of 2.0×10^{-2} meter are charged to a potential difference of 1.0×10^2 volts. Points A, B, and C are located in the region between the plates. Calculate the magnitude of the electric field strength between the plates. [Show all calculations, including the equation and substitutions with units.] [2]

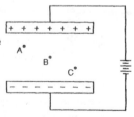

CHAPTER 11
OHM'S LAW AND RESISTIVITY

KEY IDEA 4

ENERGY EXISTS IN MANY FORMS, AND WHEN THESE FORMS CHANGE ENERGY IS CONSERVED.

PERFORMANCE INDICATOR 4.1

STUDENTS CAN OBSERVE AND DESCRIBE TRANSMISSION OF VARIOUS FORMS OF ENERGY.

CHAPTER 11 – MAJOR UNDERSTANDINGS

☆ 4.1m The factors affecting resistance in a conductor are length, cross-sectional area, temperature, and resistivity.*

☆ 4.1l All materials display a range of conductivity. At constant temperature, common metallic conductors obey Ohm's Law*.

☆ 4.1n A circuit is a closed path in which a current* can exist. (Note: Use conventional current.)

☆ 4.1p Electrical power* and energy* can be determined for electric circuits.

CHAPTER 11
OHM'S LAW AND RESISTIVITY

ALL ABOUT CIRCUITS

ELECTRIC CURRENT

The word **current** means "flow" and the words **electric current** means "flow of charge." The flow refers to the movement of either positive or negative charges. The electric current refers to the amount of charge that passes a single point in a period of time. Conventional current flows from positive to negative. Electron current flows from negative to positive. *Note:* Current references in this review book will refer to conventional current unless otherwise noted.

The *SI* unit for current is the ampere (or amp), which is the flow of one coulomb of charge per second or 6.25 x10^{18} electrons per second.

$$I = q/t$$

Where: **I** = current measured in amperes
  q = charge measured in coulombs
  t = time measured in seconds

CONDUCTIVITY IN SOLIDS

Solids vary in their ability to conduct current. The conductivity of solids depends on the number of free charges per unit volume and the mobility of the charges. In general, since metals have a large number of free electrons, they are good conductors. Nonmetals are poor conductors of electricity. Substances with few free electrons are called insulators. No solid is a perfect insulator, but in some solids, such as glass and fused quartz, the conductivity is so low that they are good insulators. Some materials whose resistivities lie between metals and insulators are called semiconductors. **Superconductors** are materials which lose all of their resistance when cooled to very low temperatures.

CONDUCTIVITY IN LIQUIDS

Liquids also vary in their ability to conduct an electric current. Pure water is not a good conductor. Many chemical compounds, called **electrolytes**, dissociate in an aqueous solution into positively and negatively charged particles, called ions. In such a solution, both positive and negative ions are free to move. The solution can conduct an electric current. Both positive and negative charges move in solution.

Note: The motion of positive charges in one direction is equivalent to motion of negative charges in the other direction.

CONDUCTIVITY IN GASES

Ionized gases conduct electric current. Gases which are normally composed almost entirely of neutral molecules may become ionized by high energy radiation, electric fields, and collisions with particles. **Ionized gases**, also known as **plasma**, are the fourth state of matter.

Plasma is the most common phase of matter in the universe. Plasma is commonly found in space. The stars, the streams of ions (that radiate from the stars), and the Van Allen belts around our planet, are examples of this fourth phase of matter. Plasma, or an ionized gas, may consist of positive ions, negative ions, and electrons which are free to move.

POTENTIAL DIFFERENCE (VOLTAGE)

A potential difference is required to create a flow of charge between two points in a conductor. The conductor must form a complete circuit to maintain a flow of charge. Work must be done on charges to move them from one charged object to another charged object. The work per unit charge is called the volt. One volt equals one joule per coulomb.

$$V = \frac{W}{q}$$

Where: V = electric potential measured in volts
W = work measured in joules
q = charge measured in coulombs

OHM'S LAW

At constant temperature, the current in a metallic conductor is directly proportional to the potential difference between its ends. **Ohm's Law** is specific for certain materials and not a general law of electricity.

$$R = \frac{V}{I}$$

Where: V = potential measured in volts
I = current measured in amperes
R = resistance measured in ohms

The resistance is the constant of proportionality in Ohm's Law.

RESISTANCE

Resistance is the ratio of the potential difference across a conductor to the current in it. The *SI* unit of resistance is the ohm. The symbol Ω is used to represent the ohm.

$$\frac{V \text{ (volts)}}{I \text{ (amps)}} = R \ (\Omega)$$

The slope of a potential difference vs. current graph is resistance. The resistance is a constant for a metallic conductor at constant temperature.

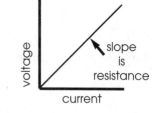

The resistance in a conducting wire can be expressed by the following formula:

$$R = \frac{\rho L}{A}$$

Where: R = resistance in ohms
ρ = resistivity in ohm • m
L = length in meters
A = cross sectional area in square meters

The resistivity of a substance is defined as the resistance of a cube, with edges 1 meter long, at a given temperature (usually 0 degrees or 20 degrees Celsius).

Resistivities at 20° C

Material	Resistivity (Ω • m)
Aluminum	2.82×10^{-8}
Copper	1.72×10^{-8}
Gold	2.44×10^{-8}
Nichrome	1.50×10^{-8}
Silver	1.59×10^{-8}

LAWS OF RESISTANCE

a   **Length (L):** As the length of the wire increases, the resistance also increases.

b   **Cross-sectional area (A):** the wire diameter increases, the resistance decreases by the inverse square rule. Since $A = \pi r^2$, the area increases as the radius is squared (r^2).

c   **Temperature:** As the metal wire temperature increases, the resistance increases. The resistance of nonmetals and solutions usually decreases with increasing temperature. At extremely low temperatures, some materials have no measurable resistance. This phenomenon is known as superconductivity.

REAL WORLD CONNECTIONS
CURRENT INVOLVED IN ELECTRIC SHOCK

The amount of electric current, in amperes, determines the severity of an electric shock. This current is determined by the driving voltage and the resistance of the path which the current follows through the body. Under different circumstances, the same voltage which produces only a mild tingling sensation can be a lethal shock hazard.

Electric Current [1 second contact, in milliamperes]	Physiological Effect
1 mA	Threshold of feeling, tingling sensation.
10-20 mA	"Can't let go!" current - onset of sustained muscular contraction.
100-300 mA	Ventricular fibrillation, fatal if continued.

Will the 120 volt common household voltage produce a dangerous shock? It depends!

If your body resistance is 100,000 ohms, then the current which would flow would be:

$$I = \frac{120 \text{ volts}}{100,000 \ \Omega} = .0012 \text{ A} = 1.2 \text{ mA}$$

This is just about at the threshold of perception, so would produce only a tingle.

But if you have just played a couple of sets of tennis, are sweaty and barefoot, then your resistance to the flow of current might be as low as 1000 ohms. Then the current would be:

$$I = \frac{120 \text{ volts}}{1,000 \ \Omega} = .12 \text{ A} = 120 \text{ mA}$$

This is a lethal shock, capable of producing ventricular fibrillation and death!

The severity of shock from a given source will depend upon its path through your body.

ELECTRIC CIRCUITS

An **electric circuit** is an arrangement where charges can flow in a closed path. The simplest electric circuit consists of a source of potential difference (such as a battery or a power source), a resistor and connecting wires. Scientists and engineers use schematic diagrams to draw electric circuits. The symbols and their meanings are listed in the chart at the right. The diagram below represents a completed circuit:

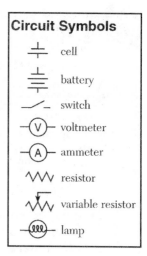

Circuit Symbols

	cell
	battery
	switch
	voltmeter
	ammeter
	resistor
	variable resistor
	lamp

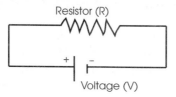

Resistor (R)

Voltage (V)

ENERGY AND POWER

Electric power is the time rate at which electrical energy is expended. The watt is the SI unit of power. It is a derived unit. Power is equal to the product of current and potential difference for any general electrical device. The power unit is the same as used in mechanics (p.165). For ohmic conductors, power can be obtained from the equation:

$$P = VI = I^2R = V^2/R$$

By substituting units into the formula: $\mathbf{P = VI}$

$$P = VI \ \frac{\text{joules}}{\text{coulomb}} \bullet \frac{\text{coulomb}}{\text{second}}$$

$$P = VI \ \frac{\text{joules}}{\text{second}}$$

$$P = \text{watts}$$

The energy used in an electric circuit is the product of the power developed and the time during which the charges flow. The work done (or the energy expended) can be calculated with the following formula:

$$W = Pt = VIt = I^2Rt$$

Where: W = work in joules   I = current in amperes

V = potential difference in volts   t = time in seconds

Since the joule is a small unit of energy, commercial electricity is usually measured in **kW-hr**. One kW-hr = 3.6 x 10⁶ J. Both the watt-sec and the kW-hr are units of energy. A joule is also a watt-second. Energy is a scalar quantity.

REAL WORLD CONNECTIONS

POWER ME UP

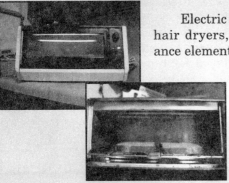

Electric heaters, such as toasters, irons, hair dryers, and heating pads, use resistance elements.

Current is passed through a high resistance heating element of nichrome wire. The heating element is placed on some insulating material such as mica. Where a long length of wire is required to produce the necessary resistance and heat, it may be made in a long coil. Most heating elements draw considerable current, and too many running at the same time can cause the circuit to "trip" (break) or cause a fuse to "blow."

☆ TRY IT

A light bulb operating at 120 volts draws a current of 0.50 amperes for 240 seconds. Determine the power rating of the lamp and the amount of energy used in the 240 seconds.

$$
\begin{aligned}
\text{Power} &= \text{Voltage x Current} \\
\text{P} &= \text{VI} \\
&= (120 \text{ volts})(0.50 \text{ amperes}) \\
&= 60 \text{ volts-amperes} = 60 \text{ watts}
\end{aligned}
$$

Note: One watt equals one joule per second.

$$
\begin{aligned}
\text{Energy} &= \text{Work} = \text{Power x time} \\
&= \frac{60 \text{ joules}}{\text{second}} \text{ x } 240 \text{ ~~seconds~~} \\
&= 14{,}400 \text{ joules}
\end{aligned}
$$

1   Using the relationships above, complete the table below.

Appliance	Power(W)	Voltage(V)	Current(A)	Resistance(Ω)
Hair Dryer	5000	120		
Microwave	900	120		
Curling Iron	1200	120		
Vacuum Cleaner		120	12.5	

REAL WORLD CONNECTIONS

"PIECE DE RESISTANCE"

Extension cords are a simple, but effective solution for temporary connections. But what is the proper choice of cord for the voltage, wattage, and amperage, especially with power tools and appliances? Inadequate extension and power cords are a major cause of fire in the home. For example, a 1,400 watt waffle iron connected to a 18 gauge extension cord could pose a fire hazard as the cord could overheat. The fuse or circuit breaker guarding the circuit would not cut off the power. They are designed only to protect the house wiring.

Why does the wire heat up? In electrical terms the gauge of the wire such as 12, 14, 16, and 18 is inversely proportional to the diameter. The higher the gauge the smaller the cross section of wire increasing the resistance. The resistance of a metal also rises with temperature. Also what about the length? Longer is not better. In a longer wire, electrons encounter and collide with more atoms in their path and therefore encounter more resistance. A too long, thin cord can waste power as the voltage has to travel farther than necessary. A voltage loss of about 2% is typical, but a higher loss can burn out an element or weaken a motor. Be sure the cord is a three prong grounding type.

FOR 120 VOLT APPLIANCES RATED	USE CORD
Up to 6 amps (0-720 watts)................	18 gauge
6-9 amps (720-1060 watts)..................	16 gauge
9-14 amps (1080-1680 watts)..............	14 gauge
14-18 amps (1680-2160 watts)	12 gauge

adapted from: *Readers Digest - Fix It Manual*, page 126

SKILLS 4.1VIII, 4.1IX, 4.1X, 4.1XIII
LAB 18 – OHM, OHM ON THE RANGE
THE PROBLEM

In this experiment, we shall study the way an electric current in a conductor depends on the potential difference. The conductor in the first part of the experiment is a metal wire, so the moving charges will be electrons. The potential difference is measured with a voltmeter, and the current is measured with an ammeter. *Note:* The voltmeter is a high resistance meter which is placed in the circuit in parallel, for measuring potential differences in volts. The ammeter is a low resistance meter which is placed in series in a circuit and measures electric current.

THE CIRCUIT

The circuit diagram at the right shows the conductor (**R**) you are testing, with a voltmeter (**V**) across it to measure the potential difference between ends of the conductor. An ammeter (**A**) is connected so that all the current in the conductor must pass through the ammeter. The rheostat is a variable device to change the potential difference across **R**. Note that you make connection to its sliding contact and to one end. **S** is a switch. If you are using a variable power source, you may eliminate the rheostat. *Note:* **E** is the energy source.

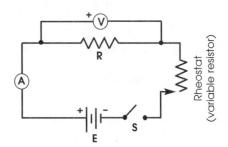

ACTIVITY

Connect the circuit as shown above. Use a conductor made of nichrome wire as **R**. Have the circuit checked by your instructor before closing the switch. Keep the switch closed only long enough to take meter readings. Change the voltage across **R** by adjusting the rheostat. Take a series of readings of current and potential difference. Record your data in a table. Plot a graph from the data.

Change to a different-sized metallic conductor at R and repeat the series of measurements.

Plot graphs of current versus voltage for both cases on the same set of axes. Interpret your graphs. What is the significance of the shape and of the slope? Do the graphs pass through the origin? Do your graphs illustrate Ohm's law? How?

Calculate the resistance of each conductor used (a) from the original data, and (b) from the graphs.

CURRENT IN A DIODE

Repeat the experiment for a non-metallic conductor, such as a germanium or silicon diode. If the diode seems not to be a conductor at all, reverse its connections without making any other changes in the circuit. Again plot and interpret a graph. Does your non-metallic conductor "obey" Ohm's law?

Skills 4.1IXI, 4.1XIII
Lab 19 - Resist Me

The Problem

The purpose of this experiment is to find how the physical character-istics of a metal wire determine its resistance.

Measuring Resistance

The resistance of a wire sample can be calculated from measurements of voltage and current, as in the preceding experiment. Set up a simple circuit as illustrated at the right. In the diagram, **R** is the wire whose resistance is being measured.

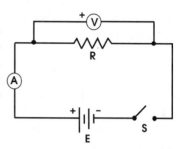

Dependence of Resistance on Length

Measure the resistance of several wires that differ only in length. How does the length of a wire affect its resistance?

How Resistance Depends on Diameter

Measure the resistance of several wires that are identical except for diameter. The thickness of a wire is expressed as a gauge number. A table of gauge numbers is listed at the right. How is the diameter of a wire related to its resistance? Be specific.

Gauge	Diameter (mm)
10	2.588
14	1.628
18	1.024
22	0.6438
26	0.4049
30	0.2546
34	0.1601

The Resistivity of Different Metals

Measure the resistance of two wires that have the same length and gauge number, but are made of different materials. Compute the resis-tivity and compare your results with the known values.

A Practical Problem

Use the principles learned above to design a five-ohm resistor. Use wire of known resistivity and gauge. Then from the resistivity and the cross-section area, calculate the length of wire needed to make a 5-Ω resistor. Measure the resistance of this length of wire and record your result and the percentage error.

A Fun Extension

Determine the resistivity of a Play-doh® wire.

CHAPTER ELEVEN ASSESSMENTS

PART A QUESTIONS

1   Conductivity in metallic solids is due to the presence of free
    (1) nuclei   (2) protons   (3) neutrons   (4) electrons

2   Which of the following is a vector quantity?
    (1) electric charge   (3) electrical potential difference
    (2) electrical resistance   (4) electric field intensity

3   When an incandescent light bulb is turned on, its thin wire filament
    heats up quickly. As the temperature of this wire filament increases,
    its electrical resistance
    (1) decreases   (2) increases   (3) remains the same

4   Which graph best represents the relationship between the resistance
    of a copper wire of uniform cross-sectional area and the wire's length
    at constant temperature?

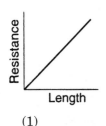 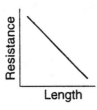 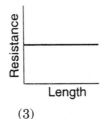 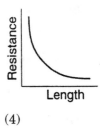

    (1)   (2)   (3)   (4)

5   A copper wire is part of a complete circuit through which current
    flows. Which graph best represents the relationship between the
    wire's area and its resistance?

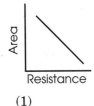 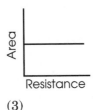 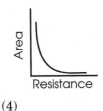

    (1)   (2)   (3)   (4)

6   The table at the right shows the length
    and cross-sectional area of four pieces
    of copper wire at the same temperature.
    Which wire has the highest resistance?
    (1) A   (3) C
    (2) B   (4) D

Wire	Length (m)	Cross-Sectional Area (m²)
A	10	2×10^{-6}
B	10	1×10^{-6}
C	1	2×10^{-6}
D	1	1×10^{-6}

7   Plastic insulation surrounds a wire having diameter d and length l as shown at the right. A decrease in the resistance of the wire would be produced by an increase in the

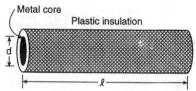

Metal core
Plastic insulation

(1) thickness of the plastic insulation
(2) length l of the wire
(3) diameter d of the wire
(4) temperature of the wire

8   A microwave oven operating at 120 volts is used to heat a hot dog. If the oven draws 12.5 amperes of current for 45 seconds, what is the power dissipated by the oven?

(1) 33 W   (3) 5.4×10^3 W
(2) 1.5×10^3 W   (4) 6.8×10^4 W

9   A metallic conductor obeys Ohm's law. Which graph best represents the relationship between the potential difference (V) across the conductor and the resulting current (I) through the conductor?

(1)   I

(2)   I

(3)   I

(4)   I

10 A simple electrical circuit contains a battery, a light bulb, and a properly connected ammeter. The ammeter has a very low internal resistance because it is connected in

(1) parallel with the bulb to have little effect on the current through the bulb
(2) parallel with the bulb to prevent current flow through the bulb
(3) series with the bulb to have little effect on the current through the bulb
(4) series with the bulb to prevent current flow through the bulb

11 A student uses a voltmeter to measure the potential difference across a circuit resistor. To obtain a correct reading, the student must connect the voltmeter

(1) in parallel with the circuit resistor
(2) in series with the circuit resistor
(3) before connecting the other circuit components
(4) after connecting the other circuit components

12 To increase the brightness of a desk lamp, a student replaces a 60-watt light bulb with a 100-watt bulb. Compared to the 60-watt bulb, the 100-watt bulb has
   (1) less resistance and draws more current
   (2) less resistance and draws less current
   (3) more resistance and draws more current
   (4) more resistance and draws less current

PART B QUESTIONS

13 A current of 3.0 amperes is flowing in a circuit. How much charge passes a given point in the circuit in 30. seconds? [1] _____ C

14 If 1.0 joule of work is required to move a charge of 1.0 coulomb between two points in an electric field, the potential difference between these two points is [1] _____ V

15 An operating lamp draws a current of 0.50 ampere. The amount of charge passing through the lamp in 10. seconds is [1] _____ C

16 A lighting bolt transfers 6.0 coulombs of charge from a cloud to the ground in 2.0 x 10^{-3} second. What is the average current during this event? [1] _____ A

17 The graph at the right represents the relationship between the potential difference across a metal conductor and the current through the conductor at a constant temperature. What is the resistance of the conductor? [1] _____ Ω

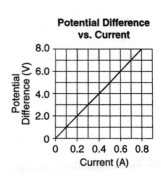

Potential Difference vs. Current

18 The diagram at the right represents a simple electric circuit. How much charge passes through the resistor in 2.0 seconds? [1] _____ C

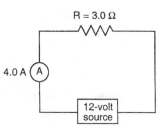

R = 3.0 Ω

4.0 A (A)

12-volt source

19 What is the potential difference across a 2.0-ohm resistor that draws 2.0 coulombs of charge per second? [1] _____ V

20 An electric motor draws 150 amperes of current while operating at 240 volts. What is the power rating of this motor? [1] _____ W

21 The heating element on an electric stove dissipates 4.0×10^2 watts of power when connected to a 120-volt source. What is the electrical resistance of this heating element? [1] _____ Ω

22 A light bulb operating at 120 volts draws a current of 0.50 ampere for 240 seconds. The power rating of the light bulb is [1] _____ W

23 An electric dryer consumes 6.0×10^6 joules of energy when operating at 220 volts for 30. minutes (1,800 seconds). During operation, the dryer draws a current of [1] _____ A

24 An operating 75-watt lamp is connected to a 120-volt outlet. How much electrical energy is used by the lamp in 60. minutes (3600 seconds)? [1] _____ J

25 The diagram at the right represents an electric circuit. The total amount of energy delivered to the resistor in 10. seconds is [1] _____ J

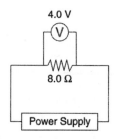

4.0 V

(V)

8.0 Ω

Power Supply

26 A 12-volt automobile battery has 8.4×10^3 coulombs of electric charge. The amount of electrical energy stored in the battery is [1] _____ J

PART C QUESTIONS

Base your answers to questions 27 through 29 on the information below.

A circuit is made with a 5.0–ohm resistor and a 24-volt source of potential difference. A single ammeter is placed in the circuit to read the total current.

5.0 Ω ⟋⋁⋁⋏⟍ | 24-volt source |

20.0 Ω ⟋⋁⋁⋏⟍ ⟋(A)⟍

27 Draw a diagram of this circuit, using the symbols with labels given at the right. [Assume availability of any number of wires of negligible resistance.] [2]

28 Determine the total circuit current. [Show all calculations, including the equation and substitution with units.] [2]

29 Determine the total circuit power. [Show all calculations, including the equation and substitution with units.] [2]

Base your answers to questions 30 through 31 on the information below.

A scientist set up an experiment to collect data about lightning. In one lightning flash, a charge of 25 coulombs was transferred from the base of a cloud to the ground. The scientist measured a potential difference of 1.8×10^6 volts between the cloud and the ground and an average current of 2.0×10^4 amperes.

30 Determine the time interval over which this flash occurred. [Show all calculations, including the equation and substitution with units.] [2]

31 Determine the amount of energy, in joules, involved in the transfer of the electrons from the cloud to the ground. [Show all calculations, including the equation and substitution with units.] [2]

32 A resistor was held at constant temperature in an operating electric circuit. A student measured the current through the resistor and the potential difference across it. The measurements are shown in the data table at the right.

Data Table

Current (A)	Potential Difference (V)
0.010	2.3
0.020	5.2
0.030	7.4
0.040	9.9
0.050	12.7

a Using the information in the data table, construct a graph on the grid, following the directions below: [3]

   1) Mark an appropriate scale on the axis labeled "Current (A)."
   2) Plot the data points for potential difference v. current.
   3) Draw the best-fit line.

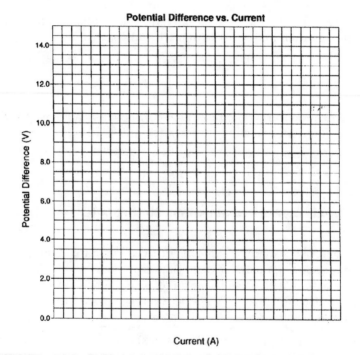

Potential Difference vs. Current

b Using your graph, find the slope of the best-fit line. [Show all calculations, including the equation and substitution with units.] [2]

c What physical quantity does the slope of the graph represent? [1]

CHAPTER 12
SERIES AND PARALLEL CIRCUITS

KEY IDEA **4**
ENERGY EXISTS IN MANY
FORMS, AND WHEN
THESE FORMS CHANGE
ENERGY IS CONSERVED.

PERFORMANCE INDICATOR **4.1** *STUDENTS CAN OBSERVE
AND DESCRIBE TRANSMISSION OF VARIOUS FORMS OF ENERGY.*

CHAPTER 12 – MAJOR UNDERSTANDINGS

☆ 4.1o Circuit components may
be connected in series* or in
parallel*. Schematic diagrams

are used to represent circuits
and circuit elements.

CHAPTER 12
SERIES AND
PARALLEL CIRCUITS

SERIES CIRCUITS

A **series circuit** is one in which there is only one current path. The current is the same in all the components of a series circuit. The sum of the potential drops in a series circuit is equal to the total applied potential difference. The equivalent resistance of the series circuit is equal to the sum of the resistance of its components and can be derived as follows.

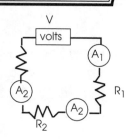

$$V \quad = \quad V_1 + V_2 + V_3 + ...$$

Where: $\quad V \quad = \quad IR$

Thus, $\quad IR_{eq} \quad = \quad I_1 R_1 + I_2 R_2 + I_3 R_3 + ...$

But, $\quad I \quad = \quad I_1 = I_2 = I_3 = ...$

So, $\quad R_{eq} \quad = \quad R_1 + R_2 + R_3 = ...$

$$I \quad = \quad I_1 = I_2 = I_3 = ...$$

$$V \quad = \quad V_1 + V_2 + V_3 = ...$$

$$R_{equivalent} \quad = \quad R_1 + R_2 + R_3 = ...$$

EXAMPLE

Three resistors of 20, 30, and 40 ohms are connected in series to an applied potential of 120 volts.

Calculate:

        a   total resistance
        b   current through each resistor
        c   potential drop across each resistor

Given: $R_1 = 20 \, \Omega$ $R_3 = 40 \, \Omega$
                     $R_2 = 30 \, \Omega$ $V = 120 \, V$

Solution:

a $R_{eq} = R_1 + R_2 + R_3 = 20\,\Omega + 30\,\Omega + 40\,\Omega = 90\,\Omega$

b $I = \dfrac{V}{R_{eq}} = \dfrac{120\,V}{90\,\Omega} = 1.3$ amperes

In the series circuit, current is the same in all parts of the circuit.

$$I = I_1 = I_2 = I_3$$

c $V_1 = I_1R_1 = (1.3\,A)(20\,\Omega) = 26\,V$
$V_2 = I_2R_2 = (1.3\,A)(30\,\Omega) = 39\,V$
$V_3 = I_3R_3 = (1.3\,A)(40\,\Omega) = 52\,V$

In a series circuit, voltage total is equal to the sum of the voltage drops across each resistor.

Check: $V = V_1 + V_2 + V_3$
$= 26\,V + 39\,V + 52\,V = 117\,V$
$V = 120\,V$

REAL WORLD CONNECTIONS
THE TINY LIFE-SAVING SENSOR

If too much current flows through a wire, it can get hot enough to set fire to surrounding materials. Fuses and circuit breakers protect against this by cutting off power to a circuit that is drawing excessive current. Circuit breakers work like thermostats, when they get hot they shut off. Fuses "blow" when a metal strip overheats and melts. The fuse and circuit breakers protect the wiring in the building. To protect a person against lethal shocks from leakage of current, a GFI outlet is installed. GFI, or ground fault interrupter, senses currents as low as 0.005 ampere. It senses when some of the current flowing out of one side of the outlet is not returning to the other side of the outlet. If the current isn't coming back, then the leakage could flow through your body to ground. The usual cause of leakage current in appliances or tools is a breakdown of insulation between the current carrying wire and the frame of the electrical device. Since water is such a good conductor, GFI outlets should be used in wet locations, such as the kitchen, bathroom, or outdoors.

Adapted from *Readers Digest Fix it Manual*, 1977. Pg 127

PARALLEL CIRCUITS

A parallel circuit is one in which there is more than one current path. The potential drop is the same across each branch of a parallel circuit. The total current in a parallel circuit is equal to the sum of the branch currents. The reciprocal of the equivalent resistance of a parallel circuit is equal to the sum of the reciprocals of the branch resistances and can be derived as follows:

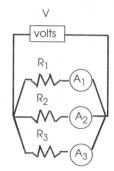

$$I = I_1 + I_2 + I_3 + ...$$

Where: $\quad I = V/R$

Thus, $\quad \dfrac{V}{R_{eq}} = \dfrac{V_1}{R_1} + \dfrac{V_2}{R_2} + \dfrac{V_3}{R_3} + ...$

But, $\quad V = V_1 = V_2 = V_3 = ...$

So, $\quad \dfrac{1}{R_{eq}} = \dfrac{1}{R_1} + \dfrac{1}{R_2} + \dfrac{1}{R_3} + ...$

$$V = V_1 = V_2 = V_3 = ...$$

$$I = I_1 + I_2 + I_3 = ...$$

$$\dfrac{1}{R_{equiv.}} = \dfrac{1}{R_1} + \dfrac{1}{R_2} + \dfrac{1}{R_3} + ...$$

Example: Three resistors of 20., 30., and 40. ohms are connected in parallel to an applied potential of 120 volts.

Calculate: a the total resistance
 b the potential difference across each resistor
 c the current through each resistor

Given: $R_1 = 20. \, \Omega \quad R_3 = 40. \, \Omega$
 $R_2 = 30. \, \Omega \quad V = 120 \, V$

Find: a R_{total}
 b V_1, V_2, V_3
 c I_1, I_2, I_3

Solution:
 a
$$\dfrac{1}{R_{eq}} = \dfrac{1}{R_1} + \dfrac{1}{R_2} + \dfrac{1}{R_3}$$

$$\frac{1}{R_{eq}} = \frac{1}{20\Omega} + \frac{1}{30\Omega} + \frac{1}{40\Omega}$$

$$\frac{1}{R_{eq}} = \frac{6}{120\Omega} + \frac{4}{120\Omega} + \frac{3}{120\Omega}$$

$$\frac{1}{R_{eq}} = \frac{13}{120\Omega} \ , \ R_{eq} = \frac{120\Omega}{13} = 9.2\ \Omega$$

b   In the parallel circuit, voltage is the same across each resistor in the circuit.

$$V = V_1 = V_2 = V_3 = 120\ V$$

c

$$I_1 = \frac{V_1}{R_1} = \frac{120\ volts}{20.\ \Omega} = 6.0\ amp$$

$$I_2 = \frac{V_2}{R_2} = \frac{120\ volts}{30.\ \Omega} = 4.0\ amp$$

$$I_3 = \frac{V_3}{R_3} = \frac{120\ volts}{40.\ \Omega} = 3.0\ amp$$

Note: In parallel circuits, the sum of the currents in the resistors is equal to the total current from the source

$$I = I_1 + I_2 + I_3$$

$$= 6.0\ A + 4.0\ A + 3.0\ A$$

$$I = 13\ A$$

Check: $$I = \frac{V}{R_{eq}} = \frac{120\ V}{9.2\ \Omega} = 13\ A$$

KIRCHHOFF'S LAWS

First Law – Conservation of Charge. The sum entering any current junction, is equal to the sum leaving. *A* represents a junction in an electric circuit. Nine amperes are entering *A*; therefore, according to Kirchhoff's First Law, nine amperes must come out of junction *A*.

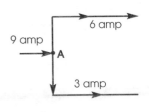

REAL WORLD CONNECTIONS
TINY NANOWIRE – MICROCIRCUITS

Millions of transistors, resistors, and conductors are assembled by a photographic process, in three dimensions. How small can you make a wire which still conducts? A 16 gauge copper wire is about 2 mm in diameter and can conduct 6 amps. In per-

spective, the human hair is 100 μm or 100,000 nm in diameter. Making micron size wires (1 μm or 1,000 nm) a factor of 100 or smaller than human hair involves the $300 billion semiconductor industry. The process of semiconductor lithography starts with a wafer of silicon. A series of circuit designs, depositions, ion implantations, and etching,

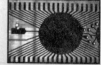

which is all done through a stencil, forms a microcircuit capable of storing and retrieving millions of bits of information.

©PhotoDisc

The microchip uses an electric circuit of micron wires made from aluminum or copper to connect the chip to a external circuit. Microminiaturization continues to drive circuits with wires as small as 100 nm to the limit of current capacity of copper – a limit of 1 million A/cm² (scales down with area). New materials made of single walled nanotubes of carbon, called Bucky tubes (1 nm in diameter), are being investigated to allow for better current carrying capacity for (billion A/cm²) future circuits of 10 nm in size.

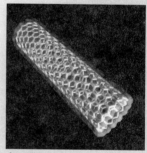

Source: *Scientific American*, Dec 2000 p.69

http://www.chem.ox.ac.uk/mom/
buckytubes/buckytubes.html
© Copyright 1995-2002
University of Oxford

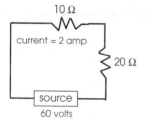

Second Law – Conservation of Energy.
The algebraic sum of all the potential drops, and the applied voltage around a complete circuit is equal to zero. According to Kirchhoff's Second Law, the applied voltage (+60 volts) minus the potential drops around the complete circuit, must equal zero.

60 volts – (20 Ω x 2 amp) – (10 Ω x 2 amp) = 0
60 volts – 40 volts – 20 volts = 0

Skills 4.1xiii, 4.1viii, 4.1xii
Lab 20 – Series and Parallel Circuits

Background
The components of a circuit can be connected in series or in parallel. In a series circuit, the parts are connected end-to-end. When elements are connected in parallel, one bridges the other. An ammeter is always connected in series. A voltmeter, on the other hand, is always connected in parallel with the part of the circuit across which it is measuring a potential difference.

The Problem
The plan of this experiment is to study series and parallel circuits. In each case, you will measure the current in each component, the potential difference across each component, and the current and potential difference for the entire circuit. The final result for each part of the experiment is a comparison between the circuit resistance as computed from your current and voltage measurements and the circuit resistance computed from the known values of the individual resistors.

Preparing for the Experiment
Select three resistors or light bulbs of different resistances. The resistance of each must be known in advance. If the resistors are not labeled, measure the resistance of each by the voltmeter-ammeter method. Set up an appropriate data table to record all measurements. Compare your actual and computed results.

Series Circuit
Connect two of the resistors in series. Measure the current in each, the voltage across each, and the applied voltage. How are the separate voltages across the resistors related to the applied voltage? How is the current through the source related to the currents in the individual resistors? Calculate the circuit resistance from your measurements and compare it with the resistance computed from the known values of the resistors.

Parallel Circuit
Connect two of the resistors in parallel. Measure the current in each, the total circuit current, and the applied voltage. Again, state the relationship of the applied voltage and current to these quantities measured for the separate resistors. Calculate the combined resistance from your measurements and compare it with the resistance computed from the known resistances of the components.

☆ Try It

Base your answers to questions 1 through 3 on the information below.

> You are given a 12-volt battery, ammeter **A**, voltmeter **V**, resistor R_1, and resistor R_2. Resistor R_2 has a value of 3.0 ohms.

1 Using appropriate symbols from the *Reference Tables for Physical Setting/Physics*, draw and label a complete circuit showing:

   a   resistors R_1 and R_2 connected in parallel with the battery [1]

   b   the ammeter connected to measure the current through resistor R_1, only [1]

   c   the voltmeter connected to measure the potential drop across resistor R_1 [1]

2 If the total current in the circuit is 6.0 amperes, determine the equivalent resistance of the circuit. [1]

3 If the total current in the circuit is 6.0 amperes, determine the resistance of resistor R_1. [Show all calculations, including the equation and substitution with units.] [2]

CHAPTER TWELVE ASSESSMENTS

PART A QUESTIONS

1 Which diagram below correctly shows currents traveling near junction *P* in an electric circuit?

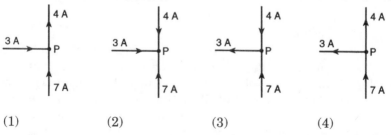

   (1)   (2)   (3)   (4)

2 An electric circuit contains an operating heating element and a lit lamp. Which statement best explains why the lamp remains lit when the heating element is removed from the circuit?
   (1) The lamp has less resistance than the heating element.
   (2) The lamp has more resistance than the heating element.
   (3) The lamp and the heating element were connected in series.
   (4) The lamp and the heating element were connected in parallel.

3 In which pair of circuits shown below could the readings of voltmeters V_1 and V_2 and ammeter A be correct?

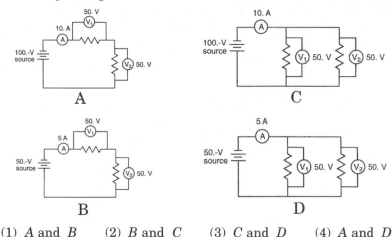

   (1) A and B (2) B and C (3) C and D (4) A and D

PART B QUESTIONS

4 The diagram at the right shows two resistors connected in series to a 20.-volt battery. If the current through the 5.0-ohm resistor is 1.0 ampere, the current through the 15.0-ohm resistor is [1] _____ A

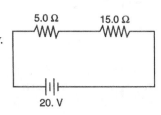

5 The diagram at the right shows a circuit with three resistors. What is the resistance of resistor R_3? [1] _____ Ω

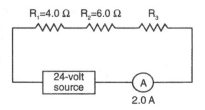

6 The diagram at the right shows three resistors, R_1, R_2, and R_3, connected to a 12-volt battery. If voltmeter V_1 reads 3 volts and voltmeter V_2 reads 4 volts, what is the potential drop across resistor R_3?
[1] _____ V

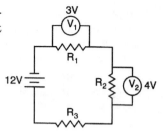

7 Identical resistors R_1 and R_2 have an equivalent resistance of 6 ohms when connected in the circuit shown at the right. The resistance of R_1 is [1]_____ Ω

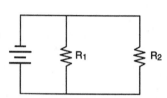

8 In the parallel circuit at the right, ammeter A measures the current supplied by the 110-volt source. The current measured by ammeter A is
[1] _____ A

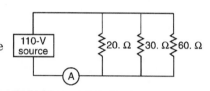

9 Three ammeters are placed in a circuit as shown at the right. If A_1 reads 5.0 amperes and A_2 reads 2.0 amperes, what does A_3 read?
[1] _____ A

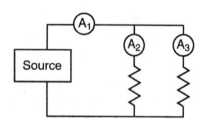

Base your answers to questions 10 and 11 on the diagram at the right, which shows two resistors connected in parallel across a 6.0-volt source.

10 The equivalent resistance of the two resistors is [1] _____ Ω

11 Compared to the power dissipated in the 1.0-ohm resistor, the power dissipated in the 3.0-ohm resistor is [1] _____

PART C QUESTIONS

Base your answers to questions 12 and 13 on the information and diagram at the right.

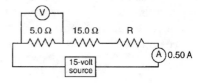

A 5.0-ohm resistor, a 15.0-ohm resistor, and an unknown resistor, R, are connected as shown with a 15-volt source. The ammeter reads a current of 0.50 ampere.

12 Determine the reading of the voltmeter connected across the 5.0-ohm resistor. [Show all calculations, including the equation and substitution with units.] [2]

13 Determine the total electrical energy used in the circuit in 600. seconds. [Show all calculations, including the equation and substitution with units.] [2]

14 Two resistors are connected in parallel to a 12-volt battery. One resistor, R_1, has a value of 18 ohms. The other resistor, R_2, has a value of 9 ohms. The total current in the circuit is 2 amperes. A student wishes to measure the current through R_1, and the potential difference across R_2.

    a Using the symbols from the *Reference Tables* for a battery, an ammeter, a voltmeter, and resistors, draw and label a circuit diagram that will enable the student to make the desired measurements. [2]

    b Calculate the value of the current in resistor R_1. [Show all calculations, including equations and substitutions with units.] [2]

Question 15 on next page

15 Using the values given in the chart below and the diagrams of the circuits, complete the table. Determine the current through the resistor, the voltage across the resistor, and the power developed by the resistor. [3]

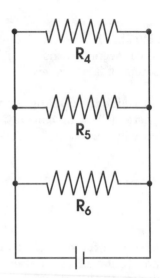

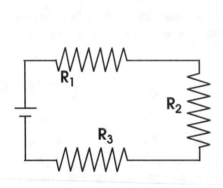

Series Circuit
Voltage Total = 195 v

Parallel Circuit
Voltage Total = 360 v

	Series			Parallel		
Resistor	R_1	R_2	R_3	R_4	R_5	R_6
Resistance Ω	13	15	11	45	180	36
Current A						
Voltage V						
Power W						

Chapter **13**
Magnetism

Key Idea **4**
Energy exists in many forms, and when these forms change energy is conserved.

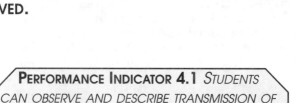

> **Performance Indicator 4.1** *Students can observe and describe transmission of various forms of energy.*

Chapter 13 – Major Understandings

☆ 4.1k Moving electric charges produce magnetic fields. The relative motion between a conductor and a magnetic field may produce a potential difference in the conductor.

CHAPTER 13
MAGNETISM

MAGNETIC FORCE

Magnetic force is a force that exists between charges in motion. All magnetic properties of any kind of material are due to the electrons orbiting the nucleus of the atoms. The electrons generate **magnetic fields** by spinning on their axis.

All substances exhibit magnetic properties. A measurement of the field intensity per area is called the **flux density**. Diamagnetic substances reduce the flux density; **paramagnetic** and **ferromagnetic** increase the flux density. **Permeability** is the property of a material which changes the flux density in a magnetic field from its value in a vacuum.

The modern theory of magnetism indicates that ferromagnetic materials such as iron, nickel, and cobalt tend to align the atoms in clusters, called **domains**. Within a domain the magnetic fields produce a relatively strong field, but normally, the axes of the domains are randomly arranged so the fields cancel each other out. These fields are due to atomic currents caused by spinning electrons. In a magnetic field, some atoms line up with the field causing some domains to grow larger at the expense of others getting smaller. This results in boundary shifts between these domains. When some domains are enlarged in respect to others a net field is produced and the object is said to be magnetized. If the boundaries persist after removal from the field, the substance is a permanent magnet. Certain natural substances, such as magnetite, are magnets.

MAGNETIC FIELDS

A magnetic field is a region where magnetic force may be detected. It can be near a magnet, or near a current carrying wire. The direction of a magnetic field is, according to convention, the direction in which the N - pole of a compass would point in the field.

The magnetic field around a bar magnet is mapped by drawing magnetic **flux lines** (lines of force). The flux lines are imaginary and always form closed paths. The direction of the magnetic field at any point is tangent to the field line at that point. The flux density is measured in the units of N/amp•m or tesla.

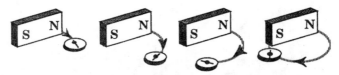

The SI unit for flux is the weber. The magnetic lines never cross each other. The field is strongest near the poles when the lines of force are closest together. The compass will point from the N (North) pole and towards the S (South) pole. Inside the magnet the lines of force go from south to north. If a magnet were broken into pieces, each piece would have a north and south pole.

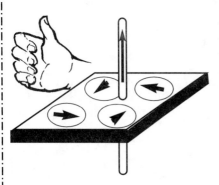

Note: Moving electric charges produce magnetic fields. The "hand rules" are a convenient way to determine the direction of these fields. If conventional current is used, the student should use the right hand rules. If electron current is used, the left hand should be used. Since most textbooks and major national tests refer to conventional current, this review book uses the right hand rules.

A magnetic field also exists around a current carrying wire. Compasses surrounding the wire would point in a circle. The magnetic field direction can be determined by the first right-hand rule for conventional current. (Electron flow - use left hand)

The **first right-hand rule** states that when you grab a current-carrying wire with your right hand, such that the thumb points in the direction of the current flow, the curved fingers will point to the direction of the magnetic field.

Using the first right-hand rule, one can determine the direction of the field around a **loop** of current carrying wire. The field is such that the faces of the loop show polarity. When the number of loops is increased, a **solenoid** is formed. The lines of magnetic flux around a solenoid emerge from the north pole of the solenoid and enter the south pole. Inside the solenoid, the lines of force are nearly parallel to its axis and perpendicular to its faces.

A magnetic field exists around a current carrying coil. The direction of the north Pole of a solenoid can also be determined by the second right-hand rule.

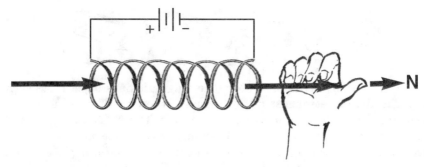

The **second right-hand rule** states if you grab the solenoid with your right hand so that your fingers point in the direction of the current flow, your thumb will point to the N-pole. A solenoid consists of many coils wrapped around a core (which could be air), and is also known as an electromagnet. The magnetic field near a current carrying coil can be made stronger by:

a inserting an iron core (increasing permeability)
b increasing the current in the coil
c increasing the number of turns

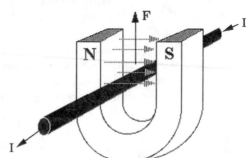

Direction of Force on a Wire Carrying Traditional Current in a Magnetic field

A magnetic field exerts a force on any moving charge. When a current carrying wire is placed in a magnetic field, a force is exerted on the conductor, (if the conducting wire is not parallel to the magnetic flux).

The force is perpendicular to both the field and the current and can be determined by the **third right-hand rule**. Placing the right hand so the thumb points to the direction (I) of the conventional current flow, the fingers point in the direction (B) of the magnetic flux (N to S), and the palm of the hand (F) indicates the direction of the force.

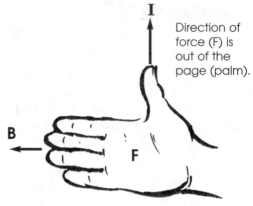

Direction of force (F) is out of the page (palm).

An **X** indicates that current (or magnetic field) is traveling *into* the page. Whereas, a • (dot) indicates *out of* the page. The magnetic field generated by the current in the wire is circular. Below the wire the magnetic flux lines add to each other. Above the wire the fields subtract, causing a weaker field above the wire than below the wire. Therefore the wire would move down.

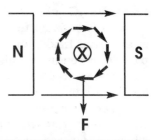

 REAL WORLD CONNECTIONS

HOW DOES MRI WORK?

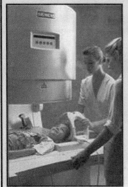

Because humans are mostly water, the frequency selected for the MRI is determined for water. Magnetic Resonance Imaging works because the single largest constituent of the human body - about 75% - is water. A molecule of water is composed of two hydrogen atoms and one oxygen atom. The nucleus of each hydrogen atom consists of a single proton. Under normal conditions, these protons are constantly spinning, which generates a a tiny magnetic field around them.

Normally, this magnetic field is randomly orientated (i.e. has no particular overall direction). Placing a person inside an MRI scanner, however - which is essentially a very large powerful magnet - makes the protons in their body line up either with or against the direction of the scanner's own strong magnetic field

MRI uses radio waves to make an image. Short bursts – or pulses – of radio waves are directed at the area being examined through a special antenna (called a coil). This knocks the protons off-balance, causing them to flip their orientation.

When the pulse is turned off, the protons return, or relax, to their original positions. As they do so, they emit weak radio signals (the MR signal) of a particular frequency, which are analyzed by a computer and combined to create a series of cross-sectional images –called scans – in any orientation.

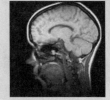

Water content differs in healthy and diseased tissue. The intensity of the MR signal from a particular body tissue is related to the density of protons in the tissue, and therefore to the water content of the tissue. The more water a tissue contains, the stronger its MR signal and the better the resulting image, which is why human (and animal) bodies are ideal candidates for MRI scanning. Different tissues contain variable amounts of water, and diseased or damaged tissue usually contains more water than healthy tissue.

Magnetic Field

It is convenient to describe the interaction between charges by means of electrical fields, and the interaction between currents flowing in two parallel wires by defining a magnetic field. We can think of one of the currents as producing a magnetic field, and the field as exerting a force on the other current. The magnetic field is measured by the force it exerts on a current. The direction of the force depends on the direction of the current, but the magnitude of the force depends on the angle at which the wire crosses the B field.

☆ The force depends on the direction of the current and varies to a maximum value. The strength of the magnetic field is defined as:

$$B = \frac{F_{max}}{IL}$$

Where: **F** = maximum force measured in newtons
           I = current in amperes
           L = length of wire in magnetic field
           B = strength of field, known as magnetic flux density

The flux density (**B**) is the number of flux lines per unit area and is proportional to the intensity of the field. Flux density is a vector quantity. The magnetic field (**B**) is commonly measured in **newtons/amp•m**, or **tesla**. Flux density between the poles of magnets is often given in Gauss, as

$$1.0 \text{ tesla} = 1.0 \times 10^4 \text{ Gauss}$$

The field strength of magnets is commonly measured in webers/meter², newtons/amp•m, or tesla.

$$B = \frac{\text{webers}}{\text{meter}^2} = \frac{\text{newtons}}{\text{amp}\bullet\text{m}} = \text{tesla}$$

Flux can be calculated from flux density.

$$\text{Flux} = \text{BA} = \text{Webers}$$

Where: **B** is the magnetic density (magnetic field intensity)
           A is the area

The magnetic field strength **B** is analogous to the electric field strength **E** and the gravitational field strength **g**. All of these fields are vector quantities, which means that they have magnitude and direction.

Gravitational field strength (g) = force per unit mass
Electric field strength (E) = force per unit charge
Magnetic field strength (B) = force per unit current element

Two current carrying wires exert a force on each other through their magnetic fields. If the currents are flowing in the same direction, the wires attract each other. Currents flowing in the opposite direction of two parallel wires cause them to repel each other.

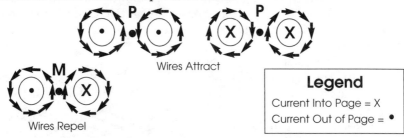

Wires Attract

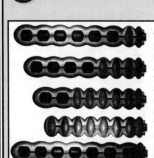

Wires Repel

Legend
Current Into Page = X
Current Out of Page = •

At point **P** in both examples above, the fields are subtractive. The wires move together or attract each other. At point **M**, the fields add together and the wires move apart.

The definition of an ampere is based on the strength of the force between two parallel wires. An ampere is that amount of unvarying current, which, if present in each of two parallel conductors of infinite lengths and one meter apart in free space, will produce a force of exactly 2×10^{-7} newtons per meter of length.

🌎 REAL WORLD CONNECTIONS

Caterpillars are made of rubber capsules with iron, magnetic suspensions. Attracted to a magnetic field, the capsules bulge and shorten, grabbing the sides of a tight space. Past the magnetic field, the capsules "spring back" to normal and the caterpillar moves ahead with it's life saving sensors.

MAGNETIC CATERPILLAR
A magnetic caterpillar to search for disaster victims has been demonstrated by an engineer at Akita Prefectural University in Japan. In the future, the magnetic caterpillar could find earthquake , mud slide, avalanche and other disaster victims because of the way it burrows through debris. Just a few centimeters wide and equipped with a nose camera the remote controlled searcher relies on a coaxial magnetic field to distort magnetic fluids inside the elastic rubber tube to propel it through tiny crevices that would thwart present search robots. To make the caterpillar move forward, the magnetic field is applied backwards from the head to the tail and the magnetic field attracts the magnetic fluid inducing a bulging which constricts the frontal portion. As the magnetic field repeats its cycle, the caterpillar springs forward as the magnetic fluid reconfigures.

Source: Catherine Zandonella, *New Scientist*, Nov, 2001, page 22

ELECTROMAGNETIC INDUCTION

If a straight conductor is moved across a magnetic field, the charge in the conductor will be acted upon by a magnetic force. This force will tend to move the charge along the conductor from one end to another. As the motion of the electrons cause an excess of negative charge at one end and a deficiency of charge at the other end, a potential difference is established between the ends of the conductor. This effect can also be observed if the conductor is stationary and the field is moving.

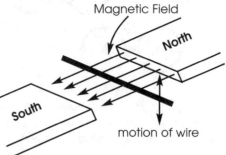

Magnetic Field

North

South

motion of wire

Therefore, any time a conductor cuts lines of flux, a potential difference is induced in the conductor. If the conductor is connected to a circuit, a current will flow around the circuit. The direction of the induced current is in such a direction that its magnetic field opposes that of the field that induced it. **Lenz's Law** predicts the direction of the induced Emf. Remembering that nothing is "free," the work done and the electrical energy produced is an example of conservation of energy.

THE GENERATOR PRINCIPLE

A conducting loop rotating in a uniform magnetic field experiences a continual change in the total number of flux lines crossing the loop. This change induces a potential across the ends of the loop, which alternates in direction and varies in magnitude, between zero and a maximum. When the plane of the loop is perpendicular to the field, the induced potential is zero. When the plane of the loop is parallel to the field, the induced potential is a maximum.

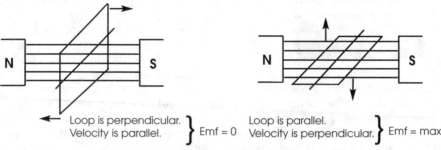

Loop is perpendicular.
Velocity is parallel. } Emf = 0   Loop is parallel.
Velocity is perpendicular. } Emf = max

The magnitude of the induced potential is proportional to the component of the velocity perpendicular to the field and the intensity of the magnetic field. When the loop is part of a complete circuit, the induced potential causes a current in the loop. Since the induced potential is alternating, the current is an alternating current. An **alternating current** is a current that reverses its direction with regular frequency.

A **transformer** makes use of the ferromagnetic properties of an iron core to efficiently raise or lower AC voltages. It cannot increase power so that if the voltage is raised, the current is proportionally lowered and vice versa.

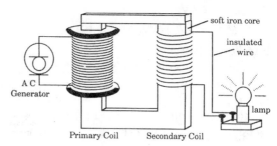

The power in equals the power out in an ideal transformer. Transformers must be powered by alternating current in the primary in order to induce a field and a current in the secondary coil. There are two basic types of transformers. A step-up transformer takes a low voltage from the power plant and raises it to a high voltage for transmission. Transmitting power at high voltage reduces energy loss in the wires. Along the way to your house and perhaps even on your street, you will see a step-down transformer. This takes a high voltage from the line current and lowers it to 120 volts for the house current. Transformers are used inside the house to further lower voltage for some appliances.

ELECTROMAGNETIC RADIATION

As alternating voltages and current are produced in rotating loops by electromagnetic induction, charges are moved back and forth in the conductor. This motion means that the charges are accelerating alternately in opposite directions. Oscillating charges produce electric and magnetic fields that radiate outward in the form of waves. This combined electric and magnetic wave is called an **electromagnetic wave** and is propagated by interchanging electric and magnetic fields. The waves make up the **electromagnetic spectrum**. *Note:* The electromagnetic spectrum is illustrated on page 344.

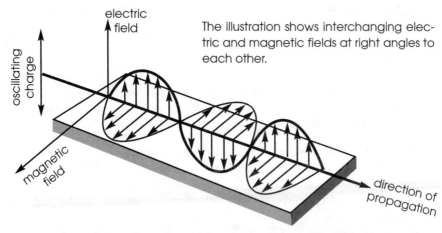

The illustration shows interchanging electric and magnetic fields at right angles to each other.

SKILL 4.1xv
LAB 21 – MAGNETIC FIELDS

BACKGROUND

The region in which a magnet experiences a force is called a magnetic field. A magnetic compass is a small magnet pivoted to swing in a horizontal plane. The direction of a magnetic field is taken as the direction of the force on a north pole. A compass in a magnetic field will turn so that its north pole points in the direction of the field.

THE PROBLEM

We shall use a small compass first to map the magnetic field in the vicinity of a single permanent magnet. The compass will then be used to compare the forces on its north pole caused by two permanent magnets at a point in the field of both. Finally, we shall determine the distance at which a bar magnet exerts the same force on a compass as does the magnetic field of Earth.

MAPPING THE FIELD OF A BAR MAGNET

Place one of the bar magnets flat in the center of a fresh page of your laboratory notebook. Mark its outline and label the N and S poles. Use the compass to map the field of the magnet. Make a dot on the page at each end of the compass needle. Next, move the compass away from the magnet until its inner point is just over the outer of the two dots. Make another dot at the other end of the needle. Continue moving the compass and making dots until you reach either the edge of the page or the other pole of the magnet.

Connect the dots with a smooth line and add an arrow head to indicate the field of direction. This line is called a magnetic line of force. Draw other lines of force until you have a uniform picture of the field of the magnet.

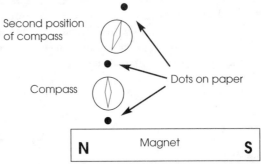

Finding the force in the vicinity of two unlike poles – On the top half of a piece of paper place two magnets as shown in Diagram 1 above. Outline the magnets and identify their poles.

Mark any point **P** as shown. Using the magnets one at a time (moving the other some distance away), find the field direction at **P** (with a compass as in the mapping exercise on page 252) caused by one magnet and then by the other magnet. Next, place both magnets on the page and find the direction of the *resultant* field.

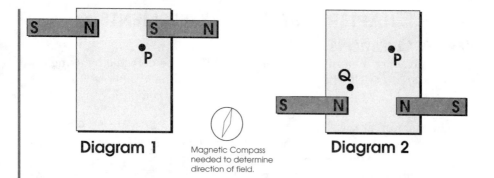

Diagram 1

Magnetic Compass needed to determine direction of field.

Diagram 2

The three directions you have determined can be used to draw the sides and diagonal of a vector parallelogram. Use any convenient length for the diagonal representing the resultant of the two fields and construct the parallelogram. Compare the forces exerted by the two magnets on the N pole of the compass needle at *P*, expressing the comparison as a ratio. Why are the two forces not the same?

Finding the force near two like poles – Repeat this same procedure with the magnets placed as shown in Diagram 2 above. Find the directions of the two separate fields at *Q* and then find the resultant direction when both magnets are in place. Compare the resultant forces determined here with those found in question 2.

Comparing Earth's field with a magnetic field – Devise and carry out an experiment for finding how far a magnet must be located from a compass so that the force the magnet exerts on the N pole of the compass needle is the same in magnitude of the force exerted by the horizontal component of Earth's field. Note that the field of Earth has been present in all your preceding work. If you did not move your paper while you were plotting the field of the single magnet, you may be able to see the effect of Earth's field in that diagram.

What modifications would you make in that part of the experiment in order to show the influence of Earth's field on a map of the field of a permanent magnet? Try out your predictions.

☆ TRY IT

1   While doing this lab, a student got the following pattern from a single magnet. Explain what would cause this pattern.

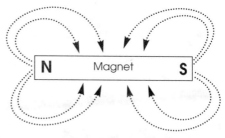

CHAPTER THIRTEEN ASSESSMENTS

PART A QUESTIONS

1   The presence of a uniform magnetic field may be detected by using a
(1) stationary charge   (3) beam of neutrons
(2) small mass   (4) magnetic compass

2   The diagram at the right shows a compass
placed near the north pole, **N**, of a bar magnet.
Which diagram best represents the position of
the needle of the compass as it responds to the
magnetic field of the bar magnet?

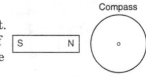

(1) S   (2) N   N◄●►S (3)   S◄●►N (4)

3   The field around a permanent magnet is caused by motions of
(1) nucleons   (2) protons   (3) neutrons   (4) electrons

4   The diagram at the right shows the
magnetic field that results when a piece
of iron is placed between unlike magnetic poles. At which point is the magnetic
field strength greatest?

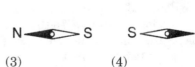

(1) A   (2) B   (3) C   (4) D

5   The diagram at the right represents
magnetic lines of force within a region of
space. The magnetic field is strongest at
point

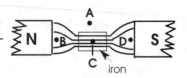

(1) A   (3) C
(2) B   (4) D

6   What is the direction of the magnetic field near the center of the current-carrying wire loop shown in the diagram at the right?

(1) into the page   (3) to the left
(2) out of the page   (4) to the right

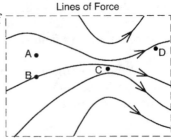

7   The magnetic lines of force near a long straight current-carrying wire are
    (1) straight lines parallel to the wire
    (2) straight lines perpendicular to the wire
    (3) circles in a plane perpendicular to the wire
    (4) circles in a plane parallel to the wire

8   The speaker in the diagram at the right makes use of a current-carrying coil of wire. The N-pole of the coil would be closest to

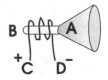

    (1) A   (3) C
    (2) B   (4) D

9   Two solenoids are wound on soft iron cores and connected to batteries as shown in the diagram at the right. When switches S_1 and S_2 are closed, the solenoids

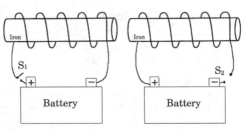

    (1) repel because of adjacent north poles
    (2) repel because of adjacent south poles
    (3) attract because of adjacent north and south poles
    (4) neither attract nor repel

10 The diagram at the right represents lines of magnetic flux within a region of space. The magnetic field strength is greatest at point

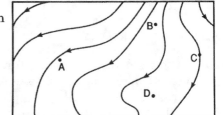

    (1) A
    (2) B
    (3) C
    (4) D

11 Which diagram correctly shows a magnetic field configuration?

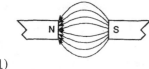

(1)

(3)

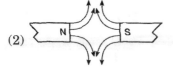

(2)

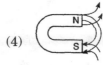

(4)

12 A magnetic field will be produced by
   (1) moving electrons   (3) stationary protons
   (2) moving neutrons   (4) stationary ions

13 In which diagram of a current-carrying solenoid is the magnetic field correctly represented?

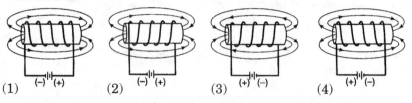

   (1) (−) (+)   (2) (−) (+)   (3) (+) (−)   (4) (+) (−)

14 An electron moving in a uniform magnetic field experiences the maximum magnetic force when the angle between the direction of the electron's motion and the direction of the magnetic field is
   (1) 0°   (2) 45°   (3) 90°   (4) 180°

15 An electron traveling at a speed (v) in the plane of this paper enters a uniform magnetic field. Which diagram best represents the condition under which the electron will experience the greatest magnetic force as it enters the magnetic field?

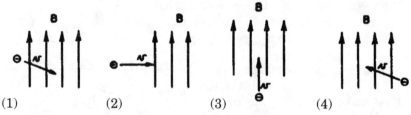

   (1)   (2)   (3)   (4)

16 If a charged particle moving through a magnetic field experiences a magnetic force, the angle between the magnetic field and the force exerted on the particle is
   (1) 0°   (2) 45°   (3) 90°   (4) 180°

PART B QUESTIONS

17 A magnet has been broken into two pieces as shown in the diagram at the right. Identify the position of the North and South Poles of each piece after the break occurred.

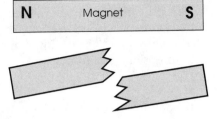

Base your answers to questions 18 and 19 on the diagram at the right which shows steel paper clips A and B attached to a string which is attached to a table. The clips remain suspended beneath a magnet.

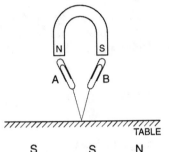

18 Which diagram best represents the induced polarity of the paper clips?

(1) (2) (3) (4)

19 As the magnet is lifted, the paper clips begin to fall as a result of
   (1) an increase in the potential energy of the clip
   (2) an increase in the gravitational field strength near the magnet
   (3) a decrease in the magnetic properties of the clip
   (4) a decrease in the magnetic field strength near the clip

20 Draw the magnetic lines of force between the two North poles. [1]

21 What causes magnetism in materials? [State your answer in a complete sentence.] [1]

22 The North Pole of a magnet picks up a nail. From this single observation, can you say that the nail is magnetic? Explain your answer. [1]

PART C QUESTIONS

23 Using a compass, a magnet, and a meter stick, devise a method to determine the relative strength of Earth's magnetic field. List your procedures and show sample data for this experiment. What assumptions did you have to make? [2]

24 In the lab, the student observed the compass reading as shown to the right. Based on this observation, label the bar magnets as North or South Poles. [2]

25 Refer to the MRI reading on page 247 to answer the following questions (*a* through *c*).

   a   What is the effect of a strong magnet on human tissue? [1]

   b   When do the protons emit an MR signal? [1]

   c   Why is the MRI used to identify diseased tissue? [1]

26 Using your knowledge of physics, write a short paragraph for each question (*a* through *c*), being sure to use complete sentences.

   a   Why is energy transmitted at high voltage and low amperage? [1]

   b   What does a "step-up transformer" do? [1]

   c   Why is it that a transformer cannot be powered by a direct current (DC) battery? [1]

CHAPTER 14
WAVE PROPERTIES

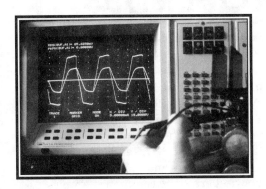

KEY IDEA 4

ENERGY EXISTS IN MANY FORMS, AND WHEN THESE FORMS CHANGE ENERGY IS CONSERVED.

PERFORMANCE INDICATOR 4.3 *STUDENTS CAN EXPLAIN VARIATIONS IN WAVELENGTH AND FREQUENCY IN TERMS OF THE SOURCE OF THE VIBRATIONS THAT PRODUCE THEM, E.G., MOLECULES, ELECTRONS, AND NUCLEAR PARTICLES.*

CHAPTER 14 – MAJOR UNDERSTANDINGS

☆ 4.3a An oscillating system produces waves. The nature of the system determines the type of wave produced.

☆ 4.3b Waves carry energy and information without transferring mass. This energy may be carried by pulses or periodic waves.

☆ 4.3c The model of a wave incorporates the characteristics of amplitude, wavelength,* frequency*, period*, wave speed*, and phase.

☆ 4.3d Mechanical waves require a material medium through which to travel.

☆ 4.3e Waves are categorized by the direction in which particles in a medium vibrate about an equilibrium position relative to the direction of propagation of the wave, such as transverse and longitudinal waves.

☆ 4.3f Resonance occurs when energy is transferred to a system at its natural frequency.

☆ 4.3h When a wave strikes a boundary between two media, reflection*, transmission, and absorption occur. A transmitted wave may be refracted.

☆ 4.3i When a wave moves from one medium into another, the wave may refract due to a change in speed. The angle of refraction (measured with respect to the normal) depends on the angle of incidence and the properties of the media (indices of refraction).

CHAPTER 14
WAVE PROPERTIES

Waves are everywhere. There are sound waves, visible light waves, radio waves, microwaves, water waves, telephone cord waves, stadium waves, earthquake waves, waves on a string, and slinky waves to name just a few. In addition to waves, there are many other phenomenon in our physical world which we call wavelike because they resemble waves so closely. The motion of a pendulum, the motion of a mass suspended by a spring, and the motion of a child on a swing are some common examples.

The goal of this unit is to develop mental models of waves and ultimately apply those models to an understanding of the two most common types of waves - sound waves and light waves.

SKILL 4.3IV - WAVES

A **pulse** is a single vibratory disturbance which moves from point to point through a medium. A **wave** is several pulses generated at regular time intervals. Waves are important in physics because waves can transfer energy without transferring mass.

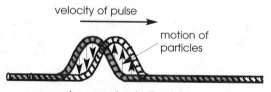

velocity of pulse

motion of particles

wave pulse - passing to the right

Some waves need material mediums in which to travel. Examples of mechanical waves that travel in mediums include water waves, sound waves or waves in a rope. The particles of the medium vibrate around a rest position. Light, radio, and other electromagnetic waves are periodic disturbances in an electromagnetic field. They need no material medium and can travel through a vacuum.

Waves are classified by the way they vibrate. The most common types are **longitudinal** and **transverse** waves.

Particles in longitudinal waves vibrate parallel to the direction of the wave motion. Each particle moves back and forth parallel to the wave direction. Sound is an example of a longitudinal wave. Seismic waves (P-waves) are longitudinal waves. Longitudinal waves are made up of compressions (where the particles are close together and rarefactions (where the particles spread out).

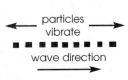

particles vibrate

wave direction

Particles in transverse waves vibrate perpendicular to the direction of the waves. Each particle moves perpendicular to the wave direction. Electromagnetic waves, such as light and radio are examples of transverse waves. Seismic waves (S–waves) are transverse waves. Transverse waves can travel in the same direction but in different planes.

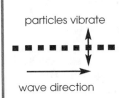

particles vibrate

wave direction

The electromagnetic wave illustration at the right has a magnetic field that vibrates in the **X** direction and has an electric field that vibrates in the **Y** direction. The velocity of an electromagnetic wave is the speed of light in the **Z** direction.

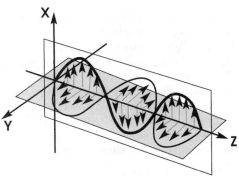

☆ TRY IT

1   The diagram at the right shows a person shaking the end of a rope up and down, producing a disturbance that moves along the length of the rope. Which type of wave is travelling in the rope?

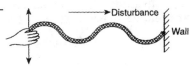

    1   torsional   2   longitudinal 3   transverse   4   elliptical

2   A wave is generated in a rope which is represented by the solid line in the diagram at the right. As the wave moves to the right, Point P on the rope is moving toward which position?
    1   A 2 B 3 C 4 D

3   In which type of wave is the disturbance of the medium parallel to the direction of travel of the wave? _____

WAVE CHARACTERISTICS

The **frequency** is the number of waves passing a point per unit time, determined by the vibrating source. The unit of frequency is hertz (or s⁻¹).

The **period** of the wave (**T**) is the time for one complete cycle to pass a point. Period is the reciprocal of frequency and is calculated from the formula, **T = 1/f**, where **T** is the period in seconds and **f** is the frequency in hertz.

The amplitude of a wave is related to energy of a wave. In a transverse wave, it is defined as the maximum distance above or below the wave axis (equilibrium position).

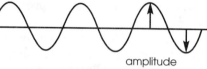

amplitude

In a longitudinal wave, the amplitude is determined by the separation of particles in the compressions and rarefactions. As the amplitude of a light wave increases, the brightness of the light increases. As the amplitude of a sound wave increases, the loudness of the sound increases.

Points on a periodic wave having the same displacement (amplitude) from their equilibrium position and moving in the same direction, are said to be *in phase* (for example, A and B or C and D). The **wavelength** (λ) is the distance between corresponding points in phase on successive waves. Wavelength is measured in meters.

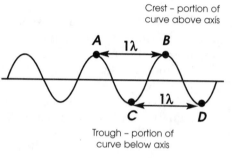

Crest – portion of curve above axis

Trough – portion of curve below axis

The **velocity** is the speed of the wave. It is determined by the type of wave medium. It is measured in meters per second. These characteristics are related to each other by the wave equation:

$$\text{Velocity} = \text{frequency x wavelength}$$
$$v = f\lambda$$

A **wave front** is the locus of adjacent points of a propagated wave that are in phase.

The **Doppler Effect** is observed when the source or the observer is moving. There is an increase in the observed frequency, when the vibrating source approaches the observer (for example, the distance between the source and the receiver is decreasing). There is a decrease in observed frequency as the source moves away from the observer (for example, the distance between the source and the receiver is increasing).

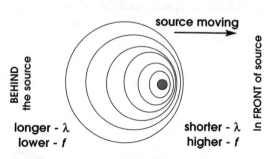

source moving

BEHIND the source

In FRONT of source

longer - λ
lower - f

shorter - λ
higher - f

If a source is moving at constant velocity, the frequency heard as it comes towards you will be a constant higher frequency than produced by the source. If the source is moving away, the frequency heard is constant but lower than the produced source.

If the source is accelerating towards you, the frequency will be higher and will continue to get higher. Accelerating away from you, it will be lower and continue to get lower.

 REAL WORLD CONNECTIONS

DOPPLER RADAR

As weather threatens to become severe, you're likely to hear about what the Doppler Radar shows. All weather radars send out radio waves from an antenna. Objects in the air, such as rain drops, snow crystals, hail stones or even insects and dust, scatter or reflect some of the radio waves back to the antenna. All weather radars, electronically convert the reflected radio waves into pictures showing the location and intensity of precipitation.

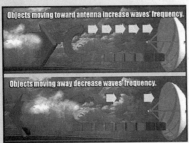

Doppler Radars are more advanced, in that they also measure the frequency change in returning radio waves. Waves reflected by something moving away from the antenna change to a lower frequency. Waves from an object moving toward the antenna change to a higher frequency. The computer that is a part of a Doppler Radar uses the frequency changes to show directions and speeds of the winds blowing around the rain drops, insects, and other objects that reflected the radio waves.

Scientists and forecasters have learned how to use these pictures to more clearly understand what is happening now and what's likely to happen in the next hour or two.

Adapted from: The *USA TODAY Weather Book* by Jack Williams

EXAMPLE

   a   Calculate the velocity of a wave that has a frequency of 6.0 hertz and a wavelength of 3.0 meters.

Given: frequency   = 6.0 hertz
                          wavelength = 3.0 meters

Find: **velocity**

Solution: $\mathbf{v = f\lambda}$
                    = (6.0 hertz)(3.0 m)
                    = 18 m/s

   b   Calculate the period of the wave in example *a*.

Given: frequency = 6.0 hertz

Find: **Period**

Solution: $\mathbf{T = 1/f}$

                $= \dfrac{1}{6.0 \text{ hertz}}$

                = 0.17 seconds

☆ TRY IT – SKILL 4.3i

Directions: Below are four transverse waves. By looking at the waveforms, you will be able to compare the various characteristics of the waves.

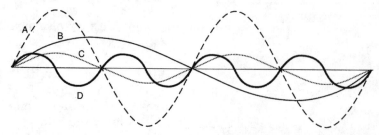

4   Rank the waves by letter (*A-D*), with the largest amplitude first.

5   Rank the waves by wavelength (*A-D*), with the longest wavelength first.

6   Rank the waves by frequency, with the highest frequency first.

7   Rank the waves by period, with the greatest period first.

8   Which waves are in phase?

Directions: On the grid below, time and amplitude are indicated. Your task will be to draw three more waves beginning at the origin with the following characteristics. The first one is completed for you.

Note: Wave *A* has been drawn with an amplitude of 5 units and a period of 2 seconds.

9 Draw a wave with amplitude 2 and a period of 4 seconds. Label it wave *B*.

10 Draw a wave of amplitude 2, a period of 4 seconds and out of phase with wave *B* by 180 degrees. Label it wave *C*.

11 Draw a wave with an amplitude of 5 and period of 1 second. Label it wave *D*.

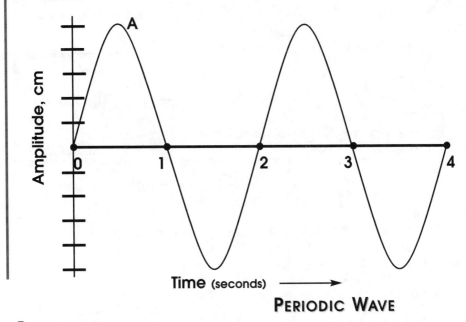

PERIODIC WAVE

PHENOMENA

Periodic waves respond to different conditions in predictable ways.

INTERFERENCE

Interference is the effect produced by two or more waves which are passing simultaneously through a region.

Superposition is the resultant disturbance at any point is the algebraic sum of displacements due to individual waves.

Constructive interference occurs at points where path distances to the two sources differ by an even number of half wavelengths. A phase difference of 0° or 360° is a wavelength. **Destructive interference** occurs when crests meet troughs or compressions meet rarefactions.

REAL WORLD CONNECTIONS – SOUND INTERFERENCE

The design of concert halls and auditoriums must take into account the destructive interference of sound waves. These halls must be designed in such a way as to reduce the amount of destructive interference. Interference can occur as the result of sound from two speakers meeting at the same location. It can also result when the sound from a speaker combines with the sound reflected off the walls and ceilings. One means of reducing the impact of destructive interference is by the design of walls, ceilings, and baffles that serve to absorb sound rather than reflect it. The best materials to use in the design of concert halls and auditoriums are those materials which are soft, such as, fiberglass and acoustic tile rather than cement and brick.

Noise reduction systems use the destructive interference of sound waves advantageously in automobiles and ear phones. Such devices capture sound from the environment and use computer technology to produce a second sound wave which one-half cycle out of phase from the original sound. The combination of these two sound waves within the headset or speaker will result in destructive interference and thus reduce a person's exposure to noise.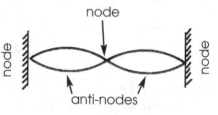

Destructive interference occurs at points where path differences to the two sources differ by an odd number of half wavelengths. A phase difference of 180° is a half wavelength. The placement of sound system speakers should take into account interference phenomena. Beats are usually heard when two sound frequencies are within 10 hertz of each other. Band members listen for beats when tuning their instruments.

Standing waves are produced when two waves of the same frequency and amplitude travel in opposite directions in the same medium. Some points, called **nodes**, appear to be standing still. Other positions called **anti-nodes**, vibrate with the maximum amplitude above and below the axis. When a wave strikes a boundary, some of the wave's energy will be **reflected**, some will be **transmitted** and some will be **absorbed**. Standing waves are most often produced by reflection of a wave train at a fixed boundary of a medium.

Resonance, or sympathetic vibrations, occur when one vibrating body sympathetically causes the other to vibrate. This occurs when both objects have the same natural vibration frequency. Most vibrating systems will vibrate at a particular frequency if disturbed. Air columns, both open and closed, provide a good example of resonance.

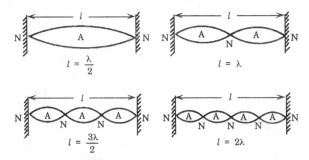

Examples of Standing Waves: different wavelengths along a rope bridge
(**N** = node, **A** = anti-node, **l** = length of bridges)

REAL WORLD CONNECTIONS
SPRINGS FOR SKYSCRAPERS

Seismologists measure the shock waves of an earthquake, but engineers have to design buildings to absorb the waves and survive a quake. The source of a quake is a fracture of rock in Earth's crust. At the moment of fracture, the stored energy is suddenly released and is dissipated by shock waves. It is precisely the vibration of the ground produced by these shock waves, which is responsible for most of the damage. The three-dimensional waves, which travel out from Earth's surface, are both longitudinal and transverse. The longitudinal waves travel faster and are called primary or P-waves. The slower transverse waves are called secondary or S-waves. The destructive waves arrive at a natural frequency, which coincides with the natural resonant frequency of most medium rise structures. At resonance, the movement of the upper floors of an uncounted building is greatly amplified. To absorb the waves engineers have placed resilient rubber mountings, like shock absorbers, at the foundation of the skyscrapers. The diagrams illustrate the buildings' movements during an earthquake.

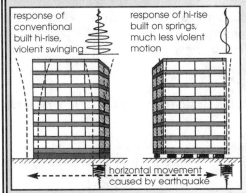

Adapted from *Physics in Technology*, 15, 177, ©1984

REFLECTION

The **law of reflection** states that the angle of incidence equals the angle of reflection, and that the incident wave, the reflected wave, and the normal, all lie on the same plane. The **angle of incidence** is defined as the angle between the normal and the incident wave. The angle of reflection is the angle between the normal and the reflected wave.

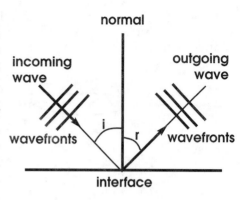

angle **i** is the angle of incidence
angle **r** is the angle of reflection

SKILLS 4.3VII, 4.3VIII

The study of waves often includes the use of a ripple tank. A ripple tank is a large glass-bottomed tank of water, used to study the behavior of water waves. A light shines upon the water from above and illuminates a white sheet of paper placed below the tank.

Because rays of light undergo bending as they pass through the troughs and crests, there is a pattern of light and dark spots on the white sheet of paper. The dark spots represent wave troughs and the bright spots represent wave crests. As the water waves move through the ripple tank, the dark and bright spots move as well. As the waves encounter obstacles in their path, their behavior can be observed by watching the movement of the dark and bright spots on the sheet of paper below. Circular waves can be observed by dipping a pencil into water.

LAB 22 – USING RIPPLE TANKS TO STUDY WAVE PHENOMENA

If you have access to a ripple tank, set the tank up and observe circular waves, straight waves, reflection, refraction, diffraction, and interference. Draw diagrams to illustrate each phenomena you observe. *Note:* it is much better to observe these phenomena directly, than simply to read about it.

If a ruler is attached to the vibrator in the tank which bobs up and down

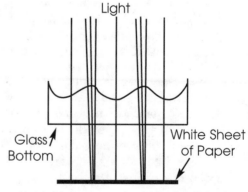

Light shining on a ripple tank will cast dark and bright spots on paper.

in the water, it becomes a source of straight waves. These straight waves have alternating crests and troughs. A pattern is formed below the tank on a sheet of white paper. The crests are the bright lines stretching across the paper and the troughs are the dark lines. These waves will travel through the water until they encounter an obstacle or a boundary surface.

THE LAW OF REFLECTION

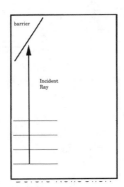 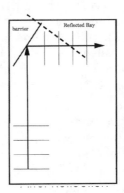

The diagram above depicts a series of straight waves approaching a long barrier extending at an angle across the tank of water. The direction which these wave fronts (straight-line crests) are traveling through the water is represented by an arrow. The arrow is called a **ray** and is drawn perpendicular to the wave fronts. When the ray reaches a barrier, these waves bounce and head in a different direction. The diagram above shows the reflected wave fronts and the reflected ray. The waves will always reflect such that the angle at which they approach the barrier equals the angle at which they reflect off the barrier as illustrated earlier. This is known as the law of reflection.

REFRACTION

Refraction is the bending of a wave as it enters a new medium obliquely. (Obliquely, means at some angle other than zero degrees.) The bending is due to a change in velocity. A wave which is traveling faster bends away from the normal. A wave which is traveling slower bends towards the normal. In the ripple tank, the depth of the water determines the speed of the wave. In shallow water, the waves travel slower.

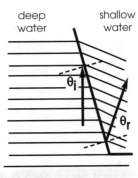

Waves enter obliquely
refraction

DIFFRACTION

Diffraction is the spreading of waves in all directions behind an obstacle.

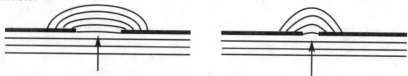

The amount of diffraction depends on the ratio between the wavelength and the slit (opening) size. If a slit is the same size as the wavelength or smaller, it will act like a point source. If the wave hits a barrier instead of a slit, it bends around the edges of the barrier producing a shadow.

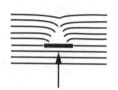

INTERFERENCE

Constructive interference occurs when the crest of one wave meets the crest of another wave. When the two waves meet, the resultant amplitude is the sum of the two crest amplitudes.

Before Interference	During Interference

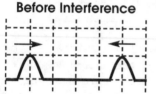 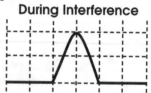

Constructive interference also occurs when the trough of one wave meets the trough of another wave. The resultant trough's amplitude is the sum of the two troughs amplitude.

Before Interference	During Interference

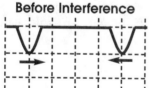 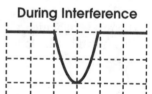

When a crest meets a trough of exactly the same amplitude, the resultant amplitude is zero.

Before Interference	After Interference

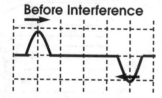 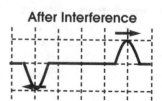

After the waves combine, in all cases, they pass through each other and continue on their way.

☆ TRY IT – LAB EXERCISE 23 – SUPERPOSITION

12 Using a ruler, complete the addition of wave *A* and wave *B*.

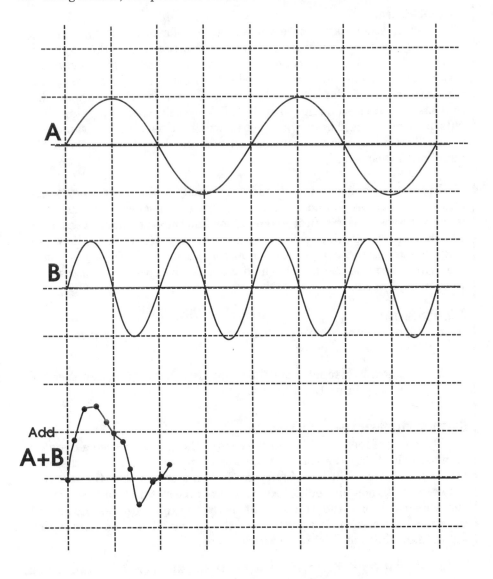

Skills 4.3ɪ, 4.3ɪɪɪ, 4.3ᴠɪ
LAB 24 – TRANSVERSE WAVES

Background

Note: All students must wear safety glasses for this activity.

Energy can be transmitted from one location to another by wave motion. Waves do not transport matter from one point to another; instead, a disturbance travels between the points. A single traveling disturbance is called a pulse. Another type of wave is called periodic and consists of a succession of pulses which follow each other at regular intervals in a medium. These wave types will be classified as transverse waves. Transverse waves are those in which the disturbance is 90° to the direction of the wave.

In this experiment you will study wave motion in a coil spring (sometimes called a snakey) and become acquainted with some basic characteristics of waves. You will first make pulses and measure their speed. You will then study standing waves of various frequencies, making the measurements required for a calculation of the wave speed. From your data, you will determine the factor which controls the speed of a transverse wave along a spring.

The Problem

a   To determine what variable controls the speed of a transverse wave in a coil spring.

b   To learn how to measure the frequency, wavelength, and speed of waves generated in a spring.

Setting the Length and Tension

Have two students hold opposite ends of the spring at such a distance along the floor that the spring has a moderate tension. A good distance between students will be 4-6 meters. It is important that the distance between the hands that hold the spring remain constant. Mark your positions on the floor and remain there throughout, unless otherwise instructed. Also, keep the position on the spring where you hold it constant. Mark that position with masking tape.

Important Note: Be careful not to stretch any portion of the spring beyond its elastic limit or it will be permanently distorted.

Generating a Pulse

Generate a pulse in the spring at one end by striking it quickly with your finger or by plucking it. Practice making pulses of various amplitudes, both crests and troughs. Quiet the spring before making each pulse. Note, especially, how a pulse is reflected at the opposite end of the spring.

Measure the Speed of a Pulse

The speed of a pulse can be determined by knowing the distance the pulse travels and the time required to travel that distance. The length of the spring can be measured easily by hanging a string next to it so that the string sags the same way, then measuring the string. (A flexible tape measure can also be used.) The time is best measured by taking the total time for a specific number of consecutive passes of the same pulse back and forth between the ends of the spring. Find the speed of three different pulses, each having a different amplitude. Record the data gathered in a data table.

Now, change the length of the spring by moving it about two meters. Do three more trials of different amplitudes and record the data.

Standing Waves

Go back to your original location. Shake the spring gently and continuously at a frequency such that the whole spring vibrates in segments or loops between certain fixed points, or nodes. The loops are often called anti-nodes. Such a wave is called a standing wave. The distance between two adjacent nodes is one-half wavelength. Thus, three consecutive nodes measures one whole wavelength. Practice making the spring vibrate in one, two, and three loops.

Does the frequency for generating each standing wave seem to be critical?

Measure the Speed of a Standing Wave

To measure the speed of the traveling waves, which are producing the standing waves, you must measure the frequency and wavelength of the standing wave. Measure the frequency of a wave by timing 10 complete cycles or vibrations, then dividing 10 by the time you get (remember, frequency is waves per second).

Analyzing the Data

Calculate the velocity of the wave pulses using the equation for average velocity. Be sure to use the time for a single pulse. Calculate the velocity of the standing waves by the relationship: $\mathbf{v} = \mathbf{f}\lambda$

Graphs

Plot a graph of wavelength versus frequency for the three different standing waves. Describe the graph in a sentence.

CHAPTER FOURTEEN ASSESSMENTS

PART A QUESTIONS

1   As a wave travels between two points in a medium, the wave transfers
   (1) energy, only
   (2) mass, only
   (3) both energy and mass
   (4) neither energy nor mass

2   Which equation correctly relates to speed v, wavelength λ, and period T of a periodic wave?
   (1) $v = \dfrac{T}{\lambda}$
   (2) $v = T\lambda$
   (3) $v = \dfrac{\lambda}{T}$
   (4) $T = v\lambda$

3   The hertz is a unit that describes the number of
   (1) seconds it takes to complete one cycle of a wave
   (2) cycles of a wave completed in one second
   (3) points that are in phase along one meter of a wave
   (4) points that are out of phase along one meter of a wave

4   Which phrase best describes a periodic wave?
   (1) a single pulse traveling at constant speed
   (2) a series of pulses at irregular intervals
   (3) a series of pulses at regular intervals
   (4) a single pulse traveling at different speeds in the same medium

5   The diagram at the right shows a transverse wave moving to the right along a rope. As the wave passes point X, the motion of X will be

   (1) up, then down
   (2) down, then up
   (3) left, then right
   (4) in a circle

6   The diagram at the right shows two pulses, A and B, moving to the right along a uniform rope. Compared to Pulse A, pulse B has

   (1) a slower speed and more energy
   (2) a faster speed and less energy
   (3) a faster speed and the same energy
   (4) the same speed and more energy

7   The diagram at the right shows a periodic wave. Which two points on the wave are in phase?
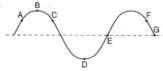
   (1) A and C (3) C and F
   (2) B and D (4) E and G

8 A transverse wave moves to the right (→) through a medium. Which diagram best represents the motion of the molecules of the medium due to the wave motion?

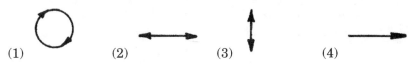

(1)   (2)   (3)   (4)

9 The diagram at the right shows a transverse water wave moving in the direction shown by velocity vector v. At the instant shown, a cork at point P on the water's surface is moving toward

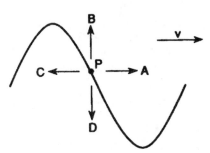

(1) A   (3) C
(2) B   (4) D

10 As shown in the diagram at the right, a transverse wave is moving along a rope. In which direction will segment X move as the wave passes through it?

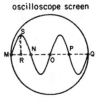

(1) down, only   (3) down, then up
(2) up, only   (4) up, then down

11 Diagram I shows a glass tube containing undisturbed air molecules. Diagram II shows the same glass tube when a wave passes through it. Which type of wave produced the disturbance shown in Diagram II?

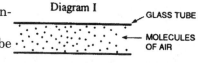
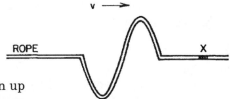

(1) longitudinal
(2) torsional
(3) transverse
(4) elliptical

12 Base your answer on the diagram which represents a sound wave and its corresponding pattern on an oscilloscope screen. What type of wave is the sound wave?

(1) elliptical
(2) transverse
(3) torsional
(4) longitudinal

13 Base your answer on the diagram at the right which represents waves generated in a spring. What type of wave is generated in the spring?

(1) longitudinal   (2) sound   (3) transverse   (4) light

14 Base your answer on the diagram of a Slinky spring shown at the right. The type of wave represented on the Slinky is a

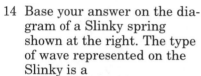

(1) longitudinal wave   (3) transverse wave
(2) light wave   (4) water wave

PART B QUESTIONS

15 In the diagram at the right, the distance between points A nd B on a wave is 5.0 meters. The wavelength of this wave is [1] _____ m

16 In the diagram at the right, a water wave having a speed of 0.25 meter per second causes a cork to move up and down 4.0 times in 8.0 seconds. What is the wavelength of the water wave? [1] _____ m

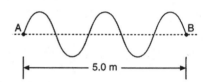

17 A wave generator located 4.0 meters from a reflecting wall produces a standing wave in a string, as shown in the diagram at the right. If the speed of the wave is 10. meters per second, what is its frequency? [1] _____ Hz

18 The graph at the right shows displacement versus time for a particle of a uniform medium as a wave passes through the medium. What is the frequency of the wave? [1] _____ Hz

19 What is the angle between the direction of propagation of a transverse wave and the direction in which the amplitude of the wave is measured? [1] _____ °

20 What is the period of a wave with a frequency of 250 hertz? [1] ___ s

21 The diagram below right shows a piston being moved back and forth to generate a wave. The piston produces a compression, C, every 0.50 second. The frequency of this wave is [1] _____ Hz

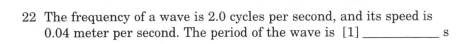

22 The frequency of a wave is 2.0 cycles per second, and its speed is 0.04 meter per second. The period of the wave is [1] _____ s

23 What is the period of a wave with a frequency of 2.0×10^2 hertz? [1] _____ s

24 A periodic wave with a frequency of 10 hertz would have a period of [1] _____ s

25 A wave which has frequency of 20.0 hertz travels with a speed of 100 meters per second. What is the wavelength of this wave? [1] _____ m

26 What is the frequency of a wave with a period of 5×10^{-3} second? [1] _____ Hz

27 What are the amplitude and wavelength of the wave shown at the right? [1]

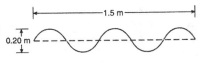

_____ m amplitude _____ m wavelength

28 Base your answer on the diagram at the right which represents a transverse wave.

How many cycles are shown in the diagram? [1] _____

29 A second wave produced by a clock chime is heard 515 m away, 1.50 s later. Determine the speed of sound of the clock's chime in air? [1] _____ °

PART C QUESTIONS

Base your answers to questions 29 through 32 on the information and diagram at the right.

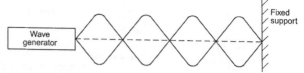

A wave generator having a constant frequency of 15 hertz produces a standing wave pattern in a stretched string.

29 Using a ruler, measure the amplitude of the wave shown. Record the value to the nearest tenth of a centimeter. [1]

30 Using a ruler, measure the wavelength of the wave shown. Record the value to the nearest tenth. [1]

31 State what would happen to the wavelength of the wave if the frequency of the wave were increased. [1]

32 How many antinodes are shown in the diagram? [1]

Base your answers to questions 33 and 34 on the information and diagram below. The diagram represents a wave generator having a constant frequency of 12 hertz producing parallel wave fronts in a ripple tank. The velocity of the wave is v.

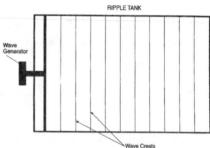

33 Using a ruler, measure the wavelength of the waves shown and record the value on your answer paper to the nearest tenth of a centimeter. [1]

34 Determine the speed of the waves in the ripple tank. [Show all calculations, including the equation and substitution with units.] [1]

35 Using one or more complete sentences, state the Law of Reflection. [2]

36 A barrier is placed in the ripple tank as shown in the diagram at the right. On the diagram, use a protractor and straightedge to construct an arrow to represent the direction of the velocity of the reflected waves. [3]

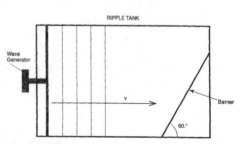

CHAPTER 15
SOUND AND LIGHT

KEY IDEA 4
ENERGY EXISTS IN MANY
FORMS, AND WHEN THESE
FORMS CHANGE ENERGY
IS CONSERVED.

> **PERFORMANCE INDICATOR 4.3** *STUDENTS CAN*
> *EXPLAIN VARIATIONS IN WAVELENGTH AND FREQUENCY IN TERMS*
> *OF THE SOURCE OF THE VIBRATIONS THAT PRODUCE THEM, E.G.,*
> *MOLECULES, ELECTRONS, AND NUCLEAR PARTICLES.*

CHAPTER 15 – MAJOR UNDERSTANDINGS

☆ 4.3f Resonance occurs when
energy is transferred to a system
at its natural frequency.
☆ 4.3n When a wave source and
an observer are in relative

motion, the observed
frequency of the waves
traveling between them is
shifted (Doppler Effect).

CHAPTER 15
SOUND AND LIGHT

SOUND IS A MECHANICAL WAVE

Sounds and music are all around us. The basis for an understanding of sound, music and hearing is the physics of waves. Sound is a mechanical wave which is created by vibrating objects and propagated through a medium from one location to another. Mechanical waves cannot travel through a vacuum.

When a ringing bell is placed in a jar and air was removed from the jar with a vacuum pump, the sound of the ringing bell can no longer be heard. The clapper can be seen striking the bell, but the ring cannot be heard because there is no air inside the jar to transport the sound.

The sound produced by the bell cannot be heard since sound cannot travel through a vacuum.

Sound can travel through many materials. As a sound is generated, pressure waves, made up of compressions and rarefactions, travel through the material. It is very difficult to draw a sound wave in a tube; so, more often the sound wave is redrawn as a pressure wave, as illustrated at the right.

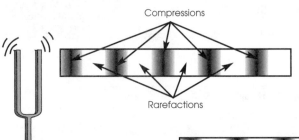

Compressions

Rarefactions

The ears are sensitive detectors capable of detecting the fluctuations in air pressure which land upon the eardrum.

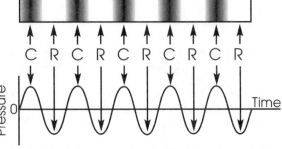

Note: "C" stands for compression and "R" stands for rarefaction.

REAL WORLD CONNECTIONS

THUNDER AND LIGHTNING

At normal atmospheric pressure and a temperature of 20° Celsius, a sound wave will travel at approximately 343 m/s. The speed of a sound wave is slow in comparison to the speed of a light wave. Light travels through air at a speed of approximately 300,000,000 m/s; this is nearly 900,000 times the speed of sound. Because of this, humans can observe a detectable time delay between the thunder and lightning during a storm. Light arrives from the location of the lightning strike almost instantaneously. The sound arrives later. The time delay between the arrival of the light wave (lightning) and the arrival of the sound wave (thunder) allows a person to approximate his/her distance from the storm location. For instance, if the thunder is heard 4 seconds after the lightning is seen, then sound (whose speed is approximated as 345 m/s) has traveled a distance of

distance = v • t = 345 m/s • 4 s = 1380 m

Longitudinal sound waves travel fastest in solids, slower in liquids, and the slowest in gases. The human ear is capable of detecting sound waves with a wide range of frequencies, ranging between approximately 20 Hz to 20,000 Hz.

VIBRATION

A vibrating string can create longitudinal waves in the surrounding air. As the vibrating string moves in the forward direction, it begins to push upon surrounding air molecules and increase the pressure. As the vibrating string moves in the backward direction, the pressure decreases. Subsequently, a guitar string vibrating at 500 Hz will set the air particles in the room vibrating at the same frequency of 500 Hz which carries a sound signal to the ear of a listener which is detected as a 500 Hz sound wave.

RESONANCE

Musical instruments and other objects can be set into vibration at their natural frequency when a person hits, strikes, strums, plucks or somehow disturbs the object. When a tuning fork is held in the air, a faint sound can be heard. When, the tuning fork is attached to a sounding box, more molecules are set into motion and the sound is much louder.

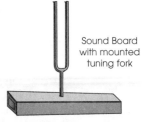

Sound Board with mounted tuning fork

A tuning fork is mounted on a sound box and set upon the table. A second tuning fork/sound box system, having the same natural frequency, is placed on the table near the first system. Neither of the tuning forks is vibrating. Then the first tuning fork is struck with a rubber mallet and the tines begin vibrating at its natural frequency.

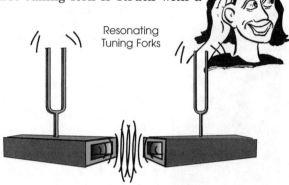

Resonating Tuning Forks

These vibrations set the sound box and the air inside the sound box vibrating at the same natural frequency. If you grab the tines of the tuning fork to stop the original vibration, the sound will still be heard. The sound is being produced by the second tuning fork – the one which was not hit.

One tuning fork forces another tuning fork into vibrational motion at the same natural frequency. The two forks are connected by the medium of air. This is an example of **resonance** – when one object vibrating at the same natural frequency of a second object forces that second object into vibrational motion.

THE DOPPLER EFFECT – SOUND

The Doppler Effect is a phenomenon observed whenever the source of waves is moving with respect to an observer. The Doppler Effect can be observed to occur with all types of waves, especially water waves, sound waves, and light waves.

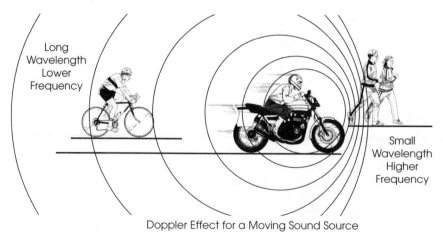

Long Wavelength Lower Frequency

Small Wavelength Higher Frequency

Doppler Effect for a Moving Sound Source

The Doppler Effect is observed because the distance between the source of sound and the observer is changing.

When the source is moving towards the observer, the observer perceives sound waves reaching him or her at a more frequent rate (higher frequency). When the source is moving away from the observer, the observer perceives sound waves reaching him or her at a less frequent rate (lower frequency). The source produces waves of the same frequency; but, the observer only perceives a different frequency because of the relative motion between them.

DOPPLER EFFECT - LIGHT

The Doppler Effect is of interest to astronomers who use the information about the shift in frequency of electromagnetic waves produced by moving stars in our galaxy and beyond in order to derive information about those stars and galaxies. The belief that the universe is expanding is based in part upon observations of electromagnetic waves emitted by stars in distant galaxies. Electromagnetic radiation emitted by such stars in a distant galaxy would appear to be shifted downward in frequency (a "red shift")

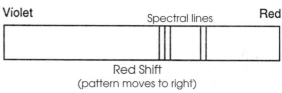
Violet
Spectral lines
Red
Red Shift
(pattern moves to right)

if the star is moving in a direction which is away from the Earth. On the other hand, there is an upward shift in frequency (a "blue shift") of such observed radiation if the star is moving in a direction that is towards Earth. The Doppler shift is one reason to believe that light is a wave phenomenon.

REAL WORLD CONNECTION - SHOCK WAVES

When the source moves at the same speed as or faster than the wave itself can move, a **shock wave** occurs. If a moving source of sound moves at the same speed as sound, then the source will always be at the leading edge of the waves which it produces. The diagram below depicts snapshots in time of a variety of wave fronts produced by an aircraft which is moving at the same speed as sound.

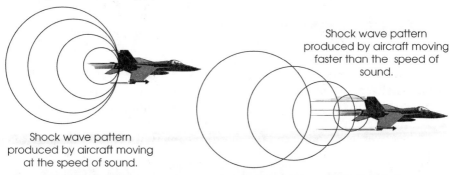

Shock wave pattern produced by aircraft moving faster than the speed of sound.

Shock wave pattern produced by aircraft moving at the speed of sound.

The circular wave fronts, which would actually be spheres, represent compressional wave fronts of the sound waves. Notice that these circles are bunched up and form a cone. This phenomenon is known as a shock wave. Shock waves are also produced if the aircraft moves faster than the speed of sound. If a moving source of sound moves faster than sound, the source will always be ahead of the wave cone which it produces. The diagram to the left depicts snapshots in time of a cone produced by an aircraft which is moving faster than sound. This cone falls behind the faster moving aircraft.

High pressure regions resulting from the piling up of compressional waves.

If you are standing on the ground when a supersonic (faster than sound) aircraft passes over-head, you might hear a **sonic boom**. A sonic boom occurs as the result of the piling up of compressional wave fronts along the conical edge of the wave pattern. The edge of the cone produces a very high pressure zone. Because the edge of the cone contains compressions followed by a rarefaction, the high pressure zone will be immediately followed by a low pressure zone. A very loud noise will be heard.

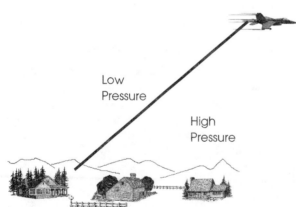

Low Pressure

High Pressure

When supersonic aircraft passes overhead, instead of the compression and rarefactions being heard at separate times, they are heard at once. This creates a sonic boom.

When you are standing on the ground, there is a slight time delay between the plane passing overhead and the actual sonic boom. These sonic booms are observed when any aircraft which is traveling faster than the speed of sound passes overhead. It does not mean that the aircraft *just* overcame the sound barrier, it means that the aircraft is traveling faster than sound.

BOUNDARY PHENOMENA

When a wave (or pulse) reaches the end of a medium, there are three possible boundary behaviors, which could occur. They are: reflection, transmission, and refraction.

ECHO

Reflection of sound waves can lead to echoes. Echoes occur when a reflected sound wave reaches the ear more than 0.1 seconds after the original sound wave was heard.

Example: Wayne shouts down a well and hears the echo of his voice .85 seconds later. How deep is the well? [*Note:* Speed of sound is 341 m/s.]

Given:

$$\mathbf{v} \text{ (sound)} \quad = \ 341 \text{ m/s}$$

$$\textbf{Distance} \ = \ 341 \text{ m/s x .85 s} = 281 \text{ m} \ \text{(distance sound traveled)}$$

$$\frac{281 \text{ m}}{2} \ = \ 141 \text{ m} \ \text{The depth of the well.}$$

  TRY IT

1   Determine the time for the echo to be heard in a 1,200 m well.

2   A student drops a stone down a 1,200 meter well. How long after the stone hits the bottom of the well will it take to hear the echo? [Show all calculations.]

DIFFRACTION

Diffraction involves a spreading out of waves as they pass through an opening or around a barrier in their path. When the wavelength of the waves is smaller than the obstacle or opening, no noticeable diffraction occurs. Diffraction of sound waves is commonly observed as sound travel around corners and into the classroom from the hallways. Many forest-dwelling birds take advantage of the diffractive ability of long-wave-length sound waves. Owls for instance are able to communicate across long distances because their long wavelength "hoots" are able to diffract around forest trees and carry farther than the short wavelength "tweets" of song birds.

REAL WORLD CONNECTIONS
ULTRASONIC BATS

Why do bats use ultrasound to hunt? The typical prey of a bat is not much larger than a couple of centimeters. As the wavelength of a wave becomes smaller than the obstacle which it encounters, the wave is no longer able to diffract around the obstacle, instead the wave reflects off the obstacle. Bats use ultrasonic waves with wave-

©PhotoDisc

lengths smaller than the dimensions of their prey. These sound waves will encounter the prey, and instead of diffracting around the prey, will reflect off the prey and allow the bat to hunt by means of echoes.

SKILL 4.3V
LAB 25 – SPEED OF SOUND IN AIR

BACKGROUND

Compared to most objects, sound waves travel very fast. It is fast enough that measuring the speed of sound is a technical challenge. One method you could use would be to time an echo. For example, if you were in an open field with a large building a quarter of a kilometer away, you could start a stopwatch when a loud noise was made and stop it when you heard the echo. You could then calculate the speed of sound. It is more convenient to resort to an indirect way of measuring the speed of sound in air by making use of its wave properties.

PROBLEM

To determine the speed of sound in air using the principle of resonance.

FINDING THE RESONANCE

A vibrating tuning fork held over an open tube may vibrate the enclosed air column at its resonance frequency. For a tube open at one end and closed at the other, resonance occurs when the air column is one-quarter the length of the sound wave. The length of the air column can be adjusted by changing the water level in the tube. The volume of the sound is loudest when the proper length is selected for resonance.

Carefully strike the tuning fork with a mallet and place it over the open end of the air column so the tines of the fork vibrate into the column. Adjust the water level until the sound is the loudest, starting with a long air column and working towards a shorter column. Record the length of the air column when the sound is the loudest in an appropriate table. Repeat several times with the same tuning fork. Repeat the experiment with different tuning forks.

ADDING IN THE CORRECTION FACTOR

Measure the diameter (**d**) of the tube. Based on the diameter, the actual sound wave forms slightly above the tube. To determine the effective resonance length use the following formula (*Note:* Be careful to use the correct units.):

Effective length = measured length + 0.4 (d)

CALCULATING THE SPEED OF SOUND

The wavelength is four times the effective length because the tube is closed at one end. Use the wave formula, which states that velocity of a wave is equal to the frequency, times the wavelength to determine the velocity of the wave in your tube.

COMPARING TO THE ACTUAL VALUE

The accepted value for the speed of sound is 332 m/s at 0°C. The speed of sound increases at 0.6 m/s for each Celsius degree above zero. Compute the accepted speed of sound at the temperature in your room. Compare your values to the accepted values.

GOING BEYOND

There are many other ways of determining the speed of sound. Plan and carry out a different experiment to find the speed of sound.

CHAPTER FIFTEEN ASSESSMENTS

PART A QUESTIONS

1   As a sound wave travels through air, there is a net transfer of
   (1) energy, only   (3) both mass and energy
   (2) mass, only   (4) neither mass nor energy

2   The diagram at the right shows a tuning fork vibrating in air. The dots represent air molecules as the sound wave moves toward the right. Which diagram best represents the direction of motion of the air molecules?

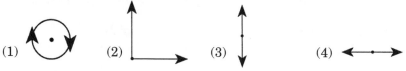

3   The amplitude of a sound wave is to its loudness as the amplitude of a light wave is to its
   (1) brightness   (2) frequency   (3) color   (4) speed

4   What type of wave is sound traveling in water?
     (1) torsional   (2) transverse   (3) elliptical   (4) longitudinal

5   Two identical guitar strings are tuned to the same pitch. If one
     string is plucked, the other nearby string vibrates with the same fre-
     quency. This phenomenon is called.
     (1) resonance   (3) refraction
     (2) reflection   (4) destructive interference

6   The diagram at the right shows an
     antenna emitting an electromag-
     netic wave. In what way did the
     electrons in the antenna produce
     the electromagnetic wave?
     (1) by remaining stationary
     (2) by moving at constant speed
         upward, only
     (3) by moving at constant speed
         downward, only
     (4) by accelerating alternately upward and downward

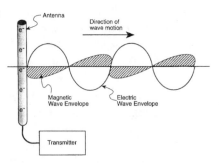

7   The driver of a car sounds the horn while traveling toward a station-
     ary person. Compared to the sound of the horn heard by the driver,
     the sound heard by the stationary person has
     (1) lower pitch and shorter wavelength
     (2) lower pitch and longer wavelength
     (3) higher pitch and shorter wavelength
     (4) higher pitch and longer wavelength

8   Light from the star Betelgeuse displays a Doppler red shift. This
     shift is best explained by assuming that Betelgeuse is
     (1) decreasing in temperature   (3) moving toward Earth
     (2) increasing in temperature   (4) moving away from Earth

9   When a tuning fork is struck with more force, which property of the
     sound is changed?
     (1) amplitude   (2) velocity   (3) frequency   (4) wavelength

10   Regions in a sound wave where particles are farthest apart are
     called
     (1) compressions   (3) depressions
     (2) condensations   (4) rarefactions

11   Sound is a form of
     (1) thermal energy   (3) radiant energy
     (2) mechanical energy   (4) electrical energy

PART B QUESTIONS

12 The frequency of a light wave is 5.0 x 10^{14} hertz. What is the period of the wave? [1] _____ sec.

13 A monochromatic beam of light has a frequency of 6.5 x 10^{14} hertz. What color is the light? [1] _____

14 For a given sound wave, the total of 4 compressions and 4 rarefactions is 120 centimeters. The wavelength of this sound wave is [1] _____ cm

15 A person sees a bolt of lightning and then hears the thunder 5 seconds later. How far away was the lightning? [1] _____ meters

16 Which wave is purely *longitudinal*?
   (1) surface waves in a shallow pan of water
   (2) sound waves in air
   (3) waves on a plucked guitar string
   (4) light waves traveling through vacuum

17 A railroad whistle is sounded. An echo is heard 5.0 seconds later. If the speed of sound is 343 m/s, how far away is the reflecting surface? [1] _____ meters

18 A nearby object may vibrate strongly when a specific frequency of sound is emitted from a loudspeaker. This phenomenon is called [1]
_____

19 A guitar string is plucked and set into vibration. The vibrating string disturbs the surrounding air, resulting in a sound wave.

		Wave in the string	Sound Wave in air
A	The wave is transmitted by particle vibrations.	no	yes
B	The wave is longitudinal.	yes	yes
C	The wave transports energy.	yes	yes
D	The wave is transverse.	no	yes

Which entry in the table above is correct? [1] _____

PART C QUESTIONS

Base our answers to questions 20 through 22 on the information below.

A 0.12-meter-long electromagnetic (radar) wave is emitted by a weather station and reflected from a nearby thunderstorm.

20 Determine the frequency of the radar wave. [Show all calculations, including the equation and substitution with units.] [2]

21 Using one or more complete sentences, define the Doppler Effect. [1]

22 The thunderstorm is moving toward the weather station. Using one or more complete sentences, explain how the Doppler Effect could have been used to determine the direction in which the storm is moving. [1]

23 Two fans are watching a baseball game from different positions. One fan is located directly behind home plate, 18.3 m from the batter. The other fan is located in the centerfield bleachers, 127 m from the batter. Both fans observe the batter strike the ball at the same time, but the fan behind home plate hears the sound first. What is the time difference between hearing the sound at the two locations? [Use 345 m/s as the speed of sound. Show all calculations, including the equation and substitution with units.] [2]

Directions for question 24: Use the diagram below of two joggers being passed by a speeding and noisy motorcycle.

A   B

24 Describe the sound heard by each jogger. [2]

Chapter 16
Refraction
and
Reflection

CHAPTER 16 – MAJOR UNDERSTANDINGS

☆ 4.3h When a wave strikes a boundary between two media, reflection*, transmission, and absorption occur. A transmitted wave may be refracted.

☆ 4.3i When a wave moves from one medium into another, the wave may refract due to a change in speed. The angle of refraction (measured with respect to the normal) depends on the angle of incidence and the properties of the media (indices of refraction).*

☆ 4.3j The absolute index of refraction is inversely proportional to the speed of a wave.*

CHAPTER 16
REFRACTION AND REFLECTION

LIGHT ENERGY

Light is necessary for sight. The objects which we see can be placed into one of two categories: luminous objects and illuminated objects. **Luminous objects** are objects which generate their own light. **Illuminated objects** are objects which are capable of reflecting light to our eyes. The candle is an example of a luminous object, while your textbook is an illuminated object.

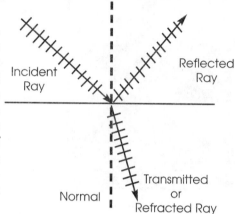

Whenever an **incident wave**, be it light, sound or water, hits a boundary three things occur. Part of the wave is reflected. Part of the wave is refracted and part of the energy is lost. In this chapter we will be concentrating on reflection and refraction. Our discussion will center around light but it can apply to water waves, as you saw in the ripple tank, sound waves or other waves in the electromagnetic spectrum.

Reflection is the bouncing of a wave off the surface of a boundary. Reflection off of smooth surfaces such as mirrors or a calm body of water is known as **regular reflection**. Reflection off of rough surfaces such as clothing, paper, and an asphalt roadway is called **diffuse reflection**. The diagram below depicts two beams of light incident upon a rough and a smooth surface.

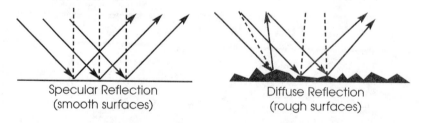

Specular Reflection (smooth surfaces)

Diffuse Reflection (rough surfaces)

These phenomena explain why it is relatively more difficult to drive at night on a wet asphalt roadway compared to a dry asphalt roadway. Most drivers are aware of the fact that driving at night on a wet roadway results in an annoying glare from oncoming headlights. The glare is the result of the regular reflection of the beam of light from an oncoming car. On dry asphalt, there is diffuse reflection, but as the water fills in the rough surface, the reflection becomes regular and the glare becomes very annoying.

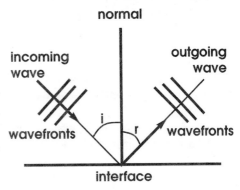

THE LAW OF REFLECTION

This very predictable nature of a reflected ray follows a law known as the law of reflection. The diagram at the right illustrates the law of reflection.

SKILL 4.3VIII

CONSTRUCT THE REFLECTED ANGLE

In the diagram, the ray of light approaching the mirror is labeled the **incident ray** (i). The ray of light which leaves the mirror is called the **reflected ray** (r). At the point of incidence, where the ray strikes the mirror, a line can be drawn perpendicular to the surface of the mirror. This line is known as a **normal line** (N). The normal line hits the surface at right angles and divides the angle between the incident ray and the reflected ray into two equal angles. The angle between the incident ray and the normal is known as the

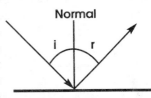

angle of incidence. The angle between the reflected ray and the normal is known as the angle of reflection. The law of reflection states that when a ray of light reflects off any surface, the angle of incidence is equal to the angle of reflection.

☆ TRY IT

1   A ray of light is approaching a set of three pieces of glass as shown in the diagram. The light ray is approaching the first mirror at an angle of 45-degrees with the mirror surface. Trace the path of the light ray as it bounces off the mirror; continue tracing the ray until it finally exits from the mirror system. How many times will the ray reflect before it finally exits?

2   A light ray is incident on a plane mirror as shown in the diagram at the right. Which ray best represents the reflected ray?

(1) *A*   (3) *C*
(2) *B*   (4) *D*

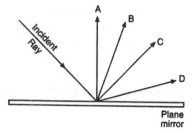

3   A ray of light traveling in air is incident on a plane mirror at an angle of 30.°, as shown in the diagram at the right. The angle of reflection for the light ray is _____°

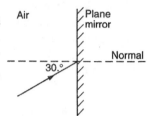

REFRACTION

As a light wave hits the boundary of a new medium, a portion of the light wave is transmitted into the new medium and a portion of the wave reflects off the boundary. When passing from air into glass, both the speed and the wavelength decrease. There is no change in the wave's frequency. The light is observed to change direction as it crosses the boundary separating the air and the glass (diagram, page 292). This bending of the path of light is known as **refraction**. Refraction is responsible for the focusing of light in eyeglasses and other lenses.

REAL WORLD CONNECTIONS

THE HUNTER AND REFRACTION

Consider a spear hunter and the fish. The hunter sights the fish in the lake. The hunter's brain interprets the ray of light from the fish as traveling in a straight line. The hunter aims along his line of sight and misses the fish every time.

Fortunately for the fish, light refracts as it travels from the fish in the water to the eyes of the hunter. The refraction occurs at the water-air boundary. Due to this bending of the path of light, the fish appears to be in a location where it isn't. But why does light refract? How can this behavior be explained?

THE MARCHING BAND ACTIVITY

A group of students formed a straight line by standing shoulder to shoulder. Each student connected themselves to their nearest neighbor by meter sticks. On the floor, a strip of masking tape was placed diagonally across the room to represent two "media." On one side of the tape, the first "medium," students walked at a normal pace. On the other side of the tape, students walked very slowly using baby steps. The group of students walked forward in a straight line towards the diagonal strip of masking tape; the students maintained a line as they approached the masking tape. When an individual student reached the tape, that student abruptly changed the pace of her/his walk. The group of students continued walking until all students in the line had entered into the second medium. The diagram below represents the line of students approaching the boundary between the two medium (the masking tape). On the diagram, an arrow is used to show the general direction of travel for the group of students in both media. Observe that the direction of the students changes at the "boundary."

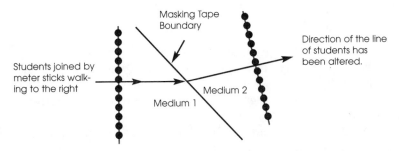

Light (and marching band students) refract at a boundary because of a change in speed. There is a cause-effect relationship: the cause is a change in speed, and the effect is a change in direction, or refraction. Refraction occurs when the wave front hits the barrier obliquely. Notice what happens when the marching band hits the masking tape barrier head on.

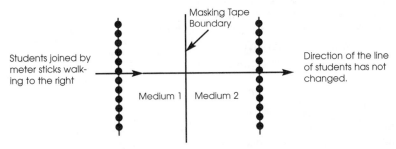

A perpendicular approach to the boundary will not result in a direction change, but the speed of the wave will change.

Photons of Light Through Media

A light wave is produced by a vibrating electric charge. As the wave moves through the vacuum (empty space), it travels at a speed of 3×10^8 m/s). When the wave runs into a particle of matter, the energy is absorbed and sets electrons within the atoms into vibrational motion. If the frequency of the electromagnetic wave matches the resonance frequency of the atom, the energy turns into thermal energy and no longer radiates. When the frequency of the electromagnetic wave does not match the resonant frequency of vibration of the electron, the energy is re-emitted in the form of an electromagnetic wave.

This new electromagnetic wave has the same frequency as the original wave. It will travel at a speed of light through the empty space between atoms. The newly emitted light wave continues to move until it hits a neighboring particle. If the energy is absorbed by this new particle, it sets the electrons of its atoms into vibration motion. If there is no match between the frequency of the electromagnetic wave and the resonant frequency of the electron, the energy is re-emitted in the form of a new electromagnetic wave.

The process of absorption and re-emission continues as the energy is transported from particle to particle through the bulk of a medium. Every photon travels between the atoms at a speed of light; yet the time delay involved in the process of being absorbed and re-emitted by the atoms of the matter lowers the net speed of transport from one end of the medium to the other. Subsequently, the net speed of an electromagnetic wave in any medium is somewhat less than its speed in a vacuum (3×10^8 m/s).

The speed of a light wave is dependent upon the properties of the medium. In the case of an electromagnetic wave, the speed of the wave depends upon the **optical density** of that material. The optical density of a medium is not the same as its physical density. The physical density of a material refers to the mass/volume ratio.

The optical density of a material relates to the sluggish tendency of the atoms of a material to maintain the absorbed energy of an electromagnetic wave in the form of vibrating electrons before re-emitting it as a new electromagnetic disturbance. The more opti-

Absolute Indices of Refraction	
($f = 5.09 \times 10^{14}$ Hz)	
Air	1.00
Corn oil	1.47
Diamond	2.42
Ethyl alcohol	1.36
Glass, crown	1.52
Glass, flint	1.66
Glycerol	1.47
Lucite	1.50
Quartz, fused	1.46
Sodium chloride	1.54
Water	1.33
Zircon	1.92

cally dense which a material is, the slower that a wave will move through the material.

One indicator of the optical density of a material is the **index of refraction value (n)** of the material. The index of refraction value of a material is a ratio of the speed of light in a vacuum to the speed of light in the material. The reference table shows values for one frequency. Since each frequency travels through material at a different speed, it will have a different index of refraction.

$$n_{material} = \frac{3.00 \times 10^8 \text{ m/s}}{v_{material}}$$

WHICH WAY DOES THE LIGHT BEND?

LIGHT TRAVELING FROM A FAST TO A SLOW MEDIUM
If a ray of light passes across the boundary from a material in which it travels fast, into a material in which it travels slower, then the light ray will *bend towards* the normal line.

LIGHT TRAVELING FROM A SLOW TO A FAST MEDIUM
If a ray of light passes across the boundary from a material in which it travels slow into a material in which it travels faster, then the light ray will *bend away* from the normal line.

BY HOW MUCH WILL THE RAY BEND?
The diagram below depicts a ray of light approaching three different boundaries at an angle of incidence of 45-degrees. The refractive medium is different in each case, causing different amounts of refraction. The angles of refraction are shown on the diagram.

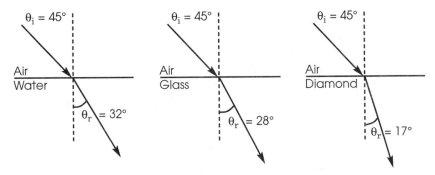

Of the three materials in the diagram above, the light ray refracts the most at the air-diamond boundary. For any given angle of incidence, the angle of refraction is dependent upon the speeds of light in each of the two materials; the speed is, in turn, dependent upon the optical density and the index of refraction values of the two materials. Snell's Law relates the angles and the indices of refraction.

SKILLS 4.3VIII, 4.3VIX
SNELL'S LAW AND THE ABSOLUTE INDEX OF REFRACTION

Snell's Law states, for a ray passing from one medium to another, the product of the index of refraction of the first medium and the sine of the angle of incidence is equal to the product of the index of refraction of the second medium and the sine of the angle of refraction.

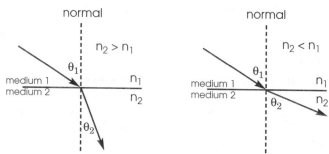

So, if the top part of the diagram is air, n_1 is the speed of light in air and if the bottom part is glass, n_2 is the speed of light in glass, both relative to the speed of light in a vacuum.

The **absolute index of refraction** is the ratio between the speed of light in a vacuum or air and the speed of light in the material.

$$n = \frac{c}{v} = \frac{\text{Speed of Light in a Vacuum}}{\text{Speed of Light in the Material}}$$

The absolute index of refraction is always a number greater than one (1). Snell's Law relates the angle of incidence and the angle of refraction.

$$\frac{\sin \theta_1}{\sin \theta_2} = \frac{n_2}{n_1}$$

$$\text{or} \quad n_1 \sin \theta_1 = n_2 \sin \theta_2 \quad \text{or} \quad n_1 v_1 = c \text{ (speed of light)}$$

$$\text{also,} \quad n_1 v_1 = n_2 v_2$$

Where:
  n = the absolute index of refraction
  n_1 = index of refraction of the first medium
  θ_1 = angle measured with the normal in the first medium
  n_2 = index of refraction of the second medium
  θ_2 = angle measured with the normal in the second medium
  v_1 = velocity of light in the first medium
  v_2 = velocity of light in the second medium

☆ TRY IT

4   Using the following formula and the values for **n** in the diagram
    below, calculate the angles of refraction and using arrows. Draw
    arrows to show the path through the layers of different materials.

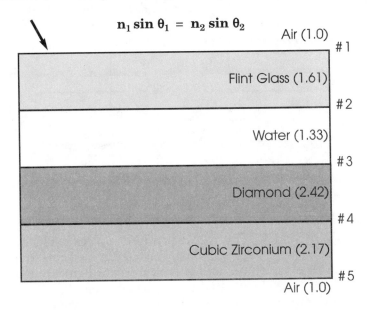

$$n_1 \sin \theta_1 = n_2 \sin \theta_2$$

Air (1.0)   #1

Flint Glass (1.61)   #2

Water (1.33)   #3

Diamond (2.42)   #4

Cubic Zirconium (2.17)   #5

Air (1.0)

TOTAL INTERNAL REFLECTION

As light travels from a more optically dense material to a less optically
dense material, the ray bends away from the normal. There exists one
angle of incidence where the angle of refraction becomes 90 degrees. That
incident angle is called the critical angle and is determined by the formula:

$$\textbf{Sin } \emptyset_c = 1/n$$

When the angle of incidence is greater than the critical angle, the
incident ray is totally internally reflected.

Refraction   Total Internal Reflection

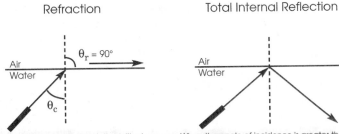

When the angle of incidence equals the critical   When the angle of incidence is greater than the critical
angle, the angle of refraction is 90 degrees.   angle, all the light undergoes total internal reflection.

REAL WORLD CONNECTIONS
TIR AND THE IMPORTANCE OF A DIAMOND'S CUT

Total internal reflection is very useful. With the proper cut and total internal reflection, a diamond reflects the full brilliance of the gemstone. Many heirloom diamonds were cut shallow and as a result lost, rather than reflected the incoming light.

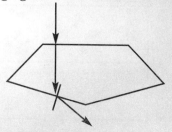

Light entering through the top facet undergoes total internal reflection (TIR) before exiting.

Light entering through the top facet exits at the second boundary since its angle of incidence is less than the critical angle.

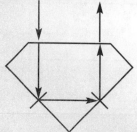

Modern **fiber optics** take advantage of this phenomenon in medicine and in communication to route light around corners and transmit high quality optical signals. A light pipe example is shown to the left.

A common demonstration set up in class uses a soda bottle and a laser. By shining the light through the bottle and out the hole, the light remains trapped in the water as the bottle empties as shown to the left.

REAL WORLD CONNECTIONS

HOW A BAR CODE SCANNER WORKS

The bar code scanner works on the interpretation of a reflected code. The laser light scans the product and the reflected light returns to the detection device. Bar code scanners are used everywhere, but do you realize you can read the code?

You may want to decode the actual bars in the bar code (at right) and map them to numbers. First of all, look at any 12-digit bar code. It is made up of black bars and white spaces between the bars.

ISBN 0-935487-75-1

90000>

9 780935 487756

Assume that the thinnest bar or space that you see is called "one unit wide." The bars and spaces can therefore be seen to have proportional widths of one, two, three or four units. If you look at any bar code you can see examples of these four widths.

The start and stop of any bar code is "1-1-1." That is, starting at the left you find a one-unit-wide black bar followed by a one-unit-wide white space followed by a one-unit-wide black bar (bar-space-bar). Following the start code, the digits are encoded like this:

0 = 3-2-1-1	**5** = 1-2-3-1
1 = 2-2-2-1	**6** = 1-1-1-4
2 = 2-1-2-2	**7** = 1-3-1-2
3 = 1-4-1-1	**8** = 1-2-1-3
4 = 1-1-3-2	**9** = 3-1-1-2

The code embedded in the example is **780935487756**. The bar code starts with the standard start code of 1-1-1 (bar-space-bar).

Seven is **1-3-1-2** (space-bar-space-bar).
Eight is **1-2-1-3** (space-bar-space-bar).
Zero is **3-2-1-1** (space-bar-space-bar).
Nine is **3-1-2-2** (space-bar-space-bar).
Three is **1-4-1-1** (space-bar-space-bar).
Five is **1-2-3-1** (space-bar-space-bar).

In the middle, there is a standard 1-1-1-1-1 (space-bar-space-bar-space), which is important because it means the numbers on the right are optically inverted!

Four is **1-1-3-2** (bar-space-bar-space).
Eight is **1-2-1-3** (bar-space-bar-space).
Seven is **1-3-1-2** (bar-space-bar-space).
Seven is **1-3-1-2** (bar-space-bar-space).
Five is **1-2-3-1** (bar-space-bar-space).
Six is **1-1-1-4** (bar-space-bar-space).
Stop character is 1-1-1 (bar-space-bar).

How a Bar Code Scanner Works

1 As product passes over the glass counter, a laser beam scans the bar code.

2 Light reflected off the code reaches the photodetector via a series of mirrors. Changes in bar width and black or white spaces causes changes in light intensity.

3 The photodetector converts the light beam into an electronic signal that is translated into a number and sent to a computer for analysis and display.

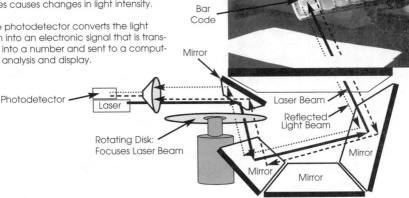

Bar Code

Mirror

Photodetector

Laser

Rotating Disk: Focuses Laser Beam

Laser Beam

Reflected Light Beam

Mirror

Mirror

Mirror

 TRY IT

5   On a sheet of graph paper, make a four-digit bar code of the year you were born.

SKILL 4.3VIII
LAB 26 – REFLECTION

As we observed in the ripple tank, when a wave is produced by a point source and is reflected by a boundary, the reflected wave seems to have originated at some point behind the boundary. If we look into a mirror at the reflection of an object, we can see that the **image** is behind the mirror. In this lab, we will be using a small laser pointer to determine the angles of the incident and reflected light. All students must wear protective eyewear. In addition, never point the laser light into a person's eye or deliberately look into the beam.

THE PROBLEM

How are the angle of incidence and the angle of reflection related?

LOCATING AN IMAGE BY REFLECTION

Draw a horizontal line in the center of your lab notebook. Label this line the mirror line. Make the arrow about three or four centimeters long and incline it at some arbitrary angle to the mirror line. Mount a mirror on the mirror line.

Look into the mirror and note the image of the arrow. To help locate the point of the arrow more precisely, stick a pin vertically in the paper at the arrow point. Now, aim the laser pointer at the pin and towards the mirror at the base of the pin. A red line should be visible on the paper to the mirror. A weaker, reflected line should be visible coming off the mirror. *Note:* Do not look directly into the laser beam.

Draw the incident ray and the reflected ray for this single beam of light. Repeat the process and point the laser pointer at the pin and towards another mirror position. (The laser beam goes by the pin if you can place a second pin so that its parallax is the same.) Remove the mirror from the mirror line. Extend the reflected line back behind the mirror to a position where they meet. Mark this point. This is the point of the arrow. Similarly, locate the images of the tail of the arrow. Draw the image of the arrow.

Compare the sizes of the original arrow and its image. Compare their distances from the mirror. Rule a line from the arrow point to its image. What angle does this line make with the mirror? Does the light by which you see this image actually come from the image location? This is why we call it a **virtual image**.

THE LAW OF REFLECTION

For each set of rays that you have drawn, draw a perpendicular (a normal) at this point where the ray is reflected from the mirror.

Compare the angle of incidence with the angle of reflection. State the law of reflection.

OTHER REFLECTION EXPERIMENTS

Devise experiments and carry them out to investigate any or all of the following:

1   When a mirror is rotated through a certain angle, what happens to the angle of reflection and in what direction does the reflected ray go?

2   When light enters a corner formed by two mirrors mounted at right angles to each other, describe the emergent ray.

3   Two mirrors mounted at right angles will produce three images of an object located between them. As the angle between the mirrors changes, what happens to the number of images?

SKILL 4.3IX

LAB 27 – REFRACTION AND THE INDEX OF REFRACTION

If you hold a pencil in a glass of water at some position other than vertical, you observe an apparent displacement of the part of the pencil seen through the glass. The bending of a light path as the light passes obliquely from one substance into a different substance is called refraction.

THE PROBLEM

How are the angle of incidence and the angle of refraction related?

MEASURING THE ANGLE OF REFRACTION

Lay the semicircular plate flat in the center of a clean page of your laboratory notebook. Draw its outline with a sharp pencil. Stick a pin in the paper near the center of the top edge of the container. Stick another pin 5 or 6 centimeters away, so that the line joining the two pins makes an angle of 30 or 40 degrees with the normal erected at the first pin. Use a ruler to sight on the pins through the curved edge of the container. Shift your sight line until it is exactly lined up with the two pins. Draw this sight line. Remove the pins and the semicircular container and draw the complete ray of light, including the line through the pins, the sight line, and the ray in the water. Measure the angle of incidence (the angle between the ray in air and the normal) and the angle of refraction (the angle between the ray in water and the normal).

Repeat for several different angles of incidence, ranging from a small angle to as large an angle as you can see. Tabulate your results. You should have enough trials so that you can use the data for drawing good graphs.

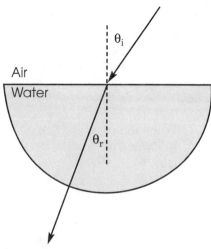

ANALYZING THE DATA
How does the angle of refraction depend on the angle of incidence? Plot a graph of angle of refraction against angle of incidence. Is there a direct proportion? Does there appear to be any steady, systematic change in the ratio? Disregard the scattering of results caused by inaccuracy in reading small angles. Does θ_i/θ_r seem to be constant over any part of the range of values?

The sort of pattern you have found is characteristic of the relationship between the ratio of two angles and the ratio of their sines. To show this, use a table of sines and choose pairs of angles, one of which is just twice the other, ranging from very small to very large. Compute the ratios of their sines. How do these ratios compare for small angles and for large angles? Make a table of your results.

Now return to your data on refraction. Plot a graph of sin i against sin r. Is the ratio constant? What is the slope of your graph? This ratio is known as the index of refraction.

MEASURING THE INDEX OF REFRACTION FOR ANOTHER SUBSTANCE
Find the index of refraction for some transparent substance. Try glass or Plexiglass. Trace the ray through the block of material. You need to obtain data for only one ray.

THE APPARENT DEPTH OF A TRANSPARENT SUBSTANCE
Stand the glass plate on edge and look through the top edge at one of the bottom corners. Draw a diagram showing why this corner appears to be higher than its actual location. Devise and carry out an experiment for using this phenomenon to measure the index of refraction of the glass. Why does a swimming pool look shallower than its true depth? Draw an explanatory diagram.

CHAPTER SIXTEEN ASSESSMENTS

PART A QUESTIONS

1   When a student looks into a plane mirror, she sees a virtual image of herself. However, when she looks into a sheet of paper, no such image forms. Which light phenomenon occurs at the surface of the paper?
(1) regular reflection
(2) diffuse reflection
(3) refraction
(4) resonance

2   Which diagram best represents Image *I*, which is formed by placing object *O* in front of a plane mirror?

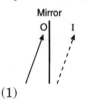
(1)

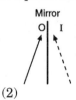
(2)

(3)

(4)

3   The diagram at the right shows light rays in air about to strike a glass window. When the rays reach the boundary between the air and the glass, the light is
(1) totally refracted
(2) totally reflected
(3) partially reflected and partially diffracted
(4) partially reflected and partially refracted

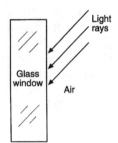

4   What occurs as a ray of light passes from air into water?
(1) The ray must decrease in speed.
(2) The ray must increase in speed.
(3) The ray must decrease in frequency.
(4) The ray must increase in frequency.

5   As a monochromatic beam of light passes obliquely from flint glass into water, how do the characteristics of the beam of light change?
(1) Its wavelength decreases and its frequency decreases.
(2) Its wavelength decreases and its frequency increases.
(3) Its wavelength increases and it bends toward the normal.
(4) Its wavelength increases and it bends away from the normal.

6   A ray of light traveling in air is incident on an interface with medium *X* at an angle of 30.°. The angle of refraction for the light ray in medium *X* is 12.°. Medium *X* could be
(1) alcohol   (2) corn oil   (3) diamond   (4) flint glass

7   The diagram at the right shows a ray of light
    (λ = 5.9 x 10⁻⁷ meter) traveling from air into
    medium X. If the angle of incidence is 30.°
    and the angle of refraction is 19°, medium X
    could be

    (1) air   (3) sodium chloride
    (2) alcohol   (4) glycerol

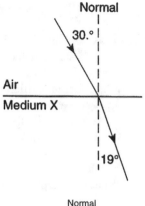

8   The diagram at the right shows a ray of
    monochromatic light incident on an alcohol-
    flint glass interface. What occurs as the light
    travels from alcohol into flint glass?
    (1) The speed of the light decreases and the ray
        bends toward the normal.
    (2) The speed of the light decreases and the ray
        bends away from the normal.
    (3) The speed of the light increases and the ray
        bends toward the normal.
    (4) The speed of the light increases and the ray
        bends away from the normal.

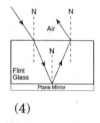

9   A ray of monochromatic light traveling in air enters a rectangular
    glass block obliquely and strikes a plane mirror at the bottom. Then
    the ray travels back through the glass and strikes the air-glass inter-
    face. Which diagram below best represents the path of this light ray?
    [N represents the normal to the surface.]

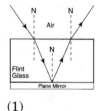
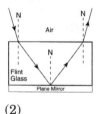
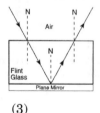

    (1)   (2)   (3)   (4)

10 A ray of monochromatic light is traveling in flint glass. The ray
    strikes the flint glass-air interface at an angle of incidence greater
    than the critical angle for flint glass. Which diagram best represents
    the path of this light ray?

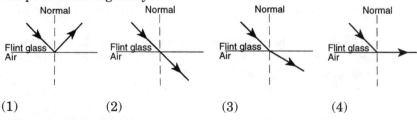

    (1)   (2)   (3)   (4)

11 A light ray passes from air into glass as shown in the diagram at the right. Which relationship represents the index of refraction of the glass?

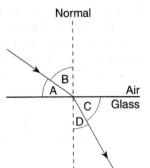

(1) $\dfrac{\sin A}{\sin C}$

(3) $\dfrac{\sin B}{\sin C}$

(2) $\dfrac{\sin A}{\sin D}$

(4) $\dfrac{\sin B}{\sin D}$

PART B QUESTIONS

12 A 2.0-meter-tall student is able to view his entire body at once using a plane mirror. The minimum length of the mirror is [1] _____m

13 A ray of light strikes a plane mirror at an angle of incidence equal to 35°. The angle between the incident ray and the reflected ray is [1] _____°

14 The speed of light in glycerol is approximately [1] _____ m/s

15 A ray of monochromatic light traveling in air is incident on an interface with a liquid at an angle of 45°, as shown in the diagram at the right. If the absolute index of refraction of the liquid is 1.4, the angle of refraction for the light ray is [1] _____°

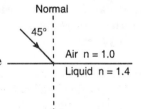

16 The absolute index of refraction for a substance is 2.0 for light having a wavelength of 5.9 x 10⁻⁷ meter. In this substance, what is the critical angle for light incident on a boundary with air? [1] _____°

Base your answers to questions 17 through 18 on the diagram at the right which represents a beam of monochromatic light (f = 5.09 x 10¹⁴ Hz) traveling from Lucite into air.

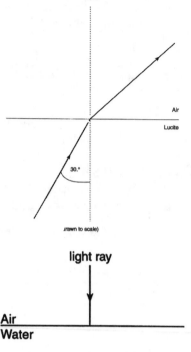

17 What is the measure of the angle of refraction? [Use a protractor or a mathematical calculation.] [1] _____ °

18 The speed of the light in Lucite is [1] _____ m/s

19 A ray of light traveling in air is incident on an air-water boundary as shown at the right.

On the diagram provided, draw the path of the ray in the water. [1]

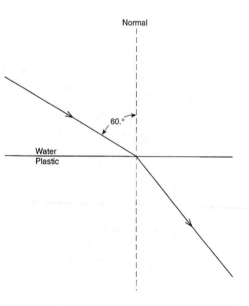

PART C QUESTIONS

Base your answers to questions 20 and 21 on the diagram at the right, which shows a light ray in water incident at an angle of 60.° on a boundary with plastic.

20 Using a protractor, measure the angle of refraction to the nearest degree. [1]

21 Determine the absolute index of refraction for the plastic. [Show all calculations, including the equation and substitution with units.] [2]

Base your answers to questions 22 through 24 on the diagram below, which shows a light ray *AO* in Lucite. The light ray strikes the boundary between Lucite and air at point *O* with an angle of incidence of 30.°. The dotted line represents the normal to the boundary at point *O*.

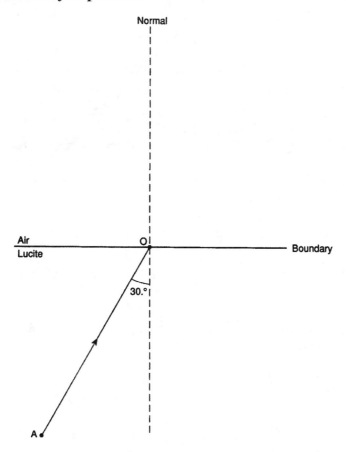

22 Calculate the angle of refraction for incident ray *AO*. [Show all calculations, including the equation and substitutions with units.] [1]

23 On the diagram, using your answer from question 22, construct an arrow with a protractor and straight edge to represent the refracted ray. [1]

24 Calculate the critical angle for a Lucite-air boundary. [Show all calculations, including the equation and substitutions with units.] [1]

Base your answers to questions 25 through 27 on the information and diagram below.

A ray of light *AO* is incident on a plane mirror as shown.

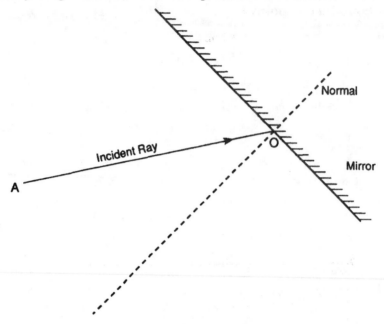

25 Using a protractor, measure the angle of incidence for light ray *AO* and record the value. [1]

26 What is the angle of reflection of the light ray? [1]

27 Using a protractor and straightedge, construct the reflected ray. [1]

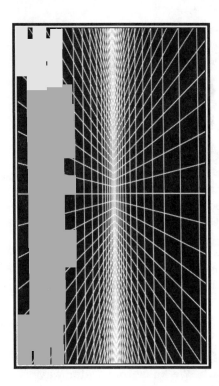

CHAPTER 17
DIFFRACTION
AND
INTERFERENCE

KEY IDEA 4
ENERGY EXISTS IN MANY FORMS, AND WHEN THESE FORMS CHANGE ENERGY IS CONSERVED.

CHAPTER 17 – MAJOR UNDERSTANDINGS

☆ 4.3g Electromagnetic radiation exhibits wave characteristics. Electromagnetic waves can propagate through a vacuum.

☆ 4.3k All frequencies of electromagnetic radiation travel at the same speed in a vacuum.*

☆ 4.3l Diffraction occurs when waves pass by obstacles or through openings. The wave-length of the incident wave and the size of the obstacle or opening affect how the wave spreads out.

☆ 4.3k When waves of a similar nature meet, the resulting interference may be explained using the Principle of Superposition. Standing waves are a special case of interference.

CHAPTER 17
DIFFRACTION AND INTERFERENCE

LIGHT – A WAVE OR A STREAM OF PARTICLES?

By the late 1800s, scientists believed that Newton's idea that light was a stream of particles was incorrect. They had a lot of proof that light was a wave. In this unit we will examine the proof in some detail. Light diffracts in the same manner that any wave would diffract. Light undergoes interference in the same manner that any wave would interfere. And light exhibits the Doppler Effect just as any wave would exhibit the Doppler Effect. Light behaves in a way that is consistent with our conceptual and mathematical understanding of waves. Since light behaves like a wave, one would have good reason to believe that it should be a wave.

DIFFRACTION

Diffraction involves a spreading out of waves as they pass through an opening or around an obstacle in their path. We know that water waves and sound waves have the ability to travel around corners, around obstacles and through openings. Do light waves bend around obstacles and through openings?

When light encounters an obstacle in its path, the obstacle blocks the light and tends to cause the formation of a shadow in the region behind the obstacle. Light does not exhibit a very noticeable ability to bend around the obstacle and fill in the region behind it with light. Nonetheless, light does diffract around obstacles. The size of the opening and the size of the wavelength determine the amount of diffraction which will occur.

SKILL 4.3VII
LAB 28 – THE LASER PENNY

A laser is a device which produces light of one wavelength (monochromatic) which is in phase (coherent). Shine the laser at a penny and project the image on a piece of paper on the wall. Draw the projected image on the paper and explain why the image is fuzzy.

Interference effects occur due to the diffraction of light around different sides of the object, causing the shadow of the object to be fuzzy. In this demonstration, light diffracting around the right edge of a penny constructively and destructively interferes with light diffracting around the left edge of the penny. The result was that an interference was created. This pattern is only noticeable if a narrow beam of monochromatic light (i.e., single wavelength light) is passed directly at the penny. Diffraction can only be explained if you assume a wave nature of light.

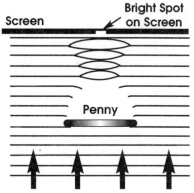

The Proof:
The diffraction of light around a penny and its ultimate interference upon a screen produces a pattern which could only be observed if light is a wave.

Wave interference is the phenomenon, which occurs when two waves meet while traveling along the same medium. The interference of waves results from the net effect of the two individual waves upon the particles of the medium. We have already discussed the basics of interference in the wave chapter.

TWO POINT SOURCE INTERFERENCE

Wave interference can be constructive or destructive in nature. Constructive interference occurs where ever two interfering waves have a displacement in the same direction. For example, if the crest of one wave meets the crest of a second wave, they will interfere in such a manner as to produce a larger crest. Similarly, the interference of a trough and a trough interfere constructively to produce a deeper trough. Destructive interference occurs at any location along the medium where the two interfering waves have a displacement in the opposite direction. For example, the interference of a crest with a trough is an example of destructive interference. Destructive interference will decrease the resulting amount of displacement of the medium.

The interference of two sets of concentric waves with the same frequency produces an interesting pattern in a ripple tank. The diagram on the next page depicts an interference pattern produced by two periodic disturbances. The crests are denoted by the thick lines; and, the troughs are denoted by the thin lines. These patterns can represent water waves, light waves, or sound waves. If you have not had an opportunity to observe two point interference in a ripple tank, this would be a good time to make that observation.

Destructive interference occurs where ever a thick line meets a thin line; this type of interference results in the formation of a **node**. The nodes are denoted by a dotted line and are labeled *N*. Constructive interference occurs wherever a thick line meets a thick line or a thin line meets a thin line; this type of interference results in the formation of an **anti-node**. The anti-nodes are located between the nodal lines. The pattern is a standing wave pattern because it appears to be standing still.

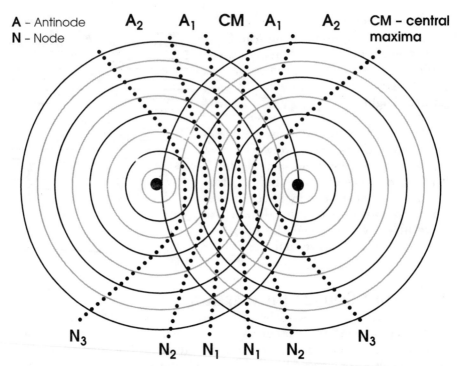

A two-point source interference pattern always has an alternating pattern of nodal and anti-nodal lines. However, there are some features of the pattern which can be modified. First, a change in wavelength (or frequency) of the source will alter the number of lines in the pattern and alter the proximity or closeness of the lines. An increase in frequency will result in more lines per centimeter and a smaller distance between each consecutive line. And a decrease in frequency will result in fewer lines per centimeter and a greater distance between each consecutive line.

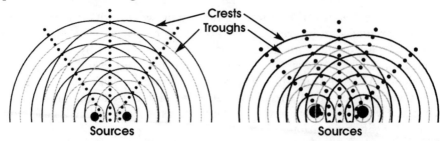

The position of the anti-nodal lines in a two-point source interference pattern is dependent upon the wavelength of the waves.

About 1800, British physicist Thomas Young showed that an interference pattern results when light passes through two narrow parallel slits while traveling through the same medium. Scientists believed that they had proved – beyond a doubt – light was a wave.

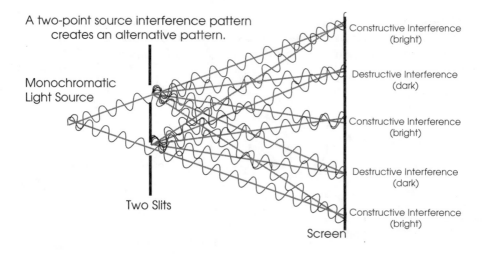

A two-point source interference pattern creates an alternative pattern.

Monochromatic Light Source

Two Slits

Constructive Interference (bright)

Destructive Interference (dark)

Constructive Interference (bright)

Destructive Interference (dark)

Constructive Interference (bright)

Screen

Young, with his double slit apparatus provided more conclusive proof that light was a wave.

 ## REAL WORLD CONNECTIONS - POLARIZATION

A light wave is an electromagnetic wave, which can travel through the vacuum of outer space. Accelerating charged particles produces light waves. An electromagnetic wave is a transverse wave, which has both an electric and a magnetic component. The transverse nature of an electromagnetic wave is quite different from any other types of waves we have already looked at. If you could view an electromagnetic wave traveling towards you, then you would observe the vibrations of the wave occurring in more than one plane of vibration.

A light wave which is vibrating in more than one plane is referred to as **unpolarized light**. Light emitted by the Sun, by a lamp in the classroom, or by a candle flame is unpolarized light. These light waves are created by an electric charge, which vibrates

A lightwave is known to vibrate in a multitude of direction...

...In general, a light wave can be thought of as vibrating in a vertical and in a horizontal plane.

in a variety of directions, thus creating an electromagnetic wave, which also vibrates in a variety of directions. Unpolarized light is rather difficult to visualize; in general, it is helpful to picture unpolarized light as a wave with half its vibrations in a horizontal plane and half of its vibrations in a vertical plane.

It is possible to block some of the vibrations from unpolarized light into **polarized light**. Polarized light waves are light waves in which the vibrations occur in a single plane. The process of transforming unpolarized light into polarized light is known as **polarization**. An easy way to visualize polarization is to consider the picket fence analogy.

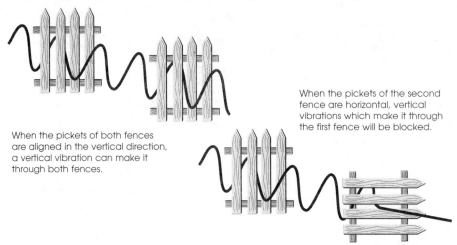

When the pickets of the second fence are horizontal, vertical vibrations which make it through the first fence will be blocked.

When the pickets of both fences are aligned in the vertical direction, a vertical vibration can make it through both fences.

The most common method of polarization involves the use of a **Polaroid filter**. Polaroid filters are made of a special material, which is capable of blocking one of the two planes of vibration of an electromagnetic wave. When unpolarized light is transmitted through a Polaroid filter, it emerges with one-half the intensity and with vibrations in a single plane; it emerges as polarized light.

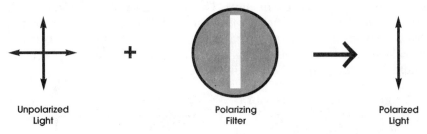

Unpolarized
Light

Polarizing
Filter

Polarized
Light

A Polaroid filter is able to polarize light because of the chemical composition of the filter material. Polarization has a wealth of useful applications besides their use in glare-reducing sunglasses. In industry, Polaroid filters are used to perform stress analysis tests on transparent plastics. Polarization is also used in the entertainment industry to produce and show 3-D movies.

Our model of the polarization of light provides support for the wave-like nature of light. It would be extremely difficult to explain polarization phenomenon using a particle view of light. Polarization only occurs with a transverse wave. Polarization is one more reason why scientists believe that light exhibits wave-like behavior.

The Electromagnetic Spectrum

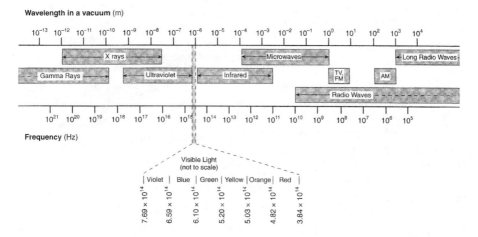

ELECTROMAGNETIC SPECTRUM

Electromagnetic waves are waves, which are capable of transporting energy traveling through deep space, unlike **mechanical waves**, which require a medium in order to transport their energy. Electromagnetic waves are produced by a vibrating electric charge and as such, they consist of both an electric and a magnetic component. Nineteenth century British physicist James C. Maxwell predicted the connection between light, magnetism, and electricity in 1870.

Electromagnetic waves exist with a large range of frequencies. The entire range of frequencies is identified as the **electromagnetic spectrum**. The subdividing of the entire spectrum into smaller spectra is done mostly on the basis of how each region of electromagnetic waves interacts with matter. The diagram above depicts the electromagnetic spectrum and its various regions. The longer wavelength, lower frequency regions are located on the right of the spectrum and the shorter wavelength, higher frequency regions are on the left. The relatively narrow region in the spectrum is the visible light region.

The very narrow band of frequencies located between the infrared region and the ultraviolet region is known as visible light. Our eyes are sensitive to only this very narrow band. Normally, when we use the term "light," we are referring to a type of electromagnetic wave, which stimulates the retina of our eyes. Each individual frequency within the spectrum of visible light frequencies is representative of a particular color. Isaac Newton showed that light shining through a **prism** will be separated into its different frequencies and will thus show the various colors of which visible light is comprised. The separation of visible light into its different colors is known as **dispersion**.

Light waves pass through a prism and separate into seven major colors: red, orange, yellow, green, blue, indigo, and violet.

This phenomenon can be observed in nature as light passes through rain drops producing a rainbow.

Each color is characteristic of a distinct frequency; and different frequencies of light waves will bend varying amounts upon passage through a prism; for these reasons, visible light is dispersed upon passage through a prism. Violet bends the most and red bends the least. Dispersion of visible light produces the colors red (R), orange (O), yellow (Y), green (G), blue (B), indigo (I), and violet (V). It is because of this that visible light is sometimes referred to as ROY G. BIV. The number seven was considered a lucky number to the ancients. There were seven days in the week and Seven Wonders of the World so it was felt that there should be seven colors in the rainbow. You should now realize that there are an infinite number of colors in the rainbow because there are an infinite number of frequencies producing them.

LAB 29 - POLARIZED ART

BACKGROUND

Polaroid lenses are everywhere, from your calculator display, to sunglasses to photographic lenses. Polarized art has long been an accepted art form. A wonderful example of these technique graces the Boston Science Museum. This activity will give you an opportunity to create piece of "art" work, which can be only observed through crossed Polaroid lenses.

OBJECTIVE

To create a piece of artwork on a sheet of overhead transparency film, using layers of transparent tape at different angles.

SETTING UP THE OVERHEAD

This activity works well when an overhead is set up at the front of the room. One piece of Polaroid film should be placed on the overhead glass. A second piece should be supported a few inches above the glass. Students should slip their "art" between the two crossed filters to observe the effects. Students should use very inexpensive tape for this activity. High quality tape does not work well.

LET'S BEGIN

As you start creating your masterpiece, take time to record your observations. How many layers do you need to make a particular color? What happens when you stretch the tape? Can you set up a complete "palette" or are you limited in your colors?

CHAPTER SEVENTEEN ASSESSMENTS

PART A QUESTIONS

1 Which diagram best illustrates wave diffraction?

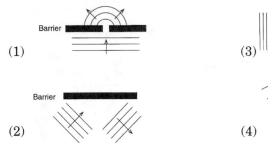

(1)

(3)

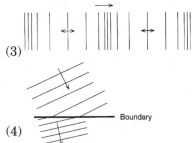

(2)

(4)

2 The diagram at the right shows two sources, *A* and *B*, vibrating in phase in the same uniform medium and producing circular wave fronts. Which phenomenon occurs at point *P*?

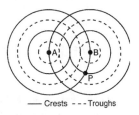

(1) destructive interference
(2) constructive interference
(3) reflection
(4) refraction

—— Crests - - - Troughs

3 The diagram at the right shows two waves approaching each other in the same uniform medium. Which diagram best represents the appearance of the medium after the waves have passed through each other?

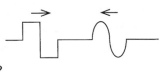

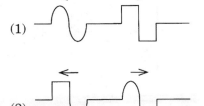

(1)

(3)

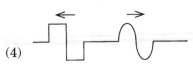

(2)

(4)

4   Which diagram best represents light in phase?

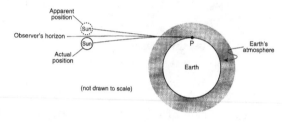

(1)   (2)   (3)   (4)

5   If all parts of a light beam have a constant phase relationship, with
    the same wavelength and frequency, the light beam was from
    (1) a laser
    (2) an incandescent bulb
    (3) a florescent bulb
    (4) a gas discharge tube

6   The diagram at the
    right shows how an
    observer located at
    point P on Earth can
    see the Sun when it is
    below the observer's
    horizon. This observa-
    tion is possible because
    of the ability of Earth's
    atmosphere to

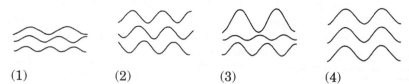

    (1) reflect light   (3) refract light
    (2) diffract light   (4) polarize light

PART B QUESTIONS

7   Two waves having the same amplitude and the same frequency pass
    simultaneously through a uniform medium. Maximum destructive
    interference occurs when the phase difference between the two
    waves is [1] _____ °

8   The diagram at the
    right shows two waves,
    A and B. The phase dif-
    ference between A and
    B is [1] _____ °

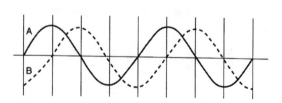

PART C QUESTIONS

Base your answers to questions 9 through 11 on the information and diagram at the right.

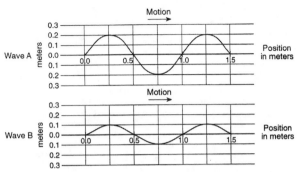

Two waves, *A* and *B*, travel in the same direction in the same medium at the same time.

9   On the grid below, draw the resultant wave produced by the super-position of waves *A* and *B*. The grid below is to be used for practice purposes only. [1]

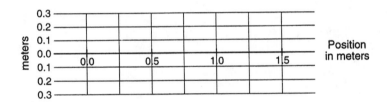

10 What is the amplitude of the resultant wave? [1]

11 What is the wavelength of the resultant wave? [1]

CHAPTER 18
MODERN
PHYSICS

KEY IDEA 5 — ENERGY AND MATTER INTERACT THROUGH FORCES THAT RESULT IN CHANGES IN MOTION.

PERFORMANCE INDICATOR 5.3 *STUDENTS CAN COMPARE ENERGY RELATIONSHIPS WITHIN AN ATOM'S NUCLEUS TO THOSE OUTSIDE THE NUCLEUS.*

CHAPTER 18 – MAJOR UNDERSTANDINGS

☆ 5.3c On the atomic level, energy is emitted or absorbed in discrete packets called photons.*

☆ 5.3d The energy of a photon is proportional to its frequency.*

☆ 5.3e On the atomic level, energy and matter exhibit the characteristics of both waves and particles.

MODERN PHYSICS

DUAL NATURE OF LIGHT

Light exhibits the characteristics of waves and particles. This duality is true for all electromagnetic radiation. It means that some phenomena are more easily explained by the use of the wave model, while other phenomena are better explained by considering light a particle. Interference, polarization, and diffraction are explained only on the basis of wave theory. The **photoelectric effect** is explained only on the basis of the particle theory.

A German physicist, Max Karl Ernst Ludwig Planck (1858-1947) at the close of the nineteenth century, developed an equation to explain the black-body radiation phenomena which could not be explained by classical physics. Planck won the Nobel Prize in 1918. Atomic oscillators emit or absorb electromagnetic radiations only in discrete amounts, called **quanta**. The energy of each quantum is proportional to the frequency of radiation. The constant of proportionality (**h**) is called **Planck's constant**.

$$E_{photon} = hf \quad \text{or} \quad E_{photon} = \frac{hc}{\lambda}$$

Where:

E	=	energy
ƒ	=	frequency
h	=	Planck's constant
c	=	speed of light
λ	=	wavelength

☆ PHOTOELECTRIC EFFECT

The **photoelectric effect** is the emission of photoelectrons (electrons that are responsive to light) from an object when a certain electromagnetic radiation strikes it. Wave theory did not explain the observations of the photoelectric effect. According to the wave theory, the maximum kinetic energy should be related to the intensity of the radiation and any radiation should cause the emission of photoelectrons if sustained long enough.

In 1905, **Albert Einstein** proposed that electromagnetic radiation is always quantized. Using this, he explained the photoelectric effect as a particle phenomena.

$$KE_{max} = E - mgh$$

The illustration above is a mechanical analogy of the photoelectric effect. The example is of a ball in a ditch which when given kinetic energy E greater than mgh, will escape from the ditch. After the ball's escape, the maximum kinetic energy is:

$$KE_{max} = E - mgh$$

The illustration at the right is a schematic view of an apparatus for observing the photoelectric effect. Electrons, collected at wire A, are ejected when light strikes plate C, causing a current.

incident light

ejected photoelectron

vacuum

ammeter

battery

The equation for the photoelectric effect is:

Energy out = Energy in – work function

(or)

$$KE_{max} = hf - w_o$$

Where:

KE_{max} is the maximum kinetic energy of the emitted electron

h is Planck's constant: 6.63×10^{-34} joule/sec

f is the incident frequency

w_o is the work function (minimum energy for an electron to escape)

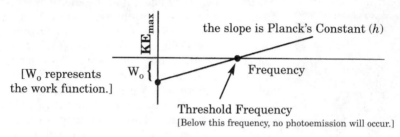

[W_o represents the work function.]

the slope is Planck's Constant (h)

Threshold Frequency
[Below this frequency, no photoemission will occur.]

In the region of the spectrum where photoemission can occur, the rate of emission depends on the intensity of the incident light. Doubling the illumination or intensity, doubles the number of electrons emitted. The maximum kinetic energy depends only on the frequency of the incident radiation.

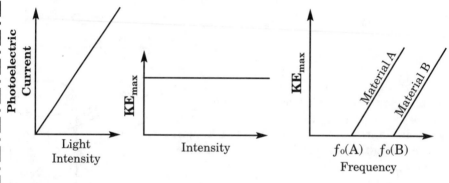

Photoelectric current plotted against the intensity of the incident light for a case in which photoelectrons are emitted.	A graph of KE_{max} of the emitted photoelectrons versus intensity of the light causing the emission. KE_{max} is constant for a given light source.	The maximum kinetic energy of photoelectrons as a function of the frequency of the incident light for two materials. Each material exhibits a threshold frequency f_o.

For each photoemissive material there is a minimum frequency below which no photoelectrons will be emitted. This is called the **threshold frequency** (f_o). The energy associated with the threshold frequency is the **work function** (w_o).

$$w_o = hf_o$$

Photon-Particle Collisions (The Compton Effect)

In 1922, **Arthur Compton** used X-rays for photon-particle collisions. The **Compton Effect** can be explained in terms of conservation of energy and momentum. The illustration at the right shows the result of a collision between an electron in an atom and a very high energy X-ray photon. Both an electron and a photon of lower energy are emitted. Energy and momentum are conserved.

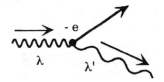

Using the equations $E = mc^2$, $E = hf$, and $c = f\lambda$, the momentum of photons is expressed as:

$$p = \frac{E}{c} = \frac{hf}{c} = \frac{h}{\lambda}$$

Where:

p	is momentum	f	is frequency
c	is the speed of light	λ	is wavelength
h	is Planck's constant	E	is energy

The momentum of the photon is inversely proportional to its wavelength. In Compton's experiments, the wavelength of the photon increased, indicating a momentum loss. Momentum is a particle property. Although the photon carries momentum and can exert a force, it does not and cannot have, rest mass. In any frame of reference in space, the **photon moves with the speed of light** and cannot be at rest.

Matter Waves (de Broglie)

In 1924, **Louis de Broglie** made the proposal that moving particles have wave properties. It was based on his intuitive feeling that nature is symmetrical. The dual nature of light should be matched by a dual nature of matter. His **matter waves** would be represented by:

$$\lambda = \frac{h}{p} = \frac{h}{mv}$$

Where:

- p is momentum
- h is Planck's constant
- λ is wavelength

The wavelength of a particle is inversely proportional to its momentum. *Note:* No particle can move at the speed of light; hence, de Broglie simply changed "c" to "v," (v is velocity) for his prediction.

Theoretically, all matter has wave characteristics. Under ordinary circumstances, the wave nature of the object is not significant. One does not notice the wavelength of a moving baseball or golf ball. The wavelength is very small since the momentum is relatively large. If the particle moving was an electron rather than a baseball, the wave movement would become significant, because of a much smaller mass. In 1927, diffraction patterns of electrons were observed by American physicists **Clinton Davisson** and **Lester Germer**. The observed wavelength was equal to **h/p**.

MODELS OF THE ATOM

In the early years of the 20th Century, British physicist Ernest Rutherford proposed a model of the atom, similar to our solar system. The nucleus was at the center and the electrons orbited the nucleus, like the planets orbit the Sun. The limitation of Rutherford's Model was that it did not account for (1) the lack of emission of radiation, as electrons move about the nucleus, and (2) the unique spectrum of each element and (3) the stability of the atom.

The electrons moving around the nucleus are accelerated and should radiate energy of changing frequency, thus the electrons should eventually collide with the nucleus. Since atoms emit only radiation of specific frequencies and do not collapse spontaneously, Rutherford's Model required modification.

In 1913, Danish physicist **Neils Henrik Bohr** (1885-1962) developed a model of the hydrogen atom which consisted of a positively charged nucleus and a single electron revolving in a circular orbit and in 1922, won the Nobel Prize for his work. In order to explain this model, Bohr made assumptions which were contrary to classical theory.

First, Bohr's orbiting electron does not lose energy even though it has an acceleration (centripetal) towards the center. According to classical physics, the electron should lose energy by emitting electromagnetic radiation and spiral into the nucleus. Bohr assumed that all forms of energy were quantized. Second, only a limited number of specified orbits of radius **r** is permitted. Each orbit represents a particular energy state. The permitted orbits are those for which the angular momentum of the electron is an integral multiple (**n**) of Planck's constant divided by 2π:

$$\mathbf{mvr} = \frac{\mathbf{nh}}{\mathbf{2\pi}} \quad \text{(mvr, angular momentum is quantized)}$$

Third, when an electron changes from one energy state to another, a quantum of energy equal to the difference between the energies of the two states is emitted or absorbed. The change in energy is given by:

$$\mathbf{h}f = \mathbf{E_1} \text{ - } \mathbf{E_2}$$

Where, E_1 and **E_2** are the respective energies of the two states and f is the frequency of the photon emitted or absorbed: absorbed when electrons move to a high energy state, and emitted when they drop to a lower energy state.

In 1914, American physicist **James Franck** (1882-1964) and German physicist **Gustav Ludwig Hertz** (1887-1975) further strengthened the concepts of stationary states or fixed energy levels, by bombarding gas molecules with electrons. They shared the 1925 Nobel Prize for their work. The gas molecules can only accept energy in discrete amounts. The process of raising the energy of atoms is called **excitation**. Excitation energies were different for different gases. Excited atoms subsequently released the energy as photons. Electrons with energies lower than the discrete excitation energies, collided elastically with gas molecules. The Franck-Hertz experiment demonstrated one way of exciting atoms. Other methods included thermal excitation, electrical discharge, and electromagnetic excitation.

In the energy level diagram, **n = 1** is the lowest possible energy level or the **ground state**. The **ionization potential** is the minimum energy necessary to remove an electron from the ground state to infinity; that is, to ionize the atom. For example, the ionization potential is 13.6 eV for hydrogen and 10.38 eV for mercury

The negative (–) signs of energy levels indicate that the electron is controlled by the nucleus with that amount of energy. Energy must be applied to ionize the electron. The amount of energy required is greatest for the ground state.

Energy Level Diagrams

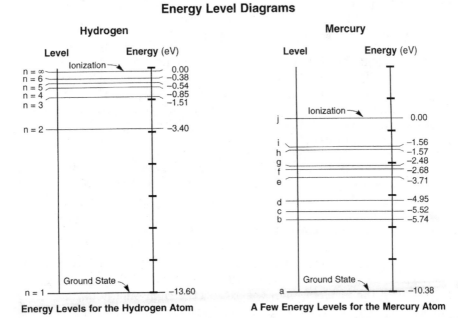

Energy Levels for the Hydrogen Atom

A Few Energy Levels for the Mercury Atom

An interpretation of Bohr's Model describes the electron as a wave. The probability of finding the electron at a particular position can be described by a standing wave, which can exist at only certain distances from the nucleus. This standing wave will only occur:

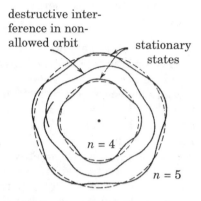

destructive interference in non-allowed orbit

stationary states

When: $\quad mvr = \dfrac{nh}{2\pi}$

So: $\quad 2\pi r = nh/mv$

$\quad$ and $\quad n\lambda = 2\pi r$

Therefore: $\quad n\lambda = nh/mv$

Thus: $\quad \lambda = \dfrac{h}{p}$

In a **Stationary State**, there is no destructive interference. The n's refer to the energy levels of the hydrogen (see Energy levels for Hydrogen).

Where, **n** is an integer, λ is the wavelength of the electron, **h** is Planck's constant, and **p** is the momentum. An electron in a standing wave about the nucleus will not radiate energy. Bohr's model of the atom did not successfully predict other aspects of the hydrogen atom, nor did it explain the electron orbits of large atoms having many electrons.

ATOMIC SPECTRA

Each element has a characteristic **spectra**. Bohr's model helped to explain the spectra of elements. Atoms with electrons, excited to an energy level above the ground state, emit energy as photons, as their electrons fall to lower energy levels.

Spectra may be classified according to the nature of their origin, i.e., emission or absorption. An emission spectrum consists of all the radiations emitted by atoms or molecules. In an absorption spectrum, portions of a continuous spectrum (light containing all wavelengths) are missing because they have been absorbed by the medium through which the light has passed; the missing wavelengths appear as dark lines or gaps.

The energies associated with the lines in an emission spectrum of an element may be determined by using an energy level diagram. The reference charts contain the energy level diagrams for both hydrogen and mercury. The emission spectra is emitted when electrons in higher energy levels fall to lower energy levels.

Any atom can absorb those photons whose energies are equal to the energies of the photon it can emit when excited. Absorbing a photon will only occur if the incident energy is exactly the right energy to raise it to a particular energy state. If a hydrogen electron in the ground state is hit by a photon of 10.5 eV or 10.0 eV, the photon will either pass through or scatter elastically. However, a 10.2 eV photon will be absorbed and the electron will jump to the n = 2 level. If any photon equal to or greater than 13.6 eV hits the hydrogen atom in the ground state, the atom will ionize. The leftover energy of the photon is then carried away by the electron as it leaves the atom.

SPECTRUM OF INCANDESCENT SOLIDS

The spectrum of incandescent solids is said to be continuous because all wavelengths are present. The spectrum of incandescent gases, on the other hand, is called a line or emission spectrum because only a few wavelengths are emitted. These wavelengths appear to be a series of parallel lines because a slit is used as the light-imaging device. Line spectra are characteristic of the elements that emit the radiation. Line spectra are also called atomic spectra because the lines represent wavelengths radiated from atoms when electrons change from one energy level to another.

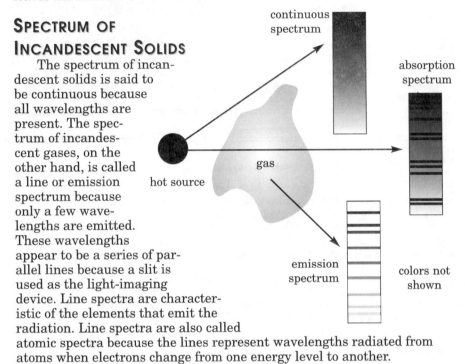

continuous spectrum

absorption spectrum

hot source

gas

emission spectrum

colors not shown

 **REAL WORLD CONNECTIONS**

BLACK LIGHTS

You have probably seen **black lights** at amusement parks, science museums and displays. Black light makes fluorescent colors "glow in the dark." A black light bulb produces "black light." If you turn on a "black light" bulb in a dark room, what you can see from the bulb is a purplish glow. What you cannot see is the **ultraviolet light** that the bulb is also producing.

Our eyes can see light in the visible spectrum ranging from red through orange, yellow, green, blue and violet. Above violet is ultraviolet light, which we cannot see. A black light bulb produces UVA light (as opposed to UVB light, which is much more harmful).

It is the phosphors which glow under a black light. A phosphor is any substance that emits visible light in response to some sort of radiation. In other words, a phosphor converts the energy in the radiation into visible light, whether it is a fluorescent poster or an invisible hand stamp or a newly-washed white T-shirt.

Normal colors simply reflect light, but a **fluorescent color** absorbs the radiation and re-emits it in the visible spectrum (sort of like a light bulb emits light), so it looks much brighter than a normal color. White T-shirts and socks normally glow under a black light because modern detergents contain phosphors that convert UV light into white light. This makes whites look "whiter than white" in normal sunlight. What you are seeing in sunlight is the normal reflection of visible white light from the cloth, as well as the emission of white light that the phosphors create from UV light in sunlight. The T-shirt really is whiter than white!

Many other substances fluoresce naturally under black light. Because of this, black lights are used to test urine and some types of paper money.

A fluorescent light works on the same principle. Inside a fluorescent light is low-pressure mercury vapor. When ionized, mercury vapor emits ultraviolet light. The light we see from a fluorescent tube is the light given off by the phosphor coating the inside of the tube (the phosphor **fluoresceces** when energized, hence the name).

Skill 5.3.1 – Interpret Energy Level Diagrams

Example: Using the energy level diagram of hydrogen, calculate the number and energy of photons possible, as an $n = 3$ state electron returns to the ground state.

$$E_{photon} = E_i - E_f$$

Solution: In returning to the ground state from the $n = 3$ level, the electron could jump directly to $n = 1$ or go to $n = 2$, and then $n = 1$. Each jump represents a different energy level photon. There are three different photons which could be emitted.

$n = 3$ to $n = 1$
$hf = E_3 - E_1$
$\quad = -1.5$ eV $- (-13.6$ eV$) = 12.1$ eV

$n = 3$ to $n = 2$
$hf = E_3 - E_2$
$\quad = (-1.5$ eV$) - (-3.4$ eV$) = 1.9$ eV

$n = 2$ to $n = 1$
$hf = E_2 - E_1$
$\quad = -3.4$ eV $- (-13.6$ eV$) = 10.2$ eV

In hydrogen, any jump to the $n = 1$ level represents high energy. The radiation would be in the ultraviolet range. This series is commonly called the **Lyman Series**. Any jump to the $n = 2$ level (from higher energy levels) represents lower energy radiation. Many of these lines are visible light. This is the **Balmer Series**. Other series have been observed as well.

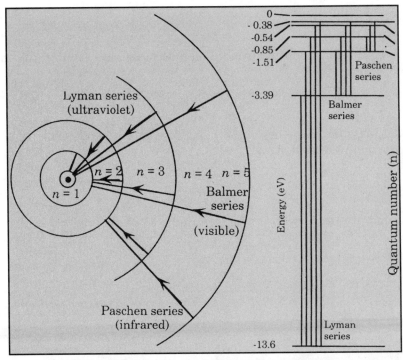

TRY IT

1   Calculate the energy level jumps possible for an electron at the d
    level in the mercury atom. [Refer to the Reference Tables and the
    material in the previous example.]

LAB 30 – CALCULATING THE FREQUENCY EMITTED
IN THE ELECTRON JUMP

Using the energies we determined for n=3 to n=1 hydrogen jump in
the above skill, we will now determine the frequency of the emitted light.

First convert the number of electron volts to joules. Then divide by
Planck's constant to determine the frequency. All that remains is to look
up the frequency on the reference table to determine the kind of electromagnetic radiation.

n=3 to n=1 equals 12.1 eV

12.1eV x 1.6 x 10^{-19} J/eV =1.9 x 10^{-18} J

E = hf

1.9 x 10^{-18} J = 6.63 x 10^{-34} Js (f)

f = 2.9 x 10^{15} hz

From the chart on the Physics Reference Table, we see that that frequency is ultraviolet.

TRY IT

2   Calculate the frequency of radiation for each of the other jumps cal-
    culated in the skill above.

3   Using the Mercury Spectrum, determine all of the jumps which pro-
    duce visible light and identify the color of each photon produced.

REAL WORLD CONNECTIONS

LASER THEORY AND OPERATION

The word laser is an acronym for Light Amplification by Stimulated Emission of Radiation. The color or wavelength of light being emitted depends on the type of lasing material being used. For example, if a Neodymium:Yttrium Aluminum Garnet (Nd:YAG) crystal is used as the lasing material, light with a wavelength of 1064 nm will be emitted.

A laser generates a beam of very intense light. The major difference between laser light and light generated by white light sources (such as a light bulb) is that laser light is monochromatic, directional, and coherent. Monochromatic means that all of the

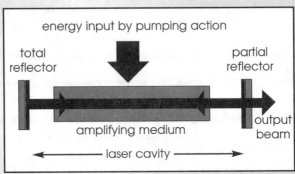

light produced by the laser is of a single wavelength. White light is a combination of all visible wavelengths (400 - 700 nm). Directional means that the beam of light has very low divergence.

Light from a conventional source, such as a light bulb, diverges, spreading in all directions. The intensity may be large at the source, but it decreases rapidly as an observer moves away from the source. The laser light travels in a single direction and maintains its intensity for long distances. Coherent means that the waves of light are in phase with each other. A light bulb produces many wavelengths, making it incoherent. Even a monochromatic light will be incoherent unless the emitted waves are in phase.

UNCERTAINTY PRINCIPLE

(HEISENBERG)

The **Uncertainty Principle** was first advanced by **Werner Heisenberg** in 1927. As a mathematical statement, it can be written as:

$$\Delta x \, \Delta p \geq h$$

Where: Δx represents the uncertainty in position
           Δp represents the uncertainty in momentum
           h   represents Planck's constant

The uncertainty principle limits how well we can know simultaneous values of the position and the linear momentum of a particle or wave. As we make the observation, a photon of light would hit the object. The photon imparts momentum to the electron. You cannot locate the electron without changing its momentum.

CHAPTER EIGHTEEN ASSESSMENTS

PART A QUESTIONS

1 In which part of the electromagnetic spectrum does a photon have the greatest energy?
(1) red   (2) infrared   (3) violet   (4) ultraviolet

2 During a collision between a photon and an electron, there is conservation of
(1) energy, only
(2) momentum, only
(3) both energy and momentum
(4) neither energy nor momentum

3 The momentum of a photon is inversely proportional to the photon's
(1) frequency
(2) mass
(3) weight
(4) wavelength

4 The four-line Balmer series spectrum shown below is emitted by a hydrogen gas sample in a laboratory. A star moving away from Earth also emits a hydrogen spectrum.

Lines in Hydrogen Spectrum

6.5   4.9   4.3 4.1
Wavelength (×10⁻⁷ m)

Which Spectrum might be observed on Earth for this star?

6.3   4.7   4.1 3.9   6.5   5.8   5.0   4.1
Wavelength (×10⁻⁷ m)   Wavelength (×10⁻⁷ m)
(1)   (3)

6.5   5.8   5.0   4.1   6.7   5.1   4.5 4.3
Wavelength (×10⁻⁷ m)   Wavelength (×10⁻⁷ m)
(2)   (4)

5 Which phenomenon can be explained by both the particle model and wave model?
(1) reflection
(2) diffraction
(3) polarization
(4) interference

6 Light demonstrates the characteristics of
(1) particles, only
(2) waves, only
(3) both particles and waves
(4) neither particles nor waves

7 The photon model of light is more appropriate than the wave model in explaining
(1) interference
(2) refraction
(3) polarization
(4) photoelectric emission

Note: Question 8 has only 3 answer choices.

8 Interference and diffraction can be explained by
   (1) the wave theory, only
   (2) the particle theory, only
   (3) neither the wave nor particle theory

9 The energy of a photon varies
   (1) directly as the wavelength
   (2) directly as the frequency
   (3) inversely as the frequency
   (4) inversely as the square of the frequency

10 Which graph best represents the relationship between the energy of a photon and its wavelength?

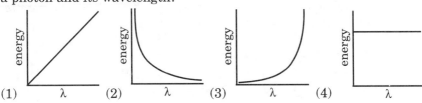

11 If the wave properties of a particle are difficult to observe, it is probably due to the particle's
   (1) small size   (3) low momentum
   (2) large momentum   (4) high charge

Note: Questions 12 and 13 have only 3 answer choices.

12 As the wavelength of a ray of light increases, the momentum of the photons of the light ray will
   (1) decrease   (2) increase   (3) remain the same

13 As the frequency of a photon increases, its momentum
   (1) decrease   (2) increase   (3) remain the same

14 According to the quantum theory of light, the energy of light is carried in discrete units called
   (1) alpha particles   (3) photons
   (2) protons   (4) photoelectrons

15 Which is conserved when a photon collides with an electron?
   (1) velocity   (3) energy, only
   (2) momentum, only   (4) momentum and energy

16 Which color of light has the greatest energy per photon?
   (1) red   (2) green   (3) blue   (4) violet

PART B QUESTIONS

17 What is the minimum energy required to excite a mercury atom initially in the ground state? [1] _____eV

18 The electron in a hydrogen atom drops from energy level $n = 2$ to energy level $n = 1$ by emitting a photon having an energy of approximately [1] _____ joules

19 A hydrogen atom could have an electron energy level transition from $n = 2$ to $n = 3$ by absorbing a photon having an energy of [1] _____ eV

20 What is the approximate matter wavelength of a 0.30-kilogram tennis ball moving at a speed of 30. meters per second? [1] _____ m

21 If the momentum of a particle is 1.8×10^{-22} kilogram-meter per second, its matter wavelength is approximately [1] _____ m

22 Blue light has a frequency of approximately 6.0×10^{14} hertz. A photon of blue light will have an energy of approximately [1] _____ J

23 What is the energy of a photon with a frequency of 5.0×10^{15} hertz [1] _____ J

24 The momentum of a photon with a wavelength of 5.9×10^{-7} meter is [1] _____ kg m/s

25 What is the approximate matter wavelength of a 0.500-kilogram tennis ball moving at a speed of 300. meters per second? [1] _____ m

26 What is the energy of a photon with a frequency of 3.00×10^{13} hertz? [1] _____ J

27 The energy of a photon which has a frequency of 3.3×10^{34} hertz is approximately [1] _____ J

28 What is the wavelength of the matter wave associated with a bird of 1.0-kilogram mass flying at 2.0 meters per second? [1] _____ m

29 An atom changing from an energy state of -0.54 eV to an energy state of -0.85 eV will emit a photon whose energy is [1] _____ eV

PART C QUESTIONS

Base your answers to questions 30 and 31 on the information below.

An electron is accelerated from rest to a speed of 2.0 x 10⁶ meters per second.

30 How much kinetic energy is gained by the electron as it is accelerated from rest to this speed? [Show all calculations, including the equation and substitution with units.] [2]

31 What is the matter wavelength of the electron after it is accelerated to this speed? [Show all calculations, including the equations and substitutions with units.] [2]

Base your answers to questions 32 through 34 on the information below.

A hydrogen atom emits a 2.55-electronvolt photon as its electron changes from one energy level to another.

32 Express the energy of the emitted photon in joules. [1]

33 Determine the frequency of the emitted photon. [Show all calculations, including the equation and the substitution with units.] [2]

34 Using the *Reference Tables for Physical Setting: Physics*, determine the energy level change for the electron. [2]

APPENDIX A
SPECIFIC RATING CRITERIA

The examples presented and discussed in Appendix A contain references to these general suggestions for rating, where appropriate.

CALCULATIONS

To receive credit for performing a calculation, the student must provide the equation, the substitution with units into the equation, and the final answer with units.

Generally, a calculation is worth a maximum of 2 credits. Allow the first credit if the student shows the equation and substitution with units into the equation. Allow the second credit if the correct answer is recorded with appropriate units.

When rating calculations, review all the student's work to be certain that the physics concepts are applied correctly. At times, a student may make two or more errors that cancel each other out, resulting in a correct answer based on erroneous physics.

Allow 1 credit if a student records the equation, substitutes with numbers only, and records the correct answer without units. Penalize a student only once per question for leaving out units. However, allow no credit if another error was made, such as recording an incorrect equation (or no equation) or making a calculation error.

The **SI (International System)** units are used in the Physical Setting: Physics Core Curriculum and in the examinations. However, students are expected to have an understanding of metric units. Where more appropriate, **cgs** units will be used. Although students are generally expected to record answers in the correct SI unit, also allow credit for the use of correct non-SI units.

GRAPHS

To receive full credit for constructing a graph, the student must be able to:

1. Label both axes with appropriate variables and units
2. Mark linear scales with appropriate scale divisions
3. Plot all points accurately
4. Draw a best-fit line
5. Calculate the slope of the best fit line at a point

Requirements vary according to the graphing questions. A partially completed graph may be provided for the student to finish according to directions given in the question(s).

1. Axes: By convention, the dependent variable should be placed on the y-axis. However, do not penalize students for not following this convention on graphs constructed for the test, unless they are specifically instructed to do so. A graph constructed without following this convention is not wrong; at times the data being analyzed are better presented by placing the dependent variable on the x-axis.

2. Scales: When a question requires students to develop the scale for one or both axis, they care expected to select appropriate scale divisions. The term "appropriate" means that most (not necessarily all) of the grid provided is used and that scale divisions allow for relatively simple estimation between lines.

3. Points: All data points should be plotted iwthin ± 0.3 grid space of their true positions. Single points are clearest, but points emphasized with circles or crosses are acceptable. Points or empty circles drawn larger than 0.3 grid space in diameter should not be accepted.

4. Best-fit line: When the best-fit line is a straight line, students must draw it with a straight-edge. When the best-fit line is a curve, students should draw it as accurately as possible, and the teacher must understand that they will be doing so freehand. A best-fit line should be continuous and have the data points distributed evenly around it if they do not fall exactly upon it. It may or may not pass through the origin, depending on the distribution of points, and it need not pass through the first and last data points on the graph. **Students should not merely connect the dots, whether with straight or curved line segments**.

5. Slope of a graph: To find the slope of a straight line graph the student must pick two points on the best-fit line and use the slope formula $m = \Delta y / \Delta x$ to determine the value, with units, of the slope. Values taken from the data table may be used *only* if the student's best-fit line passes through those data points. Credit for the slope calculation should be allowed according to the Scoring Criteria for Calculations that appear in the scoring key.

    To find the slope of a curve at a particular point, the student should draw the tangent to the curve at that point and determine the slope of the tangent line as described above for a straight line. The use of

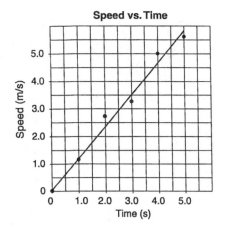

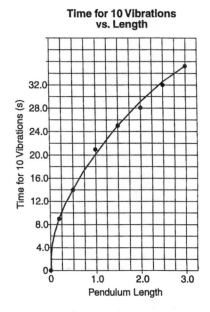

analysis (e.g., derivative of a function) may not be used to determine a slope unless the graph was derived from a specific function or is shown by the student to be derived from that function. Generally, graphs drawn from experimental data should not be assumed to represent any particular mathematical function.

Generally, a graph should have a title. Students may be required to provide a title for a graph constructed for the test. However, if no title is required in the question, credit should not be deducted if it is missing.

APPENDIX B

REFERENCE TABLES FOR PHYSICAL SETTING: PHYSICS

The follow reference tables were produced by the State of New York State Education Department, 2002 Edition.

List of Physical Constants		
Name	Symbol	Value
Universal gravitational constant	G	6.67×10^{-11} N•m^2/kg^2
Acceleration due to gravity	g	9.81 m/s^2
Speed of light in a vacuum	c	3.00×10^8 m/s
Speed of sound in air at STP		3.31×10^2 m/s
Mass of Earth		5.98×10^{24} kg
Mass of the Moon		7.35×10^{22} kg
Mean radius of Earth		6.37×10^6 m
Mean radius of the Moon		1.74×10^6 m
Mean distance—Earth to the Moon		3.84×10^8 m
Mean distance—Earth to the Sun		1.50×10^{11} m
Electrostatic constant	k	8.99×10^9 N•m^2/C^2
1 elementary charge	e	1.60×10^{-19} C
1 coulomb (C)		6.25×10^{18} elementary charges
1 electronvolt (eV)		1.60×10^{-19} J
Planck's constant	h	6.63×10^{-34} J•s
1 universal mass unit (u)		9.31×10^2 MeV
Rest mass of the electron	m_e	9.11×10^{-31} kg
Rest mass of the proton	m_p	1.67×10^{-27} kg
Rest mass of the neutron	m_n	1.67×10^{-27} kg

Absolute Indices of Refraction
($f = 5.09 \times 10^{14}$ Hz)

Air	1.00
Corn oil	1.47
Diamond	2.42
Ethyl alcohol	1.36
Glass, crown	1.52
Glass, flint	1.66
Glycerol	1.47
Lucite	1.50
Quartz, fused	1.46
Sodium chloride	1.54
Water	1.33
Zircon	1.92

Approximate Coefficients of Friction

	Kinetic	Static
Rubber on concrete (dry)	0.68	0.90
Rubber on concrete (wet)	0.58	
Rubber on asphalt (dry)	0.67	0.85
Rubber on asphalt (wet)	0.53	
Rubber on ice	0.15	
Waxed ski on snow	0.05	0.14
Wood on wood	0.30	0.42
Steel on steel	0.57	0.74
Copper on steel	0.36	0.53
Teflon on Teflon	0.04	

Prefixes for Powers of 10

Prefix	Symbol	Notation
tera	T	10^{12}
giga	G	10^{9}
mega	M	10^{6}
kilo	k	10^{3}
deci	d	10^{-1}
centi	c	10^{-2}
milli	m	10^{-3}
micro	μ	10^{-6}
nano	n	10^{-9}
pico	p	10^{-12}

The Electromagnetic Spectrum

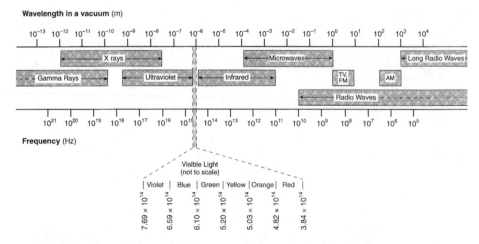

Hydrogen

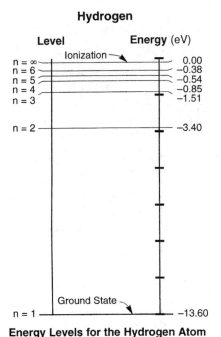

Level	Energy (eV)
Ionization	
n = ∞	0.00
n = 6	−0.38
n = 5	−0.54
n = 4	−0.85
n = 3	−1.51
n = 2	−3.40
n = 1 (Ground State)	−13.60

Energy Levels for the Hydrogen Atom

Mercury

Level	Energy (eV)
j (Ionization)	0.00
i	−1.56
h	−1.57
g	−2.48
f	−2.68
e	−3.71
d	−4.95
c	−5.52
b	−5.74
a (Ground State)	−10.38

A Few Energy Levels for the Mercury Atom

Classification of Matter

Matter
→ Hadrons
→ Leptons

Hadrons
→ Baryons
→ Mesons

Baryons → three quarks

Mesons → quark and antiquark

Particles of the Standard Model

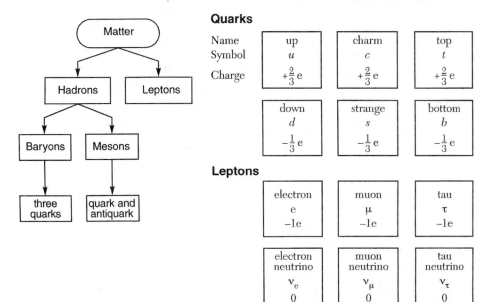

Quarks

Name	Symbol	Charge
up	u	$+\frac{2}{3}$ e
charm	c	$+\frac{2}{3}$ e
top	t	$+\frac{2}{3}$ e
down	d	$-\frac{1}{3}$ e
strange	s	$-\frac{1}{3}$ e
bottom	b	$-\frac{1}{3}$ e

Leptons

Name	Symbol	Charge
electron	e	−1e
muon	μ	−1e
tau	τ	−1e
electron neutrino	ν_e	0
muon neutrino	ν_μ	0
tau neutrino	ν_τ	0

Note: For each particle there is a corresponding antiparticle with a charge opposite that of its associated particle.

Electricity

$$F_e = \frac{kq_1q_2}{r^2}$$

$$E = \frac{F_e}{q}$$

$$V = \frac{W}{q}$$

$$I = \frac{\Delta q}{t}$$

$$R = \frac{V}{I}$$

$$R = \frac{\rho L}{A}$$

$$P = VI = I^2R = \frac{V^2}{R}$$

$$W = Pt = VIt = I^2Rt = \frac{V^2t}{R}$$

A = cross-sectional area
E = electric field strength
F_e = electrostatic force
I = current
k = electrostatic constant
L = length of conductor
P = electrical power
q = charge
R = resistance
R_{eq} = equivalent resistance
r = distance between centers
t = time
V = potential difference
W = work (electrical energy)
Δ = change
ρ = resistivity

Series Circuits

$$I = I_1 = I_2 = I_3 = \ldots$$

$$V = V_1 + V_2 + V_3 + \ldots$$

$$R_{eq} = R_1 + R_2 + R_3 + \ldots$$

Parallel Circuits

$$I = I_1 + I_2 + I_3 + \ldots$$

$$V = V_1 = V_2 = V_3 = \ldots$$

$$\frac{1}{R_{eq}} = \frac{1}{R_1} + \frac{1}{R_2} + \frac{1}{R_3} + \ldots$$

Circuit Symbols

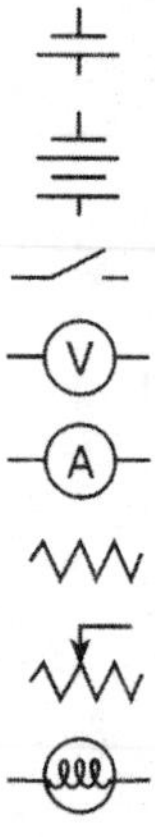

cell

battery

switch

voltmeter

ammeter

resistor

variable resistor

lamp

Resistivities at 20°C	
Material	**Resistivity ($\Omega \bullet$m)**
Aluminum	2.82×10^{-8}
Copper	1.72×10^{-8}
Gold	2.44×10^{-8}
Nichrome	$150. \times 10^{-8}$
Silver	1.59×10^{-8}
Tungsten	5.60×10^{-8}

Waves and Optics

$v = f\lambda$

$T = \dfrac{1}{f}$

$\theta_i = \theta_r$

$n = \dfrac{c}{v}$

$n_1 \sin \theta_1 = n_2 \sin \theta_2$

$\dfrac{n_2}{n_1} = \dfrac{v_1}{v_2} = \dfrac{\lambda_1}{\lambda_2}$

c = speed of light in a vacuum
f = frequency
n = absolute index of refraction
T = period
v = velocity
λ = wavelength
θ = angle
θ_i = incident angle
θ_r = reflected angle

Modern Physics

$E_{photon} = hf = \dfrac{hc}{\lambda}$

$E_{photon} = E_i - E_f$

$E = mc^2$

c = speed of light in a vacuum
E = energy
f = frequency
h = Planck's constant
m = mass
λ = wavelength

Geometry and Trigonometry

Rectangle
$A = bh$

Triangle
$A = \frac{1}{2}bh$

Circle
$A = \pi r^2$
$C = 2\pi r$

Right Triangle
$c^2 = a^2 + b^2$

$\sin \theta = \dfrac{a}{c}$

$\cos \theta = \dfrac{b}{c}$

$\tan \theta = \dfrac{a}{b}$

A = area
b = base
C = circumference
h = height
r = radius

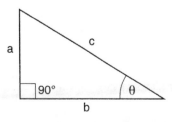

Mechanics

$\bar{v} = \dfrac{d}{t}$

$a = \dfrac{\Delta v}{t}$

$v_f = v_i + at$

$d = v_i t + \dfrac{1}{2}at^2$

$v_f^2 = v_i^2 + 2ad$

$A_y = A \sin \theta$

$A_x = A \cos \theta$

$a = \dfrac{F_{net}}{m}$

$F_f = \mu F_N$

$F_g = \dfrac{Gm_1 m_2}{r^2}$

$g = \dfrac{F_g}{m}$

$p = mv$

$p_{before} = p_{after}$

$J = Ft = \Delta p$

$F_s = kx$

$PE_s = \dfrac{1}{2}kx^2$

$F_c = ma_c$

$a_c = \dfrac{v^2}{r}$

$\Delta PE = mg\Delta h$

$KE = \dfrac{1}{2}mv^2$

$W = Fd = \Delta E_T$

$E_T = PE + KE + Q$

$P = \dfrac{W}{t} = \dfrac{Fd}{t} = F\bar{v}$

a = acceleration

a_c = centripetal acceleration

A = any vector quantity

d = displacement/distance

E_T = total energy

F = force

F_c = centripetal force

F_f = force of friction

F_g = weight/force due to gravity

F_N = normal force

F_{net} = net force

F_s = force on a spring

g = acceleration due to gravity or gravitational field strength

G = universal gravitational constant

h = height

J = impulse

k = spring constant

KE = kinetic energy

m = mass

p = momentum

P = power

PE = potential energy

PE_s = potential energy stored in a spring

Q = internal energy

r = radius/distance between centers

t = time interval

v = velocity/speed

$\bar{v}$ = average velocity/average speed

W = work

x = change in spring length from the equilibrium position

Δ = change

θ = angle

μ = coefficient of friction

APPENDIX C
PROCESS SKILLS AND
PERFORMANCE INDICATORS

This is a listing of all the Physical Setting: Physics skills referenced in each of the chapters of this *STAReview*. The skills are identified by both number and description.

PROCESS SKILLS
BASED ON STANDARDS 1, 2, 6, AND 7

Science process skills are based on a series of discoveries. Students learn most effectively when they have a central role in the discovery process.

Standards 1, 2, 6, and 7 incorporate in the *Physical Setting: Physics Core Curriculum* a student-centered, problem-solving approach to physics. It should be a goal of the student to learn the science process skills that will provide the background and curiosity to investigate important issues in the world.

This section denotes the types and depth of the process skills the students should practice throughout the school year. These process skills are an integral part of all core-based curricula. This implies that students should already have a foundation in these skills. This book reinforces these process skills by creating new situations for the student to investigate in the context of physics. During assessments, students will be presented with new situations to analyze and new problems to solve using these process skills.

PROCESS SKILLS
BASED ON STANDARD 4

Standard 4 incorporates a student-centered, problem-solving approach to physics. This list is not intended to be an all-inclusive list of the content or skills that teachers are expected to incorporate into their curriculum. It should be a goal of the instructor to encourage science process skills that will provide students with the background and curiosity to investigate important issues in the world around them.

Note: the use of e.g. denotes examples which may be used for in-depth study. The terms for example and such as denote material which is testable. Items in parantheses denote further definition of the word(s) preceding the item and are testable.

STANDARD 4—THE PHYSICAL SETTING

Students will understand and apply scientific concepts, principles, and theories pertaining to the physical setting and living environment and recognize the historical development of ideas in science.

Key Idea 4: Energy exists in many forms, and when these forms change energy is conserved.

4.1 Observe and describe transmission of various forms of energy.
   i.   describe and explain the exchange among potential energy, kinetic energy, and internal energy for simple mechanical systems, such as a pendulum, a roller coaster, a spring, a freely falling object
   ii.   predict velocities, heights, and spring compressions based on energy conservation
   iii. determine the energy stored in a spring
   iv.   determine the factors that affect the period of a pendulum
   v.   observe and explain energy conversions in real-world situations
   vi.   recognize and describe conversions among different forms of energy in real or hypothetical devices such as a motor, a generator, a photocell, a battery
   vii. compare the power developed when the same work is done at different rates
   viii. measure current and voltage in a circuit
   ix.   use measurements to determine the resistance of a circuit element
   x.   interpret graphs of voltage versus current
   xi.   measure and compare the resistance of conductors of various lengths and cross-sectional areas
   xii. construct simple series and parallel circuits
   xiii. draw and interpret circuit diagrams which include voltmeters and ammeters
   xiv. predict the behavior of lightbulbs in series and parallel circuits
   xv.   map the magnetic field of a permanent magnet, indicating the direction of the field between the N (north-seeking) and S (south-seeking) poles

4.3 Explain variations in wavelength and frequency in terms of the source of the vibrations that produce them, e.g., molecules, electrons, and nuclear particles.
   i.   compare the characteristics of two transverse waves such as amplitude, frequency, wavelength, speed, period, and phase
   ii.   draw wave forms with various characteristics
   iii. identify nodes and antinodes in standing waves
   iv.   differentiate between transverse and longitudinal waves
   v.   determine the speed of sound in air

vi.   predict the superposition of two waves interfering constructive-ly and destructively (indicating nodes, antinodes, and standing waves)

vii. observe, sketch, and interpret the behavior of wave fronts as they reflect, refract, and diffract

viii. draw ray diagrams to represent the reflection and refraction of waves

ix.   determine empirically the index of refraction of a transparent medium

Key Idea 5: Energy and matter interact through forces that result in changes in motion.

5.1 Explain and predict different patterns of motion of objects (e.g., linear and uniform circular motion, velocity and acceleration, momentum and inertia).

i.   construct and interpret graphs of position, velocity, or acceleration versus time

ii.   determine and interpret slopes and areas of motion graphs

iii. determine the acceleration due to gravity near the surface of Earth

iv.   determine the resultant of two or more vectors graphically or algebraically

v.   draw scaled force diagrams using a ruler and a protractor

vi.   resolve a vector into perpendicular components both graphically and algebraically

vii. sketch the theoretical path of a projectile

viii. use vector diagrams to analyze mechanical systems (equilibrium and nonequilibrium)

ix.   verify Newton's Second Law for linear motion

x.   determine the coefficient of friction for two surfaces

xi.   verify Newton's Second Law for uniform circular motion

xii. verify conservation of momentum

xiii. determine a spring constant

5.3 Compare energy relationships within an atom's nucleus to those outside the nucleus.

i.   interpret energy-level diagrams

ii.   correlate spectral lines with an energy-level diagram

PERFORMANCE INDICATORS FOR ASSESSMENTS

Key Idea 4: Energy exists in many forms, and when these forms change energy is conserved.

4.1   Students can observe and describe transmission of various forms of energy.

4.3   Students can explain variations in wavelength and frequency in terms of the source of the vibrations that produce them, e.g., molecules, electrons, and nuclear particles.

Key Idea 5: Energy and matter interact through forces that result in changes in motion.

5.1   Students can explain and predict different patterns of motion of objects (e.g., linear and uniform circular motion, velocity and acceleration, momentum and inertia).

5.3   Students can compare energy relationships within an atom's nucleus to those outside the nucleus.

APPENDIX D

INDEX AND GLOSSARY
FOR PHYSICAL SETTING: PHYSICS

The follow pages give a listing of the major terms and concepts covered in this *STAReview* and cross-indexed page references.

Balmer series (333): A series of related lines in the visible part of the hydrogen spectrum corresponding to energy jumps from higher energy levels to the n = 2 quantum level; after Swiss physicist Johann Jakob Balmer (1825-1898).

Baryon (14): Any of a family of subatomic particles, including the nucleon and hyperon multiplets, that participate in strong interactions, are composed of three quarks, and are generally more massive than mesons.

Beta particle (17): A high-speed electron or positron, especially one emitted in radioactive decay.

Beta decay (17): The emission of an electron or a positron from an atom.

Black light (332): Invisible ultraviolet or infrared radiation; black light causes fluorescent materials to emit visible light and is used to take pictures in the dark.

Bohr Model (328, 330): A model of the atoms proposed by Niels Bohr in which electrons revolved around a nucleus in certain allowable orbits.

Bohr, Niels Henrik David (328) Danish physicist (1885-1962); won a 1922 *Nobel Prize* for investigating atomic structure and radiations.

Boson (16): Any of a class of particles, such as the photon, pion, or alpha particle, that have zero or integral spin and obey statistical rules permitting any number of identical particles to occupy the same quantum state.

Bright line spectrum (330-331): A spectrum produced by gases at low pressures with characteristic bright lines for each element (see line spectrum).

Celsius temperature (281, 287): A temperature scale defined such that the ice point is 0° and the boiling point is 100° with 100 equal divisions between them.

Centripetal acceleration (123, 129-131, 328): A vector quantity representing $\Delta v / \Delta t$ and always directed towards the center of the circle.

Centripetal force (124, 129-131): The force which causes an object to move in a circular path; this force is always directed towards the center of the circle.

Circuit (216, 220-224, 232-238, 250): The path that charged particles follow around a closed loop.

Coefficient of friction (92, 93, 98-100): The ratio of the force necessary to overcome sliding friction to the normal force pressing the surfaces together.

Coherence (335): the property of two waves with identical wavelengths and a constant phase relationship; laser light.

Collision, elastic: see Elastic collisions.

Compton, Arthur H. (327): American physicist (1892-1962); shared a 1927 *Nobel Prize*.

Compton Effect (327): An increase in wavelength that takes place in a high energy photon when it collides with an electron; the effect illustrates that waves have the "particle" property of momentum.

Concentric waves (313): Waves emanating from a common center

Concurrent forces (33): Forces which act on the same point.

Conductivity (216-217): Ability or power to conduct or transmit heat, electricity, or sound.

Conductor (201, 222-223, 250, 251): A substance in which electrical charge flows easily.

Conservation of charge (197): A principle that states electric charge can neither be created nor destroyed.

Conservation of energy / mass (180-189): A principle that states that energy / mass can neither be created nor destroyed.

Constructive interference (265, 270, 313): The effect that occurs when two waves come together in such a way that a crest meets a crest or a trough meets a trough (in phase).

Coulomb (196, 199, 201, 203, 204, 205, 216, 220): The meter-kilogram-second unit (**C**) of electrical charge equal to the quantity of charge transferred in one second by a steady current of one ampere.

Coulomb's Law (15, 199): The force between two point charges is directly proportional to the product of the charges and inversely proportional to the square of the distance between them; after French physicist Charles Augustin de Coulomb (1736-1806) – pioneered research into magnetism and electricity.

Critical angle (299): That angle of incidence in an optically denser material that results in an angle of refraction of 90°.

Current (216, 222, 223, 224, 237, 245, 250): see electric current

Davisson, Clinton Joseph (328): American physicist (1881-1958); shared a 1937 *Nobel Prize* for the discovery of the diffraction of electrons by crystals.

deBroglie's matter waves (327): Probability wave associated with moving particles, moving matter; after French physicist Louis de Broglie, (1892-1987);1929 *Nobel Prize* for physics.

Derived unit (30): A new name for the unit made up of fundamental units; for example, a joule is a newton - meter.

Destructive interference (265, 266, 313): Effect that occurs when two waves come together in such a way that a crest meets a trough ($^{1}/_{2}$ λ out of phase).

Diamagnetic (244): Materials which are weakly repelled by a strong magnet; decrease of flux density.

Diffraction (268, 270, 285, 312-322, 324): The spreading of a wave disturbance into a region behind an obstruction; occurs when the obstruction or opening is narrow compared to the wavelength.

Diffuse reflection (292): Reflection that occurs when light strikes a rough surface; light is scattered in all directions.

Diode (223): An electronic device that restricts current flow chiefly to one direction.

Dirac, Paul Adrien Maurice (13): British mathematician and physicist (1902-1984); shared 1933 *Nobel Prize* for new formulations of the atomic theory.

Dispersion (317): The process of separating polychromatic light into its component wavelengths because of speed.

Displacement (32, 41-42, 50, 160, 161, 163, 164, 165, 169, 313): A vector quantity that represents the length and direction of a straight line path from one point to another point between which the motion of an object has taken place; total displacement is a vector sum; distance a vibrating particle is from the midpoint of its vibration.

Distance (32, 50): A scalar quantity that represents the length of a path from one point to another point.

Domain (244): A microscopic magnetic region consisting of atoms whose magnetic field are aligned in a common direction.

Doppler Effect (262, 263, 282, 283): The observed change in frequency of a moving object.

Double slit apparatus (315): Two closely spaced openings used in the study of diffraction and interference.

Dynamic equilibrium (83): The object is moving with constant velocity. The sum of all net forces and torques is zero.

Echo (285, 286): Repetition of a sound by reflection of sound waves from a surface.

Einstein, Albert (12, 13, 325): German-born American theoretical physicist revolutionized modern thought on the nature of space and time; formed a theoretical base for the exploitation of atomic energy; 1921 *Nobel Prize*.

Elastic collisions (138, 217, 329): Brief dynamic event consisting of the close approach of two or more particles, such as atoms, resulting in an abrupt change of momentum or exchange of energy; sum of the kinetic energies before a collision equals the sum of the kinetic energies after the collision.

Elastic potential energy (170-172, 184): Type of potential energy stored in a spring.

Electric circuit (220, 232-238, 250): A closed path followed or capable of being followed by an electric current; a configuration of electrically or electromagnetically connected components or devices.

Electric current (216, 222-223, 232): Amount of electric charge flowing past a specified circuit point per unit time.

Electric field (196-206, 217): Region where electrical force acts on a charged particle.

Electric field intensity (205): The force per unit positive charge at a given point in an electric field measured in N/C or V/m.

Electric field line (202): Line along which charged particle moves as a result of its interaction with the field.

Electric potential (203, 250): At any point is the work required to bring a charge from infinity to that point.

Electrolytes (216): Chemical compound that ionizes when dissolved or molten to produce an electrically conductive medium.

Electromagnet (246): Magnet whose field is produced by an electric current.

Electromagnetic induction (250, 251): Generation of electromotive force (emf) in a closed circuit by a varying magnetic flux through the circuit.

Electromagnetic spectrum (251, 283, 292, 317, 324, 328): The entire range of electromagnetic radiation from low frequency radio waves to high frequency gamma rays.

Electromagnetic waves (251, 261, 283, 296, 315, 317): Waves composed of electric and magnetic fields vibrating at right angles to each other.

Electromotive force (emf) (250): Energy per unit charge supplied by the source; see also voltage

Electron (13, 17, 23, 196, 197, 202, 204, 205, 216, 222, 244, 250, 296, 324, 325, 327, 328, 329, 330, 333, 335): A stable subatomic particle in the lepton family having a rest mass of 9.1066×10^{-28} gram and a unit negative electric charge of approximately 1.602×10^{-19} coulomb.

Electron volt (13, 204, 329, 331): Unit of energy (abbrv.= **eV**) equal to amount of work done moving an electron through a potential difference of one volt.

Electrostatics (199-200): The study of electric charges at rest.

Electro-weak Unification (15) Weak force in nuclear interaction connected to the electromagnetic force.

Emission spectrum (330): The spectrum of bright lines, bands, or continuous radiation characteristic of and determined by a specific emitting substance subjected to a specific kind of excitation.

Energy (180-186, 203, 220, 296, 324, 327): A physical quantity that has the capacity to do work.

Equality (30): The state or quality of being equal; in mathematics, a statement, usually an equation, that one thing equals another.

Equilibrium (82, 83, 150, 153, 170, 262): The state of a body or physical system at rest or in unaccelerated motion in which the resultant of all forces acting on it is zero and the sum of all torques about any axis is zero.

Equilibrant (32): The force that produces equilibrium; equal in magnitude to the resultant but in the opposite direction.

Equipotential lines (203, 204): represent positions of equal potential energy in an electric field.

Excitation (329): The process by which an electron jumps from the ground state of an atom to an excited state.

Excited state (328-329): Any allowed orbit except the one of lowest energy in the Bohr model of the atom.

Faraday, Michael (88): British physicist and chemist (1791-1867); discovered electromagnetic induction (1831) and proposed the field theory later developed by Maxwell and Einstein.

Fermi, Enrico (21): Italian-born American physicist (1901-1954); won a 1938 *Nobel Prize* for his work on artificial radioactivity; produced the first controlled nuclear chain reaction in 1942.

Ferromagnetic (244): A material which is strongly attracted by a magnet.

Fiber optics (300): Light passes through small transparent fibers. Due to total internal reflection, it does not escape.

Field intensity (205): See Intensity of an electric field.

Fluorescent light (332): A lamp that produces visible light by fluorescence, especially a glass tube whose inner wall is coated with a material that fluoresces when an electrical current causes a vapor within the tube to discharge electrons.

Fluid friction (93): The force which results from an object moving through a medium such as air or water.

Flux lines (244, 250): Imaginary closed path lines representing force around a magnet

Flux density (244, 248): A measurement of the field intensity per unit area whose units are N/amp•m, weber/m^2, or tesla.

Force (82, 163, 169): A push or a pull that changes or tends to change the state of motion of an object.

Franck, James (329): German-born American physicist (1882-1964); shared a 1925 *Nobel Prize* for discovering the laws that describe the impact of electrons upon atoms.

Franklin, Benjamin (197): American public official, writer, scientist, (1706-1790); practical innovations include the lightning rod, bifocal spectacles, and a stove.

Free-fall (61, 63): The motion of an object when the only force acting on the object is that of gravitational attraction.

Frequency (262, 264, 266, 273, 281, 282, 286, 296, 313, 314, 317, 318, 324, 326, 327): The number of cycles per unit time made by a vibrating object.

Friction (92-96, 98-100): A force that resists the relative motion of objects that are in contact with each other.

Fundamental unit (30): SI system of units including meter, kilogram, second, ampere, and Kelvin.

Gamma particle (18): A photon produced as a step in a radioactive decay chain.

Gauss (248): Centimeter-gram-second SI unit of magnetic induction, equal to one maxwell per square centimeter.

Gell-Mann, Murray (13): American physicist (b.1929); 1969 *Nobel Prize* for his study of subatomic particles.

Generator (250): A machine that converts mechanical energy into electrical energy.

Germer, Lester H. (328): American physicist (1896-1971); wave properties of electrons confirmed with Davisson.

GeV (15, 16, 18): Abbreviation for Gigaelectron Volts.

GPS / Global Positioning System (40): Worldwide radio-satellite navigation system.

Gravitational field (88, 110, 248): The region in which one massive body exerts a force of attraction on another massive body.

Gravitational mass (88): Mass measured by gravitational attraction.

Gravitational potential energy (169, 172): energy a body has because of its position.

Graviton (16): Hypothetical particle postulated to be the quantum of gravitational interaction and presumed to have an indefinitely long lifetime, zero electric charge, and zero rest mass.

Gravity, force of (87-91, 150): The force of attraction on an object by the Earth.

Ground (233): An infinite source of electrons or sink for electrons.

Ground state (329, 330, 331, 333): The lowest energy orbit available to an electron in the Bohr model of the atom.

Hadrons (14): Any of a class of subatomic particles that are composed of quarks and take part in the strong interaction.

Harmonic motion: See simple harmonic motion.

Heisenberg, Werner Karl (335): See uncertainty principle.

Hertz (264, 266, 281, 296, 317, 329): A unit of frequency equal to one cycle per second; after German physicist Heinrich Rudolph Hertz (1857-1894).

Hertz, Gustav Ludwig (329): German physicist (1887-1975); shared a 1925 *Nobel Prize* for discovering the laws that describe the impact of electrons upon atoms.

Higgs boson (16): Theoretical particle existing only at high temperatures; see boson.

Hooke, Robert (152): English physicist, inventor, and mathematician (1635-1703); formulated the theory of planetary movement.

Hooke's Law (152, 154, 170): In springs, the strength of the elastic restoring force is directly proportional to the displacement from equilibrium (elongation); i.e., the greater the displacement, the greater the restoring force; first described by English physicist Robert Hooke (1635-1703).

Horsepower (166): A unit of power in the U.S. Customary System, equal to 745.7 watts or 33,000 foot-pounds per minute.

Illuminated objects (292): substances which reflect light

Image (302): Optical counterpart of an object produced by a lens or a mirror.

Impulse (141): The product of the force and the time interval in which it acts.

Incident ray (293): Ray approaching a surface.

Incident wave (292): Wave which falls upon or strikes a surface.

Index of refraction (297, 298, 303): Property of an optical substance measured by the ratio of the speed of light in a vacuum to the speed of light in the substance.

Induced current (250): Current made by changing magnetic field near a conductor.

Induced emf (250): Potential difference produced by a changing magnetic field.

Induction (250): The generation of electromotive force in a closed circuit by a varying magnetic flux through the circuit..

Inelastic collisions (138): the normal condition that momentum is conserved in collisions, but kinetic energy is expended.

Inertia (84, 88): The property that opposes any change in its state of motion; proportional to mass.

Inphase (262): Having the same electrical phase.

Instantaneous speed (50): Speed at any given instant of time.

Insulator (201, 216): A substance which does not easily conduct electricity.

Intensity of an electric field (205): Rate at which electric potential changes with position.

Interference (265, 266, 270, 312-315, 324): The effect produced when two or more waves overlap.

Internal energy (182): The sum of the internal potential and kinetic energies of a system due to motion and position of particles.

Ion (196, 197, 198, 216, 217): An atom or group of atoms having an electrical charge.

Ionize (331, 332): To convert or be converted totally or partially into ions.

Ionized gases (217): See plasma

Ionization potential (329): The energy required to remove an electron from an atom in the ground state to infinity.

Joule (12-13, 162, 165, 168, 170, 171, 180, 182, 183, 203, 204, 206, 220, 221, 334): Unit of energy equal to the work done when a force of 1 newton acts through a distance of 1 meter; after British physicist James Prescott Joule 1818-1889– mechanical theory of heat and discovered the first law of thermodynamics.

Kilowatt hour (kW-hr) (220): A unit of electric power equal to the work done by one kilowatt acting for one hour; kW-hr = 3.6×10^6 J.

Kinematics (50-69): The branch of mechanics that studies the motion of a body or a system of bodies without consideration given to its mass or the forces acting on it.

Kinetic energy (171, 172, 180-183, 325, 326): Energy possessed by a body because of its motion.

Kinetic friction (92, 93): The force which must be overcome to keep an object moving.

Kirchhoff's laws (235-236): (1st Law) In an electric circuit, the sum of the current entering a junction is equal to the sum of the currents leaving a junction. (2nd Law) The sum of the IR drop around a loop of a circuit equals the applied Emf; after German physicist Gustav Robert Kirchhoff (1824-1887), noted for his research in spectrum analysis, optics, and electricity.

Laser (302, 312, 335): Light Amplification by Stimulated Emission of Radiation. Source of very intense, highly directional, monochromatic, and coherent beam of light.

Lenz's law (250): The direction of an induced current is such that the magnetic field induced produces magnetic forces which oppose the original forces; after Estonian physicist Heinrich Lenz (1804-1865).

Lepton (14): Any of a family of elementary particles that participate in the weak interaction, including the electron, the muon, and their associated neutrinos.

Line spectrum (331): A spectrum produced by gases at low pressures with characteristic bright lines for each element.

Lines of force (244): Imaginary lines drawn in a field such that the tangent drawn at any point indicates the direction of a force on a test unit in that field.

Longitudinal wave (260, 261, 262, 281): A wave in which the particles vibrate back and forth in the direction in which the wave travels.

Luminous objects (292): Emitting light, especially emitting self-generated light.

Lyman series (333): A series of related lines in the visible part of the hydrogen spectrum corresponding to energy jumps from higher energy levels to the n = 1 quantum level; after American experimental physicist Theodore Lyman (1874-1954); discovery played a major role in supporting Niels Bohr's quantum theory of the atom.

Magnetic field (244, 245, 246, 247, 248, 249, 250, 252): A region in which magnetic forces can be detected. The direction of the field is the direction of force on the north pole placed in that field.

Magnetic flux (244, 245): Lines of flux through a region of a magnetic field.

Magnetic force (244, 250): A force that exists between charges in motion.

Magnetic induction (248): Magnetic field strength in newtons per amp-meter (or tesla).

Magnitude (31-33, 34, 41, 50, 52, 169): The size of a quantity (for example, vector).

Mass (12-13): A specification of the inertia of an object.

Maxwell, James C. (214, 317): British physicist (1831-1879); made fundamental contributions to electromagnetic theory and the kinetic theory of gases.

Mechanical energy (180-183): The ability to do work

Mechanical waves (317): Waves that require a medium to transport their energy.

Meson (14, 18): Any of a family of subatomic particles that participate in strong interactions, are composed of a quark and an antiquark, and have masses generally intermediate between leptons and baryons.

MKS (31, 82): (Meter-Kilogram-Second) Basic clustering of international metric units in science and engineering created in 1889 by the International Bureau of Weights and Measures and adopted as the 11th General Conference on Weights and Measures (1960).

MeV (13): abbr. = one million electron volts.

Milliampere (219): Abbreviation = **mA**; a unit of current equal to one thousandth (10^{-3}) of an ampere.

Millikan oil drop experiment (205): Determined that the smallest charge possible was the charge on one electron, 1.6×10^{-19} coulombs and all charges were whole number multiples of this fundamental value; after American physicist Robert Andrews Millikan (1868-1953); 1923 *Nobel Prize.*

Momentum (138, 163, 327, 328, 335): The product of the mass of an object and its velocity.

Monochromatic (294, 313, 335): Of or composed of radiation of only one wavelength.

MRI (247): Magnetic Resonance Imaging – use of a nuclear magnetic resonance spectrometer to produce electronic images of specific atoms and molecular structures in solids, especially human cells, tissues, and organs.

Mu (98): 12th letter of the Greek alphabet; symbol for coefficient of friction (μ)

Muon (14): A lepton which interacts by means of the weak nuclear force.

Nanometer (19): One billionth (10-9) of a meter (Abbr. nm).

Negative elementary charge (196): The charge on an electron.

Neutrino (14, 17): A subatomic particle of zero mass and zero charge.

Neutron (196): An electrically neutral subatomic particle in the baryon family, having a mass 1,839 times that of the electron, stable when bound in an atomic nucleus.

Newton (82, 87, 88, 90, 92, 141, 152, 162, 199, 205, 248): The derived unit for force; one newton is equal to 1 kg.m/s^2

Newton/coulomb (201, 202, 205): SI units used in measuring electric field strength – the force (F) is measured in newtons (1 newton = 0.225 lb), and the charges (q) in coulombs (E = F/q).

Newton, Isaac (16, 84-87, 89, 312, 317-318): English mathematician and scientist (1642-1727); invented differential calculus and formulated the theories of universal gravitation (*Principia Mathematica*, 1687), terrestrial mechanics, and color.

Newton's first law (84): An object remains at rest or in uniform motion unless acted upon by an unbalanced force ($F_{net} = 0$).

Newton's Law of Universal Gravitation (87): The force of attraction between any two point masses is directly proportional to the product of their masses and inversely proportional to the square of the distance between them.

Newton's second law (84, 86, 94, 96, 124): An unbalanced force acting on an object causes an acceleration directly proportional to the force and in the direction of the force (F = ma).

Newton's third law (16, 86): Forces always occur in pairs.

Node (266, 273, 313): The points on a standing wave at which no motion occurs.

Normal (293, 297): A line drawn perpendicular to a surface or line.

Nuclear fission (17, 18): Nuclear reaction in which an atomic nucleus, especially a heavy nucleus such as an isotope of uranium, splits into fragments, usually two fragments of comparable mass, with the evolution of from 100 million to several hundred million electron volts of energy.

Nucleus (23): The positively charged central region of an atom, composed of protons and neutrons and containing almost all of the mass of the atom.

Ohm (217, 218, 222, 238): The SI Unit of electrical resistance; after German physicist Georg Simon Ohm (1789-1854); noted for contributions to mathematics, acoustics, and the measurement of electrical resistance.

Ohmic conductor (220): Conductor which obeys Ohm's Law.

Ohm's law (217, 223): At a constant temperature, the ratio of the potential difference across a resistor to the current flowing in the resistor is a constant.

Optical density (296, 297): Sluggish tendency of the atoms of a material to maintain the absorbed energy of an electromagnetic wave in the form of vibrating electrons before re-emitting it as a new electromagnetic disturbance.

Oscillation (251): To swing back and forth with a steady, uninterrupted rhythm.

Parallel circuit (235): An electric circuit connected at the same two points so there are two or more paths for the current to follow.

Paramagnetic (244): Material which is weakly attracted by a strong magnet.

Pendulum (150-154, 180): Body suspended so it can swing about an axis.

Period (150-154, 262, 264): The time for one complete cycle or oscillation. The time required for a single wavelength to pass a given point.

Permeability (244): The property of a material by which it changes the flux density in a magnetic field from the value in air.

Phase (262, 264): A condition of matter; periodic motion, the stage within each oscillation.

Phenomena (265, 293): Observable events (*pl.*); (sing. = phenomenon).

Photoelectric effect (324, 325): The emission of electrons by a surface when exposed to electromagnetic radiation.

Photoelectron (324, 326): Electrons emitted from a light sensitive material when it is illuminated.

Photoemission (326): Emission of photoelectrons, especially from metallic surfaces.

Photon (16, 18, 296, 327, 328, 330, 331, 333, 335): Quantum of electromagnetic energy, generally regarded as a discrete particle having zero mass, no electric charge, and an indefinitely long lifetime.

Pico-(21): Prefix for one-trillionth (10^{-12}): ex. picosecond.

Pith ball (197): Slang term for tight-celled foam material used for static electricity experiments.

Planck, Max (13, 324): German physicist (1858-1947); 1918 *Nobel Prize* for discoveries in connection with quantum theory.

Planck's constant (324, 326, 327, 328, 330, 335): A fundamental constant (**h**) in nature that determines what values are allowed in quantum mechanics.

Plasma (217): An electrically neutral, highly ionized gas composed of ions, electrons, and neutral particles; fourth stage of matter in which electrons are stripped from atoms leaving positive ions and free electrons.

Pion (15): A hadron which interacts by means of the strong nuclear force.

Polarity (245): Intrinsic polar separation, alignment, or orientation, especially of a physical property: magnetic polarity; ionic polarity.

Polarization (316, 324): Process of transforming unpolarized vibrations of light waves so they are are aligned into one plane.

Polarized light: see polarization

Polaroid filters and lenses (316, 318): A trademark used for a specially treated, transparent optical device capable of polarizing light passing through it, used in glare-reducing optical devices.

Positive elementary charge (196): The charge on one proton.

Positron (15, 17): A particle with the same mass as an electron, but a positive charge.

Potential difference or potential drop (203, 217, 218, 220, 222-223, 232, 250): The work done per unit charge as a charge is moved between two points in an electric field.

Potential energy (169, 172, 180-183, 203): Energy that results from position or state of an object.

Pound (82): British unit of force equal to the weight of a standard one-pound mass where the local acceleration of gravity is 9.817 meters (32.174 feet) per second per second.

Power (165-168, 220): The time rate of doing work; SI Unit is the watt; electric power is the product of current and potential difference.

Prism (317-318): An optical device used for the dispersion of light.

Projectile motion (114): The motion of an object characterized by constant speed in the horizontal direction and constant acceleration (gravity) in the vertical direction.

Propagation (251): Process by which a disturbance, such as the motion of electromagnetic or sound waves, is transmitted through a medium such as air or water.

Proton (196, 197, 203, 205, 247): A stable, positively charged subatomic particle in the baryon family having a mass 1,836 times that of the electron.

Pulse (260, 272, 273): A single non-repeated disturbance.

Quanta (324, 328): (plural of quantum) – smallest amount of a physical quantity that can exist independently, especially a discrete quantity of electromagnetic radiation.

Quantum (324): An elemental unit of energy; a photon or energy hf.

Quantum Theory (324): The theory that radiant energy is transmitted in the form of discrete units.

Quark (13): Any of a group of hypothetical elementary particles having electric charges of magnitude one-third or two-thirds that of the electron, regarded as constituents of all hadrons.

Radiation (217): Any form of energy which moves along as a wave.

Radioactivity (17-18): Spontaneous nuclear disintegration by the emission of radiation.

Rarefaction (265, 281, 284): A decrease in density and pressure in a medium, such as air, caused by the passage of a sound wave.

Ray (269): A line drawn in the direction in which a wave is traveling.

Reciprocal (234): A number related to another in such a way that when multiplied together their product is 1.

Reflected ray (293): Ray leaving a surface at the point of incidence.

Reflection (266, 268, 285, 292, 293, 302): Wave bounced off smooth hard surface; light bounced off an optical surface.

Reflection, Law of (268, 293, 303): Angle of incidence equals the angle of reflection.

Refraction (269, 285, 292, 294, 295, 297, 299, 304): The bending or change of direction of a beam of light which occurs when the ray passes obliquely from one medium to another due to a change in speed.

Regular (specular) reflection (292): Reflection off smooth surfaces.

Resistance (218, 221, 222, 223, 224, 232): The opposition to flow of electrons.

Resistivity (218): A proportionality constant used to determine the resistance of a wire.

Resistor (220, 237): A device used to control current in an electric circuit by providing resistance.

Resonance (266, 267, 282, 286, 296): The effect produced when a vibrating object is forced to vibrate at one of its natural frequencies.

Resultant (31, 32, 33, 35, 253): A vector representing the sum of several components.

Rheostat (223): A continuously variable electrical resistor used to regulate current.

Rolling friction (93): The force which which occurs when an object moves over a surface.

Rutherford, Ernest (328): New Zealand-born British physicist (1871-1937); classified radiation into alpha, beta, and gamma types and discovered the atomic nucleus; won the 1908 *Nobel Prize* in chemistry.

Rutherford's Model (328): Model of the atom as a very small, tightly packed, charged nucleus sprinkled with opposite charges in the mostly empty surrounding void (c. 1911).

Satellite (40): See GPS / Global Positioning System.

Scalar (31, 163, 169, 220): A physical quantity that is completely specified by magnitude.

Semiconductor (204, 216, 236): Any of various solid crystalline substances, such as germanium or silicon, having electrical conductivity greater than insulators but less than good conductors.

Series circuit (232): An electrical circuit in which there is only one path.

Shock wave (283): A large-amplitude compression wave, as that produced by an explosion or by supersonic motion of a body in a medium.

SI units (32, 196, 201, 216, 218, 220, 245): Abbreviation for International System of Units set up in 1960 at the 11th General conference on Weights and Measures; from the original French for Système International d'Unités.

Sigma, (Σ) (39): Greek letter used in scientific notation to represent "sum of."

Significant figures (20): Those digits in a number that are known for certain plus the first digit that is uncertain.

Simple harmonic motion (150): Repeating motion in which the acceleration is proportional to the displacement from the equilibrium position.

Slug (82): The unit of mass that is accelerated at the rate of one foot per second per second when acted on by a force of one pound weight.

Snell's law (298): Dutch scientist Willebrord Snell (1621) state that, for a ray passing from one medium to another, the product of the index of refraction of the first medium and the sine of the angle of incidence is equal to the product of the index of refraction of the second medium and the sine of the angle of refraction.

Solenoid (245): A coil of wire at frequent intervals wound around a core.

Sonic boom (284): An explosive sound caused by the shock wave preceding an aircraft traveling at or above the speed of sound.

Spectra (330-331): The distribution of atomic or subatomic particles in a system, as in a magnetically resolved molecular beam, arranged in order of masses; see emission spectrum and absorption spectrum

Spectral line (283): An isolated bright or dark line in a spectrum produced by emission or absorption of light of a single wavelength.

Spectrum (330): A range of electromagnetic frequencies.

Specular reflection (292): See regular reflection.

Speed (33, 50): A scalar quantity which represents the magnitude of the velocity.

Standard Model (14): Basic representation of the physical composition of matter.

Standing wave (266, 273): Interference effect which occurs when two identical waves travel through the same region of space but in opposite direction.

Static electricity (196, 199-200): Electricity "at rest" – no net transfer of charge.

Static friction (92): The force which must be overcome to start an object moving.

Strong force (15): The force of attraction between two nucleons in which mesons serve as the carrier.

Superconductor (216): Certain metals, alloys, and ceramics that allow electric current to flow without resistance temperatures near absolute zero, and in some cases at temperatures hundreds of degrees above absolute zero.

Superposition (265): Combining the displacement of two or more waves to produce a resultant displacement.

Tau (14): An elementary particle of the lepton family, having a mass about 3,490 times that of the electron, a negative electric charge, and a mean lifetime of 3×10^{-13} seconds.

Tension (86): A measure of such a force of stretching something tight; (mg = tension).

Tera- (21): Prefix indicating one trillion (10^{12}): ex. terahertz.

Tesla (248): SI Unit of magnetic flux density; after Serbian-born American electrical engineer and physicist Nikola Tesla (1856-1943); discovered the principles of alternating current (1881) and invented numerous devices and procedures that led to the development of radio and the harnessing of electricity.

Terminal speed (95): The speed reached by a falling object at the instant a frictional resistance force equals the weight.

Threshold frequency (326): The frequency below which electromagnetic radiation will not eject electrons from the surface of a given metal.

Total internal reflection (299, 300): When light traveling in a substance strikes the boundary of a surface in which its speed is greater, none passes into the "higher speed" substance if the angle of incidence is greater than the critical angle; all light is reflected (none absorbed).

Transformer (251): Device used to transfer electric energy from one circuit to another, especially a pair of multiply wound, inductively coupled wire coils that effect such a transfer with a change in voltage, current, phase, or other electric characteristic.

Translational kinetic energy (171): Energy due to motion from one location to another.

Transmit (266, 285): To cause (a disturbance) to propagate through a medium.

Transmutation (16): Conversion of an atomic nucleus of one element into that of another element.

Transverse wave (260, 261, 264, 272, 315): A wave in which the vibrations are at right angles to the direction of propagation of the wave.

Ultraviolet (332): Of or relating to the range of invisible radiation wavelengths from about 4 nanometers, on the border of the x-ray region, to about 380 nanometers, just beyond the violet in the visible spectrum.

Uncertainty principle (335): Some properties of atoms and their particles can be determined simultaneously only to within a certain degree of accuracy; developed by German physicist Werner Karl Heisenberg (1901-1976); a founder of quantum mechanics; won a 1932 *Nobel Prize.*

Uniform circular motion (123): Constant speed in a circular path.

Universal Gravitation Constant (**G**) (87): Masses measured in kilograms for Newton's Law of Universal Gravitation; $6.67 \times 10^{-11} \text{N-m}^2/\text{kg}^2$.

Universal Mass Unit (u) (13): A unit of mass in atomic physics described as 1/12 the mass of the carbon-12 nucleus; one u equals 931 MeV.; used in place of Universal Atomic Units.

Unpolarized light (315): A light wave that is vibrating in more than one plane.

Van Allen belts (217): Either of two zones of high-intensity particulate radiation trapped in Earth's magnetic field and surrounding the planet, beginning at an altitude of about 800 kilometers (500 miles) and extending tens of thousands of kilometers into space; after American physicist James Alfred Van Allen (b. 1914).

Vector (31-42, 50-52, 144, 161, 201, 253): A quantity that is completely specified by both magnitude and direction.

Vector diagrams (52, 200): Sketches or drawings that show the direction and magnitude of a vector quantity.

Velocity (33, 50, 52, 53, 55, 56-65, 110-116, 123, 138, 163, 169, 172, 262, 263, 273): A vector quantity which represents the time rate of change in displacement.

Virtual image (302): Type of image formed when rays of light appear to come from the image. This image can be seen but not focused on a screen.

Visible spectrum (317-318): The portion of the electromagnetic spectrum whose frequencies produce the sensations of color.

Volt (203, 204, 205, 217, 233): SI Unit of potential difference that exists between two points in an electric field; one volt is equal to one joule per coulomb.

Voltage (217): Electromotive force or potential difference, usually expressed in volts.

Voltmeter (220, 222-223, 237, 238): An electrical device to measure voltage drop across a resistor; meter is always attached in parallel.

Watt (165-168, 220): The SI Unit of power; one watt is equal to one joule per second.

Watt, James (165-166): British engineer and inventor (1736-1819); made fundamental improvements in the steam engine, resulting in the modern, high-pressure steam engine.

Wave (260): A series of pulses.

Wave front (262): locus of adjacent points of a wave that are in phase.

Wave interference (313): phenomenon that occurs when two waves meet while traveling along the same medium.

Wavelength (262, 264, 266, 273, 286, 287, 294, 314, 327, 328, 330, 331, 335): The distance between two consecutive points of a wave moving in the same direction with the same displacement.

Weak nuclear interaction (16): Nuclear reactions in which leptons (collective name for electrons, muons, and neutrinos) are emitted.

Weber (248): The SI unit of magnetic flux equal to the magnetic flux that in linking a circuit of one turn produces in it an electromotive force of one volt as it is uniformly reduced to zero within one second; after German physicist Wilhelm Eduard Weber (1804-1891) – noted for his study of terrestrial magnetism.

Weight (90): The force of gravitational attraction exerted on an object by the earth.

Work (160-165): The transfer of energy to a body by the application of a force that moves the body in the direction of the force; calculated as the product of the force and the distance through which the body moves and is expressed in joules, ergs, and foot-pounds.

Work energy theorum (183): Quantitative relationship between initial KE + PE + external force = final energy (initial energy + work by external force = final energy).

Work function (326): The minimum amount of energy required to remove an electron from the surface of a material.

W–particle (16): Carrier of the weak nuclear interaction.

X ray (317, 327): A range of deeply penetrating high frequency electromagnetic radiations.

Young, Thomas (314-315): British physician, physicist (1773-1829); revived the wave theory of light and postulated the three-color theory of color vision.

Yukawa, Hideki (15): Japanese physicist (1907-1981); 1949 *Nobel Prize* for mathematically predicting the existence of the meson.

Z-particle (16): Carrier of the weak nuclear interaction.

Zero height position (169): Ground level or the point at which an object has no gravitational potential energy.

PHYSICAL SETTING: PHYSICS
PRACTICE TEST # 1 - JUNE 2002

To the Teacher: This exam is the actual June 2002 Regents Exam as published by the State Education Department of New York. It has not been edited, altered, or corrected.

PART A

Answer all questions in this part

Directions (1-35): For *each* statement or question, select the number of the word or expression that, of those given, best completes the statement or answers the question.

1   Which is a vector quantity?
(1) distance   (2) speed   (3) power   (4) force

2   The diagram at the right shows a granite block being slid at constant speed across a horizontal concrete floor by a force parallel to the floor. Which pair of qualities could be used to determine the coefficient of friction for the granite on the concrete?

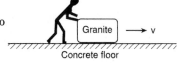

(1) mass and speed of the block
(2) mass and normal force on the block
(3) frictional force and speed of the block
(4) frictional force and normal force on the block

3   An object with an initial speed of 4.0 meters per second accelerates uniformly at 2.0 meters per second² in the direction of its motion for a distance of 5.0 meters. What is the final speed of the object?
(1) 6.0 m/s   (2) 10. m/s   (3) 14 m/s   (4) 36 m/s

4   After a rocket model reached its maximum height, it then took 5.0 seconds to return to the launch site. What is the approximate maximum height reached by the rocket? [Neglect air resistance.]
(1) 49 m   (2) 98 m   (3) 120 m   (4) 250 m

5   The diagram at the right shows a student throwing a baseball horizontally at 25 meters per second from a cliff 45 meters above the ground level.

Approximately how far from the base of the cliff does the ball hit the ground? [Neglect air resistance.]
(1) 45 m   (3) 140 m
(2) 75 m   (4) 230 m

6   A projectile is fired from a gun near the surface of Earth. The initial velocity of the projectile has a vertical component of 98 meters per second. How long will it take the projectile to reach the highest point in its path?
(1) 5.0 s   (2) 10. s   (3) 20. s   (4) 100. s

7   A 70.-kilogram astronaut has a weight of 560 newtons on the surface of planet Alpha. Which is the acceleration due to gravity on planet Alpha?
    (1) 0.0 m/s²   (2) 8.0 m/s²   (3) 9.8 m/s²   (4) 80. m/s²

Base you answers to questions 8 and 9 on the diagram and information below.

The diagram shows a student seated on a rotating circular platform, holding a 2.0-kilogram block with a spring scale. The block is 1.2 meters from the center of the platform. The block has a constant speed of 8.0 meters per second. [Frictional forces of the block are negligible.]

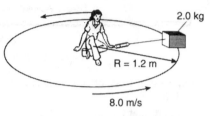

2.0 kg

R = 1.2 m

8.0 m/s

8   Which statement best describes the block's movement as the platform rotates?
    (1) Its velocity is directed tangent to the circular path, with an inward acceleration.
    (2) Its velocity is directed tangent to the circular path, with an outward acceleration.
    (3) Its velocity is directed perpendicular to the circular path, with an inward acceleration.
    (4) Its velocity is directed perpendicular to the circular path, with an outward acceleration.

9   The reading on the spring scale is approximately
    (1) 20. N   (2) 53 N   (3) 110 N   (4) 130 N

10 The diagram at the right shows a horizontal 8.0-newton force applied to a 4.0-kilogram block on a frictionless table.

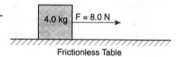

4.0 kg   F = 8.0 N

Frictionless Table

What is the magnitude of the block's acceleration?
    (1) 0.50 m/s²   (2) 2.0 m/s²   (3) 9.8 m/s²   (4) 32 m/s²

11 A 0.10-kilogram model rocket's engine is designed to deliver an impulse of 6.0 newton-seconds. If the rocket engine burns for 0.75 second, what average force does it produce?
    (1) 4.5 N   (2) 8.0 N   (3) 45 N   (4) 80. N

Base you answers to questions 12 and 13 on the diagram and information below.

The diagram shows a compressed spring between two carts initially at rest on a horizontal frictionless surface. Cart A has a mass of 2 kilograms and cart B has a mass of 1 kilogram. A string holds the carts together.

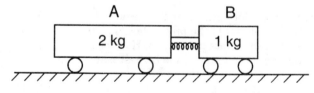

A

B

2 kg

1 kg

12 What occurs when the string is cut and the carts move apart?
    (1) The magnitude of the acceleration of cart A is one-half of the acceleration of cart B.
    (2) The length of time that the force acts on cart A is twice the length of time the force acts on cart B.
    (3) The magnitude of the force exerted on cart A is one-half of the magnitude of the force exerted on cart B.
    (4) The magnitude of the impulse exerted on cart A is twice the magnitude of the impulse exerted on cart B.

13 After the string is cut and the two carts move apart, the magnitude of which quantity is the same for both carts?
    (1) momentum   (2) velocity   (3) inertia   (4) kinetic energy

14 An object moving at a constant speed of 25 meters per second possesses 450 joules of kinetic energy. What is the object's mass?
    (1) 0.72 kg   (2) 1.4 kg   (3) 18 kg   (4) 36 kg

15 The diagram below shows a moving, 5.00-kilogram cart at the foot of a hill 10.0 meters high. For the cart to reach the top of the hill, what is the minimum kinetic energy of the cart in the position shown? [Neglect energy loss due to friction.]

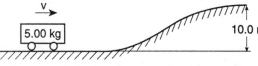

    (1) 4.91 J   (2) 50.0 J   (3) 250. J   (4) 491 J

16 A constant force of 1900 newtons is required to keep an automobile having a mass of 1.0×10^3 kilograms moving at a constant speed of 20 meters per second. The work done in moving the automobile a distance of 2.0×10^3 meters is
    (1) 2.0×10^4 J   (2) 3.8×10^4 J   (3) 2.0×10^6 J   (4) 3.8×10^6 J

17 The energy required to move one elementary charge through a potential difference of 5.0 volts is
    (1) 8.0 J   (3) 8.0×10^{-19} J
    (2) 5.0 J   (4) 1.6×10^{-19} J

18 The diagram below shows two identical metal spheres, A and B, on insulated stands. Each sphere possesses a net charge of -3×10^{-6} coulomb.

-3×10^{-6} C -3×10^{-6} C

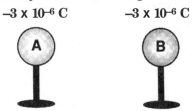

    If the spheres are brought into contact with each other, and then separated, the charge on sphere A will be
    (1) 0 C   (3) -3×10^{-6} C
    (2) $+3 \times 10^{-6}$ C   (4) -6×10^{-6} C

19 In a vacuum, light with a frequency of 5.0×10^{14} hertz has a wavelength of
    (1) 6.0×10^{-21} m   (3) 1.7×10^{6} m
    (2) 6.0×10^{-7} m   (4) 1.5×10^{23} m

20 In the diagram at the right, 400. joules of work is done raising a 72-newton weight a vertical distance of 5.0 meters.

    How much work is done to overcome friction as the weight is raised?

    (1) 40. J   (3) 400. J
    (2) 360 J   (4) 760 J

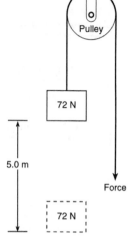

21 An incandescent light bulb is supplied with a constant potential difference of 120 volts. As the filament of the bulb heats up, its resistance

    (1) increases and the current through it decreases
    (2) increases and the current through it increases
    (3) decreases and the current through it decreases
    (4) decreases and the current through it increases

22 During a thunderstorm, a lightening strike transfers 12 coulombs of charge in 2.0×10^{-3} second. What is the average current produced in this strike?

    (1) 1.7×10^{-4} A   (3) 6.0×10^{3} A
    (2) 2.4×10^{-2} A   (4) 9.6×10^{3} A

Note that question 23 has only three choices.

23 A 30.-ohm resistor and a 60.-ohm resistor are connected in an electric circuit as shown at the right.

    Compared to the electric current through the 30.-ohm resistor, the electric current through the 60.-ohm resistor is

    (1) smaller   (2) larger   (3) the same

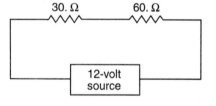

24 An operating electric heater draws a current of 10. amperes and has a resistance of 12 ohms. How much energy does the heater use in 60. seconds?
    (1) 120 J   (2) 1200 J   (3) 7200 J   (4) 72,000 J

25 If the charge on each of two small charged metal spheres is doubled and the distance between the spheres remains fixed, the magnitude of the electric force between the spheres will be
    (1) the same   (3) one-half as great
    (2) two times as great   (4) four times as great

26 The diagram at the right represents a periodic wave

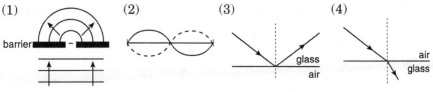

Which two points on the wave are in phase?
(1) *A* and *C*   (2) *B* and *D*   (3) *A* and *D*   (4) *B* and *E*

27 A beam of monochromatic light travels through flint glass, crown glass, Lucite, and water. The speed of the light beam is slowest in
(1) flint glass   (2) crown glass   (3) Lucite   (4) water

28 A standing wave pattern is produced when a guitar string is plucked. Which characteristic of the standing wave immediately begins to decrease?
(1) speed   (2) wavelength   (3) frequency   (4) amplitude

29 A source of sound waves approaches a stationary observer through a uniform medium. Compared to the frequency and wavelength of the emitted sound, the observer would detect waves with a
(1) higher frequency and shorter wavelength
(2) higher frequency and longer wavelength
(3) lower frequency and shorter wavelength
(4) lower frequency and longer wavelength

30 What is the smallest electric charge that can be put on an object?
(1) 9.11×10^{-31} C   (3) 9.00×10^{9} C
(2) 1.60×10^{-19} C   (4) 6.25×10^{18} C

31 What characteristic of electromagnetic radiation is directly proportional to the energy of a photon?
(1) wavelength   (2) period   (3) frequency   (4) path

32 What is the maximum height to which a 1200-watt motor could lift an object weighing 200. newtons in 4.0 seconds?
(1) 0.67 m   (2) 1.5 m   (3) 6.0 m   (4) 24 m

33 A spring of negligible mass has a spring constant of 50. newtons per meter. If the spring is stretched 0.40 meter from its equilibrium position, how much potential energy is stored in the spring?
(1) 20. J   (2) 10. J   (3) 8.0 J   (4) 4.0 J

34 How much current flows through a 12-ohm flashlight bulb operating at 3.0 volts?
(1) 0.25 A   (2) 0.75 A   (3) 3.0 A   (4) 4.0 A

35 Which diagram below best represents the phenomenon of diffraction?

(1)   (2)   (3)   (4)

barrier   glass   air
                                           air   glass

PART B–1

Answer all questions in this part.

Directions (36-48): For *each* statement or question, select the *number* of the word or expression that, of those given, best completes the statement or answers the question.

36 The displacement-time graph below represents the motion of a cart initially moving forward along a straight line.

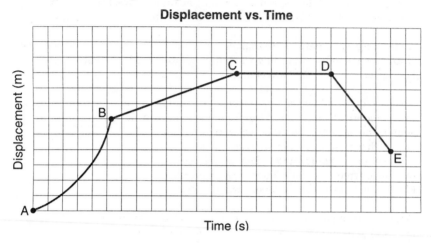

Displacement vs. Time

During which interval is the cart moving forward at a constant speed?
(1) *AB*   (2) *BC*   (3) *CD*   (4) *DE*

37 The diagram at right represents shallow water waves of wavelength λ passing through two small openings A and B, in a barrier.

How much longer is the path of AP than the length of path BP?

(1) 1λ (2) 2λ (3) 3λ (4) 4λ

Note that question 38 has only three choices.

38 In the diagram at the right, lamps L_1 and L_2 are connected to a constant voltage power supply.

If lamp L_1 burns out, the brightness of L_2 will
(1) decrease   (2) increase   (3) remain the same

39 What is the approximate mass of a pencil?
(1) 5.0×10^{-3} kg   (3) 5.0×10^{0} kg
(2) 5.0×10^{-1} kg   (4) 5.0×10^{1} kg

40 What is the minimum energy needed to ionize a hydrogen atom in the n = 2 energy state?
(1) 13.6 eV   (2) 10.2 eV   (3) 3.40 eV   (4) 1.89 eV

41 The potential difference applied to a circuit element remains constant as the resistance of the element is varied. Which graph best represents the relationship between power (P) and resistance (R) of this element?

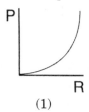
(1)
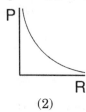
(2)
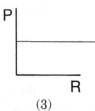
(3)
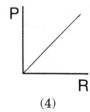
(4)

42 Which graph best represents the elastic potential energy stored in a spring (PE_s) as a function of its elongation, x?

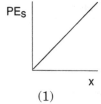
(1)
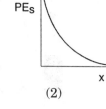
(2)
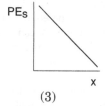
(3)
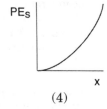
(4)

43 Which graph best represents the relationship between the gravitational potential energy of a freely falling object and the object's height above the ground near the surface of Earth?

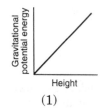
(1)
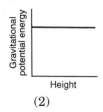
(2)
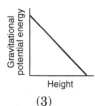
(3)
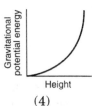
(4)

44 A force vector was resolved into two perpendicular components, F_1 and F_2, as shown in the diagram at the right.

Which vector best represents the original force?

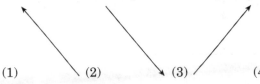
(1)   (2)   (3)   (4)

45 A beam of monochromatic light ($f = 5.09 \times 10^{14}$ hertz) passes through parallel sections of glycerol, medium X, and medium Y as shown in the diagram at the right.

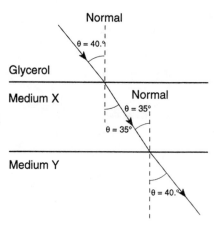

What could medium X and Y be?

(1) X could be flint glass and Y could be corn oil.
(2) X could be corn oil and Y could be flint glass.
(3) X could be water and Y could be glycerol.
(4) X could be glycerol and Y could be water.

PART B-2
Answer all questions in this Part.
Directions (46-59): Record your answers in the space provided.

46 The diagram at the right shows two compasses located near the ends of a bar magnet. The north pole of compass X points toward end A of the magnet.

On the diagram provided, draw the correct orientation of the needle of compass Y and label its polarity. [1]

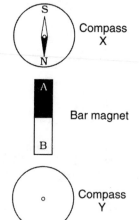

47 A ray of light traveling in air is incident on an air-water boundary as shown below. On the diagram provided below, draw the path of the ray in the water. [1]

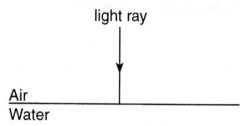

Base your answers to questions 48 and 49 on the information and the diagram at the right.

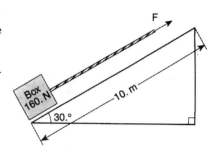

A 160.-newton box sits on a 10.-meter-long frictionless plane inclined at an angle of 30.º to the horizontal as shown. Force (F) applied to a rope attached to the box causes the box to move with a constant speed up the incline.

48 On the diagram provided at the right, construct a vector to represent the weight of the box. Use a metric ruler and a scale of 1.0 centimeter = 40. Begin the vector at point B and label its magnitude in newtons. [2]

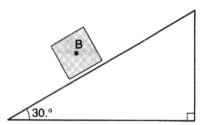

49 Calculate the amount of work done in moving the box from the bottom to the top of the inclined plane. [Show all work, including the equation and substitution with units.] [2]

Base your answers to questions 50 through 53 on the information and the table at the right.

The table lists the kinetic energy of a 4.0-kilogram mass as it travels in a straight line for 12.0 seconds.

Time (seconds)	Kinetic Energy (joules)
0.0	0.0
2.0	8.0
4.0	18
6.0	32
10.0	32
12.0	32

Directions (50-51): Using the information in the data table, construct a graph on the grid at the right, following the directions in each question.

50 Mark an appropriate scale on the axis labeled "Kinetic energy (J)." [1]

51 Plot the data points for kinetic energy versus time. [1]

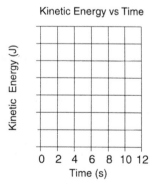

Kinetic Energy vs Time

52 Calculate the speed of the mass at 10.0 seconds. [Show all work, including the equation and substitution with units.] [2]

53 Compare the speed of the mass at 6.0 seconds to the speed of the mass at 10.0 seconds.   [1]

54 Using dimensional analysis, show that the expression v^2/d has the same units as acceleration. [Show all the steps used to arrive at your answer.] [2]

Base your answers to questions 55 through 57 on the information and the diagram at the right.

A 1.50-kilogram cart travels in a horizontal circle of radius 2.40 meters at a constant speed of 4.00 meters per second.

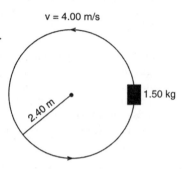

v = 4.00 m/s

2.40 m

1.50 kg

55 Calculate the time required for the cart to make one complete revolution. [Show all work, including the equation and substitution with units.]   [2]

56 Describe a change that would quadruple the magnitude of the centripetal force. [1]

57 On the diagram at the right, draw an arrow to represent the direction of the acceleration of the cart in the position shown. Label the arrow a. [1]

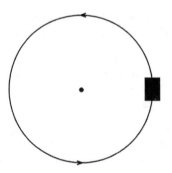

Base your answers to questions 58 and 59 on the information below.

When an electron and its antiparticle (positron) combine, they annihilate each other and become energy in the form of gamma rays.

58 The positron has the same mass as the electron. Calculate how many joules of energy are released when they annihilate. [Show all work, including the equation and substitution with units.]   [2]

59 What conservation law prevents this from happening with two electrons? [1]

PART C

Answer all questions in this part

Directions (60-69): Record your answers in the spaces provided.

Base your answers to questions 60 and 61 on the diagram at the right, which shows some energy levels for an atom of unknown substance.

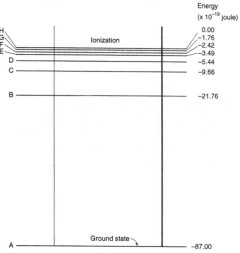

60 Determine the minimum energy necessary for an electron to change from the *B* energy level to the *F* energy level. [1]

_____ J

61 Calculate the frequency of the photon emitted when an electron in this atom changes from the *F* energy level to the *B* energy level. [Show all work, including the equation and substitution with units.] [2]

Base your answers to questions 62 and 63 on the information below.

An electric circuit contains two 3.0-ohm resistors connected in parallel with a battery. The circuit also contains a voltmeter that reads the potential difference across one of the resistors.

62 In the space provided below, draw a diagram of this circuit, using the symbols from the *Reference Tables for Physical Setting/Physics*. [Assume availability of any number of wires of negligible resistance.] [2]

63 Calculate the total resistance of the circuit. [Show all work, including the equation and substitution with units.] [2]

64 Explain how to find the coefficient of kinetic friction between a wooden block of unknown mass and a tabletop in the laboratory. Include the following in your explanation:
  • Measurements required [1]
  • Equipment needed [1]
  • Procedure [1]
  • Equation(s) needed to calculate the coefficient of friction [1]

Base your answers to questions 65 and 66 on the information below.

A toaster having a power rating if 1050 watts is operated at 120.0 volts.

65 Calculate the resistance of the toaster. [Show all work, including the equation and substitution with units.] [2]

66 The toaster is connected in a circuit protected by a 15-ampere fuse. (The fuse will shut down the circuit if it carries more than 15 amperes.) Is it possible to simultaneously operate the toaster and a microwave oven that requires a current of 10.0 amperes on this circuit? Justify your answer mathematically. [2]

Base your answers to questions 67 through 69 on the information and the diagram at the right. A monochromatic beam of yellow light, AB, is incident upon a Lucite block in air at an angle of 33°.

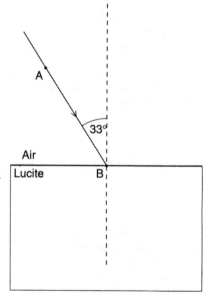

67 Calculate the angle of refraction for incident beam AB. [Show all work, including the equation and substitution with units.] [2]

68 Using a straightedge, a protractor, and your answer from question 67, draw an arrow to represent the path of the refracted beam. [2]

69 Compare the speed of the yellow light in air to the speed of the yellow light in Lucite. [1]

PART A

Answer all questions in this part.

Directions (1–35): For *each* statement or question, write on the separate answer sheet, the *number* of the word or expression that, of those given, best completes the statement or answers the question.

1   The diagram at the right shows a worker using a rope to pull a cart. The worker's pull on the handle of the cart can best be described as a force having

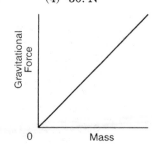

   (1) magnitude, only
   (2) direction, only
   (3) both magnitude and direction
   (4) neither magnitude nor direction

2   A car travels 90. meters due north in 15 seconds. Then the car turns around and travels 40. meters due south in 5.0 seconds. What is the magnitude of the average velocity of the car during this 20.-second interval?
   (1) 2.5 m/s   (2) 5.0 m/s   (3) 6.5 m/s   (4) 7.0 m/s

3   How far will a brick starting from rest fall freely in 3.0 seconds?
   (1) 15 m   (2) 29 m   (3) 44 m   (4) 88 m

4   If the sum of all the forces acting on a moving object is zero, the object will
   (1) slow down and stop
   (2) change the direction of its motion
   (3) accelerate uniformly
   (4) continue moving with constant velocity

5   A net force of 10. newtons accelerates an object at 5.0 meters per second^2. What net force would be required to accelerate the same object at 1.0 meter per second^2?
   (1) 1.0 N   (2) 2.0 N   (3) 5.0 N   (4) 50. N

6   The graph at the right represents the relationship between gravitational force and mass for objects near the surface of Earth. The slope of the graph represents the

   (1) acceleration due to gravity
   (2) universal gravitational constant
   (3) momentum of objects
   (4) weight of objects

7   A 1,200-kilogram car traveling at 10. meters per second hits a tree and is brought to rest in 0.10 second. What is the magnitude of the average force acting on the car to bring it to rest?
    (1) 1.2×10^2N   (3) 1.2×10^4 N
    (2) 1.2×10^3N   (4) 1.2×10^5 N

8   A spring scale reads 20. newtons as it pulls a 5.0-kilogram mass across a table. What is the magnitude of the force exerted by the mass on the spring scale?
    (1) 49 N   (2) 20. N   (3) 5.0 N   (4) 4.0 N

Base your answers to questions 9 and 10 on the information below.

A 2.0×10^3-kilogram car travels at a constant speed of 12 meters per second around a circular curve of radius 30. meters.

9   What is the magnitude of the centripetal acceleration of the car as it goes around the curve?
    (1) 0.40 m/s^2 (2) 4.8 m/s^2 (3) 800 m/s^2 (4) $9,600 \text{ m/s}^2$

10 As the car goes around the curve, the centripetal force is directed
    (1) toward the center of the circular curve
    (2) away from the center of the circular curve
    (3) tangent to the curve in the direction of motion
    (4) tangent to the curve opposite the direction of motion

Note that question 11 has only three choices.

11 The diagram at the right shows a block sliding down a plane inclined at angle θ with the horizontal. As angle θ is increased, the coefficient of kinetic friction between the bottom surface of the block and the surface of the incline will
    (1) decrease
    (2) increase
    (3) remain the same

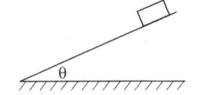

12 The amount of work done against friction to slide a box in a straight line across a uniform, horizontal floor depends most on the
    (1) time taken to move the box   (3) speed of the box
    (2) distance the box is moved   (4) direction of the box's motion

13 A 1.2-kilogram block and a 1.8-kilogram block are initially at rest on a frictionless, horizontal surface. When a compressed spring between the blocks is released, the 1.8-kilogram block moves to the right at 2.0 meters per second, as shown. What is the speed of the 1.2-kilogram block after the spring is released?
    (1) 1.4 m/s
    (2) 2.0 m/s
    (3) 3.0 m/s
    (4) 3.6 m/s

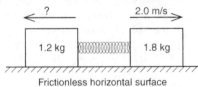

Frictionless horizontal surface

14 An object weighs 100. newtons on Earth's surface. When it is moved to a point one Earth radius above Earth's surface, it will weigh
    (1) 25.0 N   (2) 50.0 N   (3) 100. N   (4) 400. N

15 An object weighing 15 newtons is lifted from the ground to a height of 0.22 meter. The increase in the object's gravitational potential energy is approximately
    (1) 310 J   (2) 32 J   (3) 3.3 J   (4) 0.34 J

Note that question 16 has only three choices.

16 As an object falls freely, the kinetic energy of the object
    (1) decreases   (2) increases   (3) remains the same

17 Moving 2.5×10^{-6} coulomb of charge from point A to point B in an electric field requires 6.3×10^{-4} joule of work. The potential difference between points A and B is approximately
    (1) 1.6×10^{-9}V   (3) 2.5×10^{2} V
    (2) 4.0×10^{-3}V   (4) 1.0×10^{14} V

18 A 3.0-kilogram block is initially at rest on a frictionless, horizontal surface. The block is moved 8.0 meters in 2.0 seconds by the application of a 12-newton horizontal force, as shown in the diagram at the right. What is the average power developed while moving the block?

    (1) 24 W   (2) 32 W   (3) 48 W   (4) 96 W

19 The diagram at the right shows three neutral metal spheres, x, y, and z, in contact and on insulating stands. Which diagram best represents the charge distribution on the spheres when a positively charged rod is brought near sphere x, but does not touch it?

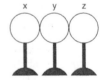

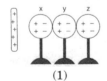

         (1)   (2)   (3)   (4)

20 Which graph best represents the electrostatic force between an alpha particle with a charge of +2 elementary charges and a positively charged nucleus as a function of their distance of separation?

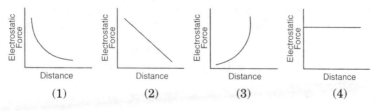

         (1)   (2)   (3)   (4)

21 When a neutral metal sphere is charged by contact with a positively charged glass rod, the sphere
    (1) loses electrons   (3) loses protons
    (2) gains electrons   (4) gains protons

22 If 10. coulombs of charge are transferred through an electric circuit in 5.0 seconds, then the current in the circuit is
    (1) 0.50 A   (2) 2.0 A   (3) 15 A   (4) 50. A

23 The diagram at the right represents a source of potential difference connected to two large, parallel metal plates separated by a distance of 4.0×10^{-3} meter. Which statement best describes the electric field strength between the plates?

    (1) It is zero at point B.   (3) It is a maximum at point C.
    (2) It is a maximum at point B.   (4) It is the same at points A, B, and C.

24 A periodic wave transfers
    (1) energy, only   (3) both energy and mass
    (2) mass, only   (4) neither energy nor mass

Note that question 25 has only three choices.

25 As the potential difference across a given resistor is increased, the power expended in moving charge through the resistor
    (1) decreases   (2) increases   (3) remains the same

26 An electric iron operating at 120 volts draws 10. amperes of current. How much heat energy is delivered by the iron in 30. seconds?
    (1) 3.0×10^2 J   (3) 3.6×10^3 J
    (2) 1.2×10^3 J   (4) 3.6×10^4 J

27 A motor is used to produce 4.0 waves each second in a string. What is the frequency of the waves?
    (1) 0.25 Hz   (2) 15 Hz   (3) 25 Hz   (4) 4.0 Hz

28 The diagram at the right shows a periodic wave. Which points are in phase with each other?
    (1) A and C
    (2) A and D
    (3) B and C
    (4) C and D

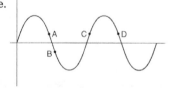

29 A surfacing whale in an aquarium produces water wave crests having an amplitude of 1.2 meters every 0.40 second. If the water wave travels at 4.5 meters per second, the wavelength of the wave is
    (1) 1.8 m   (2) 2.4 m   (3) 3.0 m   (4) 11 m

30 In a certain material, a beam of monochromatic light ($f = 5.0^9 \times 10^{14}$ hertz) has a speed of 2.25×10^8 meters per second. The material could be
    (1) crown glass   (3) glycerol
    (2) flint glass   (4) water

31 Orange light has a frequency of 5.0×10^{14} hertz in a vacuum. What is the wavelength of this light?
    (1) 1.5×10^{23}m
    (2) 1.7×10^{6}m
    (3) 6.0×10^{-7} m
    (4) 2.0×10^{-15} m

32 A radar gun can determine the speed of a moving automobile by measuring the difference in frequency between emitted and reflected radar waves. This process illustrates
    (1) resonance
    (2) the Doppler effect
    (3) diffraction
    (4) refraction

33 The diagram at the right shows a standing wave. Point A on the standing wave is
    (1) a node resulting from constructive interference
    (2) a node resulting from destructive interference
    (3) an antinode resulting from constructive interference
    (4) an antinode resulting from destructive interference

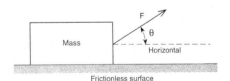

34 An object possessing an excess of 6.0×10^{6} electrons has a net charge of
    (1) 2.7×10^{-26}C
    (2) 5.5×10^{-24}C
    (3) 3.8×10^{-13} C
    (4) 9.6×10^{-13} C

35 One watt is equivalent to one
    (1) N•m
    (2) N/m
    (3) J•s
    (4) J/s

PART B-1
Answer all questions in this part.

Directions (36–50): For *each* statement or question, write on the separate answer sheet, the *number* of the word or expression that, of those given, best completes the statement or answers the question.

36 Which pair of forces acting concurrently on an object will produce the resultant of greatest magnitude?

Note that question 37 has only three choices.

37 The diagram at the right shows a force of magnitude F applied to a mass at angle θ relative to a horizontal frictionless surface. As angle θ is increased, the horizontal acceleration of the mass
    (1) decreases
    (2) increases
    (3) remains the same

38 The mass of a high school football player is approximately
    (1) 10^{0} kg
    (2) 10^{1} kg
    (3) 10^{2} kg
    (4) 10^{3} kg

39 A constant force is used to keep a block sliding at constant velocity along a rough horizontal track. As the block slides, there could be an increase in its
(1) gravitational potential energy, only
(2) internal energy, only
(3) gravitational potential energy and kinetic energy
(4) internal energy and kinetic energy

40 A photon of which electromagnetic radiation has the most energy?
(1) ultraviolet   (3) infrared
(2) x ray   (4) microwave

41 The spring of a toy car is wound by pushing the car backward with an average force of 15 newtons through a distance of 0.50 meter. How much elastic potential energy is stored in the car's spring during this process?
(1) 1.9 J   (2) 7.5 J   (3) 30. J   (4) 56 J

42 The graph at the right shows the relationship between the potential difference across a metallic conductor and the electric current through the conductor at constant temperature T_1. Which graph best represents the relationship between potential difference and current for the same conductor maintained at a higher constant temperature, T_2?

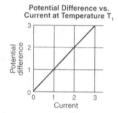

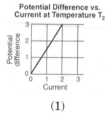

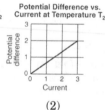

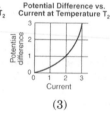

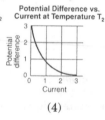

        (1)   (2)   (3)   (4)

43 The diagram at the right shows a circuit with two resistors. What is the reading on ammeter A?
(1) 1.3 A   (3) 3.0 A
(2) 1.5 A   (4) 0.75 A

44 The diagram at the right shows a bar magnet. Which arrow best represents the direction of the needle of a compass placed at point A?
(1) ↑   (3) →
(2) ↓   (4) ←

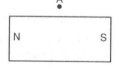

45 Which graph best represents the motion of a block accelerating uniformly down an inclined plane?

        (1)   (2)   (3)   (4)

Note that question 46 has only three choices.

46 The graph at the right shows elongation as a function of the applied force for two springs, A and B. Compared to the spring constant for spring A, the spring constant for spring B is
(1) smaller
(2) larger
(3) the same

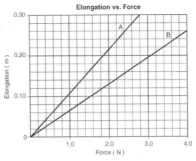
Elongation vs. Force

47 The diagram at the right represents currents in a segment of an electric circuit. What is the reading of ammeter A?
(1) 1 A
(2) 2 A
(3) 3 A
(4) 4 A

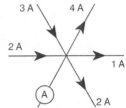

Base your answers to questions 48 and 49 on the diagram at the right, which represents a light ray traveling from air to Lucite to medium Y and back into air.

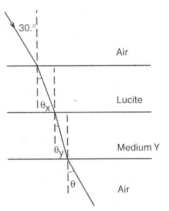

48 The sine of angle θ_x is
(1) 0.333   (3) 0.707
(2) 0.500   (4) 0.886

49 Light travels *slowest* in
(1) air, only
(2) Lucite, only
(3) medium Y, only
(4) air, Lucite, and medium Y

50 The diagram at the right shows two pulses traveling toward each other in a uniform medium. Which diagram best represents the medium when the pulses meet at point X?

(1)    (3)

(2) 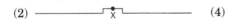   (4)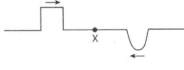

PART B-2

Answer all questions in this part.
Base your answers to questions 51 and 52 on the information below.

An outfielder throws a baseball to the first baseman at a speed of 19.6 meters per second and an angle of 30.° above the horizontal.

51 Which pair represents the initial horizontal velocity (v_x) and initial vertical velocity (v_y) of the baseball?
(1) $v_x = 17.0$ m/s, $v_y = 9.80$ m/s
(2) $v_x = 9.80$ m/s, $v_y = 17.0$ m/s
(3) $v_x = 19.4$ m/s, $v_y = 5.90$ m/s
(4) $v_x = 19.6$ m/s, $v_y = 19.6$ m/s

52 If the ball is caught at the same height from which it was thrown, calculate the amount of time the ball was in the air. [Show all work, including the equation and substitution with units.] [2]

Base your answers to questions 53 and 54 on the circuit diagram below, which shows two resistors connected to a 24-volt source of potential difference.

53 On the diagram at the right, use the appropriate circuit symbol to indicate a correct placement of a voltmeter to determine the potential difference across the circuit. [1]

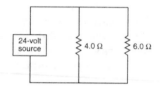

54 What is the total resistance of the circuit?
(1) 0.42 Ω   (2) 2.4 Ω   (3) 5.0 Ω   (4) 10. Ω

55 The diagram at the right shows a plane wave passing through a small opening in a barrier.

On the diagram at the right, sketch four wave fronts after they have passed through the barrier. [1]

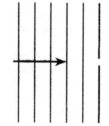

56 What prevents the nucleus of a helium atom from flying apart? [1]

Base your answers to questions 57 and 58 on the information below.

A 1.00-meter length of nichrome wire with a cross-sectional area of 7.85×10^{-7} meter^2 is connected to a 1.50-volt battery.

57 Calculate the resistance of the wire. [Show all work, including the equation and substitution with units.] [2]

58 Determine the current in the wire. [1] _____ A

Base your answers to questions **59 through 62** on the information and table at the right.

Length (meters)	Period (seconds)
0.05	0.30
0.20	0.90
0.40	1.30
0.60	1.60
0.80	1.80
1.00	2.00

In a laboratory exercise, a student kept the mass and amplitude of swing of a simple pendulum constant. The length of the pendulum was increased and the period of the pendulum was measured. The student recorded the data in the table at the right.

Directions (59–61): Using the information in the table, construct a graph on the grid at the right, following the directions below.

59 Label each axis with the appropriate physical quantity and unit. Mark an appropriate scale on each axis. [2]

60 Plot the data points for period versus pendulum length. [1]

61 Draw the best-fit line or curve for the data graphed. [1]

62 Using your graph, determine the period of a pendulum whose length is 0.25 meter. [1]

_____ s

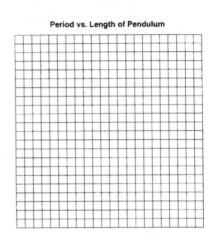

Period vs. Length of Pendulum

PART C

Answer all questions in this part.

Directions (63–78): Record your answers in the spaces provided.

Base your answers to questions **63 through 65** on the information below and diagram at the right.

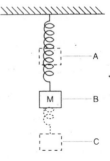

A mass, *M*, is hung from a spring and reaches equilibrium at position *B*. The mass is then raised to position *A* and released. The mass oscillates between positions *A* and *C*. [Neglect friction.]

63 At which position, *A*, *B*, or *C*, is mass *M* located when the kinetic energy of the system is at a maximum? Explain your choice. [1]

64 At which position, *A*, *B*, or *C*, is mass *M* located when the gravitational potential energy of the system is at a maximum? Explain your choice. [1]

65 At which position, *A*, *B*, or *C*, is mass *M* located when the elastic potential energy of the system is at a maximum? Explain your choice. [1]

Base your answers to questions 66 through 69 on the information below.

A force of 6.0 x 10⁻¹⁵ newton due south and a force of 8.0 x 10⁻¹⁵ newton due east act concurrently on an electron, e^-.

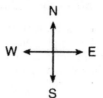

66 On the diagram at the right, draw a force diagram to represent the two forces acting on the electron. (The electron is represented by a dot.) Use a metric ruler and the scale of 1.0 centimeter = 1.0 • 10–15 newton. Begin each vector at the dot representing the electron and label its magnitude in newtons. [2]

67 Determine the resultant force on the electron, *graphically*. Label the resultant vector R. [1]

68 Determine the magnitude of the resultant vector R. [1] _____N

69 Determine the angle between the resultant and the 6.0 x 10⁻¹⁵-newton vector. [1] _____°

Base your answers to questions 70 through 74 on the information below.

A force of 10. newtons toward the right is exerted on a wooden crate initially moving to the right on a horizontal wooden floor. The crate weighs 25 newtons.

70 Calculate the magnitude of the force of friction between the crate and the floor. [Show all work, including the equation and substitution with units.] [2]

71 On the diagram at the right, draw and label all vertical forces acting on the crate. [1]

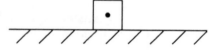

72 On the diagram, draw and label all horizontal forces acting on the crate. [1]

73 What is the magnitude of the net force acting on the crate? [1] _____N

74 Is the crate accelerating? Explain your answer. [1]

Base your answers to questions 75 through 78 on the information below.

An electron in a hydrogen atom drops from the $n = 3$ energy level to the $n = 2$ energy level.

75 What is the energy, in electronvolts, of the emitted photon? [1] _____ eV

76 What is the energy, in joules, of the emitted photon? [1] _____ J

77 Calculate the frequency of the emitted radiation. [Show all work, including the equation and substitution with units.] [2]

78 Calculate the wavelength of the emitted radiation. [Show all work, including the equation and substitution with units.] [2]

PHYSICAL SETTING: PHYSICS
PRACTICE TEST # 3 – JUNE 2003

To the Teacher: This exam is the June 2003 Regents Exam as published by the State Education Department of New York. It has not been edited, altered, or corrected.

PART A
Answer all questions in this part

Directions (1-35): For *each* statement or question, select the *number* of the word or expression that, of those given, best completes the statement or answers the question.

1   The diagram below shows a 50.-kilogram crate on a frictionless plane at angle θ to the horizontal. The crate is pushed at constant speed up the incline from point *A* to point *B* by force *F*.

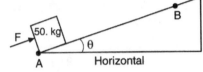

If angle θ were increased, what would be the effect on the magnitude of force *F* and the total work *W* done on the crate as it is moved from *A* to *B*?
(1) *W* would remain the same and the magnitude of *F* would decrease.
(2) *W* would remain the same and the magnitude of *F* would increase.
(3) *W* would increase and the magnitude of *F* would decrease.
(4) *W* would increase and the magnitude of *F* would increase.

2   A vector makes an angle, θ, with the horizontal. The horizontal and vertical components of the vector will be equal in magnitude if angle θ is
(1) 30°
(2) 45°
(3) 60°
(4) 90°

3   A car initially traveling at a speed of 16 meters per second accelerates uniformly to a speed of 20. meters per second over a distance of 36 meters. What is the magnitude of the car's acceleration?
(1) 0.11 m/s²
(2) 2.0 m/s²
(3) 0.22 m/s²
(4) 9.0 m/s²

4   A ball is thrown at an angle of 38° to the horizontal. What happens to the magnitude of the ball's vertical acceleration during the total time interval that the ball is in the air?
(1) It decreases, then increases.
(2) It decreases, then remains the same.
(3) It increases, then decreases.
(4) It remains the same.

5   A man standing on a scale in an elevator notices that the scale reads 30 newtons greater than his normal weight. Which type of movement of the elevator could cause this greater-than-normal reading?
(1) accelerating upward
(2) accelerating downward
(3) moving upward at constant speed
(4) moving downward at constant speed

Base your answers to questions 6 and 7 on the information below.

Projectile A is launched horizontally at a speed of 20. meters per second from the top of a cliff and strikes a level surface below, 3.0 seconds later. Projectile B is launched horizontally from the same location at a speed of 30. meters per second.

6   The time it takes projectile B to reach the level surface is
    (1) 4.5 s   (2) 2.0 s   (3) 3.0 s   (4) 10. s

7   Approximately how high is the cliff?
    (1) 29 m   (2) 44 m   (3) 60. m   (4) 104 m

8   A 60-kilogram skydiver is falling at a constant speed near the surface of Earth. The magnitude of the force of air friction acting on the skydiver is approximately
    (1) 0 N   (2) 6 N   (3) 60 N   (4) 600 N

9   An astronaut weighs 8.00×10^2 newtons on the surface of Earth. What is the weight of the astronaut 6.37×10^6 meters above the surface of Earth?
    (1) 0.00 N   (2) 2.00×10^2 N   (3) 1.60×10^3 N   (4) 3.20×10^3 N

10 A 10.-newton force is required to hold a stretched spring 0.20 meter from its rest position. What is the potential energy stored in the stretched spring?
    (1) 1.0 J   (2) 2.0 J   (3) 5.0 J   (4) 50. J

11 When a 12-newton horizontal force is applied to a box on a horizontal table-top, the box remains at rest. The force of static friction acting on the box is
    (1) 0 N   (3) 12 N
    (2) between 0 N and 12 N   (4) greater than 12 N

12 Ball A of mass 5.0 kilograms moving at 20. meters per second collides with ball B of unknown mass moving at 10. meters per second in the same direction. After the collision, ball A moves at 10. meters per second and ball B at 15 meters per second, both still in the same direction. What is the mass of ball B?
    (1) 6.0 kg   (2) 2.0 kg   (3) 10. kg   (4) 12 kg

13 A 1.5-kilogram lab cart is accelerated uniformly from rest to a speed of 2.0 meters per second in 0.50 second. What is the magnitude of the force producing this acceleration?
    (1) 0.70 N   (2) 1.5 N   (3) 3.0 N   (4) 6.0 N

14 The diagram at the right represents the magnetic field near point P. If a compass is placed at point P in the same plane as the magnetic field, which arrow represents the direction the north end of the compass needle will point?

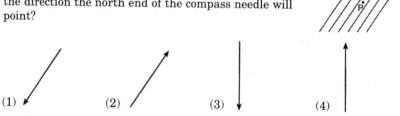

(1)   (2)   (3)   (4)

15 Which person has the greatest inertia?
    (1) a 110-kg wrestler resting on a mat
    (2) a 90-kg man walking at 2 m/s
    (3) a 70-kg long-distance runner traveling at 5 m/s
    (4) a 50-kg girl sprinting at 10 m/s

16 A child is riding on a merry-go-round. As the speed of the merry-go-round is doubled, the magnitude of the centripetal force acting on the child
    (1) remains the same   (3) is halved
    (2) is doubled   (4) is quadrupled

17 The magnitude of the electrostatic force between two point charges is F. If the distance between the charges is doubled, the electrostatic force between the charges will become

    (1) $\frac{F}{4}$ (2) $2F$ (3) $\frac{F}{2}$ (4) $4F$

Note that question 18 has only three choices.

18 As a ball falls freely (without friction) toward the ground, its total mechanical energy
    (1) decreases   (2) increases   (3) remains the same

19 A 0.50-kilogram ball is thrown vertically upward with an initial kinetic energy of 25 joules. Approximately how high will the ball rise? [Neglect air resistance.]
    (1) 2.6 m   (2) 5.1 m   (3) 13 m   (4) 25 m

20 What is the average power developed by a motor as it lifts a 400.-kilogram mass at constant speed through a vertical distance of 10.0 meters in 8.0 seconds?
    (1) 320 W   (2) 500 W   (3) 4,900 W   (4) 32,000 W

21 If 4.8×10^{-17} joule of work is required to move an electron between two points in an electric field, what is the electric potential difference between these points?
    (1) 1.6×10^{-19} V   (3) 3.0×10^2 V
    (2) 4.8×10^{-17} V   (4) 4.8×10^2 V

Note that question 22 has only three choices.

Wire

22 The diagram at the right shows a wire moving to the right at speed v through a uniform magnetic field that is directed into the page. As the speed of the wire is increased, the induced potential difference will
    (1) decrease
    (2) increase
    (3) remain the same

x   x   x   x

x   x   x   x

x   x   x   x

Magnetic field directed into page

23 A change in the speed of a wave as it enters a new medium produces a change in
    (1) frequency   (2) period   (3) wavelength   (4) phase

24 Two identical resistors connected in parallel have an equivalent resistance of 40. ohms. What is the resistance of each resistor?
    (1) 20. Ω   (2) 40. Ω   (3) 80. Ω   (4) 160 Ω

25 A tuning fork oscillates with a frequency of 256 hertz after being struck by a rubber hammer. Which phrase best describes the sound waves produced by this oscillating tuning fork?
(1) electromagnetic waves that require no medium for transmission
(2) electromagnetic waves that require a medium for transmission
(3) mechanical waves that require no medium for transmission
(4) mechanical waves that require a medium for transmission

26 In a vacuum, all electromagnetic waves have the same
(1) wavelength   (2) frequency   (3) speed   (4) amplitude

27 The speed of light ($f = 5.09 \times 10^{14}$ Hz) in a transparent material is 0.75 times its speed in air. The absolute index of refraction of the material is approximately
(1) 0.75   (2) 1.3   (3) 2.3   (4) 4.0

28 Waves pass through a 10.-centimeter opening in a barrier without being diffracted. This observation provides evidence that the wavelength of the waves is
(1) much shorter than 10. cm
(2) equal to 10. cm
(3) longer than 10. cm, but shorter than 20. cm
(4) longer than 20. cm

29 Standing waves in water are produced most often by periodic water waves
(1) being absorbed at the boundary with a new medium
(2) refracting at a boundary with a new medium
(3) diffracting around a barrier
(4) reflecting from a barrier

Note that question 30 has only three choices.

30 A sound of constant frequency is produced by the siren on top of a firehouse. Compared to the frequency produced by the siren, the frequency observed by a firefighter approaching the firehouse is
(1) lower   (2) higher   (3) the same

31 White light is passed through a cloud of cool hydrogen gas and then examined with a spectroscope. The dark lines observed on a bright background are caused by
(1) the hydrogen emitting all frequencies in white light
(2) the hydrogen absorbing certain frequencies of the white light
(3) diffraction of the white light
(4) constructive interference

32 Compared to a photon of red light, a photon of blue light has a
(1) greater energy   (3) smaller momentum
(2) longer wavelength   (4) lower frequency

33 Protons and neutrons are examples of
(1) positrons   (3) baryons   (3) mesons   (4) quarks

34 The strong force is the force of
(1) repulsion between protons
(2) attraction between protons and electrons
(3) repulsion between nucleons
(4) attraction between nucleons

35 If a deuterium nucleus has a mass of 1.53×10^{-3} universal mass units less than its components, this mass represents an energy of
(1) 1.38 MeV   (2) 1.42 MeV   (3) 1.53 MeV   (4) 3.16 MeV

PART B-1

Answer all questions in this part.

Directions (36-47): For *each* statement or question, select the *number* of the word or expression that, of those given, best completes the statement or answers the question.

36 Forces *A* and *B* have a resultant *R*. Force *A* and resultant *R* are represented in the diagram at the right. Which vector best represents force *B*?

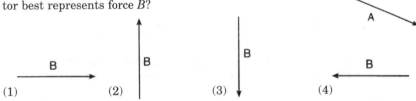

(1)   (2)   (3)   (4)

37 An object with a net charge of 4.80 x 10⁻⁶ coulomb experiences an electro-static force having a magnitude of 6.00 x 10⁻² newton when placed near a negatively charged metal sphere. What is the electric field strength at this location?
(1) 1.25×10^4 N/C directed away from the sphere
(2) 1.25×10^4 N/C directed toward the sphere
(3) 2.88×10^{-8} N/C directed away from the sphere
(4) 2.88×10^{-8} N/C directed toward the sphere

38 What is the approximate width of a person's little finger?
(1) 1 m   (2) 0. 1 m   (3) 0.01 m   (4) 0.001 m

39 The diagram at the right represents a ray of monochromatic light ($f = 5.09 \times 10^{14}$ Hz) passing from medium *X* ($n = 1.46$) into fused quartz.

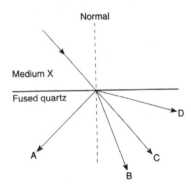

Which path will the ray follow in the quartz?
(1) *A*
(2) *B*
(3) *C*
(4) *D*

40 The graph at the right shows the relationship between the work done by a student and the time of ascent as the student runs up a flight of stairs. The slope of the graph would have units of
(1) joules
(2) seconds
(3) watts
(4) newtons

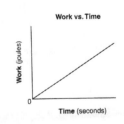

41 In the diagram at the right, two positively charged spheres, A and B, of masses m_A and m_B are located a distance d apart. Which diagram best represents the directions of the gravitational force, F_g, and the electrostatic force, F_e, acting on sphere A due to the mass and charge of sphere B? [Vectors are not drawn to scale.]

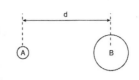

(1)

(2)

(3)

(4)

42 Which graph best represents the relationship between the kinetic energy, KE, and the velocity of an object accelerating in a straight line?

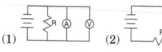   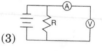   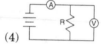

(1)   (2)   (3)   (4)

43 Which circuit diagram below correctly shows the connection of ammeter A and voltmeter V to measure the current through and potential difference across resistor R?

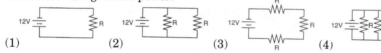

(1)   (2)   (3)   (4)

44 Identical resistors (R) are connected across the same 12-volt battery. Which circuit uses the greatest power?

(1)   (2)   (3)   (4)

45 The diagram at the right shows two pulses, A and B, approaching each other in a uniform medium. Which diagram best represents the superposition of the two pulses?

(1)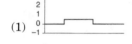

(2)

(3)

(4)

46 Which graph best represents the motion of an object that is *not* in equilibrium as it travels along a straight line?

(1)

(2)

(3)

(4)

47 Three forces act on a box on an inclined plane as shown in the diagram at the right. [Vectors are not drawn to scale.] If the box is at rest, the net force acting on it is equal to

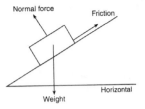

(1) the weight
(2) the normal force
(3) friction
(4) zero

PART B-2

Answer all questions in this part

Directions (48-63): Record your answers in the spaces provided.

48 The diagram at the right represents a wire conductor, *RS*, positioned perpendicular to a uniform magnetic field directed into the page.

```
         R
x   x  ┌─┐ x   x   Magnetic
x   x  │ │ x   x   field
x   x  │ │ x   x   directed
x   x  └─┘ x   x   into the page
         S
```

Describe the direction in which the wire could be moved to produce the maximum potential difference across its ends, *R* and *S*. [1]

49 Rubbing a moistened finger around the rim of a water glass transfers energy to the glass at the natural frequency of the glass. Which wave phenomenon is responsible for this effect? [1]

50 Explain why a hydrogen atom in the ground state can absorb a 10.2-electronvolt photon, but can *not* absorb an 11.0-electronvolt photon. [1]

Base your answers to questions 51 and 52 on the information below.

A hiker walks 5.00 kilometers due north and then 7.00 kilometers due east.

51 What is the magnitude of her resultant displacement? [1] _____ km

52 What total distance has she traveled? [1] _____ km

53 What is the magnitude of the charge, in coulombs, of a lithium nucleus containing three protons and four neutrons? [1] _____ C

54 A light bulb attached to a 120.-volt source of potential difference draws a current of 1.25 amperes for 35.0 seconds. Calculate how much electrical energy is used by the bulb. [Show all work, including the equation and substitution with units.] [2]

55 Calculate the wavelength in a vacuum of a radio wave having a frequency of 2.2×10^6 hertz. [Show all work, including the equation and substitution with units.] [2]

56 Two monochromatic, coherent light beams of the same wavelength converge on a screen. The point at which the beams converge appears dark. Which wave phenomenon best explains this effect? [1]

57 Exposure to ultraviolet radiation can damage skin. Exposure to visible light does not damage skin. State *one* possible reason for this difference. [1]

Base your answers to questions 58 through 61 on the information below and data table at the right.

In an experiment, a student measured the length and period of a simple pendulum. The data table at the right lists the length (l) of the pendulum in meters and the square of the period (T^2) of the pendulum in seconds^2.

Length (ℓ) (meters)	Square of Period (T^2) (seconds^2)
0.100	0.410
0.300	1.18
0.500	1.91
0.700	2.87
0.900	3.60

Directions (58-59): Using the information in the data table, construct a graph on the grid below, following the directions below.

58 Plot the data points for the square of period versus length. [1]

59 Draw the best-fit straight line. [1]

60 Using your graph, determine the time in seconds it would take this pendulum to make one complete swing if it were 0.200 meter long. [1]

_____s

61 The period of a pendulum is related to its length by the formula:

$T^2 = \left(\dfrac{4\pi^2}{g}\right) \bullet l$ where g represents

the acceleration due to gravity. Explain how the graph you have drawn could be used to calculate the value of g. [You do *not* need to perform any actual calculations.] [1]

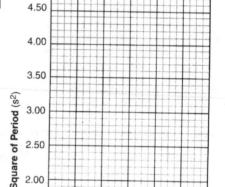

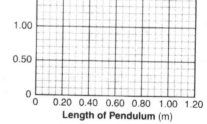

62 A student is given two pieces of iron and told to determine if one or both of the pieces are magnets. First, the student touches an end of one piece to one end of the other. The two pieces of iron attract. Next, the student reverses one of the pieces and again touches the ends together. The two pieces attract again. What does the student definitely know about the initial magnetic properties of the two pieces of iron? [1]

63 When a child squeezes the nozzle of a garden hose, water shoots out of the hose toward the east. What is the compass direction of the force being exerted on the child by the nozzle? [1]

PART C

Answer all questions in this part.

Directions (64-76): Record your answers in the spaces provided in your answer booklet.

Base your answers to questions 64 through 68 on the information below and data table at the right.

Three lamps were connected in a circuit with a battery of constant potential. The current, potential difference, and resistance for each lamp are listed in the data table at the right. [There is negligible resistance in the wires and the battery.]

	Current (A)	Potential Difference (V)	Resistance (Ω)
lamp 1	0.45	40.1	89
lamp 2	0.11	40.1	365
lamp 3	0.28	40.1	143

64 Using the circuit symbols found in the *Reference Tables for Physical Setting / Physics*, draw a circuit showing how the lamps and battery are connected. [2]

65 What is the potential difference supplied by the battery? [1] _____v

66 Calculate the equivalent resistance of the circuit. [Show all work, including the equation and substitution with units.] [2]

67 If lamp 3 is removed from the circuit, what would be the value of the potential difference across lamp 1 after lamp 3 is removed? [1] _____v

68 If lamp 3 is removed from the circuit, what would be the value of the current in lamp 2 after lamp 3 is removed? [1] _____A

Base your answers to questions 69 through 71 on the information and diagram at the right.

A ray of light passes from air into a block of transparent material X as shown in the diagram at the right.

69 Measure the angles of incidence and refraction to the nearest degree for this light ray at the air into material X boundary and write your answers below. [2]

angle of incidence = _____°

angle of refraction = _____°

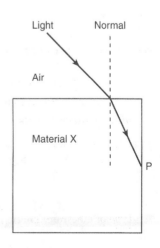

70 Calculate the absolute index of refraction of material X. [Show all work, including the equation and substitution with units.] [2]

71 The refracted light ray is reflected from the material X-air boundary at point P. Using a protractor and straightedge, on the diagram at the right, draw the reflected ray from point P. [1]

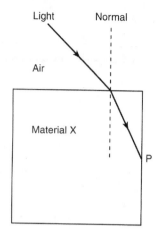

Base your answers to questions 72 through 74 on the information below.

A 50.-kilogram child running at 6.0 meters per second jumps onto a stationary 10.-kilogram sled. The sled is on a level frictionless surface.

72 Calculate the speed of the sled with the child after she jumps onto the sled. [Show all work, including the equation and substitution with units.] [2]

73 Calculate the kinetic energy of the sled with the child after she jumps onto the sled. [Show all work, including the equation and substitution with units.] [2]

74 After a short time, the moving sled with the child aboard reaches a rough level surface that exerts a constant frictional force of 54 newtons on the sled. How much work must be done by friction to bring the sled with the child to a stop? [1] _____J

Base your answers to questions 75 and 76 on the information below.

Louis de Broglie extended the idea of waveparticle duality to all of nature with his matterwave equation, $\lambda = \dfrac{h}{mv}$, where λ is the particle's wavelength, m is its mass, v is its velocity, and h is Planck's constant.

75 Using this equation, calculate the de Broglie wavelength of a helium nucleus (mass = 6.7×10^{-27} kg) moving with a speed of 2.0×10^6 meters per second. [Show all work, including the equation and substitution with units.] [2]

76 The wavelength of this particle is of the same order of magnitude as which type of electromagnetic radiation? [1]